CREATING COUNTRY MUSIC

Richard A. Peterson

Creating

Country

Music

Fabricating

Authenticity

The University of Chicago Press
Chicago and London

Richard A. Peterson is professor of sociology at Vanderbilt University, founding chair of the Culture section of the American Sociological Association, and most recently editor (with Melton McLaurin) of *You Wrote My Life: Lyrical Themes in Country Music*.

The University of Chicago Press, Chicago 60637
The University of Chicago Press, Ltd., London
© 1997 by The University of Chicago
All rights reserved. Published 1997
Printed in the United States of America

06 05 04 03 02 01 00 99 98 97   1 2 3 4 5

ISBN: 0-226-66284-5 (cloth)

Library of Congress Cataloging-in-Publication Data

Peterson, Richard A.
    Creating country music : fabricating authenticity /
  Richard A. Peterson.
        p.   cm.
    Includes bibliographical references and index.
    ISBN 0-226-66284-5 (cloth : alk. paper)
    1. Country music—History and criticism. 2. Popular
  culture—United States. I. Title.
  ML3524.P48   1997
    781.642′09—dc21   97-9675
                                                        CIP
                                                        MN

♾ The paper used in this publication meets the minimum requirements of the American National Standard for Information Sciences—Permanence of Paper for Printed Library Materials, ANSI Z39.48–1984.

Dedicated to Edna Wildman Peterson, Mom

Edna Wildman Peterson on the running board of the family Hudson with her parents (behind the hood of the car) and six of her siblings in 1917

Contents

Acknowledgments
A NOTE ON METHOD

My first memory of country music was as a small city-kid listening to a barn-dance program while visiting my grandfather's farm near Selma in Clark County, Ohio. I was puzzled at all the hilarity of those at the barn-dance because I usually couldn't tell what they were laughing about. I was fascinated, however, by the way the harmonica player simulated all the sounds of hounds and men on a coon hunt. I also loved the yarns the old hired man Earl Doster would tell as we rode along on a horse-drawn feed wagon or side-delivery rake. The stories were generally about the goings-on of men and beasts deep in the hills and hollers of his home, Ken-tuck. Earl, I later learned from Mother, was a "hillikan" of the kind that our kind avoided. But on those dusty 1940 summer days Earl sang playful rhymes while spitting tobacco for emphasis, as we rumbled along.

As a teen I was back working a summer on the farm. My kin were Quakers so there wasn't much music, but I found a bunch of records in an old wind-up Victrola stored in the abandoned tenant house near the cattle barn that reeked of coal oil, rodent droppings, and the sheep's wool stored there. I remember plaintive ballads, bluesy numbers, foxtrots, fiddle tunes, and comedy numbers. A committed New Orleans jazz-revivalist at the time, the only disk I kept was one by the Memphis Jug Band, but in all likelihood, I was listening to some Jimmie Rodgers records the year that Hank Williams died.

In the years following I became an industrial sociologist and, thanks in part to the promptings of a graduate student, Alan Orenstein, at the University of Wisconsin, and with another student, David Berger, whom I met there, I began to research aspects of the music industry. But it wasn't until some years after taking a job at Vanderbilt University in Nashville, Tennessee, that I became aware that the center of country music production was just six blocks from the Vanderbilt campus. Certainly my university colleagues didn't consider anything having to do with country as relevant to those of "our kind." But already by then a seasoned researcher of aspects of jazz, pop, and rock, I cared little about the elitist snobbery of my university colleagues of the 1970s.

While researching popular music producers and session musicians, the organizing question for the country music research became "Why Nashville?" Why should the production of country music be located in a regional center (rather than in L.A. and New York like the rest of commercial music), and why should that center be located in Nashville rather than Dallas, Atlanta, Bakersfield, Chicago, Cincinnati—or Richmond, Indiana, for that matter, where many early records were made? The easy answer, of course, was that the Grand Ole Opry was located in Nashville, but that answer just begged further questions. Why, for example, did the Opry flourish when the other larger and more important barn-dance programs of the 1930s floundered and disappeared one by one?

No single method has proved adequate to answer the questions, and so over the past twenty-five years I have made numerous interviews; I have attended concerts, recording sessions, and TV program tapings; I have consulted newspaper, company, and scholarly archives; I have made secondary analyses of available data in sources ranging from fan magazines to government surveys; and I have learned much from the rapidly growing number of detailed reports on specific artists, local scenes, and genres of country music—many completed since my quest began. Publishing bits and pieces of the work over the years has facilitated feedback from knowledgeable informants and scholars. This work also helped to put into sharper focus what I still did not understand. Giving lectures to elder-hostel groups and academic scholars, as well as teaching undergraduate seminars on country music, has greatly helped to render the huge complex of facts and speculations down to a set of ideas that can more readily be grasped and played with.

I profoundly appreciate the many people who have shared their ideas, their knowledge, and above all their enthusiasm for what is now called country music. The first was Don Light, the veteran Nashville talent agency director who, though bemused by my naivete, made it his mission to edify me. He took me backstage at the Ryman to meet Bill Monroe and to experience the chemistry of the Opry up close while Monroe, Porter Wagoner, Dotty West, and others were performing. He introduced me to Jimmie Buffett and arranged for me to spend four days on the road touring the Midwest with the Oak Ridge Boys when they were still a gospel music group and Tony Brown was their piano player.

At the Grand Ole Opry I met and extensively interviewed Bud Wendell, who was then the manager. Don also introduced me to Ronnie Light, who was then a staff record producer at RCA. Through Ronnie I attended a number of recording sessions and got to see Chet Atkins, Skeeter Davis, Waylon Jennings, Charlie Pride, and Hank Snow, among others, at work in the studio. Harold Bradley, one of the premier session guitarists, showed me something of the range of styles he had at his command, and I observed the magical manipulations of sound that were at the fingertips of the staff engineers.

It is not so much that I learned directly about the details of early country music from these people or from the brief periods of consulting with Jack Clement, Tandy Rice, Film House, and the trade magazines *Billboard* and *Radio & Records*. As with my two years of working at country music's huge annual fan-oriented bonanza, Fanfare, I gained something of a sense of what country music was and is about.

Just living in Nashville since the mid-1960s has been a great advantage for this project because I have run across a large number of profoundly important informants in the normal course of daily activities. Just two examples will have to suffice. I met one of my first informants, John DeWitt, through the Yacht Club. As a Vanderbilt engineering student, Jack had helped to build the original transmitter for WSM, home of the Grand Ole Opry, and by 1952 he was WSM's general manager when Hank Williams was fired off the Opry. The most recently found informant was Marjorie Kirby, whose late husband, Edward Kirby, was the director of publicity for WSM in the 1930s. With her husband, Marjorie helped to found the early fan magazine, *Rural Radio*. Nashville landmarks also served as inspiration: the house next to mine was first owned by Opry founder George Hay, and nearby is the place on Natchez Trace where Hank Williams holed up after his wife Audrey threw him out of the house and he got fired off the Opry.

Among the early artist interviews, the three that stand out in my memory were conducted with Paul DiMaggio the first summer he worked with me on understanding country music. One interview was with Herman Crook, founder of one of the earliest bands on the Opry, who played the harmonica as if it were a fiddle. He said he never gave up his secure day-job making cigars, because he didn't want to travel and wasn't sure the music would "last." Another was Kirk McGee, who played fiddle and did blackface comedy in the days before the Opry and who, with his brother Sam, traveled widely with the vaudevillian and first star of the Opry, Uncle Dave Macon. The third interview was with Alcyone Bate Beasley, who, as a small girl, played on the Opry with her father, Dr. Humphrey Bate. In animated tones, she told how George Hay, the creator of the Opry, made her, the daughter of a Vanderbilt graduate and medical doctor, dress up in silly rustic gingham outfits. The truth as they told it was far more interesting than the publicity spread by George Hay and others that the performers on the early Opry were a bunch of farmers who just came to town of a Saturday night to try to play on the Opry. Those three interviews provided the first lesson in the fabrication of authenticity.

I gladly acknowledge my profound debt to the numerous men and women who have devoted great amounts of time and energy to researching and reporting on one or another particular artist, group, organization, or musical scene. Some of these hold academic positions in folklore, history, English, or sociology, but as Simon Frith has observed, country music is unique among all musical genres in the number and variety of people who do painstaking scholarship out of their love for the music rather than as a part of their paid work. To cite just one example, Bradley G. Harris, a compensation and benefits officer in an Evansville, Indiana, corporation, has isolated six distinct Tennessee harmonica styles that were being performed in the 1930s. Much of what is reported in this book, as the multitude of citations in the text will show, is based on the work of these scholars.

Numerous people have generously provided bits and pieces of documentary material vital in piecing together the story of fabrication that seemed at first such a crazy quilt. The John Edwards Memorial Archive that I first researched at the University of California, Los Angeles, and more recently at the University of North Carolina, Chapel Hill, where it forms the backbone of the Southern Folklife Collection, is relatively small but rich in its holdings. The much more extensive holdings of the Country Music Foundation in Nashville have proved a gold mine in no small part because of the invaluable assistance of the people there. These include William Ivey, Bib Pinson, and Doug Green early on; and in recent years, Ronnie Pugh, Paul Kingsbury, John Rumble, and Mark Medley.

Those researchers or performers who have graciously read and commented on some parts of the manuscript in one or another of its incarnations include Duane Allen, Jan Belcher, David Berger, Johnny Bond, Pierre Bourdieu, Hugh Cherry, Daniel Cornfield, Wayne Daniel, R. Serge Denisoff, John DeWitt, Colin Escott, Richard Friedman, Simon Frith, Doug Green, Larry Grossberg, Michael Hughes, Jennifer Joplin, Ed Kahn, Michèle Lamont, Judith McCulloh, Melton McLaurin, Robert Oermann, Ruth Peterson, Nolan Porterfield, Ronnie Pugh, Joseph Rhea, Neil Rosenberg, John Ryan, Elizabeth Schlappi, Lisa Silver, Frances Simcich, Cecelia Tichi, Ann Wallace, David Wisnant, Janet Wolff, and Vera Zolberg. I am profoundly grateful to each for their comments and for their support as well. This goes many times over for the detailed comments and overarching perspectives of Paul DiMaggio, Lyn Spillman, and Charles Wolfe, who read the manuscript in its entirety.

The students-become-colleagues with whom I have batted around ideas and shared excitement about the music over years include—in the order of their appearance in my office—David Berger, Paul DiMaggio, Larry DeBord, Bo Fahs, John Rumble, Michael Hughes, John Ryan, Jennifer Joplin, and Roger Kern, and Narasimhan Anand. I've been blessed. Then there are the hundreds of students at Vanderbilt, as well as at Wisconsin, Harvard, Stanford, Leeds, and elsewhere, who have reacted to my developing ideas, helping to make the argument more articulate.

A number of agencies have graciously provided funds over the years to help this project gestate. I gratefully acknowledge the support of the Vanderbilt University Research Council, the Harold Hill Peterson Foundation for a California travel grant, the National Endowment for the Humanities, the Ministry of Education of the French Government, the Mellon Foundation, and the University of Chicago Press. I particularly appreciate the National Humanities Center in North Carolina, which allowed me the months of freedom necessary to formulate and begin writing this book.

This manuscript and I have had the benefit of the enthusiastic, caring, and expert help of the people I've worked with at the University of Chicago Press. In particular I want to thank Douglas Mitchell, Carol Saller, Sara Leopold, and Matthew Howard. Beyond what they have done, it has been a great help to feel their enthusiastic support at every stage from contract negotiations to editing, securing rights, and getting the word out about the book.

An archival work like this relies on recorded music and press accounts, but in conveying the appearance of authenticity, often an old picture is worth more than a thousand words. I greatly appreciate the artistry and skill of the photographers both amateur and professional who took the many hundreds of pictures I have viewed over the past decades. Archie Green was one of the first to recognize the value of this treasure trove of visual images and I relished each of his "Graphics" sections of the *JEMF Quarterly* as they appeared. I am most grateful to the Country Music Foundation, the Wilson Library of the University of North Carolina, as well as Les Leverett, Robert Oermann, Bob Pinson, Ronnie Pugh, Nolan Porterfield, Roger Weiss, and Charles Wolfe for preserving and allowing me to use the illustrations reprinted here.

Finally, and most important, I wish to acknowledge three wonderfully intelligent and warm people who have helped me become a more human being, and without whom this work literally could not have been possible: Paul DiMaggio, Hugh Cherry, and Claire Peterson.

In the formative days Paul shared insights and enthusiasm, and over the years since he has provided comments, perspective, and a firm nudge to get on with THE BOOK. I first met Hugh through Jerry Hopkins when Hugh was the all-night country music disc jockey at KNEW in Oakland, California. A rural Kentucky-raised pop-music jock who roared with Hank Williams, Hugh helped to define the country music disc jockey species, then became a self-made scholar of the genre in the 1970s. Through him I have learned much, not only about the country music world, but of the creative life cycle that turns a child of the tradition into a rebel and finally into a protector of the tradition. Claire has generously shared her life with me, and through her persistent and patient editing and commentaries, has taught me whatever I know about how to write.

With all this help, all I can claim authorship for is the errors and for connecting the dots.

Part One

Making the Music Commercial

CHAPTER ONE

Introduction

Finding Country Authenticity

"Authenticity, authenticity and originality."

This is the response given most often by the nine leading country record producers interviewed in 1953 when asked by a reporter for *Billboard*, the music industry trade paper, "What factors do you consider in selecting new talent?" The two who didn't use the word "authenticity" or a synonym in answering said they looked for a "distinctive" style (*Billboard* 1953h: 54).

"Authenticity" was also an answer to the next question asked of the record producers: "What do you look for in new song material?" But more often the record producers' answers had to do with the song's distinctiveness. They said they sought out songs that were "fresh and unique," "different," "original." In retrospect it seems hardly surprising that producers were looking for artists with an authentic style who could successfully deliver songs that were original. These seemingly contradictory characteristics—authenticity and originality—exactly describe Hank Williams, who that year of 1953 had been propelled to the status of country music icon by the wholly unprecedented public outpouring of sentiment following his tragic death at age twenty-nine.

Thirty years earlier when unschooled white musicians first appeared on the fledgling medium of radio and began to make phonograph records, the designation "country music" was not in use, and in fact there was no agreed understanding of the extent and nature of the genre or the physical appearance of its performers, and there was no shared understanding of the characteristics of the potential audience. For that matter there were only the rudiments of a music industry as we now know it in 1923. Records were sold at furniture stores and radio was considered little more than a novelty. Under these conditions, it was not possible for more than a handful of performers to make a full-time living from the music, and they did so largely by appearing as comedic rustics on the vaudeville stage.

All this changed between 1923 when our story begins and its finale in 1953. Authenticity and originality had been fully fabricated by 1953; the audience had been identified, and the country music industry fully institutionalized.

Home-Made to Store-Bought

In 1923 millions of people in rural areas and towns all across North America sang and played the fiddle and the guitar,[1] but "country music" was not recognized as a form of music distinct from others, and this became obvious when record company executives tried to merchandise the music. They didn't know what music to include and what to exclude, and a number of appellations were applied by the early merchandisers, ranging from "Old-time," "Old Time Tunes," "Old Familiar Tunes" and "Hearth and Home," to "Hill and Range," and "Hillbilly and Western." They did, however, make the strategic decision to market music by whites and African Americans separately.[2]

Just thirty years later, ironically, the situation was reversed. The look, sound, and lyric of country music was instantly recognizable,[3] and the music that had been entirely home-made was largely store-bought. What had been the music of noncity regions across the continent became symbolically centered in the South and Southwest. In 1953 a few hundred largely Southern professionals played and sang for a living, while millions of people attended country music concerts, listened to it on the radio, and played it—on the phonograph. In the process, authenticity had became commodified, and thousands of men and women learned how to make a living from the music not only as performers and singers, but also as songwriters, comics, instrument makers, costumers, disk jockeys, managers, promoters, producers, publicists, publishers, photographers, video makers, and the like.

FABRICATING AUTHENTICITY

The first country music record was made in Atlanta, Georgia, in mid-June 1923.[4] The New York executive overseeing the recording session pronounced the results to be "Awful" and refused to release the record, but the local record distributor prevailed on him to have 500 copies made for sale in the Atlanta region. These were all sold within days and the distributor ordered 1,000 more. When these sold out as quickly, the New York executive realized that there was an untapped market to be exploited and asked that the performer, Fiddlin' John Carson, be brought to New York to make more records.

The surprising popularity of the Carson record was not an isolated incident. In the 1920s many impresarios of popular entertainment in the United States expressed similar dismay at the enthusiastic response to what is now called country music (*Talking Machine World* 1925, 1929). They were surprised because the music and its performers seemed to break all the conventions of what made for success in the world of urbane, sophisticated commercial popular music of the time, which featured an amalgam of jazz-based dance music and vocal music featuring song stylists with opera-trained voices. In stark contrast, the musical offerings of Fiddlin' John and the other early country music entertainers relied on untrained, high-pitched nasal voices and simple musical accompaniments, evoking images of farm, family, and old-fashioned mores along with more than a dash of sexual double entendre.

Entertainment industry impresarios sensed that the essential appeal of the music was rooted in the feeling of authenticity conveyed by its performers. Accordingly, they sought out old men steeped in tradition, playing old songs in traditional ways. The performances of these old-timers, even if historically and aesthetically accurate, were, for the most part, taken by the radio audiences and record buyers as bemusing novelties. Clearly, the impresarios had misunderstood the appeal of Fiddlin' John. To the consumer, apparently, authenticity was not synonymous with historical accuracy. Numerous permutations on the theme of rustic authenticity were tried over the next three decades, and the entertainment industry's efforts to find the formulas, those that failed as much as those that succeeded, provide an excellent opportunity to understand the general process of fabricating authenticity in popular culture.

The ironic phrase "fabricating authenticity" is used here to highlight the fact that authenticity is not inherent in the object or event that is designated authentic but is a socially agreed-upon construct in which the past is to a degree misremembered (Halbwachs 1992). This tailoring of collective memory to serve the needs of the present has been studied by a number of researchers, and as they show, the process can take several forms depending on who has the power to enforce their distinctive interpretation of the past.[5] Unlike these other situations that have been researched, no authority is in a position to dictate authenticity in country music. Rather, as we will discover in the chapters that follow, it is continuously negotiated in an ongoing interplay between performers, diverse commercial interests, fans, and the evolving image.[6] As is the case in other aspects of commercial popular culture, creative people propose ideas (be they for recorded music, movies, videos, magazines, or computer games), the industry adapts them in the process of putting a product on the market, and the public chooses some while rejecting others. The entrepreneurs, in turn, try to understand why certain offerings have been accepted and others rejected in order to create more that are as much like the successful ones as possible. The disjunction between demand and supply is widest in the early days of a genre before its aesthetic has been consolidated; before, to use George Melly's phrase, what began as a revolt against social and aesthetic conventions has become mere style (Melly 1970). This was the case for jazz in the decade before 1928 (Leonard 1962), rock in the 1950s (Shaw 1987; Peterson 1990; Ennis 1992), and country music for most of the 1923–53 era under review here.

A Music for Morons

Why did it take so much longer for country music to be institutionalized than it did for these other forms of popular culture? There are a number of reasons as will be shown in the chapters that follow, but to begin with, it had to do with the prejudices of those in the entertainment business.

The popularity of Fiddlin' John Carson and the other early country music performers was very difficult for most popular entertainment impresarios to understand because they were urbane, middle-class sophisticates or recent rural-to-urban migrants who were trying to disguise their own rural origins. They did not see country music in its own terms but considered it simply the antithesis of their own aesthetic and worldview because it evoked the image of rural poverty and small-town morality that so many in the rapidly urbanizing American society were trying to escape. It was country to their city; the unchanged to their rapidly changing; traditionalism to their modernism; craft-made to their mass-produced; and aesthetically rear-guard to their avant-garde. The music's maker was the country bumpkin, rube, linthead, cracker, or hillican to their up-to-date city sophisticate. Given this mind set, the natural as-

Figure 1.1 In this portrait Ralph Peer, the talent scout who found Jimmie Rodgers, the Carter Family, and numerous rural blues artists, is shown as a cultivated man of fine taste.

sumption was that those attracted to the music were responding to representations of an unchanged past.[7]

The contempt that music industry decision makers had for those who bought the early country music records, listened to country music played over the radio, and flocked to see country musicians perform is suggested by the term "hillbilly" that was given to the music within the entertainment industry. In American slang of the time a "billy" was a rough, unschooled, and simple-minded person, and a "hillbilly" was such a person from the remote backwoods of the Appalachian Mountains. The term was applied to its performers and to its most devoted fans as well. By extension the term was applied to all persons whose appearance, mode of talking, or accent suggested unschooled rural origins.[8]

The following characterization of the music's fans appeared in a front-page article, "Hill-Billy Music," in the December 29, 1926, issue of *Variety,* the leading entertainment industry weekly of the day:

> The "hillbilly" is a North Carolina or Tennessee and adjacent mountaineer type of illiterate white whose creed and allegiance are to the

Bible, the Chautauqua, and the phonograph. . . . The mountaineer is
of "poor white trash" genera. The great majority, probably 95 percent,
can neither read nor write English. Theirs is a community all to themselves. [They are] illiterate and ignorant, with the intelligence of mo-
rons (quoted in Green 1965: 221).

Not all characterizations were this harsh, but, with rare exceptions,
the entertainment industry impresarios distanced themselves from the
country music audience. With this mind-set it is little wonder that most
did not easily understand the appeal of country music. In the chapters
that follow we will focus on the efforts of a number of those who were
most influential, including early producer/publisher Ralph Peer; the creator of the "Grand Ole Opry," George Hay; and songwriter/publisher
Fred Rose, as well as on some of the most spectacular failures in identifying country music, including car maker Henry Ford.

INSTITUTIONALIZATION

The institutional apparatus that now supports country music with its
recording companies, publishers, managers, disk jockeys, talent agencies, tour promoters, television networks, music venues, outfitters, trade
press, trade associations, award shows, and fan magazines has the look
of inevitability about it,[9] but the music might have developed quite differently. In the decades following the American Civil War there was a profound upwelling of innovation in the musical expressions of poor and
working-class people of the American South and a mixing with the commercial music of the day. By the end of the first decade of the twentieth
century three streams were being distinguished: blues, jazz, and an amalgam that would become country music (Malone 1979; Ennis 1992).[10]

Popular—Not Art or Folk Music

Though similar in their origins, blues, jazz, and country music have followed quite different paths of institutionalization in the decades since.
Jazz, which began in the marching band music of black New Orleans,
is now often performed in classical music concert halls, is taught in conservatories of music, and is played along with classical music on "good
music" radio stations, with the result that much jazz has become *art
music*.[11] The blues, which was created by rural blacks in the Mississippi
delta, is now primarily the province of folk music experts, record collectors, and a wide range of entrepreneurs devoted to renewing the music
through festivals and recorded performances. It is now, for the most part,
a *commercial folk music*.[12] Thus, both the blues and jazz have experienced

a great deal of aesthetic mobility, and neither is today appreciated much by the working-class Southern black communities that originated jazz and blues. Their place in the musical life of working-class blacks has been taken by a succession of styles including rhythm and blues, soul, funk, and rap music.

Country music is widely enjoyed by people in all walks of North American society and around the world, but its primary audience is the children and grandchildren of the poor rural Southerners that gave commercial country music its birth (Ellison 1995; Peterson and Kern 1995). How is it that country music has become an element of commercial popular music rather than follow the path of jazz or the blues to become a kind of art music or commercial folk music?[13] Commercial popular music is subject to the laws of supply and demand in the market, so why has country music not simply merged, melded, and disappeared into mainstream popular music? How is it that country music has retained in its lyrics and in the images of its leading exponents the dualistic, populist, individualist, fatalistic, antiurbane zeitgeist of poor and working-class Southern whites,[14] although most of its fans do not have these characteristics? In a word, how has it maintained its distinctive sense of authenticity?

I seek the answers to these questions by examining the distinctive ways the field was institutionalized in the years between 1923 and 1953, by examining the meaning given to authenticity in country music, and by exploring the structural conditions that can foster authenticity in the future, preserving the music as a commercial market form "in the middle" without being "absorbed" into popular music, "elevated" into art, or "ossified" as a folk music.[15]

Our Use of the Term "Country Music"

The term "country music" was not widely applied to the music until the 1940s, and not fully embraced by all those interested in the field for another thirty years, when the term "country and western" faded from wide usage. Following current practice, we use the term "country music" to refer to the stream of commercial music that began to develop rapidly in the 1920s and is now widely recognized around the world as "country."

Readers who love the music, or some eras in its development, may say that much of the music currently being produced and marketed is not really country music. This complaint has been voiced at least as far back as records have been kept, and it is ultimately a question of taste and definition. To avoid invidious or cumbersome terms such as "folk country," "pre-commercial country," "vernacular country," and the like, we will also, when appropriate, use the term "country music" in referring to the antecedent streams of music out of which commercial country music was formed. I hope that the specific meaning of the term will be clear in context.

The Production Perspective

The lens through which we will see the *fabrication* of authenticity is the production-of-culture perspective and most particularly the process called institutionalization.[16] The production perspective focuses on how the content of culture is influenced by the several milieus in which it is created, distributed, evaluated, and consumed. Law, technology, careers, markets, and industry structure all importantly shaped the development of country music.[17]

While we will be focusing on the innovative activities of a number of individuals and organizations, the production perspective leads us always to look for the structural arrangements within which innovators work and to examine how they change structures rather than to look for the roots of innovation in the rare genius of a few select people.[18] It is not a lack of talent, or motivation, or business sense, for example, that explains why so few women played leading roles in the early development of country music. Women were systematically excluded from the business side of the developing industry and for decades were expected to fit a few stereotyped performance roles (Bufwack and Oermann 1993).

To be successful the earliest artists not only had to perform for an audience, but they often had to book their own engagements, arrange transportation, plan publicity, find new songs, and collect the money owed to them. Over the years, the roles of manager, talent agent, recording producer, publicist, publisher, song plugger, disk jockey, side-man, session musician, and costumer emerged, and by the mid-1950s constituted the institutionalized "world" (Becker 1982) or "field" (Bourdieu 1984) of commercial country music, a machine that was capable of making and merchandising new records and new artists on a predictable basis using the evolving conception of authenticity.

WHAT IS TO COME

The presentation in the chapters that follow is roughly chronological, focusing on a few of the most creative forces behind country music. Part 1 shows how three new media of communication—radio, records, and the spread of hard-surface roads—made a commercial country music possible for the first time in the mid-1920s. Focusing on Polk Brockman's work with Fiddlin' John Carson in Atlanta, Georgia, chapter 2 shows the role of the fledgling radio and record industries in making it possible for the first time for a goodly number of people to make a living in country music. Chapter 3 focuses on Ralph Peer's innovative understanding of publishing that did not rely on selling sheet music and on his greatest recording success, Jimmie Rodgers. The chapter ends by showing why those who followed him could not make a living in the way Jimmie Rodgers had.

Part 2 of the story examines the creation of the distinctive country music visual image by tracing experiments over the 1920s and 1930s with the image of "old-timer," "hillbilly," and "cowboy." The image-making influences of Henry Ford, George Hay, United Studio's boss Nat Levine, and others are shown. Part 2 concludes by revealing the creative synthesis that the audience found most authentic: the young singer of plaintive hillbilly songs dressed in a cowboy outfit.

Part 3 shows the impact of radio on preserving and reshaping country music in the years of the Great Depression. The distinctive influences of the great "barn-dance" programs of the era, as well as the alternative radio-based career strategy called here "barnstorming," are detailed in chapters 7 and 8 respectively. Radio work was largely responsible for the way that country music performers relate to their audiences and for fostering the dynamic relationship between hard-core and soft-shell country music, as we see in chapter 9, where the styles of two leading groups of the "Grand Ole Opry" in the 1930s, the Vagabonds and Roy Acuff, are compared.

Part 4 brings our story to an end. It begins by examining how in the mid-1930s two new styles of music, western swing and honky-tonk, were formed in the oil boomtowns of Texas and Oklahoma and why more personal and candid lyrics evolved in this crucible. Chapter 11 focuses on Hank Williams, who was born the year that Fiddlin' John Carson cut that first record. It shows why Williams came to be seen as the personification of country music in the years that followed. Chapter 12 focuses on the field's institutionalization and the strange reasons behind the selection of the name "country" for the new field in 1953, the year of Williams's death.

The story complete, part 5 takes up some unfinished business. Chapter 13 explores academic and popular uses of the concept of "authenticity" and finds how authenticity became a renewable resource. Chapter 14 seeks the conditions that would make possible the music's survival as a distinctive form in the twenty-first century—to paraphrase the words of the old traditional hymn as sung by the Carter Family, we ask, *can the circle of authenticity be unbroken?*

CHAPTER TWO

Atlanta

Birthplace of Commercial
Country Music

Asked in 1923 whether country music could long survive, a reasonable expert would likely have answered that it could not.[1] Commercial popular music powered by brass instruments and its associated couple-dance forms, such as the two-step and the Charleston, were rapidly diffusing from the major urban centers. The one remaining large stronghold of the older, stringed instrument–based round-, line-, and square-dance music traditions was the crescent-shaped landmass stretching from West Virginia through the Carolinas, Kentucky, and Tennessee, continuing through the deep South to Arkansas and Texas, and diffusing west from Oklahoma. But in 1923 this crescent too was rapidly being penetrated by urban pop music, carried there primarily by the two new revolutionary mass media of the day, the phonograph and the radio.

If our 1923 expert lived in Atlanta, Georgia, they could, that year, witness the counterattack of stringed-instrument music via the new media. The first phonograph record by an unschooled performer, Fiddlin' John Carson, was put on sale in Atlanta early in July 1923, and Carson, along with several other country artists, could be heard performing on Atlanta's flagship radio station, WSB, throughout the year (Wiggins 1987: 69–75). Such media transmission was the death knell of authentic country music, some would argue,[2] but it was the basis of the music's survival and growth over the rest of the twentieth century as an authentic voice for millions of people. Nonetheless, the particular route of institu-tionalization of commercial country was not inevitable, as the fate of jazz and blues discussed in chapter 1 attests.

ON THE EVE

Country Could Not Be Part of Popular Music

In 1923 the commercial music industry in America was dominated by a few large New York–based music publishing houses. They produced sheet music for public performance halls, the vaudeville performance circuit, restaurants, and home pianos. All would-be country music com-posers were effectively barred from this market by the workings of the one major performance rights' organization of the day, the American So-ciety of Composers, Authors, and Publishers (ASCAP). It had recently been formed to ensure the payment of royalties to all member publishers and composers for the use of their music, and concomitantly, to exclude from the major music halls all works by nonmember composers. Virtu-ally all country music, jazz, and blues composers were systematically excluded from the benefits of ASCAP membership, and their virtual ex-clusion continued into the 1940s (Ryan 1985).

The other major component of the commercial music industry in 1923 had to do with providing live music for dances, musical theater, other entertainment, and public occasions.[3] The American Federation of Musi-cians had contracts with all the large venues in the major cities stipulat-ing that only its member musicians could be hired to perform. The lead-ership of the AFM had contempt for country music and its performers, most of whom could not sight-read sheet music. Sight-reading tests were used to exclude country music performers from the protection of union membership.[4] Thus it was not possible for country music groups to gain access to the larger halls except in the South and Southwest, where the union was weak. As a result country musicians could not play in the kinds of venues where their music might have been performed for urban audiences.

Because they could only periodically find paying work playing at barn dances, musical contests, store openings, festive occasions, political ral-lies, church functions, medicine shows, and the like, virtually all of the country performers remained amateurs or semiprofessionals in 1923. While taking the occasional jobs that were available, they had to support themselves through regular jobs outside the music field.[5]

It may seem far-fetched to suggest that if country songwriters and performers had been allowed into the most lucrative sectors of the mar-ket, country music might have been a component of popular music from the 1920s on, but it is possible. The popularity of the live radio performances of the "National Barn Dance" in Chicago and the surprisingly large record sales of Vernon Dalhart and Jimmie Rodgers suggest that there was an audience to be cultivated. In the Southwest of the 1930s country music string bands did gain access to the lucrative venues and, in the hands of Milton Brown, Bob Wills, and others, quickly evolved a hard-driving "western swing" sound that was distinct from, but analogous to, its "eastern" counterpart. If country music had taken this turn, however, it probably would have, as is the case of western swing, been more like the popular music of its day.

It may well be that by the early 1920s, even before the fledgling country music industry reified the split, there was already a fundamental divide in audience preferences between the more urbane and the more rustic. A careful analysis of the careers of a number of musicians of that period who tried to push country music toward popular music would go a long way in answering the question. For example, Clayton McMichen was a young fiddler who moved with his family to Atlanta in 1913. Prodigiously talented, his band, the Hometown Boys (named after the musical group in a newspaper comic strip popular at the time, "Toonerville Trolley"), was one of the first string bands to play on WSB in 1922. In 1923 all five of his band members won individual prizes at a Macon, Georgia, fiddlers' convention. On the air the band played a mix of sentimental, old-time, and blues numbers in a New Orleans jazzlike manner. McMichen also played with a much more traditionally oriented group, the Skillet Lickers. Significantly, their old-time tune records and hillbilly skits sold better than those of the hot band.[6]

Whether because of music industry constraints, or emerging audience predilections, or because of some combination of these and other factors, commercial country music was defined as distinct from popular music from its inception. This being true, it was in the interest of the early promoters to accentuate the differences between country and popular music and to fashion a distinctive image for the country performer in order to attract the committed allegiance of the people who did not like the more urbane popular music of the time.

Venues for Country Music

Four kinds of venues for work predominated, and these helped to shape country music in its early years. Country musicians, especially fiddlers, were commonly paid for playing music at community dances. An indication of the income that might be expected from such occasions is suggested by an anecdote told by Fiddlin' John Carson about a farmer he disliked who asked him to play for a dance. To dissuade him, Carson asked for the unusually high fee of fifteen dollars and was dismayed when the farmer agreed (Wiggins 1987: 65).[7] Clearly the pay for performing was generally much less, and no one was able to make a steady living from playing for dances. Such affairs, then as now, did, however, provide the early performing experience for most musicians.[8]

The second context where the music per se was focal was at the fiddling contest. The first contests we know of took place in the eighteenth century (Daniel 1981), and by the 1880s there were a number of well-promoted competitions, which offered as top prize a valuable instrument or a gold coin. Again it is obvious that even the most successful contenders could not hope to support themselves from their winnings.[9]

Third, some country musicians made a bare-bones existence by performing as itinerant street-corner beggars. Often blind, these street musicians sang topical tunes and sentimental ballads for passersby, usually accompanying themselves on the guitar. A remarkable number of songs were composed and instrumental techniques were developed by beggar-musicians such as Atlanta's Andrew Jenkins, who combined preaching with performing.

Finally, country music was sometimes performed in the hopes of drawing an audience to a social, political, or commercial event. The musical entertainment was provided for free to draw a crowd that could then be pitched a product by someone with something to sell. For example, John Carson, a leading figure in the development of country music in Atlanta, played to draw crowds to store openings and for political rallies before the turn of the century and eventually became a staple figure in the political campaigns of U.S. Congressman Tom Watson and—well into the commercial era—of Georgia Governors Gene and Herman Talmadge (Wiggins 1987). The son of Gid Tanner, another major Atlanta performer of the early commercial days, also recalls that on "those Saturday mornings in the early twenties, when it was 'too wet to plow,'" he and his dad would take a wagon to Atlanta. "Some merchant would ask Gid for a fiddle tune in front of his store, people would gather . . . and the crowd would grow so large that it blocked the trolley tracks until a policeman came to break it up" (Burrison 1977: 73).[10] In effect, the music was used then in the way that entertainment is used today on commercial radio and television—offered free of charge to attract listeners or viewers to an advertiser.

Perhaps the most direct analogy to commercial radio and TV performance, however, was the association of country music entertainment with the selling of patent medicine. Many prominent country entertainers, including Roy Acuff and Bill Monroe, got valuable early entertainment experience playing music and appearing in blackface comedy routines to draw crowds for medicine shows. Kirk McGee (long-time "Grand Ole Opry" regular), who in his youth toured with Dr. Walter Harris selling Aztec Indian Medicine through Tennessee, Alabama, and Georgia, told Paul DiMaggio and me in 1973 that the work was exciting and, at five dollars a day plus a bed on the wagon, the money was good for a young person in those days. Nonetheless, the medicine show work was seasonal. This is because the shows could only profitably tour the rural South in the fall when the cotton had been harvested and people had cash in hand.

Many women played fiddle and guitar, or a keyboard instrument. Far more sang. But few women performed outside the confines of family and church, and even fewer performed for money before the advent of commercial country music. As Malone (1985: 22–23) has shown, the repertoire of women's music tended to be different from that of men, and when the chance to become professionals came, many more men than women were prepared to enter the field. While there were notable exceptions, from the outset commercial country music was defined by male performers in terms of male themes, and the balance of gender voices didn't begin to be seriously redressed, as Mary Bufwack and Robert Oermann amply show (1993: 2–163), until after World War II.

Enter Radio and Records

In recent decades radio and records have complemented each other. Records have provided an inexpensive form of programming to radio, and radio airplay has provided the most effective means of advertising the availability of new records. In the 1920s, however, they were clearly rivals. Phonograph record sales boomed nationally from 1919 through 1921, but the fledgling industry was in a serious decline by 1923. Radio stations were being launched in all the major cities, and live music broadcast over the radio sounded better than did music heard on the acoustically recorded phonograph records of the time (Hughbanks 1945; Read and Welch 1959). This led to the reasoning that if people could get the music they wanted to hear free over radio, they wouldn't buy phonograph records.[11]

The record companies reacted to the competition from radio in several ways. They greatly expanded their research on alternative means of improving the sound quality of records, and they sought new markets for recorded music. These two efforts combined to encourage both the recording of folk music of several different types at diverse locations around the country, and the creation of distinct markets for black- and white-styled country music (Ennis 1992).

Now over three-quarters of a century on from those times, the path of commercialization seems to have been inevitable, but it was not. As in any entrepreneurial situation (Peterson 1981), all of the elements necessary for an innovation may be present, but they are not actualized until one or more entrepreneurs select among the wide array of available elements and, flying in the face of conventional wisdom, create a new system of production and consumption, significantly altering American and therefore world culture in the process.

CREATING A SYSTEM OF PRODUCTION

Numerous companies and individuals tried to cash in on the potential market for folk-derived music,[12] but we will focus on the efforts of Polk Brockman of Atlanta, Georgia, for three reasons.[13] First, he was the first to have made and released a phonograph record by an untrained country performer. Second, Brockman put together the mutually reinforcing, five-component industrial system of production which would later re-emerge as the basis for the triumph of Hank Williams and his peers. Third, the failure of Brockman's Atlanta development showed that its early success had depended on the contributions of each of the components. His failings also served as a lesson for other entrepreneurs, including Ralph Peer, who were looking for ways to make money out of country music.

Polk Brockman, born into an Atlanta mercantile family, spent his first three years of full-time work as a wholesale traveling representative for the Simmons Bedding Company. In 1920 he was induced to return home to Atlanta and to work for the family furniture store by the promise of being allowed to establish a department featuring the newly popular phonograph record players. As large wooden objects meant for the living room, such players were at that time regularly being merchandised by furniture stores.

While Atlanta is today a large and urbane city, it was something quite different then, populated largely by people characterized by John Burrison as "nouveau-urbanites."

> Atlanta, in the first quarter of this century, was largely a town of rural refugees. With its growing industry and business opportunities, the city was attracting into its magnetic field a flood of Georgia countryfolk, both black and white, who, because of the unstable price of cotton, the devastating effects of the boll weevil, the growing shift from near-self sufficiency to dependence on a cash economy, and ex-

ploitation by the tenant farmer system, were fleeing their small, increasingly inefficient farms to work as millhands, domestics, or tradesmen in the big city. (Burrison 1977: 59)

Brockman found that the phonograph record players attracted a good deal of attention even among the less well-to-do, since the players of the era ran on wind-up motors needing no electricity. Nonetheless, sales were slow because the regular stock of records then available to be played on them was not very attractive to the store's clientele. To secure a more appealing stock of records, Brockman acquired the Atlanta dealership for the Okeh Record Company. While Okeh had records by a range of dance bands and romantic singers, it was pioneering in releasing jazz (à la Louis Armstrong) and sophisticated blues records (à la Bessie Smith) by black performers (Dixon and Godrich 1970; Russell 1970). Blacks of the Atlanta area responding by flocking in to buy players and records, and Brockman was such a good sales manager that in 1921 the Okeh company asked him to become the regional wholesale distributor for their records.

Brockman, like other record dealers throughout the South, became involved as a "talent scout" looking for new performers to record, and this got him directly involved in commercializing country music. The emerging system of production had five major linked components: recording, radio performance, touring, song publishing, and songwriting. I will follow this sequence because it roughly reflects the route that Polk Brockman took as he became increasingly involved in the music industry.

1. Recording

While record sales of popular, operatic, and symphonic music turned down sharply across the nation in 1922 owing in part to the new competition of radio, sales of blues records, a form of music generally performed by blacks and rarely played over the radio (Leonard 1962; Dixon and Godrich 1970), remained high. Ralph Peer, Okeh's innovative producer of specialty records (records produced for specific ethnic, nationality, and religious groups), and arguably the first to identify African Americans as a distinct and potentially lucrative market, wanted to record more blues and regionally popular performers of any sort in order to compensate for lagging popular and classical music record sales. Peer sought Brockman's advice on what performers and songs to record because of his success at record merchandising in the Atlanta area.

It would have proved very difficult to bring large numbers of musical aggregations to New York from the distant regions. The way of finding talent, then as now, involved a shotgun approach followed by something like a high-powered rifle. As the system developed in the 1920s this meant recording a large number of new artists at remote locations near where they lived, using recording equipment set up temporarily in one or another city around the South or Southwest. One or two records of the new artists would be released with little promotion. Those few artists whose records sold well would then be invited to record in the company's major studio and considerable money would be spent in promoting their subsequent records.

Helped by Charles Hibbard, recording pioneer and onetime associate of Thomas Edison (Wolfe 1980: 33), the Okeh engineers devised portable recording equipment that could be shipped to a regional center and set up for a week or two in a vacant store or warehouse. The first field-recording session designed to locate regionally popular artists in the United States was set for June 1923, in Atlanta.[14] As Okeh's regional distributor, Polk Brockman was asked to scout for, and prescreen, the groups that might be recorded. Following Peer's strategy of seeking diversity, Brockman brought in a white dance band, a gospel singing group from the local black college, two female blues singers, a silent-movie theater piano player, and several novelty acts.

Brockman invited country fiddle player Fiddlin' John Carson to the improvised recording studio for Peer to hear. Brockman wanted to record Carson even though no comparable country music records had been released at that time. He reasoned that since Atlanta blacks had begun buying phonograph record players in great numbers as soon as records by blues and jazz artists were released, presumably white farmers and townsfolk would likewise be more likely to buy phonograph record players if their preferred kind of music played and sung by one of their own was available on phonograph records. This idea of recording "native Southerners" came to him, Brockman says, while he was in New York City to meet with Peer and saw a movie newsreel featuring an old-time fiddling contest in which Fiddlin' John Carson of Atlanta performed before an enthusiastic audience. Brockman then remembered that Carson had also been appearing on Atlanta's WSB for a year, so his name was widely known in the area.

Numerous colorful stories have grown up around Fiddlin' John Carson's first recording session, and even its exact date is in dispute.[15] What is important for later developments is that copies of the phonograph records made from the two songs recorded by Fiddlin' John Carson on or about June 19, 1923, and released in the Atlanta area quickly sold out, as did the subsequent pressings.

With this new record in hand, Brockman found other ways to promote the sale of record players as well. For example, soon after copies of the Carson record arrived in Atlanta, Brockman got him to appear at a fiddling contest that was part of the fifty-ninth annual national Elks Fraternal Order convention in Atlanta. Brockman placed the largest phonograph player then available in Atlanta on the stage and played the record just after Carson played live. Brockman reported that the record "sold like hot cakes." As a result of this and similar examples of Brockman's free-wheeling promotional efforts, the record continued to sell well. Peer was impressed, and, never one to put his own aesthetic judgments before his business interests, got a laudatory story about Carson and the remarkable success of his record planted in *Talking Machine World,* the leading record industry trade magazine of the day (Cohen 1974).

2. Radio

Another record merchandising device developed by Brockman involved the new rival medium, radio. Carson was attractive to radio station programmers for the same reasons other folk musicians schooled in the oral tradition were. Like amateur glee clubs, high-school bands, and the like, they were willing to play for nothing, or next to nothing. But, unlike these others who learned music from the written page, square-dance fiddlers could play for as long or as short a time as needed, having what seemed like an infinite repertoire of songs (Peterson 1975).

On March 16, 1922, radio station WSB of Atlanta went on the air—the first substantial radio station anywhere in the southern United States. There is no record of when Fiddlin' John first played on the air, but Wiggins (1987) reports that it was probably within weeks of the station's first broadcast. Certainly he had played regularly on the air for over a year before he made his first record for Brockman, and Carson had become quite a local celebrity because of the on-air promotion on WSB and in its parent company's newspaper, the *Atlanta Journal.* Evidenced, for example, in the accompanying clipping from the newspaper (see fig. 2.1). Most often Carson played on programs with performers of other types of music, but on November 29, 1922, there was what was billed as an "Old-fashioned Concert" (Wiggins 1987: 72), probably the first "all-country" radio program to air anywhere.

There is no record of Carson's having been paid for appearing on the radio, and in fact throughout the 1920s nonunion musicians were generally paid nothing more than "expense money" for performing on the air. It is clear, however, that Carson, an experienced self-promoter, realized the importance of radio for enhancing his reputation and increasing his income. He painted "Fiddlin [*sic*] John Carson—Radio and

Georgia Fiddlers Invade Radio World

Journal's Radio Truck

At the places and hours announced below, The Atlanta Journal's radio truck will receive and amplify programs transmitted by WSB, the radiophone broadcasting station of The Atlanta Journal.

Sunday

10:54 a. m., at Piedmont park.
5 to 6 p. m., at city stockade.
8 to 9 p. m., at Grant park.

Monday

7 to 8 p. m., at Riverside.

Tuesday

7 to 8 p. m., at Battle Hill sanatorium.

Wednesday

7 to 8 p. m., at Rock Springs.

Thursday

5 to 6 p. m., at Oglethorpe university.
7 to 8 p. m., at Chamblee, Ga.

Friday

7 to 8 p. m., at corner of Kennedy and Davis streets.

Fiddlin John Carson, famous champion of Georgia, and some of his cronies, who is now spreading the big name and fame far and wide with the aid of The Journal radiophone. The Fannin county mountaineer scored heavily on two of WSB's program last week and will be presented again before the picturesque gathering of old-time fiddlers at the auditorium soon.

Figure 2.1 This September 10, 1922, *Atlanta Journal* picture story pronounces the surprising success of Fiddlin' John Carson's old-time fiddling, which was being broadcast over the newspaper's fledgling radio station, WSB.

Recording Artist" on his car. Reciprocally, as soon as he had recorded his first record, Carson plugged it on the air, noting that it could be purchased at the Polk Furniture store. In turn, Brockman advertised the record as being by "Fiddlin' John Carson, famous radio artist appearing regularly on WSB."

3. Touring

Emerging country music artists of the mid-1920s typically received no money for appearing on the radio and made little money from their recordings.[16] Yet records and, even more, radio appearances, were vital in making it possible for these semiprofessional musicians to become full-time professionals. Based on the prestige of being a recording artist and based on the greatly increased name recognition and credibility gained by regular radio appearances, performers found that they could charge admissions to their concerts set up in public halls and school buildings within the range of the radio station's signal. To facilitate the process of reputation-building via radio, musicians began to announce their forthcoming personal appearances over the air. This not only ensured a larger audience at those events but demonstrated to fans and potential event sponsors in other towns that this was an act that was in much demand.

John Carson's case provides a good example of how the new media transformed the career possibilities of country musicians. Carson, who was fifty-five years old in 1923, was quite an enterprising showman, and well before the advent of the commercial era he had played at dances and store openings; he had composed and played topical songs for tips; he had been commissioned to write and perform political campaign songs for several notable Georgia politicians; and he had received wide newspaper publicity as a fiddling contest champion (Cohen 1975; Wiggins 1987; Daniel 1985). Nonetheless, all these and similar activities were not sufficiently steady or well-paying to provide Carson a full-time living from music. At various times he worked in a cotton mill, as a moonshiner, as a house painter, and at a range of other jobs. The coming of radio changed all this. It provided him and a number of his peers the means of making a living by touring, as he bluntly acknowledged in a statement quoted in the November 7, 1925, issue of *Radio Digest,* "Radio made me."

Polk Brockman was instrumental in promoting a fiddling contest in Atlanta in 1923 just after the release of Carson's first record (Wiggins 1987: 75), but there is no evidence that Brockman was ever involved in the potentially profitable business of booking live music tours for Carson or for any of the other many artists that he helped record. In fact the Atlanta fiddlers contest seems to have been primarily a vehicle for promoting the sale of phonograph record players and Carson's records (Burrison 1977). Nonetheless, performing shows at town halls, school auditoriums, and the like within the range of the radio station's broadcast signal became the prime source of income for John Carson and the other emerging professional musicians who quickly followed his example.

4. Song Publishing

Another vital element of the emerging commercial music system that was developed in Atlanta by Brockman was song publishing. What is more, the kind of publishing he engaged in was directly at odds with the song publishing practices of his day, and yet it presaged the operation of a modern music publisher. The major popular music publishers of the day were grouped together in New York along what was called Tin Pan Alley because of their brash ways of promoting songs. Each of these publishers took the new songs written by their own stable of writers and worked to get them placed in Broadway musicals, sung by the leading vaudeville artists and played by the best-known dance bands. Once songs became popular through such exposure, the publishers made most of their money by selling sheet music for performance in private homes, restaurants, dance halls, and the like. Brockman turned this around by producing lyric sheets from records. Desiring to profit from publishing songs, he had Irene Spain, the step-daughter of Andrew Jenkins, copy down the words and reduce to standard notation the music recorded by John Carson and other white and black performers in Atlanta (McCulloh 1967).

Within the folk tradition out of which commercial country music was emerging, there was no such thing as "song publishing." Songs were not written and read by trained musicians; they were just sung and heard, and gifted performers would commit many hundreds of songs to memory (Spielman 1975). Songs not only came from other local players and from touring commercial vaudeville or tent show groups but increasingly were copied from radio and phonograph records as well. Thus the available stock of song elements was continually being enriched, not only by the ever more diverse oral traditions of ethnic immigrants, but also by the reincorporation of compositions like those of Stephen Foster that had originally been written for the commercial music industry.

Musicians developed a repertoire of "their own songs," as they usually thought of them, but the songs were not so much their "compositions" as what I would call their "collages"; that is, assemblages of melody, sound styling, rhythm, and words constructed from fragments of songs in the generally available stock of song elements, edited, rearranged, and supplemented to fit their own styles and the demands of the situation.

While the pioneer record producers like Brockman and Peer accepted the song collages, they increasingly asked would-be recording artists to bring them newly composed songs, because these could be published and copyrighted. This had the effect of turning the songs as such, independent of any record version, into property, the rights to which could be bought, sold, and merchandised as sheet music or as recordings by other artists.

5. Songwriting

Not content to seek out performers capable of writing copyrightable songs, Brockman began to commission the writing of songs on topics that he thought would strike the public fancy. The emerging commercial performers could not be relied upon to come up regularly with new songs on demand, so Brockman turned to several individuals who had written poems and songs before the emergence of the commercial music business. In the process he introduced the separation of composition and performance and encouraged the emergence of full-time, professional country music songwriters.

Brockman's most prolific and successful songwriting find was Andrew Jenkins.[17] He was a blind newsboy and later revivalist preacher who for years had sung his sacred and secular songs on the street corners of downtown Atlanta. Brockman became acquainted with Jenkins's songwriting skills when he recorded several songs performed by the Jenkins Family in 1923. Soon Brockman began to commission Jenkins to write songs for John Carson and several other performers to record. Because of its commercial success, Brockman's most renowned commission was the broadsidelike (Green 1972) "event" song "The Death of Floyd Collins," written in 1925. Collins, a spelunker trapped in a Kentucky cave, became the object of national attention as newspapers around the country fed by the fledgling wire services dramatized the daily progress of the failed rescue attempt (Russell 1937). At the time the story was unfolding, Brockman was visiting in Jacksonville, Florida. He wrote to Jenkins, enclosing clippings of the newspaper article and requesting him to write a song about Floyd Collins's plight for an upcoming Okeh field-recording session in Atlanta. By the time of the recording session, April 15, 1925, Collins had died and Jenkins's tragedy song was complete. Brockman paid Jenkins twenty-five dollars for it. Brockman gave it to Carson, but Carson didn't read music and had difficulty learning a song quickly. The resulting stiff recording Carson made of the song clearly shows it, and the record sold poorly. But Brockman did not stop there. He licensed the performance rights of the song to Frank Walker of Columbia Records who then placed the song with Vernon Dalhart, a popular, classically trained interpreter of folk music, to record. The Dalhart recording was hugely successful, making Brockman quite a bit of money as the song's publisher.

The creation and commercial dissemination of "The Death of Floyd Collins" in a matter of weeks after Collins's death shows just how systematic commercial country music-making in Atlanta had become in less than two years (McCulloh 1967; Green 1965). Thus the practice of composing music on demand, which was later to make Nashville, Tennessee, the country music tune factory (Ryan and Peterson 1982), was pioneered by Polk Brockman in Atlanta, Georgia, three decades earlier.

Though the rough records of Fiddlin' John Carson are a far cry from the progressively slicker productions of Roy Acuff, Hank Williams, Loretta Lynn, and Dolly Parton, the careers of each of these, and hundreds like them, up through the 1960s, depended on the system of production constructed in Atlanta by Brockman. In effect, Brockman first put together the system for making money by transforming "home-made" music into "store-bought" commercial country music.

WHY BROCKMAN IN ATLANTA?

Atlanta's Centrality

If there was a reason for a regional center devoted to commercial country music, Atlanta was clearly the most appropriate place for it to be located. It was nearer to the geographic center of the South, which was seen by commercializers as the wellspring of the music, than any other city. But geographic centrality was not the only factor favoring Atlanta. From its origin as a railroad junction before the Civil War, Atlanta had been a point of transshipping, and with the decline of river transport after the war, it increasingly became the hub of commercial activity and light industry for the entire region. The other cities that come to mind, including Dallas, Nashville, Louisville, Charlotte, and Knoxville, were less developed, considerably smaller, or more isolated. In the 1920s, only Memphis, which was becoming the center of the blues industry, might have been a serious rival.

That a city was geographically or commercially most suitable did not mean that it would become the center of country music production. The prime reason for the rise to ascendancy of Chicago in the 1930s and Nashville from 1940 through 1970 is, I believe, the same that made Atlanta the first regional center of country music commercialization in the 1920s. That is the presence of a strong-signaled radio station that regularly played country music during the evening hours when signal quality and geographic penetration is the greatest. In Chicago it was WLS, featur-

Fiddlin' John Carson
and
Henry Whitter
Exclusive Artists

THESE two mountaineers were discovered by OKeh! Seeing the recording possibilities in their quaint style and their "Old Time Pieces" OKeh recorded some of their selections and at the same time uncovered a brand new field for record sales.

It is noteworthy that in the annual "Fiddlin' Contests" held in the South, and against the best there was, Fiddlin' John Carson was seven times awarded the championship.

Another mountain star is Henry Whitter. Throughout his native hills he is acclaimed the most novel entertainer for he plays a harmonica and a guitar at the same time and never misses a note and in between accompanies himself when he sings those quaint, "Old Time Pieces."

The craze for this "Hill Country Music" has spread to thousands of communities north, east and west as well as in the south and the fame of these artists is ever increasing. And this again gives OKeh Dealers another new field discovered, originated and made possible by the manufacturers of

OKeh Records
The Records of Quality
Manufactured by
GENERAL PHONOGRAPH CORPORATION, NEW YORK
OTTO HEINEMAN, President

Figure 2.2 Fiddlin' John Carson shown in this 1924 Okeh record company advertisement together with Henry Whitter. Note how the ad copy notes the growing popularity of "hill country" authenticity.

ing the "National Barn Dance," and in Nashville it was WSM, featuring the "Grand Ole Opry" (Peterson 1975). In Atlanta it was WSB, which in March 1922 became the first high-powered radio station anywhere in the South.

The WSB management apparently made no conscious decision to feature country music. Stations scrambled to find programs to broadcast and they turned to musical aggregations to "fill airtime." A very wide range of musical groups was called on to play, and they were invited back if they drew a large response from listeners as evidenced by phone calls, letters, and telegrams. Fiddlin' John Carson was the first country music performer to play on WSB in Atlanta, and according to the *Radio Digest* of November 7, 1925, "He made an instant hit, and before the concert was half finished the telephones in the Radio department were ringing constantly and furiously bringing in clamorous requests, and telegrams came pouring in from the outside."

Nonetheless, radio stations did not program country music performers just because they proved popular. In fact, station management and the urbane city residents typically loathed the music, seeing it as a constant reminder of the rustic rural past contrasting sharply with the sophisticated and classy urban image to which they aspired. Country musicians were programmed because they did not require complex or expensive studio arrangements, because they could be called upon to play at a moment's notice, as well as because they were capable of playing for as long (or short) a time as was required (Peterson and DiMaggio 1973). Notwithstanding country music's utility as a cheap, reliable time-filler, the radio station per se had no reason to develop the full potential for commercializing country music made possible by exposure over the radio. This required the entry of independent entrepreneurs like Polk Brockman.

Brockman's Value-Neutral Commercialism

Polk Brockman's installing a phonograph player department in his family furniture store was initially a part of the march of urban composed music into the heart of the South, the largest remaining bastion of fiddle-based music. The young and progressive manager of such a department might have been expected to champion the dissemination of Tin Pan Alley popular songs and jazz records, as many of Brockman's regional counterparts undoubtedly did.

Why then did Polk Brockman in particular work to get what was thought of as "hillbilly" music written, published, and recorded, and thus to insure the continued vitality of country music in the modern media of radio and records? While many later commercializers have said retro-spectively that they loved the music and simply wanted to spread it to new audiences, Brockman never made such a self-aggrandizing claim. In no uncertain terms he told me in 1973, "My interest in hillbilly music and black music is strictly financial." Referring to other early record com-pany men like himself, Brockman told Archie Green and Ed Kahn, who wanted to praise him and the other "folk music" record producers for preserving a vanishing culture, that:

> He never met anyone who had any self awareness of his role as a preserver of culture. . . .[He and his contemporaries in the business] were simply looking for something they could sell. . . . In response to the fact that we think of him not so much as a successful business-man [but] as a person who made a contribution to American culture, Brockman replied, "It was accidental if I did because I was at it from the commercial standpoint."[18]

Even if he was involved not for love but for money, it still took an act of insight to see what others did not, that money could be made from the music. Brockman was first and foremost a salesman. He took seri-ously the credo that "the customer is always right." As he told Green and Kahn in 1961, "I don't ever look at a thing as to what I think about it. I always try to look at it through the eyes of the people I expect to buy it. My personal opinion never enters into anything I ever have any-thing to do with when it comes to merchandising."

One final element that helped Brockman succeed relates to his com-mitment as a salesman. Whatever he was selling, he was not inhibited by the typical class and racial prejudices of his peers, the white middle class of 1920s Atlanta. Rather than revile what others saw as the "jumped up" rednecks and blacks of the new South, he catered to their new-found purchasing power. All those, black and white, rich and poor, agreed that Brockman mingled easily with all sorts of people. Even those like Irene Spain who later came to resent him for having underpaid them for their work in the early days of recording remarked on what a respectful person he was.[19]

Brockman's willingness to overcome the bonds of prejudice and dis-crimination is most clearly evidenced in the treatment he gave to those recording for him. On numerous occasions, for example, he personally drove white hill folk and blacks long distances so that they would get to recording sessions safely.[20] And on one occasion at least, he rented a special railroad car to carry blacks from Atlanta to a New York record-ing session so that they would not have to face the discomforts and humiliations of riding in one of the segregated-seating rail cars (Holston 1973).

Things Fall Apart

If you did not know better, you might by this point be prepared to believe that Atlanta has become the center of country music production and that Polk Brockman is hailed as a founding father of the form. Obviously, nothing could be much further from the truth. Nashville, and not Atlanta, is called "Music City, U.S.A.," and Brockman's name is unknown to most current performers and fans of the music.

The reason Atlanta did not continue to develop as the regional center of the commercialization of country music is not difficult to find. As has been noted, the sustained commitment of a high-powered radio station to broadcasting country music was crucial for nurturing all of the other elements that went into the development of a commercial country music system of production.

While WSB included traditional music by Fiddlin' John Carson, Clayton McMichen, the Jenkins Family, and others in its mix of programming, country music as such was not scheduled at a regular time in the day or week in the mid-1920s. Performers were billed separately along with performers of all sorts, and no generic name such as "Barn Dance," or "Country Frolic" was used to highlight or institutionalize the form on WSB. Radio broadcasting, of course, was then in its infancy and the idea of distinct types of programming scheduled at regular times was only in the process of being formulated. The first regular "Barn Dance" program was instituted January 4, 1923, by WBAP in Dallas (Malone 1985: 33).[21]

Considering the diverse talent that was featured on WSB, it would have been difficult to find a common rubric within which they would have agreed to play. The Jenkins Family sang sacred numbers, and some members of the family voiced great contempt for John Carson, who insisted that he had to get drunk and be chewing tobacco to perform. Clayton McMichen, who experimented with the latest Hawaiian and jazz forms, considered the Jenkins sanctimonious and Carson an old coot who was musically twenty years behind the times (Cohen 1965; McCulloh 1967; Burrison 1977; Wiggins 1987). It would have taken a person with great resolve and considerable tact to have brought the Atlanta musicians together regularly on one program. This sort of leadership was missing in Atlanta. Lambdin Kay, the general manager of WSB, had no great liking for the music,[22] and no other ranking member of the station's staff played the role of advocate for the music comparable to the role played by George Biggar and John Lair at WLS in Chicago and George Hay at WSM in Nashville.[23] In consequence, country music was given progressively less airtime on WSB after 1924.[24]

THE STRIP-MINING SYSTEM

Polk Brockman took part in numerous field-recording expeditions throughout the South and Southwest, and he recorded a number of artists now famous in the annals of blues and jazz history. Nonetheless, his influence and music enterprise did not grow like those of several other music industry entrepreneurs, including Ralph Peer, his friend and sometime business associate. His short-term success and long-term failures underscore the *systematic* nature of the commercializing process and his failure to appreciate it as a system. Rather, at each turn, he tried to extract as much profit from each venture without fostering the development of a self-renewing system.

But plug on he did. By 1926 the various aspects of the music business had become so important a part of the enterprise that Brockman sold the family retail furniture store to concentrate on the record, musical supply, and phonograph business. He continued to record black and white country music acts through the 1920s and continued as a major regional record distributor until 1938. He sold the musical supply business in 1943 and from that time on worked completely outside the music business. Questioned by me in 1973 about why he had progressively withdrawn from the commercial music business, he cited the privations of the Great Depression and the dislocations of the Second World War. But during those periods other entrepreneurs were founding music enterprises that would become major corporations. Why then did Brockman, the consummate commercializer, not take advantage of these new opportunities?

I think the answer is that he simply did not see the system he had helped to build. Rather, like most other record makers of the period, he viewed each development as a discreet opportunity to be exploited in the short run, not as part of a system to be developed and consolidated for long-term gain. For example, in dealing with performers, whether white or black, knowledgeable or beginners, his goal in recording was to get a single recording session from a performer; he did not nurture artists by helping them develop long-lasting careers. Brockman was not alone in this short-term strategy. Frank Walker, the major early producer of Southern performers black and white for Columbia Records, candidly described this extractive orientation in speaking of the industry men's orientation to most early artists.

Their repertoire would consist of eight or ten things that they did well and that is all they knew. So, when you picked out the three or four that were best in a man's so called repertoire you were through with that man as an artist. . . . You might come out with two selections or you might come out with six or eight, but you did it all at that time. (Evans 1982: 72)

Brockman treated the writers of songs in much the same way. He bought individual songs from writers outright, typically for ten or twenty-five dollars, so that he could get the money due both to the writer and to the publisher.[25] While writers might be glad to have the money in the short run, this system had the effect of alienating writers over time. If nothing came of the song, the writer might feel the song had failed because of the way it was recorded. If it became successful as a record or as sheet music, the writer could reasonably feel exploited.[26] Thus, ironically, Brockman's practice systematically alienated most of those writers capable of writing commercially successful songs.

Another piece of evidence suggesting that Brockman did not understand the commercial music business as a system but as so many discreet elements is that, having been successful with one particular song, he tried to repeat his success with other songs in exactly the same mold. This strategy of repeating a successful formula although conditions were changing, not uncommon among entrepreneurs in any field (Peterson 1981), quickly exhausted the novelty of subgenres, so that successive songs on the theme tended to have progressively less market success. The most outstanding example of such myopia in Brockman's work was his experience with what came to be called "disaster" or "event" songs (Wolfe 1995). He followed the immensely successful "Death of Floyd Collins" with recordings of several dozen more disaster songs, most of them also commissioned from Andrew Jenkins, author of the original hit. None of the later works enjoyed great success. Along with other record makers, Brockman repeatedly return to the genre in the late 1920s and the early 1930s (Wolfe 1995), and he tried to stage a reentry into the recording business in 1949 with yet another topical tragedy written by Andrew Jenkins for the occasion, "The Death of Little Kathie Fiscus." This was fully two dozen years after the first hit and a decade after any contemporary disaster songs had had any great success (McNeil 1987; Wolfe 1995). Characteristically, his only comment to Green and Kahn in 1961 concerning the comeback try was to complain about the amount of money he personally had lost on the venture.

The final example of Brockman's short-term pragmatic rather than systematic orientation to the music business is his practice of taking the profits from the music ventures and investing them in other lines of activity. In 1961, for example, he had a company with a plant in Ackworth, Georgia, Lovable Toys, which manufactured dolls. By 1973 he was out of toys and "retired" but dabbling in real estate, particularly in suburban central Florida shopping malls—near the site of Disney World.

If Polk Brockman is remembered in the music circles at all, it is through Ruby Bloom's song caricature of him as "The man from the south with a big cigar in his mouth . . . (who) said come here son, I'm gonna make you a star." In the end, it turns out that his goal was not to produce a star who would enjoy continuing success. Looking at all of Brockman's activities in retrospect, it seems that they more nearly resemble the old story of the person who, having bred a goose that could lay golden eggs, proceeded to butcher the goose.

CONCLUSION

This accounting of the activities of Polk Brockman of Atlanta, Georgia, his failings as much as his successes, gives clear support to the assertion that the commercialization process does not take place gradually, but rather occurs in bursts when a whole set of mutually reinforcing elements are put into place over a short period of time. Roger Wallis and Krister Malm (1984) and Jeremy Marre and Hannah Charlton (1985), in their two remarkable studies of the commercializing forces impinging on oral music traditions in twelve and thirteen countries around the world, give ample evidence that the systemic nature of the commercialization process described here for the American South of the 1920s is not an exceptional development.

CHAPTER THREE

Renewable Tradition

The Carter Family and
Jimmie Rodgers

*They want these old-fashioned things. . . . Love songs
and plantation melodies and the old river ballads.
Well, I'm ready with 'em. And I've got some new ideas
for songs, too.—Porterfield 1992: 2*

his is Jimmie Rodgers, who would eventually be anointed the "Father of Country Music," writing home to his wife Carrie in 1927, after his first meeting with Ralph Peer. He writes in the voice of a professional entertainer who is prepared to deliver what is required rather than that of a person expressing his own feelings in song. He does, however, understand Peer's expectations very well. Peer was looking for old songs that had not yet been copyrighted and newly written songs that sounded old-fashioned to fill the recently discovered demand for "old-time tunes." By 1927, Ralph Peer had come to see traditional music as a renewable resource, and he developed a system of production that committed creative singer-songwriters to the quest for new old-sounding songs. The most successful group within the system as he envisaged it was not Rodgers, but an unassuming aggregation from Maces Spring, Virginia, the Carter Family.

In this chapter, we will first explore the emerging idea of tradition as a renewable resource. We will then draw illustrations from the Carter Family's experience wherever appropriate in describing Peer's system. Finally, in the third part of the chapter, we will focus on Jimmie Rodgers's contribution in molding the first complete (but failed) picture of the commercial country music artist: the easygoing railroad worker singing blues songs in a pop artist's outfit.

TRADITION AS A RENEWABLE RESOURCE

The interdependent five-element Atlanta system of production developed in 1923 was already beginning to disintegrate by 1925 for the reasons just discussed, but a system was being perfected that relied less on radio and more on record making as the prime means for performers to become known to prospective concert audiences. The central business people in this alternative system were the phonograph record company "talent scouts" or "A&R men"[1] who ranged across the South and Southwest looking for songs to record. In the popular music field of the 1920s the job of the A&R department was to match an "artist" with the appropriate "repertoire." In the emerging country field, such persons were most often called "talent scouts" and they played a much more proactive role in finding artists to record, culling among their songs, and coaching performers on how to shape selections to the constraints of record making and the preferences of the buying public as they understood it.[2]

The early record company music prospectors who came to find new talent in the South, men like Fred Walker, Ralph Peer, Art Satherley, Henry Speir, and Eli Oberstein, sought out performers with songs that weren't already copyrighted so that they would not have to pay royalties to another author and publisher. For the first several years of Southern field recording this caused no great difficulty because there seemed to be an inexhaustible supply of songs. Asked whether a song was original, the singer typically said it was his or her song. In time the record makers came to realize that many different persons claimed authorship of essentially the same traditional song, and what is more, that numerous so called "original" songs were, in fact, derived from copyrighted older popular songs that had entered the oral tradition.

Strip-Mining

Although the early A&R men may have thought so, the performers were not lying to them about song authorship. Rather, the record people and the performers thought of song "ownership" quite differently. Within the American oral tradition shared by both whites and blacks, melodies and lyrical elements are considered common property from which a performer can draw in putting together her or his own work. As Gene Wiggins notes in discussing the traditional performers' notion of authorship: "Sometimes when they say 'wrote' they mean 'crystallized a personally meaningful version'" (1987: xvi).

Such semantic differences, however, could be quite consequential. When a song already under copyright became a hit, the original copyright holder would threaten to sue for copyright infringement and ask for compensation. This happened, for example, to Ralph Peer when he allowed Jimmie Rodgers to record his rendering of "Mother Was a Lady" under his own title, "If Brother Jack Were Here" (Porterfield 1992: 119).

As the search for songs that were different and uncopyrighted became common practice, this aboriginal mother lode of commercially interesting available songs was essentially mined-out in a few short years. Because the rate of extraction was so accelerated, the sheer number and variety of new releases were tremendous. Pekka Gronow (1983) estimates that in 1929, the peak pre-Depression year for the industry, Victor and Columbia released over a thousand new records in the United States, and that over 10,000 new records were released by all companies. Focusing specifically on the old-time country field, Charles Wolfe estimates that 3,500 distinct titles had been issued by the seven major U.S. phonograph record companies by the end of 1929 (Wolfe 1980: 57).

The Simulation of Tradition

For the country musicians such as John Carson, Uncle Dave Macon, and Ernest "Pop" Stoneman whose styles were set before 1910, there was no question about appearing "old-fashioned." That is simply how the music they played appeared to others. But this was a real problem for many of the younger performers. As Norm Cohen notes, Clayton McMichen, the youngest member of the Atlanta-based Skillet Lickers, considered Gid Tanner and Fate Norris of the group twenty years behind him musically, and he wanted to play modern rather than traditional music. Frank Walker of Columbia records cautioned him that there were far better bands in New York playing pop music and that he had brought the recording equipment all the way to Atlanta to record country, not popular music (Cohen 1965: 240).

In response to the dwindling supply of unrecorded songs, A&R men began to put a premium on finding artists who could fashion songs that *seemed* old-fashioned. As Porterfield (1992: 99) notes: "Pressured to produce material that was new [that is, uncopyrighted] yet somehow authentic to their temperament and traditions, aspiring rural artists such as Jimmie Rodgers and the Carter Family fell back on two obvious sources: either they dredged up old, half-forgotten relics of the past, or they composed original songs that sounded like the old ones—music that connected with the past and extended the tradition."

Those performers, like Vernon Dalhart and Jimmie Rodgers, who could quickly learn the newly composed "old-time songs" were highly prized, and the A&R men found it possible to pair a traditional singer with a person able to compose songs that sounded authentic. As Frank Walker noted: "There were a very few who could learn or could adopt something that somebody else might be able to do but not record. So you put these two together, so that one might be able to teach the other and you come up with a saleable or recordable article" (Evans 1982: 72).

Many of the most experienced performers were not able to learn new material quickly and perform it in a convincing manner. This was the case for Fiddlin' John Carson. His version of Andrew Jenkins's tragedy song "The Death of Floyd Collins" was not convincing and sold poorly. In sharp contrast, the rendition cut a few weeks later by Vernon Dalhart under the direction of Frank Walker became a national hit (Malone 1985: 49) and eventually went on to sell over 306,000 copies, more than any other record in Columbia Records' Old Familiar Tunes series.[3] Dalhart was a paragon of adaptability. Eschewing an exclusive contract with a single record company so that he could profit from making multiple recordings of the same song, Dalhart, who had been born Marion Try Slaughter, eventually recorded under seventy-nine names and as part of twenty-four named aggregations. A rural Texas-bred, classically trained singer, he began making records in a light operatic vein in 1916 (Walsh 1960), and in the early 1920s he had a number of hits singing songs in "Negro" dialect. Following the success of Carson's first country record in 1923, Dalhart began recording country songs in what he termed his "native dialect" (Haden 1975: 78).

Charles Wolfe (1979) has made a detailed analysis of the sources of the 1,452 songs appearing in Columbia record's 15000-D series of "Familiar Tunes—Old and New" between 1925 when Frank Walker initiated the series and 1931.[4] This gives a solid empirical reading of the mix of new and old, traditional and commercial, which constituted country music in the period. An average of just under half of all the secular recordings were traditional songs in each of these seven years. In the first two years popular songs accounted for a bit over 40 percent, a share that drops thereafter, while over the seven years the percentage of original songs doubles from 12 to 24. The change in the proportion of original songs is not as great as I had expected, based on the evidence for blues recording,[5] but the general figures mask two countertrends. By far the best-selling type of newly composed song in 1925 was the "disaster" or "event" song, led by Vernon Dalhart's version of "The Death of Floyd Collins." All of the original songs recorded in 1925 were of this special type, but the fad for event songs quickly passed and by 1931 thirty-four of the thirty-six original country songs were more representative of emerging trends in country music.[6]

DEEP-SHAFT MINING: RALPH PEER
AND THE CARTER FAMILY

All the leading A&R men of the late 1920s understood that the control of copyrights was important in keeping recording costs down. Ralph Peer alone fully appreciated how to make the control of copyrights profitable for himself and for the performers as well. In giving performers a financial stake in writing and finding new songs, he gained their personal loyalties and ensured the steady flow of new songs. Thus Peer, more than any of the other record producers, transformed tradition into a renewable resource. Here we shall see how Peer found the way to feed the golden-egg-laying geese. Illustrations are drawn from his work with the group that most perfectly illustrates his system in action, the Carter Family.

Peer's Idea

In 1925, two years after that fateful first Okeh trip to Atlanta, where he recorded Fiddlin' John Carson, Peer found himself at odds with the president of Okeh Records and he quit the company. Counting bonuses, he had been making the princely sum of $16,000 a year and had a good deal of money saved, so he loafed for several months. He then worked briefly as sales manager promoting a sports car named "Norma." This didn't work out, and he found no one to back his forward-looking scheme for selling apple pies nationally. Finally he approached Victor Talking Machine Company, by far the biggest record company in the world. They wanted to get into the growing hillbilly market, but saying that the treasurer of the company made $7,500 a year, they offered Peer about $5,000.[7] Peer refused to work for less than a third of what he had been making at Okeh, and the negotiations were at an impasse.

Still fascinated with the possibilities of making money in the music business, Peer realized that records, like radio and live performance, were just a medium of exposing music and "essentially this was the business of copyrights."[8] His earlier experience with Polk Brockman had showed him that the key to making money out of country music over the long haul was as a publisher, because the person who owned the copyright to a song profited not just from the selling of sheet music, but also from each commercial use of the material. With this idea in hand, he went back to Victor and offered to work for them for one dollar a year.[9] He did this on condition that Victor would allow him to copyright the music that was recorded. They readily agreed, reasoning that the profits from sheet-music sales of country and blues music would be negligible so that the copyrights would be virtually worthless.

Peer set up the Southern Publishing Company. He says that at the time he did not use his own name as part of the publishing company's title so that the auditors at Victor wouldn't realize how much money he personally would be making from the arrangement. And he did make a great deal of money working "for nothing." In 1959 he told Lillian Borgeson that for the three-month period a year after the relationship with Victor was finalized, the royalty payment to Southern Publishing for the songs he had recorded came to a quarter of a million dollars.

All the A&R men were asking for new songs, but the artists might, or might not, comply. The general practice was to buy songs outright from composer-performers, and if the records sold well, the artists felt cheated because the company got all the money. In order to give performers an incentive to keep bringing in good songs Peer never bought songs from them.[10] Rather he gave his artists fifty dollars as a performance fee for each side they recorded. This was as much or more than country and blues artists had been given for selling their songs outright to the other companies.[11] But under the arrangement with Peer, artists also retained songwriter rights and thus shared in all royalties from record sales and other commercial uses of their music.[12] There can be no doubt that this arrangement was attractive to prospective artists, as an illustration from 1927 clearly shows. When few artists showed up for Peer's first Victor recording session in Bristol on the Tennessee-Virginia boarder, he noted in a local newspaper article about his recording plans that the Stoneman Family, a well-known country music aggregation from the area, had received $3,600 for the past year's record sales (Wolfe 1972). "It worked like dynamite," Peer remembers. "The very next day I was deluged with long-distance telephone calls from the surrounding mountain region. Groups of singers who had not visited Bristol during their entire lifetime arrived by bus, horse and buggy, trains, or on foot" (Wolfe 1972: 12). Among the throng eager to record were two acts that were to prove the most influential of the period—the Carter Family and Jimmie Rodgers.

A New Kind of Publishing Company

Peer's strategy of building a publishing company around the royalties from record sales was an entirely new way for a publishing company to operate. Ordinarily publishers bought songs, kept writers under contract, and paid a crew of song-pluggers, all these requiring money in advance of any returns from sales of sheet music, but Peer's invention required no capital advances at all. His kind of publishing company was simply a named entity for holding copyrights. Ingenious as it was, this sort of publishing company did not spread right away, probably because in the popular music field the large profit came from the sale of sheet music.

Ironically it was not until nearly twenty years later that Acuff-Rose Publishing Company in Nashville would begin to make this kind of publishing company the norm in the entire commercial music industry.

If Peer worked for Victor "for nothing," he also managed the careers of his artists "for nothing." Peer signed all those he worked with to exclusive writer-publisher and personal management contracts that specified that they could record only for him. Although it was standard practice, Peer did not charge the artists a fee for being their personal manager, a fact that he continually reiterated to them. This "generosity" too was part of his plan because, being under contract to him, performers could not sell songs to other publishers or record for other record companies as Vernon Dalhart and Carson Robison regularly did (Walsh 1960).

Peer's deal with Victor changed the sorts of songs he looked for in one important way. Frank Walker and the other A&R men, who worked on salary, were looking for copyright-free material so that their company would not have to pay fees to a copyright holder. For them, a song in the public domain was perfectly acceptable. But this was not true for Ralph Peer because all of his income now came from the records made using the copyrighted songs in his new Southern Publishing Company. He wanted songs that he could copyright,[13] ones that were likely to enjoy considerable record sales. More than any of the other A&R men, Peer had a personal incentive to keep abreast of trends and to look for artists who were likely to produce hits. The need regularly to come up with old-sounding new songs gave a great stimulus to creative talent that otherwise would not have had such a wide-reaching channel of expression. Porterfield concludes, "The ultimate consequence [of Peer's activity] was to significantly influence the evolution of a major segment of our native culture—its popular music—and to set basic patterns that shaped the future of country music as an industry and as an art form" (1992: 99).

The Kinds of Songs Peer Sought

In the 1920s, as in every decade since, country music was influenced by the ebb and flow of styles in commercial popular music. The jazz dance fad had destabilized the industry, and many in the industry did all they could to discredit jazz. A few enterprising New York publishing firms, most notably that of Witmark, were able to render jazz songs as sheet music (Witmark and Goldberg 1975), but most of the old-line firms had not been able to adapt their sheet music sales techniques to this innovative dance form. They tried to fight the spreading popularity of jazz-based dance music, which was displacing a generation of operatic-voiced singers in the mold of Enrico Caruso and threatened their sheet music sales of the latest conventional Tin Pan Alley songs (Leonard 1962: 31).

While liking country music no more than they liked jazz, industry analysts in 1925 saw in the unprecedented nationwide popularity of old-time songs a harbinger of the end of the "jazz fad" and a return to a taste for ballads and sentimental love songs of the sort they were geared to produce. An unsigned editorial in the *Talking Machine World* of December 15, 1925, titled "What the Popularity of Hill-Billy Songs Means to Retail Profit Possibilities," is worth quoting in detail because it probably influenced Peer's thinking at the fateful recording session in Bristol seventeen months later.[14] The editorial begins,

> The advent or revival or what ever you choose to call it of what are described as the "hill-billy" songs signifies more than the mere vogue of such publications. The "Death of Floyd Collins," "Wreck of the Shenandoah," "At My Mother's Grave," and other such songs which have had fairly widespread popularity may mark the initial move in the passing of jazz, . . . a grasping out on the part of music purchasers for something besides the generally over-arranged jazz offerings.[15]

The author then notes the recent popularity of other unspecified nonjazz songs,

> the outstanding characteristic of which was that [like the hillbilly hits] they were in the most simplified song form. In fact, some of the outstanding record sellers to-day and for the past few months have been solo numbers with minor accompaniment. All of this undoubtedly shows the earmarks of a new phase of the popular music and record business.

Summarizing, the author suggests the opportunities open to the discerning industry executive like Ralph Peer who could look beyond an aesthetic prejudice against the music. The analysis continues:

> The fact that the public or a fair portion of it has decided on a funeral dirge type of offering should not be taken as an atavistic tendency. It is rather a desire for something different. This desire can be taken advantage of by both the popular music publisher and record maker, and songs of good ballad order, love songs and other numbers particularly lending themselves to solo voices with a minimum of arrangement should meet the situation and bring on a period of prosperity that would be far larger than the results obtained by merely catering to what may be a limited vogue for songs of pathos.

In Jimmie Rodgers with his clear and winning country-sounding voice and spare guitar accompaniment, Peer had found such a solo voice with a minimum of arrangement, and in the Carter Family he had tapped a treasure trove of old-sounding ballads and love songs.

Carter Family Neotraditional Songs

When A. P. Carter drove the family car the twenty-five arduous miles over the mountain to Bristol from his home in Maces Spring, Virginia, to try to record for Ralph Peer, he and his wife Sara had been singing together for ten years, and they had tried out unsuccessfully for the Brunswick company a few months earlier.[16] Unable to make much money out of music, A. P. made a living variously working as a blacksmith, a carpenter, and selling fruit trees. In addition to their two youngest children, they carried with them on that trip Maybelle, Sara's pregnant eighteen-year old guitar-playing cousin, who was married to A. P.'s brother, Eck. Maybelle had been playing with them for several months.

Looking as backwoods as any of the hundreds of people who were presenting themselves to the early A&R men, the Carters did not impress Peer. As Peer recalled years later, "They wander in, he's dressed in overalls and the women are country women from way back there. They look like hillbillies. But as soon as I heard Sara's voice, that was it. I knew it was going to be wonderful" (Wolfe 1987: 3). It is very unlikely that A. P. wore overalls,[17] but Peer's recollection is not all ex post facto bravado. The contemporary evidence that Peer was impressed with the Carter Family is that he cut (and Victor released) six songs by the Carter Family though he swore to Jimmie Rodgers several days later that it was the company's unbreakable rule to cut only two songs on a new artist.

Over the next few years of working together, the Carters sold more records than any other RCA Victor country music group except for Jimmie Rodgers. They had hits on an amazing variety of songs, including genuine folk songs, gospel songs, old sentimental pop songs, cowboy songs, and newly written love songs. With few exceptions, A. P. Carter was listed as songwriter and one of Ralph Peer's companies was listed as publisher of all of these. Thus the Carter Family represented ideal artists within Ralph Peer's system. But they did so without being prolific songwriters. In fact experts can agree on only a very few songs that A. P. actually composed. Sara and Maybelle contributed a few more. Leslie Riddle, an African American guitar player, contributed several songs and he also taught Maybelle Carter how to play melody and pick rhythm on the guitar at the same time—a style for which she became famous. A. P. got more songs out of old hymnals and songbooks, but the vast majority A. P. "collected" on what he called "song-catching" trips around the area where Virginia, Tennessee, and Kentucky come together. Riddle also accompanied A. P. Carter on a number of his song-catching trips, and being able to learn the melody of a song the first time he heard it, made it possible for Carter to forage rapidly. This range of song-getting activities illustrates just how well Peer's incentives to artists worked in producing copyrightable material.

At the same time, the Carter Family's experience shows the limits of Peer's system that focused on songwriting, song publishing, and record making. Even though they were very successful in Peer's terms, for the first decade of recording the Carters were not able to make a full-time living out of music. In 1929 A. P. went to Detroit for six months looking for carpentry work, and soon after this Maybelle went with her husband to Washington, D.C., where he worked for a railroad. For the next several years the three got together primarily for their semiannual recording sessions (Atkins 1975).

Two elements vital to the "Atlanta system of production" described in chapter 2 were missing from the Carter's professional activities. These were regular radio appearances (to gain name recognition and promote their upcoming live shows) and extensive touring (to make money). In the early years when their records sold best, the Carters did not establish a relationship with a powerful radio station,[18] and most of the live engagements they made were arranged by A. P. near their remote Virginia home in churches, schools, and clubs.[19] Thus, while the "original" Carter Family of Sara, Maybelle, and A. P. recorded a wealth of music that has directly inspired several generations of performers, their incomes from music did not make them financially secure.[20]

JIMMIE RODGERS: THE POPULAR-COUNTRY SYNTHESIS

If the Carter Family best exemplified Ralph Peer's system of song production and record making, another artist who found Peer at the same 1927 Bristol, Tennessee, sessions became hugely successful by adding live touring and image-making to Peer's prescription. This, of course, was the charming and self-aggrandizing, tubercular, Meridian, Mississippi, ne'er-do-well, James Charles "Jimmie" Rodgers.[21] In his later years, Ralph Peer said on more than one occasion, "I made Jimmie Rodgers."[22] With equal veracity, Jimmie Rodgers could have said, "I made Ralph Peer." Certainly each was responsible for the bulk of the money made by the other in the six years until Jimmie died. More important, the music they made in this time clearly established country music as something more than a romantic, backward-looking "ethnic" music primarily merchandised to rural white Southerners.

The Crucible of Creativity

After he became a successful performer billed as "The Singing Brakeman," Rodgers said that he had been a railroad worker like his father until his advancing tuberculosis made it impossible for him to engage in strenuous activity. But Porterfield (1992) shows clearly that from his youth Jimmie Rodgers had striven to be an entertainer. After winning an amateur singing contest in his hometown, Meridian, Mississippi, at the age of twelve, he put together his own neighborhood carnival, then bought an expensive sidewall tent on his father's credit and took the show on the road. Unimpressed with Jimmie's entrepreneurship, his father tracked the boy down in a nearby town and brought him home. Jimmie soon ran away, joining a traveling medicine show on its way to Birmingham, Alabama. He quit the show, he wrote his aunt a few weeks later, when the showman treated him unfairly. Continuing, he assured her using his own spelling that he had since found a job as a stock boy and "I have many frends and a Sweet little girl to" (Porterfield 1992: 4). His father came to fetch him home again. Now thirteen, he was given two alternatives: going back to school or going to work on a railroad section crew with his father. He had little enthusiasm for either, but opted for the adventure of working on the rails.

Over the next dozen plus years Rodgers picked up railroading jobs from Mississippi to the West Coast, played guitar or ukulele, and sang in a wide range of aggregations from pop dance bands to blackface minstrel shows and even a down-and-out touring "Hawaiian carnival." Figure 3.1 shows Jimmie Rodgers—on the left—with one of his numerous short-term associates. The traveling life made possible many forms of petty larceny. Jimmie would show his proficiency on guitar at a music instrument store and arrange to pay for it in installments. Then he'd hock it at a pawn shop for cash just before leaving town. In 1917 he was briefly married to a well-to-do farmer's daughter, Stella Kelly,[23] and three years later eloped with a minister's daughter, Carrie Williamson. In the summer of 1923 he arrived home broke from a tent-show trip to find their second daughter had died of diphtheria, and a few months later his chronic cough was diagnosed as tuberculosis—a death sentence in those days.

This string of tragedies would have crushed most people, but Rodgers seemed to face all adversity with cheerful optimism and boundless self-confidence over the next several years. He concentrated all his energy

Figure 3.1 Jimmie Rodgers (on the left), not yet the "Father of Country Music," with an unidentified associate in the mid-1920s on the road in one of his numerous ventures to make a living as an entertainer.

on getting lucky as an entertainer. Early in 1927 Rodgers heard of work in Ashville, North Carolina, a major mountain summer resort of the era. The work he found was as a janitor, but he soon was appearing with Helton's Old Time String Band, which played on Ashville's brand new radio station. Porterfield (1992: 9) says, "Rodgers was not interested in 'old timey' stuff" and arranged a radio program playing "novelty selections" and "specialty numbers" as a duet with one of the band members. He soon linked up with the Tennava Ramblers, three young musicians from the area, and convinced them to join him as "Popular Radio Artists," but their radio show was soon canceled.

Optimistic as usual in defeat, Rodgers proposed to go on the road touring the area with the trio, which he jocularly called his "hillbilly ork." He told his wife, Carrie, "If I can't get 'em in town, we'll go to the woods" (Porterfield 1992: 9). The tour of the "Jimmie Rodgers Entertainers" was for the most part a disaster—in one town no one showed up for the performance (Blaustein 1996: 5)—but they found by accident that Victor was recording in nearby Bristol, Tennessee. Ralph Peer said he was willing to audition the group, but by the time of the session the next day Rodgers and the group were no longer together.[24]

Peer recorded nineteen groups on that trip to Bristol, but there is no record of how many groups were auditioned and rejected. If Peer's comment that he was "deluged" with people wanting to record is credited, however, he must have rejected quite a few. Why did he reject those, while recording Jimmie Rodgers, a singer who had lost his band between their initial interview and the recording session the next day? There is no evidence from the time of the Bristol sessions that Peer thought Rodgers would be more successful than any of the other performers recorded there for the first time (Wolfe 1972, 1987; Porterfield 1992; 1995).[25]

Rodgers used the money he earned for recording the two songs to take his family to Washington, D.C., and for the next several months he sought work in the area without much success. Having not heard from Peer for three months, Rodgers packed his family off to New York City, where he checked into the posh Manger Hotel and brazenly asked the clerk to bill the charges to the Victor Talking Machine Company. Calling Peer on the phone, he mentioned that he was in town and just happened to have some spare time for a recording session. As it happened, his record had been selling moderately well and Peer had been looking for Rodgers, so a recording session was soon arranged. At this session Rodgers's landmark blue yodel "T for Texas, T for Tennessee" was cut, ensuring Rodgers's career as a recording artist, and a few months later he performed his first big theater show in Washington to rave reviews, which resulted in a contract to tour on the major Southern vaudeville circuit. By the end of 1928 his recording royalties alone reached $2,000 a month. Jimmie Rodgers had really made it at long last.

Song-Finding

The more successful Rodgers became, the more important it was for Peer to insist on Jimmie coming up with new songs. Always the optimist, Rodgers repeatedly assured Peer that he had a large number of new songs or knew where he could get them; Peer, however, was regularly exasperated to find that Jimmie did not have enough songs written. Eighty-three percent of Jimmie Rodgers's recorded songs credit him as author or coauthor, but in Porterfield's (1992: 119) words, "he actually wrote very little of the material."

In addition to rearranging old songs and buying new ones from admiring fans and aspiring songwriters, Jimmie was able to charm, coax, and beg a number of songs from his sister-in-law, Elsie McWilliams. McWilliams was a proficient musician and songwriter. She had performed with Rodgers around Meridian, but she was reluctant to claim authorship on any of the blue yodel songs because she considered them indecent.

By 1930 Jimmie Rodgers was making what seemed a fortune from his songwriting, record making, and touring. Nevertheless he was in continual pain from the advancing tuberculosis. So why did he drive himself to work so hard? Ralph Peer was "generous" with Rodgers in a way that made him dependent on returning to record just as often as possible. Peer's technique, not unlike the Hollywood movie industry's way of keeping successful stars of the era hard at work, was quite simple. As he told Lillian Borgeson, Peer "gave [Rodgers] all the money he asked for and warned him when he got in too deep." That is, Peer advanced Rodgers money in anticipation of the royalties Rodgers would earn on his forthcoming songs. This practice is directly analogous to the share-cropping system by which plantation owners kept laborers, both black and white, working at a subsistence level for eighty years after the end of slavery.[26] Given Peer's generosity with advances, Rodgers quickly learned to spend great amounts of money, so that even in his final months when he was in ill health and suffering great pain, he drove himself to record as many songs as possible in order to maintain his acquired lifestyle.

Who Was Responsible for Creating the Jimmie Rodgers Sound?

Performers were asked to bring in new songs, but the question still remains, who selected among those offered for recording, and who decided on the accompaniment and on the general sound of the music? In the words of Mike Seeger (1973: 8), "Who chose those records?" This question arises especially in the case of Jimmie Rodgers because in addition to numerous sentimental songs about home and family, in addition to songs of unrequited love, in addition to smoother popular-style numbers, Jimmie Rodgers recorded a large number of blues songs, songs with a Hawaiian sound, and songs with jazz backings quite at variance with Peer's notion of country music as an old-fashioned sound à la Fiddlin' John Carson, Vernon Dalhart, and the Carter Family.

Since the era of Chet Atkins and Owen Bradley in country music, it is the A&R person, now called "producer," who has generally played a dominant role in tailoring an artist's sound. But the A&R person did not play so proactive a role in the 1920s and 1930s. Reviewing the descriptions given by all the early A&R men, the comments of artists, and the evidence of the material in the files, a pattern emerges.[27] The A&R men gave clear instructions about the general sort of music that they wanted, and, not surprisingly, they generally suggested making music much like that which was currently most popular. After the surprising early success of Jimmie Rodgers's yodeling songs, for example (Coltman 1976a), Ralph Peer insisted that Sara Carter yodel as well (Wolfe 1993).[28] Beyond such suggestions, producers did what they could to make the artists comfortable in the studio, whether this meant praying with them before recording or sharing a bootleg pint of whiskey.

And yet this first generation of A&R men did not try to impose their own aesthetic standards, either during the recording process or in the process of selecting which of the cuts to release.[29] It is not that they were enlightened or that they were lazy. Their reason for not interfering was much more basic. In most instances they didn't like the music, didn't understand it, and had no respect for its audience. Ralph Peer, for example, was circumspect in public while he was active, but in later life he voiced great contempt for the blues and country artists he recorded and for the music they produced.[30] When Lillian Borgeson in her 1959 interview asked Peer for the names of "hillbillies" whom he had recorded, for example, he replied, "Oh, I tried so hard to forget them, and you keep bringing them up." Peer explained to Borgeson that the A&R work on hillbilly records was just a means to an end. "I was always trying to get away from hillbilly and into the legitimate publishing field because the big profits, until recently, in music publishing have come from selling sheet music, not the records." In effect then, because of the snobbish attitudes of A&R men like Peer and others, Jimmie Rodgers and the generation of artists who began to record in the 1920s had great artistic freedom, greater freedom, in fact, than has been enjoyed by any later generation of beginners in country music.

Nolan Porterfield (1992, 1995) shows that Peer gave only general suggestions on accompaniment and was not even present at several recording sessions. Peer's two documented interventions are, however, instructive because they give an insight into his understanding of the market for country music. In November 1927 at Rodgers's second recording session Peer strongly resisted the recording of the first blue yodel, "T for Texas, T for Tennessee." It didn't fit with Peer's image of country music. But Rodgers argued that it never failed to get a rousing response from an audience. It was finally included just to fill out the session time, but proved to be Rodgers's first big hit and the first of a set of blue yodels. The other intervention came five years later when Rodgers was enjoying great success. Peer was talking about a European tour and possibly a New York network radio show. He insisted on pairing Rodgers with smooth popular players who were members of the musicians' union, although Rodgers had wanted Clayton McMichen and a guitar player who understood his out-of-meter singing style. The straight-time New York musicians never fit in, and prospects for a radio show were soon scuttled.

Rodgers often recorded alone with just his own guitar. He also recorded with a wide range of backing aggregations. In addition to Clayton McMichen, he was paired with the Carter Family, the Blue and Grey Troubadours, an amateur country aggregation, a Hawaiian band, a jug band, a musical saw, and with jazz great Louis Armstrong. While it was Ralph Peer's suggestion that he record with Armstrong, who had recently been signed to Victor, Rodgers had already recorded successfully with a pickup jazz combo that he had met while barhopping in the days preceding one of his recording sessions.

Jimmie Rodgers sang with a clear, self-assured, nasal voice, honed by eighteen years of work in front of audiences, before he first recorded in Bristol in 1927. He was not a good musician, he could not read music, and he couldn't keep time. Rodgers's gift was the ability to take a song and by bending the melody, breaking meter, finding guitar work that fit, and adding his signature yodel (Coltman 1976a), to make his music seem an expression of his own personal feelings, and those of the listener as well. Just how much his singing inspired empathy is suggested by Ernest Tubb's comment to Hugh Cherry that Rodgers had such "sincerity in his voice that he made you believe what he was singing. When [as a youth] I first heard Jimmie Rodgers's song 'T for Texas,' I felt so bad for the jilted singer who sang 'I'm going to shoot poor Thelma' that I immediately started to dislike Thelma, whoever she was, for hurting him like that. He made it true."[31]

One final thing needs to be said about Jimmie Rodgers's sound. Listened to from the perspective of the late 1990s, the clear, white, Southern rural accent is unmistakable, but the dominant element in the sound is blues or even jazz, and not country as it is now understood.[32]

Creating the Pop Visual Image

From their first appearance to their last over a decade later, as shown in figure G1.3, the original Carter Family dressed in the formal attire that a country person would wear when attending church or going into town. Not so Jimmie Rodgers. Whether he had money or not, he always took pains to be a sharp dresser.[33] From 1928 on, he was a headliner in shows that featured a number of live entertainment acts along with a movie, as is shown in figure 3.2, or he appeared in traveling shows featuring a variety of acts that sang, danced, told jokes, or performed with dogs and other props. Having worked off and on as an entertainer in a number of different types of shows for many years before he became a recording artist, he was then prepared to craft a visual image befitting the music he recorded.

Rodgers had contempt for everything that was not up-to-date, and it is no surprise that he did not choose to look the part of a farmhand. The railroad, however, was then still a prime symbol of modernity, and Jimmie had worked on railroads off and on for years, so it was not inappropriate for him to image himself as "The Singing Brakeman." Thus personified he could appear to be a fast traveling man, a rambler, and a bit of a rake, but also seem to be a responsible working man (the kind who

Figure 3.2 Just eighteen months after his first record was released Jimmie Rodgers, center, is shown in this New Orleans newspaper along with other popular entertainers. The accompanying article begins: "America's famous singer and yodeler of 'blues' songs, Jimmie Rodgers, recording artist, headlines an all star vaudeville program. . . . Those familiar with his singing hail his appearance as one of the notable events of the current season."

would send money home to his wife and family, visiting his dear old mother whenever he could get home). This image fit very well the range of sentiments he expressed in song.

If the Singing Brakeman persona had the virtue of appearing authentic, it clearly labeled Rodgers a blue-collar working stiff. Genuinely popular male entertainers, depending on their age and the particular venue, wore generic "college boy" attire or formal dinner dress. Wanting to broaden his appeal, Rodgers dropped the railroading persona and, like many other entertainers before and since, adopted the persona suggested by his most distinctive songs—in his case the blue yodels. Briefly becoming "The Mississippi Blue Yodeler," he soon came to bill himself "America's Blue Yodeler." But what is the visual image of a blue yodeler? In an earlier decade, the image might well have been blackface "stage Negro" attire, but in Rodgers's fabrication the bluesman is imaged as the dapper white boy we see in the photo gallery 1.

CONCLUSION

In his ability to make every song he sang into an expression of his own personal feelings, Jimmie Rodgers is comparable to Roy Acuff in the 1930s, Hank Williams in the 1940s, and Elvis Presley in the 1950s. Like them, he projected the image of a tough yet tender, flawed man struggling with all his might against great adversity and personal pain. Jimmie Rodgers died alone on May 24, 1933, in a hotel room drowned in his own blood, the hemorrhaging due to the effects of advanced tuberculosis and compounded by years of hard living and heavy drinking.

In all, Rodgers released just 110 songs, but through them he was forging a new music. Melding the sounds and sentiments of blues, jazz, and traditional country music, he created a new kind of music that in its musical informality and earthy sentiments stood in stark contrast to the standard Tin Pan Alley–based urban popular music of the time.[34] Virtually all country artists of his era, and for two generations after, were directly influenced by Jimmie Rodgers. They copied his meter-free song styling, his yodel, and his informal but professional stage manner, and like him they strove to make the songs they sang personal expressions of their own feelings.

Even before his untimely death, however, the prime vehicle of Rodgers's popularity, the phonograph record, was suffering great commercial reverses owing to the Great Depression. Total record sales in the United States, which reached $75 million in 1929, plummeted to just $6 million, less than one tenth of the 1929 figure, by 1933.[35] For all practical purposes, country music record making in the mode exemplified in the work of Ralph Peer died with Jimmie Rodgers. Record making didn't begin to make a comeback for five years after Rodgers's death, and then it was sparked not by record sales to consumers but because of the widespread playing of phonograph records in jukeboxes. By then, as we will see below, the ways of making music and the kinds of music produced had changed greatly.

Beginning with Polk Brockman's innovations in Atlanta and continuing right through the Depression, however, country music flourished by combining radio exposure and live concert tours. Then in the mid-1930s, the western films of Gene Autry and his followers proved another major avenue for projecting country music. These media, however, made for a music and an image quite different from the blues-singing, popular-music stage persona projected by Jimmie Rodgers. As the next three chapters will show, the images projected by radio and the movies accentuated the *regional* and *rustic* nature of the music, its performers, and its audience.

The Folk versus Pop Look

G1.1 Participants, including Fiddlin' John Carson at the right, at the 1925 Mountain City, Tennessee Old Time Fiddling Contest sponsored by the Ku Klux Klan.

G1.2 Fiddlin' John Carson, and his daughter, Rosa Lee, who toured as "Moonshine Kate," and their touring Ford auto.

G1.3 The Carter Family in an early promotion photo seated out of doors on their Maces Spring, Virginia, home place. From the left Maybelle, Sara, and her husband A. P.

G1.4 The musically eclectic Tenneva Ramblers, including a bespectacled Jimmie Rodgers, in a May 1927 publicity photo taken shortly before they approached Ralph Peer to make their first recordings.

G1.5 For vaudeville appearances, Jimmie Rodgers, billed as "America's Blue Yodeler," sometimes appeared in a tuxedo and bowler hat.

G1.6 In reference to his working on the railroads, Jimmie Rodgers was presented as "The Singing Brakeman."

G1.7 More often Jimmie Rodgers's publicity images featured him in a boater and bow tie, as seen in this billboard for his May 1930 appearance in Borger, Texas.

Part Two

Fabricating the Image of Authenticity

CHAPTER FOUR

Old-Timer Image of Authenticity

Jimmie Rodgers was far and away the most widely copied country music artist up to World War II. Although every aspect of his music-making was imitated by numerous performers, no legion of disciples donned boaters and blazers. Rodgers-like tuxedos didn't come back until the 1960s, when Nashville-based performers such as Jim Reeves tried to distance themselves from the fury of rockabilly. Clearly, in the mid-1930s, the Jimmie Rodgers pop-artist *look* was a dead end.

Here in Part 2 we focus on the search that took place from the mid-1920s through the 1930s for the right *look* for the country music artist—a look that, to be seen as authentic, had to fit the image implied in the music, in the lyrics, and most important, in the expectations of audiences.

From the outset, country music was seen as a rustic alternative to urban modernity. If the music had been commercialized in 1823, rather than a century later, the image would have been that of the leatherstocking mountaineer as depicted in the frontier novels of James Fenimore Cooper[1] and personified in the stories about Daniel Boone. With a century of industrial change, however, there were a number of different ways of imaging the alternative to urban modernity.

By the 1920s, the hearty Eastern mountain man was seen as little more than a relic, an *old geezer,* whose wisdom was filtered through generations of inbreeding and corn liquor. He did have two offspring, however. The one—increasingly referred to as *hillbilly*, stayed fairly close to the old mountain home farming the bottomland, cutting timber, working in the coal mines, and taking work in the cotton mills. The hillbilly's venturesome sibling moved on west with the frontier, and though wearing a wide range of outfits from fur trapper to gold miner, the Westerner[2] came to be seen in the heroic image of the *cowboy*.

Each of the three chapters of part 2 is devoted to one of these three constructions of authenticity. Here in chapter 4 we go back to the early 1920s to focus on the conception of country music authenticity as located in the person of old performers playing what was taken to be traditional music. We will see that while the working-class audience for the music quickly tired of performers in this image, the image of old-timer was supported for a number of years by middle-class antimodernists who tried to perpetuate the old-timer image as part of their own ideological agendas.

IMAGING AUTHENTICITY AT THE DAWN OF THE MEDIA ERA

Early 1920s performances by skilled, unschooled country performers met with an immediate positive response in venues from Texas and Georgia to Chicago and Detroit. This, for example, was the response to the first radio appearance of Fiddlin' John Carson: Ernest Rogers, who put Carson on the air in Atlanta in 1922, reported that Carson "played and sang until, shall we say,[3] exhaustion set in. But not before he had scored a signal triumph and the phones were jumping up and down with requests from listeners" (Wiggins 1987: 70). Bradley Kincaid, then a college student in Chicago, recounts a similarly startling public response to his ballad-singing. In 1926 he was asked to sing on the fledgling "National Barn Dance." Obliging, he reports, "I sang 'Barbara Allen' and a few of the other old-timers. . . . One day after I'd been singing there for three or four weeks, . . . the girl at the outer desk said, 'Bradley, there's some mail back there in the back room for you.' Here was this basket full of fan mail. I took all I could carry home with me, and everywhere I read where they said, 'You're the best singer on the air' " (Jones 1980: 20). A few months later, Kincaid was induced against his own better judgment to book a personal appearance. "When I walked up to the theater, there was a line several blocks long and people were being turned away. I crossed the street and asked a fellow what was going on. He said, 'Why that radio singer from WLS is going to be here' " (Jones: 1980: 32).

One reads an unending stream of astonished reports of this sort in the contemporary accounts of media and live performances in the 1920s. Some are probably apocryphal, but others are verifiably genuine. Taken together, they show that radio performances and the live appearances associated with them had revealed a huge unsatiated thirst, but just what exactly was it a thirst for?

There was a great deal of trial-and-error experimentation from 1922 to 1926 in an effort to understand the appeal of the music. Since most of the decision makers were urbane middle-class sophisticates or first-generation college graduates who were using their education to escape from a rural past, they tended to see country music and its makers, as we noted in chapter 1, as the mirror image of their own aesthetic and goals. It was country to their city, the unchanging past to the rapidly changing present, the rear-guard to their avant-garde. The contrast of modern with unchanging is suggested in gallery figures G2.1 and G2.2, which pair auto innovator Henry Ford with Mellie Dunham, and radio man George Hay with Uncle Jimmy Thompson. Given this mind-set, the natural assumption was that audiences were responding to representations of the unchanged past. And that was the kind of artist the enterprising music promoters sought out.

Old-Time Fiddling Contests

Old-time fiddling contests were popular public displays throughout the South and much of the Midwest, and so the model of the musical old-timer that was clearly visible to the promoters was the old-time fiddling contestant. The annual contest in Atlanta provides instructive information on the difference between image and reality in the contests. Contests were treated as hard news in the Atlanta press, which gave a great deal of attention to the winners and included large pictures. The music was called "old-time" and "traditional," although it was then undergoing rapid stylistic change (Spielman 1975). The contestants were characterized as mountain men or farmhands, although many, including the female performers, lived and worked in the cities; the case of John Carson is a good example. Although rural-born, he had lived most of his life in Atlanta and had been employed primarily in the city's largest and most technologically advanced cotton mill (Wiggins 1987). Finally, the contestants were depicted as old men and a dying breed.

The clear difference between image and reality was shown graphically in the coverage of the annual Atlanta Old Time Fiddlers Convention and Contest of 1924. More accurately, it is *not* shown in the region, because the Atlanta press suppressed the story of the eventual winner. The Atlanta newspaper coverage that year followed the usual pattern over the days of the contest, but when Marcus Lowe Stokes, aged twenty-two, won the contest with the tune "Hell's Broke Loose in Georgia," the *Atlanta Journal* carried no story at all. Lowe's defeat of Carson and the other older men did, however, run in the *New York Times* and was reprinted in the *Literary Digest* in its "Sports and Athletics" section. To recoup as much as possible of the image, the *New York Times* story noted that the "mere novice" had "come down from the Blue Ridge foothills primed with all the Southern tunes that he had learned from his grand-dad" (*Literary Digest* 1924: 70). In fact, none of this was true. The young Stokes at the time lived in Atlanta and was a member of the modernizing faction of fiddlers that gathered around Clayton McMichen. Also, "Hell's Broke Loose in Georgia" was not an ancient Smokey Mountain tune. It was Carson's favorite contest song, so Stokes, in effect, beat the old champ with his own stick (Wiggins 1987: 92).

This triumph of youth over age in the performance of old-time music seemed so striking at the time that Stephen Vincent Benét made Stokes's victory over Carson and the others into a lengthy narrative poem, "The Mountain Whippoorwill" (Wiggins 1987: 88–89). Like the newspaper accounts, the poem strained to make the age anomaly understandable by having the youthful victor (the product of the union of a fiddle made of mountain-laurel wood and a whippoorwill) come from even farther back in the aboriginal Appalachian forest. Thus the best music was seen to be carried by a pure youth newly come from a more remote mountain region. In the Benét poem the idea of mountain purity is further accented because—paralleling the standard fiddle contest story that pits the Devil against the brash youth—the old champion signals his own defeat by handing his fiddle to the youthful winner (Benét 1925).[4] Clearly the idea of a place uncontaminated by urban-industrial society and peopled by unchanging descendants of Daniel Boone-like old-time folk was lodged firmly in the American imagination.[5]

Old-time fiddling conventions and contests continued to be staged as popular entertainments through the mid-1930s, but increasingly the guise of a free and fair competition was dropped in favor of staged "showdowns." In some, a visiting group of professionals would challenge all players from the local area, with the balance of winning and losing modulated to maintain crowd interest. Other showdowns took on the aspect of a professional wrestling match, with "good guys" taking on "bad guys." Clayton McMichen and Curly Fox were often cast as good guys with Nachee, the Indian, cast as the bad guy who tried to win through trickery (Wolfe 1977b).

With the demise of the fiddling contests as popular entertainments,[6] the dominant image of the country music artist as a backwoods old geezer was eclipsed as well. The old-timer enjoyed another life, however, in the middle-class imagination, as we will see in the next section.

"OLD-TIME" MUSIC AND "LOST" WAYS OF LIFE

The 1920s witnessed a widespread fear of the loss of white Anglo-Saxon Protestant hegemony in American political life and culture, and attempts to reassert white Protestant dominance took a number of forms, ranging from a revitalized Ku Klux Klan (Boorstein 1973: 302) to the campaign for Prohibition against alcohol use (Gusfield 1986). By the 1920s there was already a well-established movement to preserve and propagate pure Anglo-Saxon musical forms. David Whisnant (1983) shows the efforts of social workers in the Appalachian Mountains who worked to preserve and to propagate all that in their narrow judgment was both "native and fine." Here we focus on three efforts of the late 1920s to use the old-time image of country music for these ideological purposes.

Henry Ford's Use of the Old-Time Image

Perhaps more than any other individual, Henry Ford helped bring to an end the agrarian way of life and usher in urbanism (Jardim 1970). His rugged and inexpensive Model T auto, introduced in 1908, accounted for 57 percent of all autos manufactured in the United Sates by 1923, and by 1926, thirteen million had been produced (Nash 1970: 154). These cars penetrated to the heart of the American backcountry, helping to give millions of people in the country their first regular contact with urbanizing influences (Wik 1972). At the same time, the mass-production methods of manufacture, which at a stroke dropped the time of assembling a Model T from twelve hours to ninety-three minutes (Nash 1970: 154) and drove the price of the touring car down to $360 (Lewis 1976: 44), showed the way for the mass production of all sorts of merchandise, bringing affordable manufactured goods within reach of the mass of the population. Thus, as with music, which was increasingly available via radio and phonograph records, goods were increasingly store-bought rather than home-made.

At the same time, Henry Ford saw the modern city as a "pestiferous growth" and contrasted the "unnatural," "twisted," "and cooped up" lives of city people with the "wholesome" life of "independence" and "sterling honesty" that the agrarian life offered. Summing up the point, he editorialized in his *Dearborn Independent* newspaper: "The real United States lies outside the cities" (Nash 1970: 157).[7] As Nash (1970: 154) puts it, "The nostalgic, backward-looking Henry Ford repeatedly de-plored the very conditions that Ford the revolutionary industrialist did so much to bring about."

Rather than see the auto and mass production as having any part in the changes, he saw the problems as stemming from alcohol, tobacco use, and sexual license—all three fostered in the atmosphere created by jazz dancing. But who was responsible for all these ills? Ford saw the culprit in "foreigners," African Americans, recent immigrants, and partic-ularly what Ford often termed the "international Jew" (Dahlinger 1977: 107). In an effort to substantiate his views, he reprinted in his *Dearborn Independent* sections of "The Protocols of the Learned Elders of Zion, a purported master-plan for Jewish domination." What is more, he contin-ued reprinting sections of it for a year after it had been exposed as a complete fabrication (Nash 1970: 156; Wik 1972: 138–40; Lewis 1976: 138–41).[8]

If, for Ford, the problem was urban vices and the cause was foreign values and cultural influences, the solution was equally simplistic: to reintroduce the older agrarian folkways. This effort took several forms, but as Lewis (1972) notes, none generated more free publicity for the Ford Motor Company than his efforts to displace jazz by old-time fid-dling and to substitute old-time square and round dancing for close-couple jazz dancing. In 1925 Ford announced that he would lead a cru-sade to bring old-fashioned dances back into public favor. He enrolled friends and Ford Motor Company executives into classes. He brought 200 Michigan and Ohio dance instructors to Dearborn to learn the old-time steps, and he published a guidebook with the long and declamatory title " 'Good Morning': After a Sleep of Twenty-Five Years Old-Fashioned Dancing Is Being Revived by Mr. and Mrs. Henry Ford." Besides illustrat-ing the appropriate moves for square dances, it condemned as promiscu-ous the newer jazz dances such as the Charleston and the associated flapper lifestyle. Proper deportment, according to Ford, minimizes physi-cal contact, the gentleman's "right hand should be placed at his partner's waist, thumb and forefinger alone touching her" (Nash 1970: 162). Act-ing much like a time-and-motion-study engineer who analyzed the movements of craftsmen in order to build standardized assembly-line machines that could be operated by semiskilled workers, Henry Ford brought thirty-nine fiddlers to Dearborn over the course of eighteen months "whom we wish to study so that we can 'standardize' our revival of the old-time dances" (*Literary Digest* 1926: 34).

In large part through Ford's efforts, old-fashioned dancing briefly be-came an urban rage, and thirty-four institutions of higher learning, in-cluding Radcliffe College, the University of Michigan, and the University of North Carolina, added courses in traditional American dance to their curricula. Not everyone, however, was enthralled. The *Cincinnati Times-Star* lampooned the fad in an article with the headline, "Just a Reel at Twilight When Your Flask is Low" (Lewis 1976: 226).

In conjunction with the promotion of old-style dancing, Ford highlighted old-time fiddlers. Through his nationwide auto dealerships, he ran a series of local and state championships that culminated in a February 1926 national competition in which John (Uncle Bunt) Stevens of Lewisburg, Tennessee, won out over 1,875 other contestants. But to his consternation, Ford found that many of the old-time fiddlers were far from paragons of Elizabethan virtue, and a number of the local and state winners were rather unsavory old characters. Would Henry Ford have provided the alcohol necessary to get Fiddlin' John Carson limber enough to play, and how could he have explained to Mrs. Ford the meaning of "When the old hen cackles, the rooster's going to crow"? Another state winner wrote Ford that he was currently driving a Chevrolet and thought it appropriate that he be given a new Ford car.[9] A number of the winners used the prize as a basis for greatly increasing their performance fees (for example, Jep Bisbee upped his performance fee from three to thirty-five dollars [Daniel 1986: 23]), and several landed vaudeville contracts based on their new-found celebrity status. Finally, the contests caused loud cries of fraud from many of the losers, cries that sometimes received local press coverage.[10]

Retreating from this gaggle of problematic old-timers, Ford fixed on Allison Mellen (Mellie) Dunham of Norway, Maine, for special publicity treatment. Dunham, seventy-two years old and the maker of the snowshoes that Admiral Robert Peary wore on his expedition to the North Pole, was a dedicated, modest, morally upstanding, and photogenic gentleman. Observing the dress and deportment of Dunham and his wife, the *Boston Herald* noted, "Their manners are naive, straightforward and honest. Their minds are those of kindly, sequestered country folk somewhat past their prime, and their clothes are just their 'Sunday suits,' not costumes devised to attract attention." (See photo G2.1.) The reporter concluded, "Both the Dunhams are real" (*Literary Digest* 1926: 38). "Real" or not, Dunham was no one's fool. Returning from the widely publicized visit to Ford's home and ready to sign a vaudeville contract, he is quoted as saying, "I came to make money and make no bones about it, since me and Ma have had honor enough" (Lewis 1976: 228).

While the Fords continued to have monthly old-time dances with guests dressing in formal attire for another fifteen years, the fiddling contest and old-time dancing craze was over by 1927 (Lewis 1976: 228). The numerous old-time fiddlers who earned vaudeville show contracts at the height of the craze were off the hard boards in months, and none of the fiddlers who recorded exclusively old-time dance and fiddle contest tunes enjoyed substantial record sales (Blaustein 1975). Clearly, the promoters had misgauged the huge outpouring of acceptance noted at the beginning of this chapter. People weren't responding to what was *literally* old-fashioned.

Elizabethan Relic, Jilson Setters

The experience of the itinerant Kentucky fiddler called Jilson Setters illustrates just how willing urban Americans and their press were to embrace the old-time image.[11] In 1927, as she recounts it, Jean Thomas was a circuit court stenographer and amateur song collector of Ashland, Kentucky, who came across a singing fiddler, Jilson Setters, who had been blind from birth. In February 1930 Thomas authored an article in *American Magazine* entitled "Blind Jilson: The Singing Fiddler of Lost Hope Hollow." It tells of how Thomas found Setters and describes in Setters's words how Thomas arranged for an operation that gave him sight, and how he appeared on a radio broadcast from New York. The piece ends with what is purported to be the radio announcer's words. "Jilson Setters, whose Elizabethan ballads broadcast over a hook-up from coast to coast and relayed half way around the world, delighted millions last night. . . . Jilson Setters is a modern survival of the ancient minstrel. . . . Who knows but that his primitive tunes have paved the way for American grand opera!" (Thomas 1930: 167).

In 1931 Thomas took Setters to London, where he performed in the Albert Hall at a folksong festival. On his return, Harvard professor George Lyman Kittering pronounced Setters's composition "London Town" "a classic of American folk song" (*Literary Digest* 1932: 27). By 1934 Thomas was affecting Elizabethan garb and Setters had become the featured performer at the National Song Festival organized by Thomas under the aegis of her American Folk Song Society, which included on its board literary and critical luminaries including Carl Sandberg, Stephen Vincent Benét, Paul Green, Ida M. Tarbell, and Irving S. Cobb.

Jean Thomas had subtitled her *American Magazine* article of 1930 "A True Story That Is Stranger Than Fiction," but most of the story was her own fabrication. To begin with, Thomas first asked another Kentucky fiddler, Ed Haley, to take on the persona of a character she was creating, Jilson Setters.[12] When Haley refused, Thomas turned to J. W. "Blind Bill" Day. He was not blind from birth as she said; rather, his sight had failed while he was young, and Jean Thomas arranged to have the cataracts removed from his eyes. There is no such place in Kentucky as Lost Hope

Hollow, and Day was not so much a mountaineer as a town beggar (*Newsweek* 1935a: 20; *Time* 1934: 54). Like the other itinerant, blind street musicians of the time, such as Andrew Jenkins, Day made money from his music not by performing primarily ancient ballads, but by playing a mixture of sentimental songs, novelties, and topical songs of his own composition.[13] Finally, Thomas was not a circuit court stenographer, as claimed in the 1930 story. Rather, she was a Hollywood scenario writer and amateur folklorist (*Newsweek* 1935a: 20).

While "Blind Jilson" had been accepted as authentic by the national press for five years, and was something of a celebrity, Setter gained no notice in Kentucky newspapers. Accompanied by the excellent songwriter and guitarist Carson Robison, Day recorded ten traditional songs for Victor in New York City in February 1928 using the Setters name.[14] But there is no record of his ever appearing on live country music shows, or performing with other hillbillies on the radio. Was that because Jean Thomas, who had him under contract, wanted him to be represented as an Elizabethan relic, or was it because the fans of the emerging country music didn't "buy" his image or many of his records? Very likely both were true (*American Magazine* 1933).

By 1935 Jean Thomas had given up interest in Day and was promoting a nineteen-year-old Harrison Elliott as a "French-Huguenot-Scottish-Irish Kentucky mountaineer, [and] authentic mountain composer [of] America's first folk opera, 'The Call of the Cumberlands.' " The piece was performed that August over the NBC network (*Newsweek* 1935b: 31).

The Quest for Authentic "Native" American Music

Henry Ford might be considered a rich eccentric and Jean Thomas an enterprising opportunist, but their views of about the moral superiority of old-time music were widely shared (Whisnant 1983). In the 1920s there was a great concern about America's dependence on Europe for models of artistic inspiration. To remedy this, many influential critics contended that U.S. artists should find inspiration in authentic American works of the common people. A lively debate developed over which music "of the common people" should be considered authentically American and taught to future generations.

America and Her Music, by the acclaimed composer-conductor, Lamar Stringfield,[15] mirrors the attitudes held by "Americanist" academic musicologists of the time. This handbook was circulated by the University of North Carolina Press in 1931 as one in a series of bulletins intended for individual and group study. It shows what was considered "native and fine" and how this music was to be brought to the population at large.

Each of the fifteen brief chapters is followed by a set of suggested phonograph records, topics for discussion, subjects for study, and a list of references. While the document is jingoistic, racist, sexist, and musicologically inaccurate at many points, it is worth reviewing to get a sense of the ideas then prevailing among middle-class white Americans.[16]

Stringfield asserts that a strong and united nation must have a national music, but that a distinctively American music had not yet developed. Most serious "native" American composers traveled to Europe for training because of the prestige associated with foreign training. Consequently, "the work of native artists was tinged with foreign characteristics. . . . [To counter this foreign influence] it is well that efforts be made to encourage the development of a nationalism in American music" (19).[17]

Since Stringfield argued that a national music will come from the "ground emotions of the people" (14), he reviews the available sources of a music of the American nation. The music of Native Americans was considered and rejected as a source because "Nationalism in music cannot be established if it is based on the ideas and themes made by a vanishing race" (34). The music of African Americans is also rejected because the "rhythms and almost monotonal expressions with their voices" that African Americans brought to this country from Africa were so primitive that they learned to mimic the music of white people (24). Thus, Stringfield concludes, "The Negro's lack of originality in music prevents his songs from being carried on from generation to generation, long enough to establish them as folk-music" (25). Jazz is also rejected as a source. "Jazz [according to Stringfield] is a mathematical and commercially concocted music and, as opposed to sincere music, is artificial. . . . Its appeal is dependent upon the suggestiveness of the lyrics. . . . [Thus] there is no way of classifying jazz as being part of musical contribution" (39).

Stringfield also rejects the assertion that Negro spirituals are representative of America. "Since the emotions of the Negro race are foreign to the white man, an essentially Anglo-Saxon nation derives its nationalism in music only from its own people" (43). The bulletin concludes with a chapter on collecting "American folk-music" which, as the reader has undoubtedly guessed, turns out to be what has here been called old-time music. "Naturally, the least affected of the folk-music that now exists in America is preserved by the people in the mountainous country, or on the plains. Lack of modern transportation has left these people in a natural state of human feeling and their music free from minstrelsy" (13).

This idea of there being a pure folk music was an illusion, more the

Figure 4.1 Though later in life he did not have to put on makeup to look the part of an authentic old-timer, Louis Marshall Jones played the Grandpa Jones part from his early days with Bradley Kincaid, as shown in this photo from the late 1940s with a youthful band that included Billy Grammer (over Jones's shoulder).

product of the ideological needs of the times than of the reality of peoples' musical lives. American vernacular music always has been, like the American people themselves, a complex mix. No dryland town or mountain fastness was too isolated in 1931, or a century earlier for that matter, to regularly exchange musical ideas with other sources.

CONCLUSION: OLDWEAR

Music reformers and promoters like Henry Ford, Jean Thomas, and Lamar Stringfield, as well as other nativists like them, sought out authenticity in the music of unschooled old people performing old music. In order to distill what they considered "native and fine," the promoters had to discard most of the what the oldsters were actually performing, so in the end, the music they "preserved" was more a reflection of their own ideological choices than a representation of the aesthetic choices of older musicians or of the lives of the country music audience.

The music of the fiddling contest performers discussed in the first part of this chapter more accurately reflected the musical preferences of the audience, but since it was committed to being old, it soon seemed outdated rather than authentic to the rising generation of the audience as well as to younger musicians.

Nothing has been said about the costume that represents the old-timer image of authenticity. Since they were supposed to be genuinely old-fashioned, no loud costume was appropriate. The conventional clothing of the old-timer was the conservative dress-up, going-to-town clothes of a farm person. This was the conventional outfit of the fiddling contest participant, as it was of virtually all country performers from Vernon Dalhart[18] to Fiddlin' John Carson and the Carter Family in the mid-1920s. Only with the success of Jimmie Rodgers did the visual image of the performer become an issue for artists, promoters, and audiences alike, and some young performers began to dress "old" in the 1930s. The most successful was Louis "Grandpa" Jones, depicted in his stage outfit in figure 4.1. But the two images that came to dominate in the 1930s, the hillbilly and the cowboy, were quite at variance with both the old-timer and the dapper Jimmie Rodgers look.[19]

CHAPTER FIVE

Hillbilly Image of Authenticity

While the image of the old-time music-maker found little lasting popular appeal, two other personifications of the country musician created in the 1920s, the hillbilly and the singing cowboy, proved more appealing to the audience. "Old-time" implied an old person dressed in an out-of-style outfit performing traditional songs; "hillbilly" and "cowboy" both suggest a region of the country, an occupation, and a way of life. The hillbilly and the cowboy images proved to be more malleable than the image of old-timer, however, both because the implied lifestyle could be continuously updated, and because they did not so tightly constrain the limits of the music that was appropriate.

The physical appearance of these sibling images is so different that it is important to underline the traits they share in common. Both hillbilly and cowboy suggest a self-reliant (most often male) child of nature, unfettered by the constraints of urban society—an image that has been a distinctive element of American fictional heroes at least since James Fenimore Cooper's *Last of the Mohicans* was published in 1826. Both depend on friends and family rather than on written law and officialdom. Both find little use for formal education in their environment, relying on knowledge that comes from a oneness with nature and its creatures. Finally, both feel at a loss in an urban environment, not only unschooled in its appropriate ways of behavior, but also unrefined in dress, speech, and manners.

At least since the eighteenth century and the time of the Enlightenment, Western civilization has had a profoundly ambivalent feeling about such primitives. On the one hand they are derided for their superstition and sloth, and on the other they are admired for their natural purity. As Tom Paine, one of the ideologues of the American Revolution, put it in his 1791 *Rights of Man,* "The artificial Noble shrinks into a dwarf before the Noble of Nature." The common ancestors of the media hillbilly and cowboy were created in the philosophy of Locke, Wordsworth, and Thoreau, were seen in the politics of Andrew Jackson, and were given life in the novels of James Fenimore Cooper and Herman Melville. The fictionalizing portrayal of a buckskin-clad Daniel Boone, the first systematic explorer of the trans-Appalachian wilderness of Kentucky and Tennessee, was the immediate progenitor of our siblings.[1]

It needs to be kept in mind as we proceed that few working cowboys played guitar or fiddled and sang, and while a large number of Southerners of the 1920s were musical, most of them were not unlettered, shiftless hillfolk. Rather the singing cowboy and the hillbilly character were deliberately constructed images created selectively out of available symbolic resources and contemporary styles. This and the next chapter show the process of their creation in the years before World War II.

The Imagined Hillbilly

The hillbilly character has been perpetuated not only by radio and record showmen but by the Lil' Abner comic strip and, more recently, the "Hee Haw" and "Foxworthy" television shows. He is, in a sense, the linear descendant of the country rube who has a long career in satire. For example, the term "Yankee Doodle" was used derisively by British administrators before the American Revolution to refer to unsophisticated colonists. Archie Green (1965) has shown that the specific term "hillbilly" was first found in print in the April 23, 1900, issue of the *New York Journal.* The term has a range of connotations, however, so it is useful to explore how it was understood by the entertainment industry in the 1920s. The December 29, 1926, issue of *Variety* gives the following characterization in a first-page article entitled "Hill-Billy Music":

> The "hillbilly" is a North Carolina or Tennessee and adjacent mountaineer type of illiterate white whose creed and allegiance are to the Bible, the Chautauqua, and the phonograph. . . . The mountaineer is of "poor white trash" genera. The great majority, probably 95 percent, can neither read nor write English. Theirs is a community all to themselves. Illiterate and ignorant, with the intelligence of morons, the

sing-song, nasal-twanging vocalizing of a Vernon Dalhart or a Carson Robison on the disks, reciting the banal lyrics of a "Prisoner's Song" or "The Death of Floyd Collins," biggest hillbilly song-hit to date, intrigues their interest. (Quoted in Green 1965: 221)

Variety's vitriolic 1926 attack on country music and its fans was not unusual. The popular music establishment was as partisan in its attack on the innovation of jazz a few years earlier (Leonard 1962), on rock music in the mid-1950s (Curtis 1987), on punk and disco in the 1970s (Laing 1985) and again on rap and heavy metal music in the 1980s and 1990s. In all these instances the new music has threatened the careers of established artists and the value of the songs copyrighted by established firms. It is notable, however, that the *Variety* writer presumed that only backwoods people liked country music, even though in the cash-poor 1920s, most such people didn't have enough money to buy the many country music records that were being sold. This and other evidence shows that the appeal was to a broad class of people and not just to those living in the fertile crescent of country music (Peterson and DiMaggio 1975).

In this chapter, we will show that the "hillbilly" was a consciously constructed image that could instantly be recognized by the audience like any of the other stock characters of vaudeville and the popular stage. While numerous people around the country took on the garb and demeanor of the hillbilly rube, the fabrication of the hillbilly image can best be illustrated in the work of two men who self-consciously worked to institutionalize the type, George Hay in Nashville, Tennessee, and Glen Rice in Beverly Hills, California.

GEORGE HAY AND THE "GRAND OLE OPRY" HILLBILLY

From Old-Timers to Hillbillies

With the craze for old-time fiddling, a number of radio stations began to program the form in the mid-1920s. The single performer on the first Saturday-evening country music program aired on WSM from Nashville, Tennessee, on November 28, 1925—the time slot that became the "Grand Ole Opry"—was the seventy-seven-year-old fiddler Uncle Jimmy Thompson.[2] Not only was he old in years, Uncle Jimmy's playing was assuredly old-time: he had learned some of his songs during the Civil War. In the climate of the mid-1920s quest for authenticity in old-time music and quixotic characters, he was, as Charles Wolfe (1994: 49) notes, "a press agent's dream: white-bearded, outspoken, hard-drinking, barking a challenge to the champion of the latest national fiddling contest sponsored by Henry Ford. (See photo G2.2.) 'Let him come to Tennessee,' Uncle Jimmy boasted, 'and I'll lie with him like a bulldog.' "

Uncle Jimmy started right in playing a string of jigs, breakdowns, and hornpipes. When after two hours George Hay, the announcer, tried to get him to conclude his performance, Uncle Jimmy said he knew 2,000 tunes and was just getting limbered up (Hay 1945). Such songs were the perfect accompaniment at a country dance and could hold the attention of a fiddling contest audience, but coming out of a radio speaker or heard with earphones, stripped of all social context, the unadorned cold fiddle sounds must soon have bored all but the most devoted students of old-time fiddle styles.

A month after his original appearance, when WSM began its regular Saturday-night country music program, Jimmy Thompson played, but so did a number of other performers, none of whom were old-time fiddlers. There were banjoists, harmonica players, guitarists, singers, and fiddlers who performed with other instrumentalists in string bands. Thompson continued to play on the show regularly during 1926, often accompanied by his niece Eva (Wolfe 1975b), but he appeared less frequently in 1927, and in 1928 he made just one guest appearance. What is more, no other old-time fiddler took the place he and another old-time fiddler, Uncle Bunt Stephens, occupied during the first several months of the program (Peterson and DiMaggio 1973).[3]

It is both ironic and significant that when in 1926 the WSM program began to be called a "barn dance," most of the music was no longer appropriate for square dancing. In effect, the show had become a rustic variety show based more on the model of vaudeville than on that of a community barn dance (Peterson and DiMaggio 1973). Clearly, WSM's barn dance (which by 1927 had been dubbed the "Grand Ole Opry"), WLS's "National Barn Dance," and a growing list of similar radio programs of the time were popular not because they faithfully adhered to old-time music. Rather, they were considered authentic, I believe, because they evoked in the listener a nostalgic remembrance of community dances, medicine shows, and street-corner singers packaged respectfully and in a fast-paced format appropriate to "the electronic marvel of the age," radio.

Media-Made Image

While radio could create an image with words and song, live appearances and movies demanded that an artist also look and act the part to be accepted as authentic. Radio station management too, although it is an aural medium, in these early days demanded that its announcers and actors look the part of the persons they were playing. BBC news readers of the 1920s, for example, were required to work dressed in tuxedos. To lend an air of genteel respectability, studios built after the first experimental months were decorated with expensive, plush furnishings and hung with crystal chandeliers.

Following this logic, performers appearing on the air were asked to dress in clothes appropriate to persona suggested by their musical style (Barnouw 1966). This may simply be because they made most of their incomes from live engagements based on their radio appearances, so they had to sound right in accent, grammar, and vocabulary in their on-air patter and had to look right in their publicity photos. Nonetheless, working in the emerging radio aesthetic of the day, hillbilly radio producers might well have evolved the "radio hillbilly" even if artists had never needed to appear in live performance. This is suggested by an article appearing in the March 1924 *American Magazine* about the number of social occasions being created for listeners to meet performers and announcers on Chicago's powerful new radio station, KYW. Citing numerous examples, the article asserts that "Radio 'fans' are not content with *hearing* the entertainers; they want to *see* them at close range" (Weatherbee 1924: 60).

As Archie Green (1965) has convincingly shown, the word "hillbilly" was not in common usage until the early 1920s, and a study of the early days of the "Grand Ole Opry" that Paul DiMaggio and I made (1973) showed that the *image* of hillbilly was a fabrication of the later 1920s. The description given here is drawn from our study, unless otherwise noted, and the use of the first person plural here refers to DiMaggio and myself.

George Hay's Opry: 1926–28

While he did not use the term "hillbilly" in the 1920s or even later when it had become the generally used term for country music, preferring instead the term "old-time music," George Hay was the most self-conscious architect of the radio hillbilly. In his role as master of ceremonies on the WLS Chicago "National Barn Dance" in 1924 and 1925, Hay fashioned himself the "Solemn Old Judge" and helped artists define identifiable characters. Hired in November 1926 as what would now be called station manager of Nashville's fledgling WSM, he went on to create the "Grand Ole Opry." In numerous interviews, press releases, and in his book, *A History of the Grand Ole Opry,* Hay (1945) asserted that in the 1920s

"Grand Ole Opry" presentations were informal affairs at which anyone in from the farm on a Saturday night could pick and sing his or her brand of old-time music.[4]

In order to examine this romantic image of informality and amateurism, we will focus on the Opry of 1928.[5] In its third year of operation, the Opry had evolved some consistency in format but had not yet been established as *the* Nashville voice of country music.[6] That year is also of interest because in 1928 WSM was assigned one of the forty national cleared channels, with the low wavelength of 650 kilohertz. The clear-channel status and low wavelength meant that during the evening the station could be heard throughout most of the country (DeWitt 1972). Finally, the late 1920s form a most interesting transitional period in which radio and the automobile were just beginning to have a major impact on country music and on the careers of its performers. While radio advertised the music and the performers, the automobile and ever-improving roads made regular touring practical.[7] Yet in 1928 the singing guitarist backed by a string band who worked on the radio to gain a reputation and made a good living by regularly touring had not emerged as the iconic form of country performer.

Building a Regular Cast

The 1928 "Grand Ole Opry Diary" indicates that the program was divided into from six to ten segments, lasting from fifteen to forty-five minutes each, and each segment featured one performer or group. Erasures and the notation "did not show" appear by some of the listings, suggesting that segments were arranged at least days in advance of show time. This is corroborated by several early Opry participants, who said Judge Hay asked them to appear every other week. Final proof that the Opry was not a catch-as-catch-can, walk-on free-for-all is provided by the fact that as early as 1926, Nashville daily newspapers and the one weekly of the era were listing Opry participants several days in advance of the Saturday show time.

The program usually opened with virtuoso black harmonica player DeFord Bailey (Morton 1991) or with Obed Pickard, who was billed as a "one man orchestra." The last segment of the evening was often a Negro-dialect comedy routine by George Hay and Ed McConnell, who played ragtime piano and spoke the part of "Uncle Wash," a shiftless but cunning older black character who was called before Judge Hay.[8] On numerous other occasions the last segment was a visiting vaudeville act, such as crooner Nick Lucas, or the Maunakia Hawaiian Serenaders.

It is impossible to say just how many individuals appeared during that year because band members are not always listed, but at least 140 individuals can be counted. Approximately seventy acts appeared, but again this number is not precise because several aggregations had overlapping memberships. Roy Hardison, for example, not only played with the Gully Jumpers, but also participated in eight other unnamed groups. In a sense he served as a staff banjoist.

DeFord Bailey played forty-nine of the fifty-one weeks the Opry aired in 1928.[9] No one else played nearly as often.[10] It is notable that Uncle Dave Macon, usually identified as the featured performer of the Opry in this era, appeared only three times during 1928.[11] The Crook Brothers, Theron Hale, Grady Moore, and Paul Warmack might have appeared more often on the Opry that year had they not also been appearing regularly on another Nashville radio program, WLAC's competing barndance show (*Radio Digest* 1928). Though there were a number of groups that played regularly on the "Grand Ole Opry," over half of the aggregations appeared only once during the year. Several of these one-time guests, like Uncle Jimmy Thompson, had earlier been Opry regulars. A number were professional performers who appeared on the Opry in conjunction with their vaudeville appearances in Nashville.[12]

Opry booking in 1928 was fully in the hands of George Hay.[13] According to all accounts, he knew little about music. As one of our interviewees commented, "To lay it on the line like it was, Judge Hay didn't know music; he couldn't memorize tunes. He wouldn't know the difference between 'Turkey in the Straw' and 'Steamboat Bill.' He liked rapid tunes because he thought the man that was making the most racket was making the most music." Ironically, this apparent deficiency was probably Hay's greatest talent, to bypass what experts might find the most aesthetically pleasing or technically proficient in favor of that which would hold a radio audience. His programming philosophy is probably best expressed in his often-repeated instructions to musicians just before airtime, "All right, let's keep it close to the ground tonight, boys."

An official roster of Opry performers was created only years later, but as early as 1928 there was a discernible cluster of Opry regulars. The members of the leading groups received five dollars apiece for "expenses," and the October 1928 *Radio Digest* "Who's Who in Broadcasting" listed eleven "Grand Ole Opry" acts among WSM's staff. All performers for whom we can find information either were hired directly by a WSM official or were introduced by other Opry regulars. Thus, although by 1928 there was clearly a surfeit of people willing to play for no more than the prestige of appearing on the "miracle of radio," few of these got the chance to appear on the Opry. As one of our informants put it, "There were very few Saturday nights when somebody didn't come around hoping to get to play with somebody else, or get on themselves.

But very few of them ever got the opportunity to play. Some of them were really good, too."

Nascent Professionalism

Among the Opry regulars of the 1920s, only Uncle Dave Macon had made his living primarily from playing music before going on the Opry. The others were, however, far from inexperienced amateurs. All whose early careers we have been able to trace had already played for money at local events such as ice cream socials, annual furniture store sale days, schoolhouse shows, fairs, union hall concerts, political rallies, and the like. A considerable number, including Dr. Humphrey Bate, the McGees, Sid Harkreader, and the Crook Brothers, ventured beyond middle Tennessee to work on patent medicine shows, Cumberland riverboat cruises, fiddling contests, and the like. For example, in the years before the Opry, Kirk McGee, then a teenager, toured Alabama and Georgia with Dr. Walter Harris's Medicine Show, which sold Aztec Indian elixir (a laxative that probably contained cocaine). Kirk worked variously as a buck-and-wing dancer, skit performer, and guitarist. Earning five dollars a day and all expenses, Kirk, the son of an old-time fiddle contest winner, felt he was getting rich. The medicine show was seasonal work, however, because the shows profitably worked the territory only for the few weeks after the farmers had received cash for their cotton crops.

While such medicine show work did not bespeak professionalism in the modern sense, the fact is that there was no more professional outlet for any but a very few country music entertainers before records and radio combined with generally rising levels of wealth to expose and develop the market for country music. The singular importance of radio in creating the possibility for full-time professional careers in country music is examined systematically in chapters 7 and 8 below. It can, however, be traced in the careers of the early Opry regulars.[14] For some, the Opry was a training ground for a fully professional career, while for others it remained a supplement to their regular "day job."

Hillbilly Origins?

If our discussion of professionalism is somewhat obscured by the fact that modern career patterns for the professional country performer simply did not exist in the period with which we are dealing, the question of the social class background of barn-dance performers is equally complicated by the fact that the rural status system of the 1920s bears little relation to our contemporary class system. Many who by modern standards might be considered impoverished were then considered relatively well off. Such people fit into the class of "respectable God-fearing poor," and socially they were a clear notch above the "poor white trash" that provided the model for the hillbilly stereotype.[15]

It emerges quite clearly from all of the background data we have been able to collect that the Opry performers of 1928 were not recruited from the rural "poor white trash" caricatured in the Lil' Abner cartoon and in *The Beverly Hillbillies* television show. In fact, a substantial majority of those who would become Opry regulars were not even rural residents in 1925, a full year before WSM went on the air. Instead, they were steadily employed residents of Nashville who worked at a wide variety of urban trades ranging from barber, cigar maker, and railroad dispatcher to insurance salesman, watchmaker, and physician.

Performers who regularly journeyed to Nashville from the surrounding counties were sons of farm owners or small-town tradespeople. While they may have been rustic by the standards of New York sophisticates, we have been able to identify only one who came from the poorer elements of rural society. Thus the early recruits of the Opry seem to have come from a more well-to-do segment of Tennessee society than most Opry newcomers during the 1940s and 1950s.[16]

Hillbilly Image

If the Opry regulars of 1928 weren't actually hillbillies, who manufactured the hillbilly image and for what purpose? The answers to both questions are not hard to find. Although he did not use the term, George Hay nurtured the hillbilly image to fit a commercially successful format derived from vaudeville. American popular theater had long depended on a set of stereotyped characters, including the Yankee, Irishman, Negro, Chinaman, Jew, Indian, Swede, city slicker, and country bumpkin.[17]

Like other impresarios of the unidimensional radio medium, Hay tried to create easily identifiable characters who could be visualized though unseen. As a quite young man, for example, he fashioned for himself the character of the Solemn Old Judge. He also christened the Gully Jumpers and the Fruit Jar Drinkers (see gallery figures G2.3 and G2.4 for images of the latter, both before and after their rustification by Hay). In like manner, Hay changed Dr. Bate and His Augmented Orchestra to the Possum Hunters, and the Binkley Brothers Barn Dance Orchestra (fig. 5.1) was renamed the Dixie Clod Hoppers.[18] The Crook Brothers band was the only regular string band that did not have its name changed. The only reason our informants were able to offer was that the Crook Brothers had played dual harmonica for some years and thus had established a local reputation. Herman Crook told Charles Wolfe that George Hay con-

Figure 5.1 The Binkley Brothers string band, which George Hay dubbed the "Dixie Clod Hoppers." Here the hillbilly image is in the process of being assembled. Gale Binkley with his homemade gag fiddle, overalls, and corncob pipe is closest to having a complete outfit, but even he, like the rest, is wearing a tie under his checked shirt. Their aspiring young guitarist, Jack Jackson, is uncompromising in his fashionable business suit, bow tie, sheer stockings, and polished shoes.

sidered their group's family name comic enough.[19] Certainly the designation "Brothers" gave the aggregation the appropriate amateurish ring.[20]

So long as the Opry was defined simply as a radio show, Hay paid no attention to aspects of image beyond those of name, musical sound, and verbal repartee that could be heard over the air. The earliest pictures of the Opry members show them in dark suits, white shirts and ties. The style of their clothes would make them indistinguishable from other townspeople. Only when the show began to cater to a studio audience— about 1928—did Hay begin to insist that group members look the part of hillbillies. For example, Alcyone Bate Beasley, who played piano with her father's Possum Hunters, recalls, "The only time I saw a performer dress up in coveralls and kerchief was when it was a costume. They always dressed in their best clothes to come to the station." Hay asked her and another little girl who sang with Ed Poplin's group to "always wear a little apron or little bonnets or something like that."

We see that by 1928 the format and sound of the Opry was already

Figure 5.2 The Cumberland Ridge Runners, seen in this 1931 photo with the group's founder-manager, John Lair (with the jug), in the type of hillbilly performance outfits characteristic of the Midwest and the WLS "National Barn Dance," where they were featured

firmly established. Our findings suggest a different picture of the early Opry than that promulgated by George Hay and others. What we have found is that the show was more tightly programmed and less casual than they said. There was also more variety and less pure old-time music. What is more, the performers were both more professional and less rural than the image that Hay fostered. Thus Hay's Opry of 1928 was more hillbilly in its image than it was in fact, and Hay's talent for crafting a commercial product in the guise of informal amateurism is seen in all these aspects of the early Opry.

GLEN RICE AND THE BEVERLY HILLBILLIES: 1930–33

Hay was not the only person to consciously craft the radio hillbilly image. A number of artists and promoters working in vaudeville played an important role in the process, but by all odds one of the most flamboyant and certainly the most blatant fabricator of the radio hillbilly was Glen Rice of KMPC, Beverly Hills, California.[21]

In 1930 Rice was the station manager of KMPC, one of a number of radio stations that were struggling for Los Angeles–area listeners. Country and western music were being played on several of them as a minor part of the programming mix, and Rice decided to introduce country music to KMPC with a special promotion. He let it be known to radio listeners that he was about to take a week's vacation riding in the then extensive wilderness stretches of the Santa Monica hills. He did not return after a week and there was increasing on-air speculation about his whereabouts and his safety.

After more than two weeks had passed, an excited announcer stated that Rice had returned with a fantastic story of his adventures and would recount them the following day. Rice said that deep into the hills he had gotten lost, but had finally come upon a small, primitive "hillbilly" community complete with log cabins, blacksmith shop, and church. Rice opined that the community members, who originally hailed from the Arkansas Ozarks, had been out of contact with civilization for perhaps a hundred years. Some in the community were excellent musicians, Rice said, and they had given a qualified "perhaps" to his invitation to ride their mules out of the mountains and appear on the station. The suspense grew over the next few days because the hillfolk were expected to arrive at any time. Then on Sunday, April 6, 1930, Rice announced that he was certain they would appear that night. "As a matter of fact I think they are coming up Wilshire Boulevard right now. Yes, yes, I see them getting off their mules, and there they are. Ladies and gentlemen, may I present the hill billies!" (Griffis 1980: 5).

Not hillbillies, the musicians were actually established Los Angeles performers and movie hopefuls hailing from San Francisco, up-state New York, and elsewhere who regularly performed music in a number of jazz, pop, and country styles. The nightly KMPC performances of the group, soon formally dubbed the Beverly Hill Billies, proved extremely popular, and large crowds came to the studio. One of the musicians represented himself as a horse doctor and thereafter regularly received letters requesting advice on the ills of animals. One evening, another band member, "Jad," mentioned that his "'ol' cabin burnt to the ground last night.' The next day, much to their dismay, the station parking lot was covered with lumber, furniture, bedding, and food donations for 'ol' Jad' and his family" (Griffis 1980: 7). People were curious about the Hill Billies' current lodgings, so Rice developed the story that he met them and their mules at a trail end and brought them into town in a car. This cover story created another problem for the performers. Fans began to hang around for hours after the show hoping to follow them out, and the musicians could not leave the station. Finally one devised the simple expedient of doffing his rube outfit and walking through the waiting crowd in street clothes, totally unrecognized.

Several months after their first appearance, one of the most popular musicians left the group, and Glen Rice met this crisis with his usual promoter's flair. He said the departing musician was homesick for the Ozarks and that he would accompany him home to scout for a suitable replacement. His "find" was a lanky fifteen-year-old, yodeling, harmonica-playing, fiddling, Los Angeles resident. With much fanfare and newspaper headlines such as "KMPC Finds New Billy/Takes Hubert's Place— 10,000 Greet 'Hill Billy,'" Rice flew in with him, landing at the Burbank airport.

Over the next two years there were many more changes in the group, and in September 1932 the Beverly Hill Billies left KMPC for another Los Angeles station, KTM. Undaunted by their desertion, Glen Rice started all over again with another pseudo-hillbilly. This time Rice "found" him in the L.A. Salvation Army mission band and built a new group dubbed Zeke and His City Fellers. As shown in the following newspaper item for a major 1933 benefit concert at the Hollywood Bowl, Rice never tired of accenting the hyper-rustic image of the performers.

> An eleventh hour addition to the crowded list of attractions will provide thrills for radio fans. Little Elton, famous yodeler from the Ozark mountains, known to every radio fan in America, will perform in person through the courtesy of the Los Angeles Theater. Robert Gumbiner, manager of the theater, will rush the boy star to the Bowl in a fast car, instead of permitting him to ride the slower mule to which he is more accustomed. (Griffis 1980: 12)

The members of the Beverly Hill Billies were good musicians, and several were excellent singers. Rice's fifteen-year-old "Ozark discovery," for example, was Elton Brit, who went on to have an extensive career as a country music soloist. Griffis (1980) credits the Beverly Hill Billies as firmly establishing country music on the West Coast and contributing to the founding of the most famous of the California groups of the 1930s, the Sons of the Pioneers. But what is most important for our purposes here is that as is shown by the public reception of these synthetic characters, the audience, or at least a large part of it, seems to have believed the promotional hoopla surrounding the Beverly Hill Billies and accepted their music as authentic.

CONCLUSION

From the backwoods like the old-timer, the hillbilly differed from the elderly geezer in being in contact with contemporary life. This made the hillbilly a much more potent dramatic persona for the popular culture industry and for the audience. Being set off against and often triggered by the intrusion of urban ways, the hillbilly's humor, aggression, and love laments could change with the times.[22]

George Hay worked hard to disguise the fact that performers on the early Opry were playing a part, and in so doing showed how to create characters that could remain believable over decades-long careers even when audiences knew they were playing a part. Minnie Pearl, who joined the "Grand Ole Opry" in 1940, is perhaps the most widely known example of Hay's work, but in the crucible of Hay's Opry, many other artists learned how to disguise first-class performance skills behind a rough-cut naive down-home exterior.

In sharp contrast, Glen Rice of Hollywood, like the great nineteenth-century impresario P. T. Barnum, drew an audience by the tactic of the "big lie," a fabrication so preposterous that for a moment it seems believable. Like Barnum, Rice could not build acts with a sustained popularity, but could continue drawing attention only by moving from sensation to sensation.[23]

CHAPTER SIX

Cowboy Image of Authenticity

The trans-Mississippian West of the American imagination has been a vast and variegated territory peopled by Spanish estate holders, Native Americans, immigrant homesteaders, wild trappers, gold prospectors, sheep ranchers, Mormon saints, cavalry units, railroad builders, town pacifiers, outlaws, and speculators of all sorts.[1] But among this wide array of half-imagined characters it is the cowboy who has most often held center stage in the western world of the imagination, while one or more of these other actors create plot and add dramatic contrast.

The fortunes of the imagined cowboy and his hillbilly sibling proved quite different in the 1930s. The hillbilly often seemed close to breaking under the combined weight of depressed agricultural prices and the march of industrialization into the rural hinterland. The dominant image alternated between the sullen, displaced farmer and the comedic buffoon. At its best, the music created in this caldron of despair was vital and richly varied. In stark contrast, the cowboy, always serious, alone, and unfettered by communal responsibilities, seemed to grow in stature. But the songs he sang proved singularly unappealing.

In this chapter we focus on the fabrication of the media cowboy, showing how the singing cowboy was shaped in the hands of Republic Studios. Finally, we see how a crisis in the development of country music was averted by dressing the singer of heartfelt hillbilly songs in the heroic cowboy outfit.

FABRICATING THE MEDIA COWBOY

The cowboy, bereft of family responsibilities, worked as a hand on a ranch or hired out as a scout, Texas Ranger, U.S. Marshall, or county sheriff, thus becoming an ambivalent-primitive-loner turned agent-of-civilization. The fictionalized exploits of Indian scout and buffalo hunter Bill Cody were first presented in a 1869 dime novel and serialized in the *New York Weekly*. The cowboy soon became one of the most frequent heroes of such pulp adventure novels (French 1951). In 1872 Cody himself appeared in a staged western drama, "Scouts of the Prairie," and soon after toured nationally as the featured performer of "Buffalo Bill's Wild West" show. In 1901 Teddy Roosevelt, who styled himself a cowboy, became president. In 1902 Owen Wister's *The Virginian*, the first "literary" western novel, was published, and it became the best-selling book of the year (Cawelti 1976: 215). A year later *The Great Train Robbery*, a western and the first extended narrative film, was released to great acclaim. A spate of one- and two-reel melodramatic western movies followed, with Tom Mix emerging as the first movie cowboy hero (Young 1980).

The 1910 anthology *Cowboy Songs and Other Frontier Ballads* was the first widely distributed, full-length publication that featured the image of cowboy as *singer*. In his introduction to the anthology, John A. Lomax presents the stock romanticized depiction of cowboy ways: "They loved roaming; they loved freedom; they were pioneers by instinct; an impulse set their faces from the east, put a tang for roaming in their veins, and sent them ever, ever westward" (Lomax 1910: xxi).[2]

This media cowboy kept his heroic qualities through the first half of the twentieth century by upholding the higher ideals of justice shared by both the communal order of the ancient leatherstocking and by the laws of urban civilization. He used the cunning of the old communal ways in order to defend the civilizing process against both the outlaw bad seed of the West and against civilization's unscrupulous progeny who used statute law against the higher ideals of justice shared by both the communal order and civilization. Imbedded in this scenario is the tragic realization that the cowboy, in working as an agent of civilization, is bringing about the demise of the older communal ways in which his way of life is imbedded. Seen in "The Lone Ranger," "Tom Mix," and many more, this Marxian tragedy is typified in Sheriff Matt Dillon of the long-running television series *Gunsmoke.*

The Singing Cowboy

More so than in any of the other popular media, the westerner of western *music* was depicted as a cowboy. But this singing cowboy came late on the scene. Working cowboys talked and sang to their cattle to calm them and to fill the lonely voids of the land where they worked—a land where, to quote R. J. Young, "there are more cows and less butter, more rivers and less water, and you can see farther and see less than any place on earth" (1980: 139). Cowboy songs represent this world; as Johnson (1981: 79) notes, "Western music is essentially the music of men, their work, their land, and their death—outside the pale of civilized society."

In spite of the popularity of the singing cowboy, in touring shows[3] and on screen, cowboy songs had little impact on the development of commercial music (Lomax 1910; Young 1980: 147). In fact, the leading historian of country music, Bill Malone, says flatly, "The cowboy contributed nothing to American music" (1985: 152). As Malone notes in the same passage, the cowboy did, however, contribute "the fabric of usable symbols which surrounded him." That is to say, the ten-gallon hat, the silver-studded leather wear, the distinctive cut and decoration of clothes and boots, the six-shooter, the horse with western saddle, the impassive look, and the imperious, legs-spread-wide stance.

There were commercial singing cowboys performing in live shows and on the radio by the mid-1920s. From 1927 through 1936 John I. White of Washington, D.C., most often using the moniker "The Lonesome Cowboy," had a regular NBC network program featuring western as well as hillbilly songs. From 1930 through 1936 his songs were used as interludes in dramatic presentations about the West, which he initially narrated as the "Old Ranger" on the radio program "Death Valley Days." The prime sponsor of this program from 1930 on was the Pacific Coast Borax Company, maker of "20 Mule Team Borax," a water softener and kitchen deodorant mined in Nevada. Following close behind White, "Tex" Ritter gained a national audience in 1932 with his melodic East Texas accent, narrating and singing on a western musical and dramatic radio program much like television's *Death Valley Days* (Malone 1985: 151).

White, Ritter, and others made records singing songs with cowboy motifs, but what really popularized the image of singer as cowboy across the nation was the advent, in the 1930s, of talking movies featuring singing cowboys. Ken Maynard is credited with having been the first cowboy to sing, in the 1930 film *The Wagon Master,* but his singing was an aspect of a particular role he was playing rather than part of his persona as a performer. The two who defined and personified the singing cowboys were Gene Autry and Roy Rogers, both of whom were launched as cinema singing cowboys by the fledgling Republic Studio.

THE SINGING COWBOYS OF REPUBLIC STUDIOS: 1934–37

Numerous silent films with cowboy and western plots starring the likes of Tom Mix and Ken Maynard were made at each of the major studios in the 1920s. With the advent of sound, however, all the majors except Paramount simply eliminated the genre, reasoning that such films' projected viewership did not justify the greatly increased costs of making a sound film. While many of the small independent film companies went bankrupt with the advent of sound, others adapted by making movie serials and B films that served as the second part of the movie bill (Tuska 1982). One of the most successful in this market was Republic Pictures, formed in 1934 by Herbert Yates from the foreclosure purchase of several failed independents, including Monogram.

John Wayne, Reluctant Singing Cowboy

One of the aspiring actors under contract to Monogram's Lone Star Productions was John Wayne.[4] At the time of the consolidation with Republic, Wayne was completing a set of eight films in which he played the part of "Singin' Sandy," a cowboy who sang songs from time to time. Wayne, who at the time had no alternative prospects, had begun the singing series as a gag, but his singing cowboy image soon became a big draw, much to Wayne's chagrin. " 'They finally got up to four songs in one picture,' Wayne recalled, 'and before you knew it, they had me going on public appearances, and over top of my horse crappin' on the stage, everybody's screamin': 'Sing! Sing! Sing!' " (Young 1980: 146). It may be, as some western buffs insist, that another had sung while Wayne lip-synched the part before the cameras. In any case, when in 1935 it came time for Wayne to renew his contract, he was adamant about not singing. He is reported to have said to Herbert Yates, the principle owner of Republic Pictures, which now held his contract, "I've had it. I'm a goddamned action star, you son-of-a-bitch. I'm not a singer. Get yourself another cowboy singer" (Young 1980: 146). At the urging of Nat Levine, its head of production, Republic spent considerable time and money to do just that.

It seemed desirable to Nat Levine to get another singing cowboy, not just because Wayne's singing had proven attractive to audiences, but because the singing cowboy persona promised to solve several pressing problems faced by moviemakers. On the one hand, by 1935 the "all-talking, all-singing, all-dancing" extravaganzas of Busby Berkeley were setting the standard for all films (Young 1980: 147). On the other hand, the effort to "clean up" the sex, violence, and leftist slant of films, spearheaded by the National Legion of Decency of the Catholic Church, had every filmmaker and distributor checking the nuances of each inch of celluloid (Stanley 1978: 192–96). Locating the films in the "old" West rather than in contemporary cities also allowed filmmakers to address contemporary issues without seeming to be polemical (Lenihan 1980).

The cowboy who sang and played for dances fit the musical mode. The politics of the cowboy hero could quite naturally be "200 percent American"; sexual interest could be represented simply by focusing on comely young people; there could be lengthy horseback chase scenes across wide-open spaces; and more violence was tolerated because it was set in a bygone era (or at least away from the politically sensitive big city), with the virtuous hero always triumphant in the end. With this formula Republic could deliver an entertaining product that distributors could schedule without question. There was no financial inducement to make these films any better than what was required to keep distributors ordering the next set of films. This is because distributors paid B filmmakers a flat rental fee for each showing, rather than basing payment on box office receipts (Stanley 1978: 126).

The singing cowboy formula was attractive to Republic for yet another essential reason. The costs of production had to be kept to a minimum on B films. Singing cowboy westerns, or "horse operas," as they came to be called, could be produced quickly, out of doors, and on simple sets, without the cost of large groups of dancers and expensive orchestral musicians. Finally, the music could consist of old songs in the public domain requiring no royalty payments, or offerings by songwriters who were used to selling their work for next to nothing.

Choosing Gene Autry

Nat Levine began the search for an actor who could sing and also ride a horse. He found singing actors and riding actors but none that could do both. Herbert Yates considered this no problem, because a singing actor could be taught to sit on a horse, and a double could film all the action shots, or the singing voice of the riding actor could be dubbed. Perhaps mindful of John Wayne's problems at personal appearances, Nat

Levine, over Yates's objections, chose Gene Autry, the one candidate who could both sing and ride. Yates strenuously objected, because Autry could not act, but his objection soon vanished as Autry went on to be a tremendous hit as a horse-opera actor. His mostly small-town and youthful fans empathized with the awkward, halting style of acting that made him seem always out of place in modern settings of domesticity and work. He became animated only when he could escape civilization and get away on his trusted horse with some buddies on some adventure.[5] By 1939 Gene Autry's box-office appeal rivaled that of the reigning movie stars of the era, Clark Gable, Bing Crosby, and Gary Cooper.

When selected by Nat Levine, Autry, then twenty-seven, was a stranger to moviemaking, but he was an experienced performer.[6] He spent his early years in and around the west Texas town of Tioga, singing in his grandfather's Baptist church and, while still in high school, touring briefly with a medicine show. Not thinking of a professional career in music, he worked for three years as a railroad telegrapher in Oklahoma. He played guitar and sang to while away the lonely hours on the night shift until a chance encounter with an admiring Will Rogers induced him in 1929 to go to New York for an audition. Counseled to get experience working a microphone and come back in several years, Autry found work at a Tulsa radio station, and within a year he was invited to join the "National Barn Dance" cast at WLS in Chicago. Autry soon made records and issued the first of a number of songbooks. These sold millions of copies in the early 1930s, when they were included along with a guitar instruction manual, and later a "Gene Autry Roundup" guitar, in the Sears and Roebuck mail order catalog.[7]

During his time on the "National Barn Dance," Autry was dubbed "Oklahoma's Singing Cowboy," but western songs were only a minor part of his repertoire. Initially he patterned his singing style after the preeminent country artist of the day, Jimmie Rodgers, and he sang a number of Rodgers's songs, including "In the Jailhouse Now," "Any Old Time," "Rheumatism Blues," and several of his idol's blue yodels. In all, Autry recorded twenty-eight Rodgers compositions between 1929 and 1937. Ronnie Pugh (1987) has found that seven of Autry's covers recorded between 1930 and 1933 were recorded *before* the Rodgers originals were released. Pugh conjectures that Ralph Peer, Rodgers's publisher, delivered the songs to Autry as soon as possible. The exposure of the songs via the "National Barn Dance" on which Autry performed regularly, as well as the sale of Autry's records, would net Peer more as publisher than any loss of the mechanical royalties on Rodgers's American Record Corporation (ARC) releases.

In addition to the songs composed by Jimmie Rodgers, during his four years on the "National Barn Dance," Autry recorded sentimental tunes ("The Tie That Binds"), folksongs ("Methodist Pie"), novelty numbers ("Slue-Foot Sue"), and even a labor ballad ("The Death of Mother Jones"). His biggest hit of the period was a duet with Jimmy Long, the sentimental ballad "That Silver-Haired Daddy of Mine," a plaintive lament of a prodigal son's love for his aging father. Thus when Autry went to Hollywood in 1935, his musical identity was that of an eclectic singer in the mold of Jimmie Rodgers, not that of a singing cowboy (Malone 1985: 143).

Autry's most successful songs had been recorded on the various labels of the ARC company, which was, along with Republic Studios, owned by Herbert Yates. Thus when Nat Levine chose Autry to mold into Republic's replacement for John Wayne as its featured singing movie cowboy, he had solid evidence of Autry's ability and popularity as a radio and recording artist. In addition, the company stood to profit from the promotion of Autry's songs via his movies.

Molding Autry into a singing cowboy actor proved easy for Levine. Building on the image of "Oklahoma's Singing Cowboy," Levine asked him always to appear in public in western clothes and to sing exclusively songs with western motifs. (See photo G2.3.) He tested Autry's cinematic appeal by giving him a minor singing part in a 1934 Ken Maynard film, *In Old Santa Fe*. The positive response was so great that he gave Autry the featured role in a twelve-part movie serial. This placement meant that Autry would be before the national audience for twelve weeks in a row. Autry's first feature-length vehicle, *Tumbling Tumbleweeds*, followed early in 1935. The movie was a success, and the record of the title song also sold well (Whitburn 1986: 40). His popularity grew so rapidly that by 1937 Autry was voted the movie industry's top western star, and by 1939 he was receiving as many as 12,000 pieces of mail a week, and he was making more money from product endorsements than from his movies and records combined. For example, in that year over two million cap pistols bearing his name were sold (Johnston 1939).

The Squeaky-Clean Singing-Cowboy Formula Film

Nat Levine's prime task was reshaping the movie western form to accommodate this *singing* cowboy who couldn't act and to satisfy the newly stricter demands of movie industry censors (Stanley 1978: 195). To simplify the acting assignments and pacify censors, Autry played himself. That is, he played Gene Autry, an open-faced, trusting fellow, rather than the typical rugged bad man turned hero by the love of an Eastern beauty in distress that was characteristic of the genre (Cawelti 1970). Since he played himself, the plots had to be placed in the West of the present or to involve some sort of time-space travel, as in his first serial production, *The Phantom Empire.* The usual plot line ran as follows: riding his horse, Champion, and surrounded by a group of fellow musicians, Rogers was forced by circumstances to champion the interests of those exploited or victimized by unscrupulous businessmen.

The businessman-as-villain was chosen by the process of elimination. Because of the growing sensitivity about media images, foreigners, ethnics, and religious minorities could not be safely depicted as villains. Also because of the very real threat of censorship, the good will of politicians, law enforcement officials, and journalists had to be cultivated by the movie industry, so these occupational roles could not be portrayed as corrupt. In this Depression era of great financial hardships, individual businesspersons, if not the business class itself, seemed the natural villain. This casting was all very explicit, as is shown by Johnston's 1939 article on Autry: "The ideal villain of today should be white, Protestant, native-born of native parents, of Anglo-Saxon stock, and engaged in business, preferably banking" (1939: 75).

Shaping the Music

The choices made in creating the formula film constrained the kinds of music that could be featured. Interludes of singing, particularly singing love ballads to the female lead, would bring the action to a halt and engender the wrath of the vociferous young male element of the audience. But the Republic directors wanted to use the films to promote the phonograph records of Autry singing. They found numerous ingenious ways of tying the music into the story line. For example, music was used to quell an incipient riot, it was used to send a coded message, it was the occasion for mending a rift between band members, it was paid for by the bad guys to advance their as yet undetected nefarious purposes, it formed the substance of a duel with the bad guys, it provided the occasion for flashbacks to scenes of the Old West, and so forth.

Such plot devices, together with the expectations of the audience, constrained the music, and the songs created for and popularized in western films of the 1930s generally dealt with images of the West and provided descriptions of cowboys in action. They did not deal with the joys and travails of heterosexual love relations, the preeminent theme of country music lyrics (Rogers 1989).

Substituting Roy Rogers

When his contract with Republic was up for renewal in 1938, Autry asked for considerably more money. Herbert Yates's reaction was typical of media executives of the day. Believing that it was his promotion and production team at Republic Studios that had made Autry a nationally known movie star, he refused to meet Autry's demands and, to chasten his jumped-up star, began the effort to find another "unknown" to fashion as a singing cowboy. Although numerous auditions were conducted, the successor was found right on the Republic lot. This was Leonard Slye, charter member of the Sons of the Pioneers, who had appeared in a number of westerns.

Slye was first rechristened Dick Weston, and finally Roy Rogers by the Republic image-makers. Rogers, born in Cincinnati, Ohio, in 1912, had moved to southern California with his family in the early days of the Great Depression. There he teamed with two other musicians to form the Pioneer Trio. When two more musicians were added, the name was changed to the Sons of the Pioneers in order to escape the confining "old-time" connotation of "pioneer" and to fit in better with the youthful age and sophisticated harmonic stylings of the group (Green 1976).

So that Rogers might quickly replace the recalcitrant Autry, Yates did not require the customary budget restrictions on a novice actor, allowing him to receive full star treatment from the beginning. The strategy worked. Rogers, soon joined by his comely wife, Dale Evans, and his horse, Trigger, and supported by his old singing group, the Sons of the Pioneers, quickly became a hit in the world of B movies. Rogers's boyish good looks are apparent in figure 6.1 and in the publicity photo of him with Evans and Trigger (gallery figure G2.7).

Capitalizing on his difficulties at Republic and box-office appeal, several movie executives asked Gene Autry to become a romantic lead, but he steadfastly refused, saying, "A cowboy, if he doesn't let his public down, is good until he is fifty years old. A matinee idol doesn't last five years" (Johnston 1939: 75). Within a year Autry resigned from Republic with terms that allowed him to keep his increasingly large income from personal appearances and from licensing items with his name or image. In effect, movies became for Gene Autry (and later Roy Rogers) what radio was for so many country artists, a way to keep his name before the public so that he could make money from personal appearances, recordings, songbooks, and promotional items, and he was very successful in doing so (Page 1965; Fessier 1967).

HILLBILLY SAVED BY DONNING HIS COWBOY SIBLING'S CLOTHES

In the 1930s, many performers from the Southwest cultivated an image of links to cowboy life. For example, Woodward Ritter from the cotton-

Figure 6.1 Roy Rogers (in the light outfit), "King of the Cowboys," reared in Duck Run, Ohio, and the Cactus Cowboys, together with Hank Snow of Nova Scotia (in front with guitar), sport the cowboy image of authenticity.

growing area of east Texas, who had attended Northwestern Law School, took the name "Tex" and consciously cultivated the aura of a cowboy. As Bill Malone (1985: 151) notes, "Ritter was not a cowboy, but was instead a very believable interpreter of cowboy songs. Impressionable easterners were easily convinced that he came, not from a small East Texas community and a college background, but from a working cattle ranch." In order to get on the western bandwagon, many country musicians of the 1930s completely reworked their pasts to fit the image. For example, Arkansas-reared Rubye Blevins renamed herself Patsy Montana and thereafter cultivated an identity with that state. Likewise, Dolly and Millie Good (née Goed), from East St. Louis, Illinois, rewrote their biographies to have come from Muleshoe, Texas, and took on the identity of the Girls of the Golden West (Malone 1985: 144–45; they are shown in their fashionable westernwear in gallery figure G2.6). Wisconsin-born accordion-playing bandleader Pee Wee King (né Frank Kuczynski) so admired the complex close-harmony singing of the female duo that he named his band the Golden West Cowboys (Green 1976: 90).

These claim-jumpers were not no-talent performers trying to get a few dates by adapting to the latest show-business fad. Ritter and King are both in the Country Music Hall of Fame, and Patsy Montana had a long and successful career as the first female country artist to have a million-selling record, with her assertive "I Want to Be a Cowboy's Sweetheart" (Oermann and Bufwack 1981).

The trend to the cowboy identity did carry many lesser talents along with it, and the spread of the cowboy image was so complete that virtually all country artists, male and female alike, dressed in western outfits through the 1940s and tried in every way to project a cowboy rather than a hillbilly persona. A study of the names of the 428 country music bands playing on radio stations around the country in 1950, for example, showed that 53 percent of the bands had names with identifiable geographic loci such as the Blue Ridge Ramblers and the West Texas Rangers. Of these, fully 60 percent referred to locations in the Southwest, and 26 percent referred to locations in the Central South, including Kentucky, Tennessee, Alabama, and Mississippi. What is more, groups with names evoking a place in the Southwest predominated in all regions of the country, from southern California to New England, *except* for the original home of the hillbilly, the Central South and the South Atlantic states (Peterson and Gowan 1971: 3–6).

In the mid-1930s the hillbilly look still predominated on the "Grand Ole Opry," but there were many in westernwear on the "National Barn Dance," as can be seen in figures 7.1 and 7.2. Over the protests of many hillbilly traditionalists, including George Hay, bands with western outfits were even coming to predominate on the stage of Nashville's "Grand Ole Opry" in the 1940s. Roy Acuff, then the leading performer on the Opry, was one of the more vocal holdouts. When he went to California with his band, the Smoky Mountain Boys, in 1940 to help make a movie for Republic titled *The "Grand Ole Opry,"* Roy refused to have his band dressed in western outfits. Reflecting on the experience in 1943 he said, "I am very annoyed when someone calls me a cowboy. You can see that there is nothing cowboy about me" (Schlappi 1978: 176).

The Unpopular Western Song Lyric

In spite of their repeated exposure to millions of moviegoers, the western songs performed by Autry, Rogers, and the legion of other movie singing cowboys who followed, with rare exceptions, did not sell well. As Douglas Green (1976: 104) notes, "Surprising as it may seem, western music just didn't seem to sell well on record." For example, Roy Rogers—for all of his movie success—had no hit songs (Whitburn 1986: 374).[8]

Autry, who sold more records than any of the other singing cowboys, early in his Hollywood years had several western hits, including "Back in the Saddle Again," and "Tumblin' Tumbleweeds." But his most successful songs all explored nonwestern themes,[9] ranging from "That Silver Haired Daddy of Mine," recorded in 1931 while he was still with the "National Barn Dance" in Chicago, to his mid-career love songs such as "Be Honest with Me," and "South of the Border (Down Mexico Way)" to his numerous later seasonal novelties such as "Rudolph the Red-Nosed Reindeer."

The songs performed in 1930s western films were a mix of older public domain songs such as "Oh Susanna" and "Streets of Laredo (The Dying Cowboy)," and lyrics newly written for the films, whose plots were hardly heavy on sexual tension. The movie plots set man against man in a wide, unforgiving natural environment. The songs accented the dependence on pals—human ("Texas Plains") and animal ("Give Me a Pinto Pal")—a changeable land of privation and dust ("Tumblin' Tumbleweeds," "Cool Water," "Dust"), and nostalgia for a passing cowboy way of life ("Back in the Saddle Again," "Cimaroon").[10]

Many of the songs were written by professional songwriters used to working with the Tin Pan Alley lyrical formula that accented abstractions and tight lyrical rhymes, and many of the songs seem to have been written after looking at postcards of the West or skimming a Zane Grey novel. Since the songs were written to be played by actors in B movies, there was little pressure for them to be commercially viable on their own, and writers began to build a western B-movie aesthetic of abstraction, or as Douglas Green calls it, "poetic escapism,"[11] which soon suffused the music. Perhaps the basic reason that western B-movie music was not all that popular is that it was not created primarily to be popular.

Why the Hillbilly Donned Westernwear

If western and cowboy songs were not popular, why did the singing cowboy outfit, ever more completely divorced from the garb of a working cowboy, with its increasingly bright colors and growing profusion of piping, silver, and rhinestones, became the standard costume for country-music performers right across the nation? Why did most hillbilly bands shed their coveralls, gingham dresses, brogan shoes, and straw hats for cowboy clothes, western boots, and Stetson hats? R. J. Young suggests what the problem was with the hillbilly image:

> "Hillbilly" had long been a pejorative term, not only to those who played and listened to it, but to an even larger audience who sneered at it. Autry's success, however, opened up a brand new audience and proved that it wasn't so much the music as the hillbilly *style* that

turned off a greater audience. Thus the hillbilly music-makers followed Autry's lead by simply changing their dress code. (1980: 152)

Bill Malone suggests why, in the 1930s, the cowboy image was more
appealing than that of his sibling, the hillbilly.

> From New York to California, individuals responded to the western
> myth and "cowboy" singers. . . . "Western" became a rival and often
> preferred term to "hillbilly" as a proper appellation for country music.
> It is easy to understand, of course, why "western" would be preferred
> to the seemingly disreputable backwoods term. "Western," specifi-
> cally, suggested a music that had been developed by cowboys out on
> the Texas Plains; more generally, it suggested a context that was open,
> free, and expansive. In short, the term fit the American self-concept.
> (1985: 152–153)[12]

In 1935 Gene Autry showed that the cowboy could not only lend
dignity to country music but could literally defend it as well. In *Tumbling
Tumbleweeds,* his first feature film for Republic Pictures, while singing
"That Silver Haired Daddy of Mine," Autry is beset by a couple of rough-
looking hecklers who disparage his daddy. Autry lays down his guitar
and beats up them both. In doing so, Douglas Green notes, "He is fighting
for the dignity of the country music song and country singer" (Green
1976: 105–6).

If the cowboy image greatly increased the legitimacy and appeal of
country music in the 1930s, it also affected the music and the careers
of many performers as well. The featured singing cowboys played guitars
rather than fiddles or banjos, bringing this instrument to prominence
for the first time. Nick Lucas and Jimmie Rodgers were the only guitar-
playing performers with national reputations in the 1920s, and it was
not until Gene Autry's mid-1930s success as a singing movie cowboy
that the sales of guitars began to grow rapidly (Green 1976: 105). In
addition, as Douglas Green (1976: 107) notes, "the financial success enjoyed by the singing cowboys, especially Autry, helped make 'hillbilly'
music a respectable way of life to the musically talented and their families, thus fostering the careers of many entertainers who have followed
the singing-cowboy era."

CONCLUSION

Part 2 began with an examination of the politics of imaging the country
music artist as an old-time geezer, relic of the leatherstocking of the

1820s. This old person playing old songs proved to have limited appeal to the country music audience.[13] Chapter 5 examined a much more pliable image, that of the hillbilly, and in this chapter we have focused on his sibling, the cowboy. We concluded by suggesting that in the late 1930s the two siblings had begun to merge in a way that proved extremely important for the development of country music.

The importance of fusing music elements drawn from the hillbilly tradition with the visual image of the cowboy can clearly be seen in the experience of the most prominent singing cowboy of the 1940s, Jimmy Wakely. Though he sang a number of western songs, Wakely never had a song with a western theme on the music charts. His two big hits were honky-tonk confessionals of the sort that would later propel Hank Williams to stardom, "One Has My Name (The Other Has My Heart)" and "Slippin' Around." Like Gene Autry and the other successful singing cowboys of the 1930s and 1940s, Wakely and Ernest Tubb (Pugh 1996) found the most success singing hillbilly songs while wearing a cowboy's clothing.

Geezers, Hillbillies and Cowboys

G2.1 Old-time fiddler and snowshoe maker Mellie Dunham of Norway, Maine, is seen here with his admiring patron, auto maker Henry Ford.

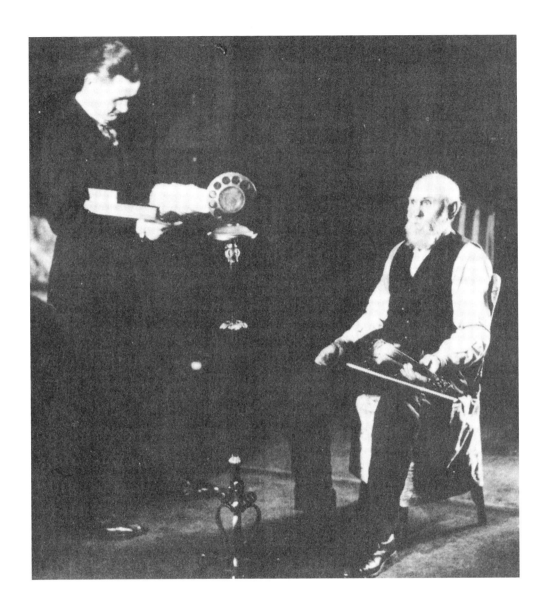

G2.2 Fiddlin' Uncle Jimmy Thompson, venerable fiddle champion who was the first performer on the Saturday night radio program that came to be called the "Grand Ole Opry," with George Hay, architect of the program and the image of its performers.

G2.3 *(top)* The Fruit Jar Drinkers in their best street clothes as they appeared at early Opry performances. Only the name had been made rustic by the time of this first publicity photo.

G2.4 *(bottom)* The Fruit Jar Drinkers in hillbilly overalls but still without the stereotypic hillbilly straw hats in their second publicity photo.

G2.5 Gene Autry was a leading artist on Chicago's WLS "National Barn Dance" before he moved to Hollywood, donned western outfits and became the paradigmatic cinematic singing cowboy.

G2.6 Dorothy (Dolly) and Mildred (Millie) Goed (Good) were Illinois farm girls who sang tight harmonies on WLS and throughout the Midwest. Following the advice of a manager, they dressed western, claimed Muleshoe, Texas, as their birthplace, and called themselves the "Girls of the Golden West."

G2.7 Roy Rogers, Trigger, and Dale Evans display the fully developed western look that was seen in the numerous singing cowboy films, concerts, and rodeos of the 1930s and 1940s.

Part Three

Radio-Made Country Music in the 1930s

CHAPTER SEVEN

Barn Dance in the Air

Prices for agricultural products trended downward through the 1920s so that the stock-market crash of November 1929 only aggravated an already depressed rural economy. Bob Miller's popular song of the time, " 'Leven Cent Cotton and Forty Cent Meat," said bluntly that what a farmer had for sale was nearly worthless, yet what he had to buy in the store was very expensive. By the early 1930s, everyone was affected by these conditions, and as a consequence, attendance at vaudeville and similar entertainments was sharply down, and the bottom fell out of the record business.[1]

Radio was the one entertainment medium that continued to flourish. With the founding of national networks in 1927, national advertisers found radio to be a cost-effective means of selling consumer products (Sanjek 1988: 169), and for the reasons discussed in chapter 2 above, country music was included in the programming mix of both network and independent stations.[2]

For the potential consumer, radio entertainment had the great advantage of being free of charge, an especially important consideration in those Depression years. Country music played over the radio had an almost magical power for rural people growing up in the 1930s, drawing families together and at the same time opening isolated communities to the larger world beyond the county and even the state. Elmer Bird of

Putnam County, West Virginia, eight years old in 1930, described to Charles Wolfe the Saturday-evening ritual of climbing the highest hill around to capture the sounds of the barn dance in the air.

> Uncle Walter had the first radio in that part of the country, and he had it rigged up to run off a car battery. As we got up to the top of the hill he would start hooking up the radio. Meanwhile, other people would begin arriving from other directions; some of them would walk three or four miles to get up there, up where we could get good reception. And we'd gather in. And at nine o'clock we'd start listening to the Grand Ole Opry. And the different ones of us that played different instruments liked the different acts . . . and some just liked to hear the jokes of old Judge Hay, the man who ran it. All of us would sit up there under the stars and listen to it until it went off the air after midnight. It was fine. (Wolfe 1994: 41)

More than phonograph records or movies, radio showcased country music to millions of listeners and provided hundreds of performers the chance to make a living from playing it. In the process radio profoundly shaped country music in the Depression decade leading up to World War II. While few performers could support themselves by playing on the radio exclusively, radio performance was the context in which performers had a chance to perfect their skills with other would-be professionals, to become experienced in the ways of commercial entertainment, to attract the attention of record producers, and most important, to become well enough known among the public to make a living from playing shows and dances.

For all these reasons and more, as we will see in part 3, live performance on radio most importantly shaped country music in the 1930s. In this chapter the focus is on the influence of the large "barn-dance"[3] programs of the era. Chapter 8 examines the influence of an alternate radio format and way of making a living that we call "barnstorming." Finally, in chapter 9 we identify hard-core and soft-shell styles in 1930s radio music, and show how their dialectical interaction continued to renew country music decade by decade.

1930s BARN DANCE ECLECTICISM

The leading performer of the precommercial era was the fiddler who played for dances and performed in contests. But the solo fiddle sound, which animated dancers in live performance so much that the instrument was called by many of God's Southern ministers "the Devil's box," quickly proved to be extremely monotonous when listened to over early radio receivers. Fiddlers who could also sing, like Fiddlin' John Carson, and bands like the Skillet Lickers, who could provide instrumental variety within a tune, soon displaced the old-time square-dance fiddler as the staple fare on radio programs of country music.

Barn Dances Not for Dancing

The "barn dance of the air" that had become a standard format in the 1930s took this call for variety one step further, dictating that there be variety from song to song in type, instrumentation, and personnel. In this context it was easy to insert informal banter among performers, humorous skits, announcements of upcoming live performances, and an increasing number of commercial advertisements. The addition of a live studio audience helped to lend verisimilitude to the event, and many performers felt more relaxed playing to a live audience rather than to an inanimate microphone in a well-padded studio. Also, studio audience reaction gave the radio audience the sense of being in on something very exciting. Finally, the promotion of products by barn-dance stars with whom the audience identified greatly facilitated product sales.

When what would come to be called the "National Barn Dance" went on the air from WLS, Chicago, on April 19, 1924, as the "Radio Barn Dance," it was intended by station director Edgar L. Bill to "simulate an old-fashioned country barn dance." A band was assembled and Tom Owen called the squares (Biggar 1964: 9). Apparently calling squares was dropped, because it is not mentioned further except that once each year from 1926 through 1929 the square-dance callers' contest formed part of the program. I know of no 1930s radio barn-dance program where the listening audience was actually invited to dance to the instructions of a caller. In all likelihood the radios generally available at the time could not generate enough sound to fill a hall of adequate size for a real barn dance. By the late 1930s barn-dance programs often had performers who danced to such tunes, but they clogged and ran their squares without the aid of a caller, performing largely for the entertainment of the studio rather than the radio audience.

As it evolved, the radio barn dance was a kind of rustic variety show designed not for dancing but to be listened to. This fact is underlined by an early handbill announcing a performance by members of the WSM "Grand Ole Opry" in Louisville, Kentucky. Following a listing of the featured artists is the announcement "Big Barn Dance After Show" (Harkreader 1976: 18). Thus, beyond its evocation of a rustic situation, the radio barn dance had very little in common with its namesake. In form it had much more in common with vaudeville because of the fast-paced sequence of diverse acts. What is more, like all commercial radio and

TV, it also had much in common with the old live medicine show because an audience was first attracted by free entertainment and then was pitched products to purchase.

The first way to show the eclecticism of barn-dance programs is to describe the sound[4] and the image projected by two of the most influential and distinctive programs, the "National Barn Dance" broadcast from Chicago and the "Grand Ole Opry" broadcast from Nashville.

The "National Barn Dance"

One of the earliest, and by all odds the most widely heard, of the 1930s barn dances was the "National Barn Dance" broadcast from Chicago's clear-channel 50,000-watt station, WLS. It is not surprising that a program broadcast from the Midwest was more popular than any of those broadcast from the South, because while fully 45.2 percent of all Midwestern farm families had radio sets by 1930, the comparable figure for white Southern farmers was estimated to be 10 percent (Patterson 1975: 12). Beginning September 30, 1933, six years before a segment of the "Grand Ole Opry" achieved network status, an hour of the "National Barn Dance" program sponsored by Alka-Seltzer was broadcast over the NBC Blue Network (WLS [n.d.]: 2). Thus the program, if not a "barn dance" in the traditional sense of the term, was, nevertheless, genuinely "national."

From its earliest months the WLS "Barn Dance" was eclectic in sound (Patterson 1975). As George C. Biggar, who was involved in programming the early programs, has noted, "Traditional country dance tunes, interspersed with heart songs and sweet ballads—popular within the memories of most listeners—were featured."[5] Beyond the square-dance caller mentioned above, and Tommy Dandurand's fiddle band, there was a wide range of performers. Chubby Parker, accompanying himself on a five-string banjo, sang updated versions of traditional ballads such as "Little Old Sod Shanty on the Claim," "I'm a Stern Old Bachelor," and the Scottish comic ballad, "Nickety Nackety Now, Now, Now." Ford and Glenn sang sentimental older pop ballads; Cecil and Ester Ward played Hawaiian-style guitar songs. Tom Corwine imitated barnyard animals; Walter Peterson, "The Kentucky Wonderbean," told jokes and sang novelty tunes, accompanying himself on the harmonica and guitar; Ralph Waldo Emerson played such songs as "Silver Threads among the Gold" on the pipe organ; and Grace Wilson, a popular contralto who was widely known from her earlier vaudeville and radio performances, sang such songs as "In the Shade of the Old Apple Tree," and "I'd Love to Live in Loveland with You." The final element of eclecticism, according to Biggar, was provided by occasional ten-minute broadcasts remote from the

Hotel Sherman's College Inn featuring Maurice Sherman's ballroom dance orchestra. The professional orchestra was kept on the ready in case "the barn dance entertainers tired."

Bradley Kincaid, billed as "The Kentucky Mountain Boy with His Houn' Dog Guitar" joined the "Barn Dance" in 1926. Singing ballads learned in his youth near Berea, Kentucky, Kincaid was an instant hit on the radio, receiving amounts of fan mail unprecedented for a newcomer (Jones 1980: 20). Kincaid's appeal, according to Biggar, led WLS programmers to seek out other performers whose accent, grammar, and vocabulary projected a folk image. Such was Claude Moye, billed as "Pie Plate Pete," who sang railroad and hobo songs. And a sense of how authenticity was defined by the WLS programmers is suggested by another addition, Olaf the Swede, whose forte was singing contemporary popular songs of the day in a Swedish accent (WLS Artists Bureau 1933).

In 1928 the *Prairie Farmer* magazine bought WLS, reconfirming the station's commitment to rural radio entertainment, and a number of new young acts joined the "Barn Dance" in the next several years. The most famous of the country music additions was Gene Autry, who, as noted in chapter 6, then sang hillbilly and sentimental numbers in the fashion of Jimmie Rodgers rather than the western songs with which he later became identified. Other performers included Arkie the Arkansas Woodchopper, a hillbilly comedian; the Georgia Wildcats, led by Clayton McMichen; George Goebel, then billed as "The Little Singing Cowboy"; and the Cumberland Ridge Runners, who are pictured in figure 5.2 dressed in their midwestern-style stage hillbilly outfits. All of these additions, with the exception of Goebel—then a thirteen-year-old local singing sensation—had in common considerable prior experience as professional performers and came to WLS as seasoned radio performers. These artists were drawn to the "National Barn Dance" not as an avocational diversion as some of the earliest performers had been, but as a means of making a living and furthering their professional careers as performers.

The 1930s "Grand Ole Opry"

The "Grand Ole Opry" of WSM in Nashville, Tennessee, was different in emphasis but not different in form from the "National Barn Dance."[6] Founded three years later, it was patterned on its Chicago counterpart, but its more meager financial resources, as well as the more willing amateur musical resources of middle Tennessee, helped to make the Opry distinctively different from the outset. The rustic eclecticism of George Hay's 1920s Opry was described in chapter 5 and need not detain us here. Suffice it to say that there was an accent on stringed instruments, from fiddles to hammer dulcimers, and there was an absence of brass

Figure 7.1 Hillbilly outfits predominate in this 1936 photo of the "National Barn Dance," but a number are in western outfits, and a wide range of other outfits are in evidence, ranging from a blackface porter in the center to storm trooper–like outfits at the lower right.

and drums. Thus, what was apparently acceptable on the Opry in the early 1930s seems to have been determined more by instrumentation than by lyrical, rhythmic, or melodic content. Differences in size, diversity, and appearance between the "National Barn Dance" and the "Grand Ole Opry" are suggested by comparing figures 7.1 and 7.2.

While founder George Hay was associated with the Opry for nearly another twenty years, intermittent bouts of depression prevented him

from personally selecting the groups that would appear on the Opry, and he increasingly devoted himself to the duties of master of ceremonies and promoter of the Opry image. In 1928, or soon thereafter, according to our informants, Harry Stone began to take over the task of auditioning and booking artists. Stone was more concerned with producing a popular show than with adhering to tradition.

Most of the Nashville-based string bands continued to play in the mid-1930s, but no new amateur Nashville area string bands were added. And most of the new bands, including Zeke Clements and his Bronco Busters, Curly Fox and Texas Ruby, and Pee Wee King and his Golden West Cowboys, dressed in the newly fashionable western outfits.

Figure 7.2 The "Grand Ole Opry" cast, c. 1935. Most of those who aren't in some version of hillbilly attire are in street clothes. Note that none are in western outfits.

A number of comedy specialists were added to the Opry roster. These included Edna Wilson and Margaret Waters playing hillbilly ingenues "Sarie and Sally," the first women to be featured on the Opry. Comedian Robert Lunn brought his ever changing "Talking Blues." Some of the comics continued the tradition of blackface comedy begun by George Hay. Lasses (Leroy) White teamed with several different partners on the Opry and for several years had a program, "Lasses White and His All-Star Minstrel Show," just before the Opry program. What is more, for

several years, the Opry was interrupted by NBC's "Amos 'n' Andy." According to WSM engineer Aaron Shelton, this Negro dialect show performed by a pair of white men was simply too popular not to air, but it
also fit with the tradition of such humor as part of the Opry.

The popular close-harmony trio the Vagabonds joined in 1931, followed by the Melody Boys—Jack (Shook), Nap (Bastien) and Dee (Simmons)—the duo Asher Sizemore and Little Jimmie, and the Delmore
Brothers. All of these groups featured harmony singing with a minimum
of instrumental accompaniment and with nary a fiddle among them.
Even the singers in the new string bands, including Texas Ruby and Zeke

Clements, sang in a style more like that of Bing Crosby and the other emerging pop crooners than like the older ballad singers.

Each of these vocal groups proved very popular with Opry listeners and they were featured more and more. Thus in the mid-1930s, the balance of styles on the Opry was changing. The string-band sound was less evident, while vocalists and professional comedians were coming to the fore. What is more, the new western-dressing bands progressively incorporated more of the emerging big swing-band music of the day that in the West would come to be known as "western swing."

In summary, the barn-dance eclecticism of the 1930s "National Barn Dance" and the "Grand Ole Opry" was not static. Old-time fiddlers had been phased out, and string bands were less prevalent. Solo and harmony singers as well as professional comics were more in evidence. The program managers had developed the sense of a barn-dance formula, and most performers showed a generally higher level of radio-centered professional careerism.

THE RADIO BARN DANCE FORMULA AND ITS EFFECT ON CAREERS

The conditions of work on the radio affected country music in a number of ways. Several of these have already been suggested in our review of the Chicago and Nashville barn dances. Singers were displacing instrumentalists in the limelight, and one-line jokesters were displacing slapstick comics. Both of these changes were made possible by the move to radio. Radio technology, work routines, and barn-dance formula all had an impact on performers and their careers in country music.

Microphone-Made Singing Styles

The microphone is the organizing reality of performance on radio. Early performers had to learn how to stay "on mike," and some older performers who were attuned to providing a lively show for a live audience found this very difficult. Uncle Dave Macon, the leading act of the early Opry, for example, was the bane of radio engineers when as he played banjo, sang, yelled, and jumped about the stage with no regard for the microphone. In fact, Macon, like many of his vaudeville colleagues, had great contempt for mikes because their use allowed small-voiced singers to come to the fore. To the delight of studio audiences and the horror of radio engineers, Macon would kick over microphones, and the radio audience heard hilarious laughter accompanying what sounded like a violent fight on stage.

To get enough volume to fill a large hall in the days before electronic amplification, singers had used a shouting style[7] that depended on clearly enunciating words. They conveyed emotion largely through physical gestures, rather than words. On the strictly aural medium of radio it was, of course, impossible to convey emotions through gestures, but the microphone made it possible to sing more softly and with much more nuanced emotion in the tone of the voice. At a stroke the vocal skills of a generation of performers were made redundant as their style became defined as forced, corny, and distinctly old-fashioned. The emerging "crooning" style of singing was softer, mellower, and more intimate, suggesting to each member of the audience that the words were meant for him or her alone.[8]

Crooning gave the advantage to the younger, small-voiced performers who learned how to work close to the microphone to get the desired feeling. The acuity of the newly invented mikes also made it possible for radio audiences to appreciate intricate vocal harmonies and for them to be recorded accurately as well. This development in technology made for an explosion in harmonizing duets, trios, and quartets. In his autobiography, Alton Delmore (1977) comments that he and his brother had little voices, and he acknowledged the importance of amplification in the creation of the Delmore Brothers' sound. Speaking of the early 1930s, Bob Coltman (1976b: 9) notes:

> The microphone's exclusiveness encouraged soft, expressive, modulated voices, music with nuance and suggestion. The old shouters and straightaway pickers began to tumble from grace, even on the radio barn dances, whose new headliners were supple, sweet singers like Bradley Kincaid, the Delmore Brothers, Scott Weisman, and the Vagabonds. The new small-town radio stations emulated the larger stations and the networks in their programming, demanding that their local artists, including country musicians, conform to professional standards of on-the-air presentation: polish, smoothness, command of the current performing idiom.

Comedy was also affected by the radio in a parallel way. Much stage comedy depended on exaggerated outfits and broad visual effects. While these routines could be transferred to the medium of silent film, they were, of course, incomprehensible to an unseeing radio audience. Radio gave the advantage to those comics who developed characters who could be conveyed in a few words and who delivered one-line jokes working with a "straight" person in a minimalist style. On the "Grand Ole Opry," this sort of duet-comedy was represented early by Sarie and Sally, and later by Minnie Pearl working with Rod Brasfield.[9]

The Barn Dance as an Opportune Work-Site for Youth and Women

Most of the musicians and singers drawn to radio in the early 1930s were young people who could afford to work for next to nothing while perfecting their craft. Since all major-station radio music was created live in the studio,[10] novices could regularly observe and learn from the styles of dozens of other country and popular music performers, and they could get immediate feedback on their experimental efforts. Thus, "radio, unlike records, was a fluid medium tending to keep musical form, style, and sound shifting, rather than fixing or preserving them. Now that everyone was hearing everyone else, the pace of musical development was quickening" (Coltman 1976b: 11).

Women had been fully involved in precommercial country music played in and around the home, but in the 1920s they were disadvantaged by the low esteem in which professional performers were held and by the prejudice against women performing in public (Malone 1985). Those who did try to perform in public met active discrimination (Bufwack and Oermann 1993). Many, like Sara and Maybelle Carter, and "Moonshine" Kate Carson, who did venture forth as professionals, did so as part of family aggregations.

The relative safety of the radio studio and the support of barn-dance casts of the 1930s gave several hundred women the opportunity to develop their talents and attract fans. This environment nurtured the development of harmony-singing sister acts such as Millie and Dolly Good, the Girls of the Golden West, and with the commercial success of Patsy Montana, it became possible for women to front bands of their own. Nonetheless, many aspiring young women found the best way to avoid harassment and maintain performance opportunities was to marry another performer. The "National Barn Dance" of the mid-1930s had a larger proportion of aspiring young women than did the "Grand Ole Opry," and Daniel (1993) reports that through 1937 fully sixteen "National Barn Dance" female artists married other performers they met while working at the station.

Variety Shows from Specialist Performers

In 1932, WHO of Des Moines, Iowa, began to broadcast a barn-dance program, "The Iowa Barn Dance Frolic." From its range of performers to its way of paying them, it was in every way a copy of the "National Barn Dance," as Patterson (1975) shows in detail; and as Malone (1985: 97) notes, it was just one of a number of spin-offs of the basic design.

Clearly by the early 1930s, the barn dance had become a recognized genre of radio programming.[11] It is useful to detail the barn-dance formula because it had such a very important effect in shaping both the development of country music and the ways in which performers of the 1930s could make careers in country music.

The formula program was based on the model of vaudeville—a quick succession of individuals and groups performing different sorts of music interspersed with comedy and informal banter between performers and the master of ceremonies about upcoming show dates and other items of interest. Studio audience laughter and applause, encouraged by the gestures of the master of ceremonies, and on some shows by a flashing applause sign, helped give the home radio audience a sense of being part of a live happening.

It was most convenient for the barn-dance managers to have acts that could be relied on to deliver a single sort of performance. This way program elements could be ordered in an appropriate sequence, and elements could be added or dropped as audience reaction indicated their waxing or waning appeal. To most easily fit the formula, acts were asked to deliver only the performance for which they were typecast. The vaudeville-trained performers may have been content to do their one bit, but the musicians who played on the Opry in the mid-1930s whom I had the chance to interview were vexed with their stereotyped roles. Herman Crook, for example, was very frustrated at being asked to perform only breakdowns and not being able to perform the old popular tunes, blues, novelty numbers, and religious songs that he enjoyed much more. Kirk McGee and Blythe Poteete said much the same thing. DeFord Bailey, the only black who has ever been an Opry regular, was very bitter that George Hay would let him play only his fast, trick harmonica tunes and would not allow him to perform anything from the rest of his harmonica repertoire or play banjo or guitar (Horton 1991).[12]

While wanting the freedom to express themselves beyond their single stereotyping specialty, most performers strongly defended the system because it gave them the security of an uncontested place on the show. However, a number of individuals who made major contributions to country music, including Bradley Kincaid, the Pickard Family, and the Delmore Brothers, chafed so much at being narrowly typecast that they gave up their relative security to strike out on careers in radio outside the confines of the barn-dance format. Such performers are the focus of the next chapter.

Three kinds of acts could most easily fit the demands of the barn-dance formula for specialization. The first kind of specialists were the semiprofessionals, persons who played on the barn dance but who relied for their income primarily on jobs outside the music field. By the late 1920s all such semiprofessionals were gone from the "National Barn Dance." In contrast, most of the performers on the WSM barn dance as late as 1928 were semiprofessionals, and a few of these, like Herman Crook, played on the Opry until they died in the 1970s or 1980s. No semiprofessionals were added to the Opry after 1930.

The second successful adaptation to the demand for specialization consisted of individuals or small aggregations of professionals who built their careers from delivering their one specialty on the barn dance and in live performance. Many such as Lasses White, Uncle Dave Macon, and later Rod Brasfield, came to radio from the vaudeville stage, while others, including Gene Autry, George Goebel, and Zeke Clements, used their work in radio as a stepping-stone to careers in films and television.

The third type of specialist included individuals and groups who held regular jobs on the radio station as staff musicians or announcers and simply assumed rustic character roles for their barn-dance appearances. Examples include Grace Wilson, Ralph Waldo Emerson, the Vagabonds, and the members of Jack Shook's Missouri Mountaineers.

Consequences of Specialization

One of the consequences of specialization was that members of the cast competed directly with only a few others to hold their positions on the show, and, in a sense, all regulars had an interest in defending the reputations of the others against the encroachments of aspirants to the cast.[13] This may be why so many barn-dance veterans describe the cast as a "family." There were great rivalries, but these tended to be, as in most families, between those who aspired to preeminence in the same specialist role. Such "sibling" rivalries, however, were not simply the result of the commercialization and star-making machinery of recent decades. George Hay, for example, describes with some exasperation the problem of having two old-time fiddlers, Uncle Jimmy Thompson and Uncle Bunt Stephens, on the Opry in 1927. "For many months we nursed two elderly male prima donnas who couldn't see each other for the dust in their eyes" (Hay 1945: 20). To the many individuals and groups vying to get a spot on the show, however, this "tight-knit family" appeared as a cold, self-protecting, and uncaring clan.

Another consequence of the development of a barn-dance formula was that even with a flow of individuals and groups on and off the program, the sound of the show would not vary for months and even years at a time. Programmers and program regulars alike would feel safe in the program's predictable sameness. Nonetheless, bit by bit the cast and audience would feel less excited about the show as "predictability" became formula and a loss of authenticity. Then from time to time, a fresh new act would so excite the audience that the formula would be broken and country music would undergo a significant change. Such dramatic changes on the "Grand Ole Opry" include the coming of the Vagabonds in 1932, then Roy Acuff, Eddy Arnold, Hank Williams, and Elvis Presley, all in a little over two decades.

The same logic of predictability that made for the system of specialization also dictated that incumbent specialists would not be displaced as long as they continued to deliver their stereotyped performances. Such security, however, was often relatively short-lived because specialists were vulnerable to the continual shifts in aesthetic taste. Habituated to providing one kind of performance, they might not be able to change with the times. And often their efforts to evolve with changing aesthetic tastes were not appreciated by barn-dance programmers and loyal fans.[14]

Because of the accent on tradition and continuity in country music, its performers are probably less vulnerable than performers in popular music to being displaced by the exponents of new forms of music. Most older performers on country music barn-dance programs, however, have found themselves shoved ever farther from the limelight and pressed into ever more confined specialist roles on the program. By the 1970s, for example, the remnants of the once-dominant string bands of the 1920s that still performed were grouped together as "The Old-Timers." The group was never featured; instead they just played jig tunes behind the clog dancing teams who often closed program segments.

MAKING A LIVING OFF THE "BARN DANCE"

The 1930s were a time of extreme hardship for most Americans, and the biographies of many musicians starting out in that time show intermittent periods of work in music and work at other sorts of jobs. For some, playing music began as a means that laid-off workers used to make some money while looking for other forms of employment. Many others, seeing the success of Jimmie Rodgers and the barn-dance stars, hoped to be able to make a living at music. For the likes of Alton Delmore and Bill Monroe, the father of the bluegrass style of music, factory work was viewed as a temporary expedient when music jobs played out (Delmore 1977; Rosenberg 1985). The exigencies of making a marginal living from music profoundly affected the music itself.

In the earliest days, country music performers were not paid for appearing on barn dances. Grace Wilson says that payment for appearances on the "National Barn Dance" began thanks to the notorious Chicago gangster Al Capone. "A girl friend of Capone's was a singer at the Sherman Hotel's College Inn and she was asked to guest on the 'Barn Dance' one night. Capone watched the performance with smiling approval which later turned to suggestive firmness when he asked the producer, 'Well don't she get paid?' She did. [Wilson asked for equal treatment and] . . . thereafter, a full talent payroll was established" (Asbel 1954: 25). Payment for appearances on the Opry didn't begin until 1927 and amounted to just five dollars. This was understood to be "for expenses" rather than as a compensation for professional services, and was instituted to guarantee that artists would appear on the Opry rather than on the rival Nashville barn dances.

Even on the "National Barn Dance," payments could not be considerable because, in the 1930s, the program did not generate much revenue either from advertising or from the sale of admissions to watch the broadcast. The makers of Aladdin kerosene lamps had inaugurated in 1931 what was probably the first sponsored thirty-minute segment (Malone 1971: 222), but even in the mid-1930s with advertising and the network hookup, weekly "Barn Dance" appearances did not provide enough income to sustain a performer. Here we examine the things that barn-dance musicians most often did to augment their incomes, because each had an effect in shaping the country music of the 1930s.

Staff Musician Work

To build their incomes, many "Barn Dance" artists performed on other programs broadcast from the station. One of the models of multiple radio-role activity was Linda Parker, who was billed as the "Sunbonnet Girl" when she appeared with the Cumberland Ridge Runners on the "National Barn Dance." At the same time she appeared as a comedian on the "Coon Creek Social," as an anonymous "Old-Fashioned Girl" on "Swift & Co. Time"; and as Jeanne Munich, she sang blues as "The Red-Headed Bluebird" (Samuelson 1995: 17). Other "National Barn Dance" regulars of the early 1930s who performed on other programs included, among others, Gene Autry, Bradley Kincaid, Grace Wilson, Henry Burr, Hal O'Holloran, the Maple City Four, Mac and Bob (the Knoxville Blind Boys), the Hoosier Sod Busters, Little George Goebel, and Ralph Waldo Emerson.[15]

Opry artists who performed on other WSM programs in the 1930s included the Vagabonds, members of the Missouri Mountaineers, and the comedy duo Sarie and Sally. Probably only one or two of these staff musicians were able to make a comfortable living from their radio appearances. The others had to find other ways of making a living from music, principally record making, songwriting, songbook selling, and public appearances.

Most WSM musicians were paid just five dollars for each show on which they appeared, so there was an incentive for them to perform in many different styles so that they could appear on as many programs as possible. As Betty Waggoner, an aspiring popular music soloist of the era who sang on the Opry, recalls,

> I began to organize a girls trio, we had a late-in-the-night show—called "Dream Shadows." It is the kind of music that makes you feel dreamy, and comfortable. . . . Then I got with a trio of boys for an act called "Betty and the Dixie Dons." We did very fast popular music. Then we put the boys and my girls trio together and did all Hawaiian music. . . . I had worked up enough versatility to have seven different type programs a week [including one that appeared on the Grand Ole Opry], and $35 a week sure helped keep the wolf away from the door.[16]

Record Making, Songwriting, and Song Publishing

Most of the performers who appeared regularly on the major barn dances in the early 1930s made phonograph records, but their income from this work was slight. In the austere early 1930s, they usually were paid less than fifty dollars for each side recorded, and when they received royalties these were usually meager at best. For their first Columbia recording session of four sides made in 1931, for example, the Delmore Brothers received twenty-five dollars, and the one record released paid no appreciable royalties, having sold just 511 copies. As Charles Wolfe notes in his introduction to Alton Delmore's biography, "This was not especially a failure, as most of the issues during that year sold around this amount—an indication of how the Depression was affecting the record industry" (Delmore 1977: 41).

The slight contribution of record making to an artist's income in the mid-1930s is suggested by an incident from the early career of Bill Monroe. Eli Oberstein, who had replaced Ralph Peer in making most field recordings for RCA records, wanted the Monroe Brothers to record while he had the portable RCA equipment in Charlotte. Bill Monroe recalled that he "threw away the first several letters they wrote us." In desperation Oberstein sent a telegram and followed it with a phone call. "We finally went up to their studio in Charlotte, but we told 'em we didn't have much time, that we had to get back in time to play a school that night" (Wolfe 1994: 60). Oberstein obliged by interrupting a session by the Delmore Brothers and fiddler Arthur Smith to record ten numbers by

the Monroe Brothers (Rosenberg 1985: 33). The brothers may have received no more than ten dollars a side and no royalties for this, their
first recording effort.

Many country music performers composed songs, and a few like the
Vagabonds were active in song publishing but, as we have seen, even
the industry-wise Ralph Peer could not make money in publishing country as sheet music. The money in publishing country music then, as later,
came from record sales, and since in the bitter years of the Depression
record sales were so low, there was precious little money to be made from
songwriting and publishing. This trio of activities that was so central to
the development of the music industry beginning in the late 1930s was
unimportant in financially sustaining performers in the depths of the
Depression.

To say that records were financially unimportant to country music at
this time is not to say that their impact was inconsequential. A whole
generation of rising performers played and replayed the songs of Jimmie
Rodgers, the Delmore Brothers, the Georgia Wildcats and others as a
prime way of learning their craft.

Individualized Songbooks

A related printed music form, personalized songbooks, did, however,
provide income to some barn-dance regulars. Popular minstrel show and
vaudeville singers had long been able to supplement their incomes by
selling songbooks in conjunction with their stage appearances, and artists carried this practice over in the new medium of radio. The most
popular books consisted of a large number of widely known songs and
a few that were identified with the particular artist or group. The first
few pages often included pictures and information about the artist, and
the cover featured a photo, the artist's name, and the phrase "as sung
by." Country artists who received a great amount of fan mail were aware
of the large number of requests for songbooks that came into the station.
There was not a significant market for instrumental arrangements, so the
old-time fiddlers and string bands could not supplement their incomes
in this way. But, as we have seen, country singers and singing groups
were coming to the fore on barn dances, and the more enterprising
quickly took advantage of the opportunity to put out songbooks.

Gene Autry, the Vagabonds, Bradley Kincaid, and the Pickard Family
all made a good deal of money from songbooks that they promoted over
the air. So much so, in fact, that differences with station management
may have contributed to the latter two groups' leaving the relative security of the barn dance and seeking other kinds of radio work. Because
songbooks were so important to many of these independent barnstorm-

ers discussed in the next chapter, we will discuss the strategy of song-book selling in more detail there.

Touring

By far the most common means of profiting from the name recognition and legitimacy that came from performing on the radio was to play live music engagements. Elaborating the pattern that we have seen developed at WSB in Atlanta, most artists made a living by giving live performances at various types of venues within the hearing range of the radio station. In the early 1930s WLS was especially ingenious in promoting itself and its "Barn Dance" artists. On the opening night of the 1933 Chicago Worlds Fair, for example, Clayton McMichen and his Georgia Wildcats broadcast a segment of the "Barn Dance" from an airplane circling Chicago (WLS [n.d.]). Because of its strong radio signal and such inventive promotion, a 1933 WLS booklet was able to boast that at the 1932 Indiana State Fair "6,000 people crowded the Coliseum Building to see and hear a group of ["National Barn Dance"] artists. The receipts were over $3,000 for the one night" (WLS Artists Bureau 1933: 2).

In order to make a well-rounded show for live appearances, a number of the specialty groups would be packaged together, simulating to a large degree a WLS "Barn Dance" program. There was a problem for barn-dance specialists, however, because smaller venues could not afford such a large retinue of performers. In response, the most resourceful specialist groups made efforts to develop a more complete show for their live appearances. For example, the Cumberland Ridge Runners, organized by John Lair, were described by a 1933 Artists Bureau booking promotion thus:

> (5 persons) Old-time numbers with guitar, banjo, fiddle and mandolin accompaniment. Suitable for dancing or good novelty act for theaters. Personnel are as follows: Ramblin' Red Foley, popular and comedy numbers with guitar and singing; Carl & Harty, the Renfro Valley Boys; Slim Miller, comedy talk and trick fiddlin; Linda Parker, the Kentucky Sun-Bonnet Girl, old-time folk songs with guitar accompaniment. 20 to 40 minutes act.

The group that was the model for the Vagabonds, the Maple City Four, was described as:

> The popular WLS quartet, featured on all WLS programs, also Barn Dance. Act consists of harmony singing, comedy talk, novelty musical instruments, also spiritual and minstrel numbers. Can do any length program. (WLS Artists Bureau 1933: 3)

As a consequence of these contradictory demands of their specialist radio barn-dance appearances and live performance dates, many acts were being pushed in two different directions. On the air they were expected to perform one specific sort of fare, while on the road, they could be successful only if they were able to perform a much wider range of offerings. Many of the older troopers like Uncle Dave Macon carried on as if they were oblivious to the differing demands being made on them (Wolfe 1975a, 1975b). The younger performers who were trying to establish a reputation and make a living greatly resented the conflicting demands.[17]

As early as 1927, Opry artists began to use the "Grand Ole Opry" identification in billing themselves at personal appearances, but not until 1933 did WSM form an Artists Service Bureau to coordinate cast tours. Like its WLS counterpart, it charged 15 percent of the artists' fees in compensation for getting dates, organizing schedules, and providing advance publicity. George Hay was appointed its first head, and while he had his staunch defenders, many artists felt that he favored other acts over them, arranged packages poorly, took kickbacks from acts in exchange for bookings, didn't understand the entertainment market, and did virtually nothing to promote tours.[18] In all fairness, the same litany of accusations was leveled by some disgruntled performers against his successor, David Stone, and each of the Artists Bureau heads that followed.[19] Nonetheless, it seems clear from all the available evidence that artists could count on only a meager income from touring under the aegis of the WSM Artists Bureau.

SUMMARY

The radio barn dances became the single most conspicuous crucible for the development of country music in the depression-plagued 1930s, and they profoundly shaped country music. The use of microphones fostered the development of softer, more intimate crooning and elaborate harmony styles of singing. Major-station radio work facilitated artistic growth by putting young performers in contact with diverse other musicians, and it provided a relatively congenial environment for women performers. While the shows were eclectic, performers were typically asked to be specialists, and country artists of the 1930s were not well compensated for this radio work. They typically used the imprimatur of barndance membership to earn money giving live shows, and for those successful in establishing a reputation, this income was often supplemented by selling personalized songbooks, cutting phonograph records, and songwriting.

The notoriety gained from being a star on the "Barn Dance," and the steady employment afforded by being a regular, were very gratifying. Some artists, including Roy Acuff and Minnie Pearl, made barn-dance membership the focus of their professional careers. Many other country music artists, however, chafed under the restrictions such work imposed. They disliked the role of radio specialist that was forced on them, they resented the percentage cut that the station took on their songbook sales, and they felt that they were not being well served by the barn-dance's booking agency. Some, like the Delmore Brothers, who were not making enough money to live, left the barn-dance format station for other stations where they could have their own programs and promote their own live performance dates. Others, among them Bradley Kincaid and the Pickard Family, who had been successful on barn-dance shows, also left in hopes of making a better living at independent stations. This career strategy, "barnstorming," is the focus of the next chapter.

CHAPTER EIGHT

Radio Station Barnstorming

"**B**arnstorming" is a nineteenth-century theatrical term referring to performing in a sequence of small towns having no regular theaters. The term was also used following World War I by returning Air Corps pilots to refer to making a living by flying from town to town across rural America and offering brief plane rides to the venturesome among the startled onlookers who gathered in the pastures where they landed.

The term "barnstorming" is not regularly used in country music, but will be used here because it nicely captures the experience of most country music professionals working in the 1930s.[1] A review of their careers over the Depression decade shows that most performed at a sequence of radio stations having no regular barn dance. Like the other sorts of barnstormers before them, the novelty of what they had to offer typically created a good deal of excitement when they first reached a town, and they were able to make enough money to support themselves. Then, as people became used to their acts, they commanded less attention and their income slipped, so they moved on to another territory which promised greener pastures only to repeat the cycle once again. In his autobiography Alton Delmore (1977: 140) describes one such cycle of radio station barnstorming: "So we moved to Greenville, South Carolina [playing on station WFBC] and we lived there for about three or four months. We enjoyed our stay there very much and got along real well. But we couldn't stay in one place very long because we would play the territory out. That is, we would run out of show dates to play."

In the pages that follow, we shall explore the impact of station barnstorming on artists' careers and on their music. Illustrations will be drawn from the careers of a number of artists and groups, but the focus will be on three who broke away from a major barn dance to go it alone, Bradley Kincaid, the Pickard Family, and the Delmore Brothers; and on three who were not associated with a barn dance in their formative years, the Carter Family, Bob Wills, and the Monroe Brothers.

In some ways barnstorming was similar to the radio work described in chapter 7, but barnstorming did not provide acts the protection inherent in barn-dance work of being part of an ongoing, large cast. First, barnstormers had to personally attract a specific advertiser. Second, the barnstorming act had to put on a whole show for the audience, so diversity, not specialization, was rewarded. Third, since barnstormers had to move frequently from town to town, the advantage went to versatile, small aggregations that could work together under adverse conditions, and the most enduring of these proved to be multitalented sibling groups such as the Delmore and Monroe Brothers. After detailing the consequences of barnstorming work for the development of country music, the chapter concludes by examining innovations in the late 1930s that spelled the end of barnstorming.

IMAGE CONTROL BY SPONSORS

Advertising Enters the 1930s Radio Field

In the 1930s three kinds of radio stations could be distinguished: network stations that originated programs for the affiliated stations of the net; passive network affiliates that, in exchange for the programming provided, were obliged to transmit a high proportion of the programs complete with advertisements fed to them by the network; and independent stations not affiliated with a network.[2] Most independents were licensed to broadcast with limited power, but several in the early 1930s, such as KWKH of Shreveport, Louisiana, and KFKB of Milford, Kansas, were quite powerful,[3] as were the superpowerful stations operating from just across the border in Mexico (Kahn 1973; Fowler and Crawford 1987). The largest and most long-lasting barn-dance shows originated from stations in Chicago and Nashville that fed programs to the rest of the network. Barnstormers worked primarily from passive network stations and independents.

Radio networks were created in the late 1920s so that stations could pool the costs of producing programs. In 1930 there were just over 600 radio stations in the entire United States, and in 1940 there were not quite 800. However, in this period of a decade, the proportion of stations with a network affiliation climbed steadily from a bit over 20 percent to almost 60 percent. NBC fielded "Red" and "Blue" networks; and two other webs, MBC (Mutual) and CBS (Columbia), spread across the nation with an aggregate listenership of millions of people.

The networks proved a major means of fostering advertising over radio, luring major consumer-products manufacturers to shift some of their advertising budgets from magazines and billboards to radio. For the most part, prospective advertisers did not pay to have promotional spots read or sung on the air in the 1930s.[4] Rather they sponsored whole programs of from fifteen to sixty minutes duration, to which they typically attached their corporate or product name. Examples of such sponsor-originated programming include the "Maxwell House Hour," the "Palmolive Hour," the "General Motors Family Party," the "Wrigley Review," and the "Eveready Hour." Shorter programs and programs that originated from individual stations often featured musical groups named after the sponsor. Early examples include the Lucky Strike Orchestra, the Ipana Troubadours, and Cities Service Orchestra, the A&P Gypsies, and the Ray-O-Vac Twins.[5] These advertisers were usually intimately involved in every aspect of what they considered their own programs, and frequently exercised their explicitly stated right to approve program scripts.

Most independent stations had a small signal radius and most were located in the smaller cities and towns across the country. Copying the developing practice of larger network stations of selling blocks of time to advertisers, they sought out local advertisers and local dealers of national concerns. In the Depression many independent station advertisers paid in kind rather than cash. For example, a hotel allowed WEXL of Royal Oak, Michigan, to use its rooms for a studio in exchange for regular plugs on the air, and restaurants paid for ads with meal tickets. In turn, station announcers as well as musicians worked in exchange for free lodging and meal tickets.

These independent stations looked to get programming for as little money as possible, but costs were rising. The novelty of radio was also wearing off for both performers and listeners. While in the medium's first several years people would listen with rapt attention to any signal, now they would stay tuned only if they felt they were being informed or entertained. Likewise, the novelty of a radio appearance no longer drew performers to volunteer their services. What is more, Musicians

Union performers were now explicitly prohibited from playing gratis. For this reason, independent station programmers, even though most had little affection for country music, often turned to country artists, because, with rare exceptions, they were not then members of the Musicians Union.[6] The owners of the Royal Oak station noted above, for example, programmed country artists not only because they cost less than union musicians but also because they were even cheaper than maintaining a record library (Barnouw 1966: 236).

Barnstormers would sometimes play on a station on a "sustaining basis," that is, they would appear on a program without a commercial sponsor, receiving little or no compensation. Beginners might work on this basis in order to perfect their skills, but experienced professionals would work on a sustaining basis only reluctantly and then only long enough to gain a sponsored program and attract sufficient name recognition in the listening radius of the station to garner live show dates.

Advertisers Use Country Music

Modeled on the pattern of network programming, some local retail stores, particularly those with a farm and working-class clientele, began to sponsor country music groups on independent stations. Sponsors included feed and seed stores, ready-made clothing stores, hardware stores, furniture stores, flour mills, equipment repair shops, and the like. The country music group was paid by the sponsoring concerns to play a regular program and was often asked to assume a persona representing the sponsor. Thus, for example, Jimmy Wakely and Johnny Bond for a time in Oklahoma City played as the "Bell Boys" sponsored by the Bell Clothing Company (Griffis 1970).

Flour Mills. Perhaps the most famous sponsorship of the early 1930s involved Bob Wills, Milton Brown, and W. Lee O'Daniel. Though the program lasted for nearly a quarter of a century, beginning Wills's trek to the Country Music Hall of Fame and O'Daniel's to the governorship of the state of Texas, the program's shaky start shows the hardships of the early days of barnstorming. In January 1931 Bob Wills's friends persuaded Burrus Mills, makers of Light Crust Dough, to sponsor Wills and his band on KFJZ, Forth Worth.[7] The first few programs received a great deal of favorable mail and Wills began to call the band the "Light Crust Doughboys." O'Daniel, general manager of Burrus Mills, wrote all the ad copy for the program, but two weeks after the program first aired he fired the band and canceled the show because he "didn't like their hillbilly music" (Townsend 1976: 69). KFJZ continued the programming on a sustaining basis because of the audience response, and the band played gratis to build its reputation.

Wills went to see O'Daniel and was forced to wait in the latter's outer office for two or three days before finally gaining an audience, only to have O'Daniel opine that musicians were a lazy lot. When Wills replied that he and the band were willing to work hard for their pay, O'Daniel said they could have their sponsored program back if the band members would all work forty-hour weeks in the mill at $7.50 a week. After a few weeks the band members revolted because the mill work was so hard on their hands that it made it impossible for them to play their instruments well. O'Daniel then said they didn't have to do manual labor, but they would have to put in a forty-hour week at the mill practicing. Remarkably, O'Daniel's dislike for the music and disdain for the musicians lead to his paying Wills and the others to perfect their evolving western swing style of music.

After a great deal of urging, O'Daniel visited a broadcast and went to the band's dance that followed. Excited by the audience approval and the direct tie between the band's popularity and Light Crust Dough sales, he bought new "baker boy" uniforms and had a touring bus fashioned with an extra-large promotional billboard and state-of-the-art public address system. What is more, O'Daniel began to tour as the band's master of ceremonies. In the next year he moved the band to the powerful clear-channel station WBAP in Dallas, and soon the program was carried over a regional network as well.

All the while, O'Daniel thought of the band as company employees. When he raised their wages to twenty-five dollars a week he forbade them from playing at dances and other outside events. In compensation he built them a better practice studio for their forty-hours-a-week practice sessions. Milton Brown quit to form his own band because he could easily make forty dollars playing a weekend dance. When Wills left the protection of O'Daniel's paternalism some months later, he had worked out most of the elements that would over the next decade transform his essentially eastern string band into the leading band in the development of jazz-colored western swing.

If Lee O'Daniel was unusual in the extent of his support of a country band, he was not unusual in doing so as part of a promotional strategy rather than with any view to fostering the development of the music and its performers, for, as we have noted earlier, radio programmers were attracted to country artists because they were inexpensive to hire and because, unlike many comparably trained performers, they could play for as long as was needed.

Patent Medicines. If flour mills and retail stores were among the first to support country musicians in any numbers, as the 1930s progressed, the most aggressive users of the music were the makers of patent medicines and related nostrums, an association that was a natural carryover from the era of medicine shows. Just as country music had been used to draw and hold an appreciative rural and small-town live audience so that the "Doctor" could pitch his medicine, now the music was used to draw radio listeners to hear the pitch over the air.

While there were many such advertisers, by far the most important for country music was Crazy Water Crystals of Mineral Wells, Texas.[8] The laxative powers of this mineral water were discovered late in the nineteenth century but not commercialized beyond the local area until much later, in the form of a powder made of mineral salts evaporated from the water. Starting in 1930, the company developed an aggressive campaign of radio advertising, sponsoring country music groups on independent radio stations ranging from New York to Oklahoma. Print advertisements for the product, such as the one in figure 8.1, show it being shipped from the factory in railroad boxcar lots, and by 1934, according to *Business Week* (1935), the company was spending $283,000 a year on radio advertising, and gross sales reached $3 million (Fowler and Crawford 1987: 102).

The company not only sponsored the radio performances of country artists, but it developed a number of practices designed to enhance the audience's identification of the product with the performer. First, the company induced a number of groups to put the word "Crazy" in their group name. Several incorporated place-names, such as the Crazy Blue Ridge Hillbillies (later to attain fame as the Blue Sky Boys), and others like the Crazy Hickory Nuts did not. The "Crazy" band name gained such cachet that fledgling bands not sponsored by the company sometimes tried to coopt the aura by incorporating the name, the most notable case in point being Roy Acuff's "Crazy Tennesseans."[9] In addition to sponsoring individual programs, the company developed a "Crazy Water Crystals Barn Dance" broadcast from WBT, Charlotte, North Carolina, which was eventually carried over fourteen stations in Georgia and the Carolinas.

Although the practice varied from case to case, the company generally did not pay musicians for performing on the air. Instead it helped them book engagements within the reach of the radio station and paid their traveling expenses. The company also worked to increase the performers' loyalty to the product by developing promotional material for the acts that depicted the barn-dance performers as one big happy family. One band was described thus:

From Mineral Wells, and Thorndale, Texas
TO MILLIONS EVERYWHERE

Crazy Water Crystals Are Shipped in Car Lots to Distributors in U. S. and Canada

What is Crazy Water?

More than 56 years ago, the original Crazy Well was discovered. A pioneer family, James Alvis Lynch, and his wife, Amandy, dug a well for drinking water. Mrs. Lynch, who had been in poor health, was the first to discover its unusual powers.

The fame of this mineral water spread; soon a little tent city sprang up around the well. Now, more than 56 years later, a thriving health resort has grown up around the Crazy Water Hotel, built at the site of the original Crazy Well. Year after year, thousands of the sick and near sick from all over America, suffering from many disorders brought on or made worse by faulty elimination, make the journey to the Crazy Wells.

What Are Crazy Water Crystals?

Crazy Water Crystals are the minerals which are taken from natural Crazy Mineral Water from our wells at Mineral Wells and Thorndale, Texas, by simply evaporating the water away. Nothing is added. You simply dissolve them in ordinary drinking water, and make your drinking water contribute to your physical well-being. At home, at work, wherever you are, you can drink Crazy Water—at just a few cents a gallon.

From the beginning of the practice of medicine doctors have recognized the importance of cleansing the bowels as the first step in treating almost every ailment. If you suffer from rheumatism, neuritis, arthritis, biliousness, constipation, acid and upset stomach, extreme nervousness, kidney trouble, or any other disorder brought on or made worse by sluggish, clogged up bowels, drink Crazy Water frequently, made from Crazy Water Crystals.

Try Crazy Water Crystals — See What Nature Can Do!

39 orth Tryon
HARLOTTE, N. C.

21 Arcade Building
ATLANTA, GA.

OF THE CAROLINAS AND GEORGIA

Figure 8.1 The Crazy Water Crystals Company sponsored radio programs and bands all across the South and Southwest in the 1930s selling a boxcar load of mineral laxative a day, they said, largely owing to promotion on hillbilly radio shows.

Homer Sherrill's Crazy Hickory Nuts are "adopted children" in the great "Crazy Water Crystals Family." They hail from Hickory, N.C., the furniture city, at the gateway to the mountains. Homer and his boys have been broadcasting daily from Radio Station WWNC Ashville, N.C. at 12:00 noon. You will also have the privilege of hearing this popular band on most of our Barn Dance programs, and in various personal appearances throughout the Carolinas. (Ahrens 1970b: 5)

The company moved groups from station to station both to aid their careers and to further the company's marketing strategy. The company also pioneered in the use of remote broadcasts transmitted to local stations via telephone lines and transcriptions—a kind of sponsor-controlled network—so that bands could be heard over the air at their scheduled times without actually being in the radio station's studio. For example, the increasingly popular Monroe Brothers were heard simultaneously on at least four stations, in Charlotte, Atlanta, Greenville, and Raleigh (Rosenberg 1985: 32).

Clearly by 1935 the Crazy Water Crystals Company was well on the way to developing a distinct form of presenting country music on the radio, one that was not so rigid as the major barn dances and at the same time was not so chaotic as the alternative, freelance barnstorming from station to station. Yet this system of promotion using country music was dismantled almost as rapidly as it had been developed. The company had roundly defeated its rival, Texas Water Crystals, with its marketing blitz, but at the same time it was under heavy attack from the American Medical Association and the federal government for marketing a useless but habit-forming purgative (*Business Week* 1935). In fear that the pending federal Food and Drug Act would make it impossible to advertise Crazy Water Crystals over U.S. radio stations, the company (with W. Lee O'Daniel a silent partner) diverted its radio promotional funds to purchase the Mexico border station XEAW. With a broadcasting output of 150,000 watts, it was three times as powerful as WLS, WSM, and the other clear-channel stations in the United States. The station hired hillbilly talent and pitched Crazy Water Crystals until 1943, when the Mexican government shut the station down (Fowler and Crawford 1987: 104–13). Thereafter the company advertised on established barn-dance programs, including the "Grand Ole Opry," until at least 1945, but had no further importance in furthering performers' careers.

Self-Sponsorship in Selling Songbooks

Enterprising artists sought other sources of income. Some sold products in their own names. Acuff, for example, promoted a product made by Cherokee Mills as "Roy Acuff Flour" (Schlappi 1978: 172), and Bob Wills successfully marketed "Play Boy Flour" for several years throughout the Southwest (Townsend 1976: 94–95). Some artists, most notably Bradley Kincaid, formed troupes of performers that toured from town to town as tent shows (Jones 1980: 64). By far the most successful product for a number of barnstormers of the 1930s, however, was the personalized songbook.

Gene Autry, Bradley Kincaid, the Pickard Family, and the Vagabonds all made a good deal of money from songbooks that they promoted over the air, but the group that relied on this means of making money more exclusively than any other came to prominence on WSM billed as "Asher Sizemore and Little Jimmie." Asher, the father, strummed his guitar and chatted with his son Jimmie, who spoke in a childish voice much like that of Shirley Temple. Then they would sing a special selection from their songbook of sentimental numbers that featured pictures of a proud father beaming at his big-eyed pudgy son dressed all in silk. Finally, they ended their program with a prayer. As Jimmie grew and his voice deepened, his younger brother "Buddy Boy" became the center of on-air adoring attention.[10]

In the early 1930s, radio airtime was being defined less as a service valuable for enhancing the station owner's reputation and more as a commodity to be sold to advertisers. Given this new definition, station management began to demand a percentage of the receipts for songbooks sold over the air. And there was often a great dispute between the artists and management over finding an equitable arrangement. Asher Sizemore solved the problem for his group by, in effect, sponsoring himself. He bought program time on the air and rented phone lines to receive orders for songbooks (Hay 1945: 26). This was clearly quite lucrative for Sizemore: on good weeks he received 40,000 pieces of mail (Wolfe 1994: 51). Sizemore continued the practice of selling songbooks as he moved from station to station.

If Asher Sizemore was the master at selling songbooks over the air through hokum with his children, many more musically respected artists, including Vernon Dalhart, Jimmie Rodgers, the Carter Family, Bill Monroe, the Pickard Family, the Oklahoma Cowboys, and Carson Robison, also marketed such books. But Bradley Kincaid devoted more effort to finding songs to include and received more money from selling songbooks than any other performer of the 1930s. Kincaid began collecting traditional songs in eastern Kentucky while a student at Berea College years before he thought of a career in music. The WLS management helped him produce his first songbook while he was on the "National Barn Dance" and took a considerable cut of the proceeds because the books were being pitched on their airtime. That arrangement may have figured in his decision to leave WLS in 1930, because in moving to WLW in Cincinnati he asked to receive no income for broadcasting but instead to be able to promote his songbooks and tour dates on the air in exchange for which he would give WLW a percentage on the sales of his songbooks (Jones 1980: 38).

While Kincaid and the Sizemores made considerable amounts of money from songbooks, this medium was of limited value for country musicians generally. As noted above, it was not a feasible medium for those who were primarily instrumentalists. Beyond this, sales came after a group had established a reputation and were not helpful in building a reputation the way, for example, record sales could be. Also, seeing a new source of revenue, music publishers, including Foster, Mills, and Stamps Baxter, began to produce stock songbooks that an artist could personalize with a distinctive cover, a few photos, a fan-oriented blurb and a few signature songs. Such books began to flood the market.[11] Finally, all songbook promoters found that following an initial period of success, radio-promoted book sales would dwindle as all the potential buyers within a station's range were reached. The only way to continue to sell songbooks under such circumstances was for the artist to move periodically to another radio station in a territory where books had not yet been sold (Jones 1980).

The Sponsor-Dictated Squeaky-Clean Image

Country music of the 1920s ran the gamut from sanctimonious to risqué. Recall that the first record by Fiddlin' John Carson paired a nostalgic song about the old homestead with a song of barnyard sexuality, and that when his daughter went on the road with him, he dubbed her "Moonshine Kate." While the biggest-selling records were about tragedy, records featuring comedic skits—often mixing in illegal alcohol use— by the Skillet Lickers and others sold very well. Some groups, including the Carter Family, kept a pristine image, and others like Charlie Poole singing "If the ocean were whiskey, and I was a duck, I'd swim to the bottom and never come up" were more or less openly dissolute. But most artists were more like Uncle Dave Macon, who played the role of the sorely tempted child of God. One of the widely circulated Uncle Dave stories is that once on the way to a show, the car's brakes began to give out near the top of a winding mountain road. Taking out his hip flask, Uncle Dave proclaimed that if he survived, he'd give up liquor forever. Once at the bottom, he averred that he better have a nip to steady his nerves.

While the music of Jimmie Rodgers was being widely acclaimed in the early 1930s, country music artists were generally considered to be no better than traveling carnival entertainers and gypsies (Wolfe 1982: 17). If the fiddle was considered "the Devil's box," and "thick as fiddlers in Hell" was a common expression of the day, the guitar was becoming a symbol of seduction as well. The Danville, Virginia, sheriff, voicing this popular concern, said that every man seen drunk or carrying a guitar should be immediately arrested (Grundy 1995: 1610). Thus, while many people apparently enjoyed and identified with the music, they thought that anyone who played for a living was, by definition, a ne'er-do-well (Tribe 1984: 17).

To counter the stereotype associated with country artists, radio programmers tried to assure audiences that their country music acts were good God-fearing people, and barn-dance masters of ceremonies went to great lengths to tell audiences that their shows were wholesome family entertainment. Being firm with problem artists could even be turned into an image-making advantage. The Opry's dropping of rowdy and intemperate acts, as was done with the leading fiddler, Arthur Smith, in the 1930s and Hank Williams in the 1950s, served to affirm the barn-dance show's image of propriety.

The image problem was even greater for barnstormers, because they had no barn-dance affiliation to buffer the relationship with the advertiser and with the audience. The barnstormer directly represented the particular advertiser to the audience, and so the sponsor was often directly involved in hiring the performer and shaping the show. Prospective sponsors tended to be less concerned with the music than with making sure that the performers were reliable, punctual, well-spoken, appropriately attired, and well groomed.

The mix of songs was affected by the concerns of broadcasters and advertisers. The numerous social commentary songs of the era were avoided, as were songs celebrating alcohol and drug use, and the quickest way for groups to affirm their wholesome status was to add religious songs. As Zeke Morris, a barnstormer of the era, put it years later to an interviewer:

> You were out there to entertain people with clean, wholesome entertainment. And so we just figured that if we put a couple or three gospel tunes in there that people would like that better. They would kind of figure us out as good people, which we always tried to be, good people. We never intended to be roughnecks or anything like that. (Grundy 1995: 1607)

The musicians themselves had a very direct and easily monitored reason for presenting an enthusiastic, sincere, positive personality on the air, because they were often asked to pitch advertiser's products themselves. Since advertisers often paid the station only on a "per inquiry" basis, musicians who could draw listeners with music and then convince a goodly number of them to write in for Hamlin's Wizard Oil, Black Draught, Carter's Little Liver Pills, Pe-Ru-Na Tonic, or whatever, would be assured of keeping their programs. The Delmore Brothers, Clayton McMichen, Patsy Montana, Lew Childre, Roy Acuff, the Monroe Brothers, Molly O'Day, Little Jimmy Dickens, Porter Wagoner, and the Sons of the Pioneers are just a few of the future featured performers who, in this way, learned the techniques of selling products (songs and themselves) with sincerity (Wolfe 1994; Fowler and Crawford 1987). Country music pitchman Paul Kallinger recalls the imperative of such sales techniques that linked the reputation of the artist to the audience response to the product in just four words—"pull mail or perish" (Fowler and Crawford 1987: 179).

The practice of evaluating bands in terms of their success in eliciting a response from potential consumers was pervasive for barnstormers by the late 1930s. Consider the following excerpt from a three-page promotional brochure apparently printed by WIS, the NBC affiliate in Columbia, South Carolina.

> The biggest mail puller on our station recently is the J. E. Mainer Mountaineers who are sponsored Monday through Friday by the Chattanooga Medicine Company. As a result of these morning broadcasts plus daily sustaining programs just after noon, this group received a total of 8,305 pieces of mail during the six months from October, 1937, to March, 1938, without benefit of contests or free offers. (Ahrens 1970b: 3)

Did Artists Fit Advertiser or Listener Interests?

Sellers of patent medicines had a special interest in vilifying the drinking of alcohol, because abstinence built the demand for their "medicines," some of which approached a 50 percent alcohol content. Nonetheless, advertisers generally had a direct interest in seeing that artists and the music they performed were pleasing to audiences. Pamela Grundy (1995: 1595) suggests that the shifting mix of songs accenting conventional bourgeois morality which were played on 1930s radio programs must have reflected the interests of audiences. Perhaps. It is difficult now to know what radio audiences of the 1930s asked for, because, although hundreds of thousands of song requests were made by postcard, letter, telegram, and phone call in the 1930s, no one apparently thought to make a systematic analysis of even a fragment of this information.

There does seem to be a difference in the relative popularity of song types between record sales and radio song requests—the latter being more conventional and the former more often being risqué. This may be in part because, as Grundy (1995: 1613) suggests, radio respondents (and presumably the larger radio audiences as well) were disproportionately women. But which came first, the programming or the gendered audience? Many of the medical and household-product advertisements were targeted at women, so it may be that music that would appeal to women was accented, making for a more female audience that then requested the softer and more conventional songs. Since record sales were so small in the 1930s, it meant that radio music demands set the parameters of what the music could be in that era.

Contrary to Grundy's view, the 1936 experience of the Nashville teen group the Deason Sisters suggests that radio listeners were more openminded than were radio advertisers. The group worked up the Carter Family's "Jealous Hearted Me" for their appearance on WSIX, but the program manager "cut the teen team off the air in midperformance" because of the line "it takes the man I love to satisfy my soul" (Bufwack and Oermann 1993: 177). Listeners called in to protest, and the Deason Sisters were given their own fifteen-minute early-morning show. Just how far radio advertisers and programmers could be out of step with public tastes is shown by what happened eighteen years later when the leading Deason sister, now performing as Kitty Wells, had a hugely successful record "It Wasn't God Who Made Honky-Tonk Angels." In spite of the song's singular success in phonograph record sales, in jukebox plays, and in Wells's live shows, the radio program censors wouldn't allow her to sing it on the "Grand Ole Opry" (Bufwack and Oermann 1993: 178).

Whether advertiser- or audience-driven, it was clearly in the interest of barnstormers to wholeheartedly endorse the products that sponsored their airtime, to happily fill conventional song requests, and to enthusiastically promote their upcoming performance dates in the listening range of the station. There was no place for sexual innuendo, social satire, political commentary, aloof professionalism, or rebel stance in this work environment. Thus the radio work of the 1930s helped to fix the image of the country artist as open, down-home, and utterly conventional— all characteristics that have been part of the country image ever since (Ellison 1995).

THE IMPACT OF BARNSTORMING ON THE MUSIC

If barnstormers were to make enough to survive as professional musicians, they had to supplement their radio-station income from other sources. Personalized songbook sales were important for some artists and record sales unimportant. In this section of the chapter we focus on the consequences of combining radio work with touring.

Touring Out

All barnstormers "touring out" from their radio-station bases made live appearances at local schools, town halls, or theaters, and since the take from each show was so small, the tendency was to fit in as many engagements as humanly possible. Bill Monroe recalls the pace in 1936: "We had two programs a day on radio, one in Greenville, South Carolina, and one on WBT, Charlotte, North Carolina, really early in the morning. We drove about one hundred miles from one place to the other, and then we played schools at night" (Wolfe 1994: 60). Self-assured professionalism developed rapidly in this crucible of numerous performances in quick succession in widely differing situations. But the toll was heavy; a number of musicians were killed or incapacitated in auto accidents while hurrying from an evening show to make an early-morning radio program, and most musicians of the era experienced more than one wreck.

Bradley Kincaid, like hundreds of other barnstormers of the 1930s, found that he was in great demand for live appearances in the months following his move to a new station, and that the audiences dwindled steadily thereafter. As soon as the market would begin to reach saturation—usually in about eighteen months—Kincaid would move to a station in another territory. He kept up barnstorming from 1930 until 1944, when he joined the "Grand Ole Opry." From the proceeds of his barnstorming activities, he was able to buy a major interest in a radio station in Springfield, Ohio, in 1949 and quit the road (Jones 1980).

Few barnstormers were able to manage their careers as successfully as Kincaid. Most tried to stay on at a station, but the irony was that the longer a barnstorming group stayed at a station after its initial burst of success, the smaller the audiences became—and consequently the more difficult it was to find another station willing to program them. When business would begin to turn down many such barnstormers blamed ineffective managers, bad weather, the deepening Depression, differences with fellow musicians, domestic quarrels, alcohol, or just the quite reasonable desire to stop wandering and plant roots where growing children could find good schools. Each of these elements figures in the litany of woe recounted by 1930s barnstormer Alton Delmore (1977), in his autobiography.

Smaller Groups Accenting Vocals

The exigencies of barnstorming made quite different demands on the music than did the barn dance. As part of a large and varied barn-dance cast, groups were pressured to become specialists in a single style of performance. Barnstorming groups, both on the air and in their live appearances, played alone or with a few other musicians. This put a premium on groups providing great variety in songs and incidental banter. The easiest way to satisfy the demand for variety would have been for groups to hire a number of performers having the range of talents required. The economics of barnstorming, however, pressed in the opposite direction. Since a band was ordinarily paid as a unit, the smaller the number of members, the larger the take per individual. Again, since barnstormers regularly moved from station to station, the fewer the members, the less the difficulty of simultaneously breaking households and moving families.

Many of the changes taking place in country music in the music of the 1930s can be traced to these exigencies. First, the primary sound became the human voice. 1920s-style string bands with no featured vocalist survived on the barn dances as an ever smaller part of the total mix, but they were completely absent from the ranks of professional barnstormers. The vocalists had to be versatile in their ways of singing, because while they could rely on a microphone in radio broadcasts, microphones were generally not available to amplify the voice on their live dates. Public address systems didn't come into wide use until late in the 1930s.

Second, the size of aggregations diminished from four or five to two or even to a solo individual. The Delmores and Bradley Kincaid illustrate the trend toward "miniaturization" among barnstormers. At the same time, both these acts, like many others of their time, often toured as part of troupes or package shows and augmented their performances with other musicians as economic conditions allowed. Under these conditions duets flowered as never before or since. Characteristically both members of the duo were accomplished musicians playing instruments with contrasting sounds—many pairing guitar and mandolin—and both sang solo and harmony so that the duo, in effect, had four voices to blend and contrast in the search for continual variety in their presentations.

Sibling Groups

A third consequence of these barnstorming working conditions was that many of the groups that endured were siblings. Think, for example, of the Delmore Brothers, the Monroe Brothers, Dolly and Millie Good (the

Girls of the Golden West), Bill and Earl Bolick (the Blue Sky Boys), the Blackwood Brothers, the Weaver Brothers and Elviry, the Casanova trio (the Three Georgia Crackers), the Dixon Brothers, and the Callahan Brothers, among many others (Malone 1985: 108–16). Growing up together, siblings could have much of their blended sound worked out before turning pro, and one of the characteristics of such sibling duos was their virtually flawless harmonizing in which each song was honed over the years. Also, in the process of growing up together, siblings could establish a system of working together that made it possible for them to stay together over a number of years.

Not all sibling duos, of course, worked smoothly. Perhaps the most innovative and commercially promising ever, the pairing of Charlie and Bill Monroe, ended in bitter acrimony in less than four years (Rosenberg 1985: 35). The Delmore Brothers stayed together for over two decades, but their frequent drunken fights often impaired their performances (Acuff 1983: 91–93), lost them radio jobs, and probably kept them from securing the lucrative show dates that their talents could have commanded (Delmore 1977: 148–55). Such vicissitudes notwithstanding, over two dozen brother duos gained notoriety in the Depression decade (Malone 1985: 103–35), and there were several female kin groups as well. Most notable among the latter were the Girls of the Golden West, and the Carter Family, featuring Sara and her cousin, Maybelle.

The Effects of the Periodic Moves

Less clear in its effect on barnstormers was the periodic change of work site. On the one hand, they might learn from the other musicians in the area; on the other hand, they might play safe by performing their songs in the way that had brought their prior success. Some groups like the Delmores and the Monroes seemed to incorporate something of the sounds of those around them. The Delmore Brothers, who in 1930 had a sound modeled on Jimmie Rodgers, two decades later had a boogie-woogie sound that was just a short step from rockabilly.

Other barnstormers, including Bradley Kincaid and the Carter Family, changed hardly at all. As John Atkins (1975: 109) notes concerning the original Carter Family's final recording session in 1941,

> Amazingly, after fourteen years of recording—after which time almost three hundred of their songs had been issued, and a period during which the rest of country music had changed radically from its late-twenties format . . . the Carters were able to go into the studio and record using exactly the same instrumentation, exactly the same vocal lineup, and exactly the same style as they had in Bristol in 1927.

Alternatives to Barnstorming in the Southwest

Most of the barnstorming discussed in this chapter took place in the states east of the Mississippi. In most sections to the west of the river musicians found the population too sparse, and in the dust-bowl areas too poor, to make a regular living by barnstorming. The dramatic effect that the working conditions had on the music is illustrated by what happened to country music where the barnstorming system of broadcasting was not possible—in the vast reaches of the Southwest. There the differing working conditions fostered distinctively different styles of music.

Superstations. The Carter Family and a number of other country music aggregations spent some time in the 1930s performing on the superpowered radio stations that beamed signals of 100,000 to 500,000 watts from just across the border in Mexico (Koon 1974). While the signal beamed the music over much of the United States, the populations within practical touring distance were too small to make performing live engagements a practical source of money. Thus the Carters and the others did not have to try to please the evolving live audience exposed to a wide range of new trends in music. They simply had to satisfy the demands of the radio patent-medicine advertisers; and since the advertisers were trying to reach older rural people, they generally favored sentimental, old-style songs. Thus, while superstation exposure gave these artists greater name recognition and facilitated their record sales, it gave them no impetus to keep up with evolving audience tastes.

Canned Music. Some phonograph records were played over the air, but the practice was not widespread except at the smallest stations through the 1930s (Barnouw 1968). Another form of canned music, however, did develop out of border radio. The superstations had transmitters in Mexico but had their studios on the U.S. side of the line. For quite different reasons the United States and Mexican governments from time to time restricted the flow of artists, advertising material, or telephone connections across the boarder. To ensure that broadcasts would be aired as planned, several of the superstations invested in the latest sound transcription equipment and prerecorded all of their musical programs. Transcriptions were cut on 33 1/3 rpm 16-inch disks. Established artists like the Pickards and the Carter Family would record a fifteen-minute musical program complete with announcements and comments between songs, being careful not to mention the place, date, or time of day.

While the transcriptions were made at first as a tactical expedient in the war with the governments to stay on the air, several programmers soon saw an opportunity to make money from them.[12] They made numerous pressings of these transcriptions and sent them to subscribing radio stations around the country, where the local announcers would read advertisements and introduce the band as if it were right there in the local studio.[13]

If the transcription services increased the competition for a dwindling number of more lucrative broadcasting slots, barnstorming was finally killed off by the resurgence of country music on phonograph records. Many small establishments that had featured live bands one or two nights a week installed jukeboxes so that customers could have music whenever they wanted it, and the music was spread far and wide in establishments ranging from soda fountains to bus terminals via the jukebox.

Beginning later, but developing in parallel to this substitution of canned for live music in places of entertainment, radio stations increasingly played the new country music records on the air. With this new system, fans everywhere, simply by putting a nickel in the jukebox or flicking the radio dial, could enjoy the latest recordings cut in Dallas, Louisville, Hollywood, or Nashville by the most popular artists. Beyond putting an end to barnstorming, these developments had far-reaching effects on the music and its performers, as we will see in part 4.

CONCLUSION

Country music artists to this day still play one-night engagements, and a few play live on the radio, but the system of barnstorming that provided many hundreds of would-be country artists employment and a chance to perfect their skills was rapidly coming to an end before World War II and was virtually a thing of the past soon after the war. The reasons for its demise are not hard to find. The growing practice of linking several stations together meant work for fewer performers and greater exposure and incomes for those who survived. Barnstorming was finally killed by the rapidly spreading practice of substituting recorded music for live bands in the decade following World War II.

Barnstorming had two main consequences for country music. First, it ingrained into the emerging tradition of country music a focus on noncontroversial lyrics, an enthusiastically positive orientation to commercial interests, and an appreciation for audiences. Second, the impoverished, unstable, and highly mobile conditions of barnstorming work brought to the fore multitalented and sober sibling groups who could withstand the rigors of the working conditions. Thus, as we have seen, while barn-dance work tended to press groups into being specialists of one stereotypic sort or another, the effect of barnstorming was to foster multitalented generalists. Both kinds of radio work accented country music as wholesome family entertainment rather than risqué or rowdy fare.

CHAPTER NINE

Soft Shell vs. Hard Core

The Vagabonds vs. Roy Acuff

The development of country music in the twentieth century conventionally traces a more or less linear trajectory from more folklike to more commercial and poplike music.[1] But we have already noted that the popularity of the rich, operatic stylings of Wendell Hall and Vernon Dalhart *preceded* that of the more old-fashioned renditions of Fiddlin' John Carson and the Carter Family. Malone (1985) argues with considerable justification that this particular anomaly was due to the fact that the commercial interests in record producing and radio broadcasting only gradually learned the extent of the demand for more authentic-seeming country music.

But this does not explain why the same phenomenon—more traditional groups becoming popular *after* more poplike ones—has continued to occur repeatedly over the many decades since. To cite but one recent major case in point, the more poplike stylings of Barbara Mandrell, Kenny Rogers, Ann Murray, the Oak Ridge Boys, and Alabama, which were most popular in the first half of the 1980s, were supplanted in the last half of the '80s by more traditional-sounding artists such as Ricky Skaggs, Randy Travis, George Strait, and Dwight Yoakam. These leading artists of the late 1980s have been called neotraditionalists, and the "neo" is as important as the "traditional" in the characterization, for while they hark back to older lyrical themes, ways of playing, and performance images, they do so in ways that profoundly change and update the "traditional" elements.

At the very least such anomalies suggest that the theory of linear modernization should be questioned, and a theory more consonant with the facts should be sought. To begin the process, it is useful to abandon the word "traditional" because, as I will try to show in this chapter, many of the elements of the music that is called "nontraditional" or "pop-oriented" are every bit as old as those called "traditional" and have a historical continuity of their own. Bill Malone (1985: 16–23) shows that in the era before the development of record- and radio-disseminated country music, two clearly distinct types of country music coexisted. The one he calls "parlor" or "domestic" and the other he calls the "assembly" or "frolic" tradition. The first was carried primarily by the human voice and consisted largely of ballads, old popular songs, lullabies, and play songs. Women mostly performed these kinds of music. The second was carried primarily by instrumental music played at barn dances, fiddling contests, and similar festive public occasions where male performers predominated. Malone notes that it was music of the frolic sort played by fiddlers and string bands that first received commercial acceptance via phonograph records and radio in the mid-1920s. The radio formats of the 1930s described in the last two chapters accenting clean "family entertainment," however, brought back into favor many of the elements of the domestic or parlor tradition. Because both styles of music represent venerable traditions, the word "traditional" cannot be used to distinguish between them. Accordingly, the sort that appeals to "rustic" assembly or frolic tradition is here called *hard core* and the more pop-music-like parlor or domestic tradition is called *soft shell.*

Barn-dance programs were variety shows, and so they provide an excellent context in which to examine the interplay between hard-core and soft-shell elements. In this chapter, we begin to understand the differences between the two and the dialectical relationship between them by focusing on the contest between soft shell and hard core taking place on the "Grand Ole Opry" during the era of radio-made country music in the 1930s.

THE ASCENDANCY OF SOFT-SHELL COUNTRY

The conventional story of changes on the "Grand Ole Opry" parallels in microcosm the conventional story of the development of country music nationally in suggesting a linear progression. Starting with an old-time fiddler, Uncle Jimmy Thompson, so the story goes, the show became the province of a number of ever more proficient fiddle bands that did not accent vocals. Then on February 19, 1938, Roy Acuff took the microphone as a singer supported by a band. Acuff's popularity, it is argued, set the model for other lead singers, from Eddy Arnold and Hank Williams on down to the present.

Vito Pellettieri, long-time stage manager and music director of the Opry, is quoted as saying, "The string bands were the main thing. What little singing there was began with Uncle Dave [Macon], the Delmores, and Sam and Kirk [McGee]. But there wasn't a lot of it . . . until the coming of a curly headed fiddler Roy Acuff" (Schlappi 1978: 37). Bill Malone in his scholarly *Country Music U.S.A.* lends weight to this view (1985: 190), and Acuff himself has contributed to the popularization of this version of collective memory. In his introduction to Jack Hurst's *Grand Ole Opry*, Acuff says, "When George D. Hay first started the Opry there was some singing, but most of the numbers they featured were instrumental. I was possibly the first one that came there with what they call a voice" (Hurst 1975: 10).

This common assertion that Acuff was the first featured singer on the "Grand Ole Opry" takes much away from the contributions of a number of earlier artists, as we will see. It also obscures not only the reasons why, though he auditioned several times, Acuff failed to get on the Opry for a number of years, but also why, when he was finally allowed to perform, he was instantly popular with Opry audiences and soon became a model for numerous other aspiring artists. The answers to these questions nicely reveal the dynamic interplay between soft shell and hard core.

The Soft-Shell Drift of the Opry Early in the 1930s

The numerous string bands that played on the Opry in the late 1920s and well into the 1930s, such as the Possum Hunters and the Skillet Lickers, provided a driving barn-dance sound that instantly identified the program as hard-core country music. Many of their songs included vocals, but, as with most of the comedy songs of Uncle Dave Macon, a number of the vocals were fragmentary or oft repeated blues lines. At the same time, a number of solo performers and singing groups on the Opry did contribute versions of old ballads and hymns as well as sentimental and heart songs that had been the vogue in urban popular music over the preceding decades.

The Pickard Family. One of the earliest and best of such singing groups featured on the Opry was the Pickard Family from Ashland, Tennessee. Obed "Dad" Pickard first appeared on the program in 1926 only months after its founding and was joined by his wife and growing circle of children for several extended periods through 1933.[2] Obed could play fiddle, but more often sang and played the Jews' harp. Other family members played the piano, accordion, banjo, string bass, and rhythm guitar. All contributed to the vocal sound on a mix of ballads, minstrel songs, old popular songs, and hymns including the likes of "Barbara Allen," "The Little Rosewood Casket," "Sourwood Mountain," Froggy Went a-Courtin'," "Turkey in the Straw," and "I'm Gonna Walk the Streets of Glory." While the group were always pictured in conservative middle-class attire, "Dad" Pickard, in their 1934 song folio, characterized the family's repertoire as "old time Hick and Hoe down Hill Billy Songs."[3]

The Pickard Family's music is soft shell in that, while cast as country music, it comprised songs that were, or had been, heard in parlors all across the country, not just in rural areas. Their singing style was more polished and less nasal than that of hard-core singers like Jimmie Rodgers. The instrumentation, while that of a country string band more than a popular orchestra, was always a background accompaniment to the singing. As is typical of the soft-shell aesthetic, the accent was on sonorous, polished, and dignified interpretations of songs rather than on the hard-edged outpouring of raw emotion.

The widespread appeal of the Pickard Family's music made it possible for them to use the Opry as the springboard for a commercial career singing on network stations in Buffalo, Chicago, New York, and Philadelphia, ending in the late 1930s (like other old-time singing groups, including the Carter Family) performing on a superpowered station on the Mexican border (Fowler and Crawford 1987: 173). The close-harmony brother duo the Delmore Brothers, while not strictly soft shell, were invited to join the Opry in 1933 to replace the Pickards when they left Nashville's WSM for the "National Barn Dance" broadcast from Chicago (Delmore 1977: 48). Other notable soft-shell singers on the Opry of the early to mid-1930s included Asher Sizemore and his two sons, Jack Jackson, and the Vagabonds.

Why the Softening Drift?

The more soft-shell-oriented WLS "National Barn Dance" broadcasts of the 1930s enjoyed a far larger audience than the "Grand Ole Opry." George Biggar of WLS regularly made careful studies of the audience appeal of "National Barn Dance" groups and cut or added acts accordingly. He also studied the formatting of the "Grand Ole Opry" to get ideas on how to stay ahead in the competition. For their part, the WSM managers understandably saw WLS as a rival that might steal its featured artists.[4] But there is no evidence that there was a conscious policy in the early 1930s to alter the mix of sound on the Opry to mimic the success of the "National Barn Dance."

More likely, changes on the Opry reflected changes taking place in the programming of country music in the 1930s. WSM's sound was becoming slicker and more professional. In 1930, Harry Stone, a station announcer, was named station manager, and the professionalism of the popular music and the service programming aimed at farmers, business people, and homemakers developed rapidly (Peterson 1975; Hurst 1975: 104). Professional popular music performers were attracted to play on the numerous music programs broadcast by the station, a set of versatile staff musicians developed, and many of these played on the Opry, as we have seen in chapter 7.

Innovations of the Vagabonds

Like any of the other WSM programs in the Harry Stone era, the "Grand Ole Opry" was open to staff musicians who could put together a credible country music act. One of the first, and by far the most influential, staff musician groups to appear regularly on the Opry was a male harmonizing trio who used only a spare, finger-picked guitar accompaniment. The Vagabonds began as a college group in the mid-1920s singing popular songs, sentimental ballads, and sacred songs. They appeared in the Chicago area singing at YMCA religious retreats and the like, sometimes on the same program with Bradley Kincaid. During the late 1920s, the group appeared on a number of Chicago radio stations, including WLS, and after experiencing some change in personnel, included in their program a number of comedic songs.[5] In 1929 the group moved to KMOX in St. Louis, where in January 1930, the membership of the trio became fixed, with second tenor Harold Goodman, baritone Curt Poulton, and the one surviving original, first tenor Dean Upson. While primarily a popular music group, as early as the Chicago days they appeared on the NBC "Farm and Home Hour" singing old familiar favorites. Their ability to tailor their repertoire is suggested by the fact that at the same time they appeared regularly on programs called "School Days," "Memory Lane," and "Covered Wagon Days." When they moved to WSM in 1931 they sang on a number of the station's popular music broadcasts but also appeared regularly on the "Grand Ole Opry."

While many of the other groups of staff musicians like Jack Shook's aggregation, which took the name "Missouri Mountaineers" and dressed in rustic outfits for Opry appearances, the Vagabonds always appeared under that name and dressed in suits or natty collegiate outfits (like those in the publicity photo shown in gallery figure G3.1) for the Opry program and on personal appearances. The ways in which the Vagabonds were introduced to audiences so that they would better fit the Opry image is suggested by George Hay's several paragraphs on the group in his 1945 fan-oriented *A Story of the "Grand Ole Opry."* Hay writes that

> A NEW turn in the Opry road was reached in 1931 when the Vaga-
> bonds . . . joined the company. . . . [Each was] the son of a minister
> of the gospel, and the boys were thoroughly familiar with sacred num-
> bers and heart songs. . . . [Noting that] their backgrounds varied
> somewhat from the other members of the company, in that they re-
> ceived more formal education, . . . [Hay acknowledged that] they
> could hardly be called "country boys," but they loved folk music, [and
> accompanying themselves] with a mellow home made guitar[6] . . . their
> voices blended so well and their enunciation was clear [so that] . . .
> the Vagabonds told a story with each song. (Hay 1945: 228–29; em-
> phasis in the original)

The musical influence of the Vagabonds on country music is hard to assess. Certainly their harmony style of rendering a song was not distinc-tive. But this style, presented regularly as part of the South's premiere country music radio barn dance by a group of comely, energetic, nattily dressed, and clearly successful young men, must have been a model for any number of aspiring vocalists and groups of the region. Alton Del-more, Red Foley, and Roy Acuff acknowledge their debt to the Vaga-bonds' sound and it must have played a part in inspiring the rapid prolif-eration in country (and gospel) music of singing groups in the 1930s (Malone 1985: 108–16). The musical influence of the Vagabonds is not confined to their song styling. The early style of guitar finger picking developed by Curt Poulton is said to have been a major early influence on the developing style of the youthful Chet Atkins.[7]

While it may be difficult to assess accurately the Vagabonds' musical influence, they clearly served as a model of professionalism to the per-formers and staff of the Opry of the early 1930s. They used a wide range of devices to make money from their reputation and to increase it further. Beyond performing on the radio, on records, and at live appearances, they early had their picture on sheet music over the words "Featured by the Vagabonds, the popular radio trio." And as early as 1928 a music trade magazine featured them in an advertisement for an electrically am-plified guitar. When they got to Nashville they were beginning to write songs; one, a weeper entitled "When It's Lamp Lightin' Time in the Val-ley" which tells about a repentant son remembering his home and mother to whom he can never return because of his unnamed sin, became a great success.

The Vagabonds formed their own publishing company, released their own songbooks, and put other artist-writers, most notably the Delmore Brothers, under contract. Their practice of promoting their songbooks on the Opry was the model for the practice, which the Sizemores further perfected. While the Vagabonds' Old Cabin Publishing Company did not survive for long in the depths of the Depression, it served as an early model for Fred Rose, a novice staff pianist at WSM and budding pop songwriter who would eventually become Hank Williams's mentor, business partner of Roy Acuff, and the most influential individual in the institutionalization of country music in Nashville. As John Rumble notes in his dissertation on Rose, Rose spent a good deal of time with the Vagabonds and their "business acumen provided Rose with an excellent example not only of how a pop-to-country transition could be made, but also of how country music could be marketed" (Rumble 1980: 34).

The Vagabonds used a number of devices to build their following which were then novel on the Opry. These included cultivating a fan club, handing out publicity photos, reproducing favorable press clippings, and composing stories that could be planted in newspapers. One of the latter began with the tabloid-like headline: "Three Preachers' Bad Boys." The first sentence of the article explained that they weren't really bad, just full of mischief. As Hay (1945: 28) notes in explaining their rapid rise in popularity on the Opry, "Having had considerable experience in show business, they were publicity conscious. . . . They went in for pictures and stories which added to their build-up." A number of aspiring Opry artists, including Alton Delmore and Roy Acuff, have noted the professional acumen of the Vagabonds and tried to emulate their business practices.

The trio received considerable press coverage while in Chicago, and in St. Louis were voted—after several national radio celebrities including Amos 'n' Andy and Rudy Vallee—among the most popular radio entertainers. None of their records, however, became hits. It is difficult to assess accurately the popularity of the Vagabonds on the Opry in the mid-1930s. Alton Delmore, who was trying to get on the program, calls them "the hit act on the station" (Delmore 1977: 47). Wolfe (1975b: 117) calls them "one of the most popular groups on the [Opry] in the early '30s. . . . [and] on a stage where most of the singing had hitherto been the traditional old time type of Uncle Dave Macon and the Pickards, the Vagabonds were a sensation." One clear evidence of the appeal of the Vagabonds is provided by the 1933 WSM Artists Service Bureau rate book. The Vagabonds could command seventy-five dollars for a single performance, which was more than any other individual or group—pop

or country—with the exception of the widely known blackface vaudeville comedy act of Lasses and Honey (Leroy White and Lee Davis
Wilds).[8]

Further Soft-Shell Drift

In the years between the coming of the Vagabonds in 1931 and Roy Acuff
in 1938, the "Grand Ole Opry" trended ever more from its hard-core
string-band sound. The coming of Asher Sizemore and Little Jimmie, the
Delmore Brothers, and the pop-staff band that for Opry appearances
styled itself "Smiling Jack (Shook) and his Missouri Mountaineers" have
already been mentioned.

While humor and comic skits had long been an Opry staple, for the
first time minstrel show and vaudeville-inspired performers who specialized in humor became part of the Opry. Most prominent among these
was the act of Lasses and Honey; Lasses White and his several partners,
most particularly Honey Wilds, were white men who wore blackface and
acted skits in a Southern African American dialect. Women were represented on the Opry in comic guise when in 1933 Sarie and Sally (Edna
Wilson and Margaret Waters) brought the tradition of outspoken country women to the show.[9] Robert Lunn introduced a line of commentary
through humor in performing his one number, "The Talking Blues."
Lunn was adept at molding the words to fit the political and social mood
of the moment, though his verses were not as politically pointed as those
of Uncle Dave Macon, and unlike those of Uncle Dave, his skits did not
always reflect his own views.

Another innovation that broadened the appeal of the 1930s Opry was
the appearance of western-dressing groups. Zeke Clements, a smooth
country crooner, came from the "National Barn Dance" with a band
called the Bronco Busters. They were the first regulars to break the hillbilly dress code of the Opry by wearing western outfits on the program.
Soon thereafter fiddle-playing showman Arnim "Curly" Fox, and his
bluesy-voiced wife, Texas Ruby (Owen), also dressed western, as did
the Golden West Cowboys, the Opry's first western swing band, led by
accordion-playing, Wisconsin-born Pee Wee King (né Frank Anthony
Kuczynski). King had come to the Opry from Milwaukee via radio stations in Louisville and Knoxville.[10] With all these changes, the Opry
seemed to be on a straight course toward becoming pop music.

THE HARD-CORE REVIVAL OF ROY ACUFF

In the mid-1940s Roy Acuff was hailed variously as the "King of the
Hillbillies," the "Backwoods Sinatra," and the "Caruso of Mountain Mu-

sic," and in 1952 he was featured on the cover of *Newsweek*.[11] This was a remarkable reversal of fortune, because until late in 1937, by which time he had already made a number of records and was appearing regularly on the radio in Knoxville, Tennessee, he was unable to land even a guest appearance on Nashville's increasingly prestigeful "Grand Ole Opry"—the institution with which he is now inseparably identified. Acuff's failure and subsequent success tells us much about the dynamics of soft shell and hard core.

Difficulty Getting on the Opry

From 1934 on, Acuff traveled one or more times annually to audition for the Opry, but all to no avail.[12] Given Opry management's quest for a soft-shell sound, his failure is understandable. His fiddle playing was not as good as that of the best string-band fiddlers on the Opry, and his voice had none of the polish of the other recent recruits, including the Vagabonds, Robert Lunn, and the Delmore Brothers. They sang in the newly popular "crooning" style that had been made possible by advances in microphone technology and use. The appealing intimacy of this singing style was striking, particularly when compared with the full-voiced sounds of their operatically trained predecessors, such as Enrico Caruso and Vernon Dalhart, as well as the older Opry rustics, such as Uncle Dave Macon, who were used to projecting their unamplified voices to fill large rooms.

On the advice of Joe L. Frank, leading artist manager of the time, who had met Acuff when the Golden West Cowboys headed by Frank's son-in-law were playing on the radio in Knoxville, the Opry managers invited Acuff to play a guest spot on the program substituting for one of its premiere fiddlers, Arthur Smith, who was put off the Opry to deal with his recurrent bouts of alcohol abuse (Wolfe 1977b: 44–45). Acuff nervously played a fiddle tune and then went into his most popular piece, "The Great Speckled Bird," but to be in fashion, Acuff sang it, as best he could, in the popular crooning style. This proved a disaster—Acuff himself says "my voice sounded to me like a whining pup's"—and the band returned to Knoxville never expecting to hear from the Opry management again (Acuff 1983: 68).

Nonetheless, the Opry still needed a temporary replacement for Arthur Smith, and Alton Delmore was given the privilege of naming which one of four recent guests he would like to give the spot.[13] Echoing Acuff's judgment, Delmore realized that the Crazy Tennesseans had "sounded really pitiful. . . . The other bands had played better, but they didn't seem nearly as sincere as Roy did" (Delmore 1977: 119–20). As he recalled later, Delmore asked for Acuff because "He was just as friendly as a puppy, and he was marked all over with pure and simple sincerity" (Delmore 1977: 117). Delmore reports that David Stone was shocked at his decision, saying, "'I'll be god damned if I think I will ever be able to understand you crazy hill billies. Here you are, picking the worst band that played. And I *know* you know better. Is there something about Roy Acuff that has you charmed or something?' 'No.' [Delmore reports replying.] 'But . . . that old boy will crawl to make good. I just know he will and I think he deserves a chance' " (Delmore 1977: 121).

Acuff was not then aware of what was going on behind the scenes at WSM, and so it was to his great surprise that the band was invited back early in 1938 for another appearance on the Opry. This time Acuff sang "The Great Speckled Bird" in the full-voiced and emotion-filled manner he had learned while working without a microphone as a medicine show entertainer. The radio audience response via telegrams and letters was immediate, and Acuff was signed to a temporary spot on the Opry and given a daily early-morning show. The audience response continued to grow and within a year his band was the most acclaimed on the Opry. Within eighteen months he became the first acknowledged star performer of the show when, in October 1939, NBC network began to carry a thirty-minute segment of the Opry, with Acuff as its host (Malone 1985: 191).

Fabricating the Hard-Core Sound

Over the first months on the Opry the hard-core elements in Acuff's act were consolidated. The musicians who championed the band's crooning and jazzlike sound left and were replaced by more hard-core (and more expert) musicians. The most risqué and pop-oriented songs were cut from the repertoire and additional old tunes, or old-sounding tunes, and religious songs were introduced. Each of these changes made the band's presentation more acceptable for radio airplay in the 1930s.

Acuff put great emotion into each rendition, often crying openly while singing songs such as the moralistic tragedy song "Wreck on the Highway." Acuff paid great attention to image as well. The band changed its name from the Crazy Tennesseans to the Smoky Mountain Boys and changed its dress from a mixture of westernlike and comedic outfits to more consistent checked shirts and work jeans or overalls appropriate for a hillbilly band of the era.

Acuff reformed the band in the image of a hard-core string band—a performance unit that was given fixed form by regular radio work and live appearances in the late 1920s. However, the Smoky Mountain Boys were not built to *be* a 1920s string band, but rather, within the sensibilities of the late 1930s, to *seem like* what by then had become a "traditional" string band. Like most string bands, the fiddle took the lead in an aggregation of stringed instruments. But Acuff made innovations. For example, Acuff introduced the dobro to the Opry string band. This is a metal-topped guitar that is played flat with a steel bar across the strings, its whining yet mellow tone being redolent of the "Hawaiian" band sound that was extremely popular throughout the United States in the early part of the twentieth century. In 1938 the dobro represented a nostalgic sound, which, laced with sweeping glissando, also fit with the nasal sonorities of Southern speech, singing, and fiddle playing. To cement the connection of dobro to hillbilly with the Opry audience, Pete Kirby, the dobro player, was dressed in bib overalls and dubbed with the rube name "Oswald." He is shown center stage in his rube outfit in gallery figure G3.2.

Rustifying the Image

Acuff was careful to accent the rural and small-town origins of band members in all their publicity and in the comments he made during performances, and he fabricated rustification where the reality did not fit the stereotype. The recasting of an early band member, Rachel Veach, seen with the band just behind Oswold in gallery figure G3.2, provides an excellent case in point. Rachel had never been far from her central Tennessee home. She was unfamiliar with inside plumbing, tall buildings, elevators, store-bought clothes, and the conventions of regular shoe wear. These all would be the natural basis for country bumpkin comedy in a man, but it did not work with a woman since there were strict limits on how much a woman could be the butt of jokes. Initially, she was billed as "Rachel, Queen of the Hills," and two of the band members were billed as "Pap and Oswald, Rachel's Two Country Comedian Boy Friends." Soon Acuff found fans expressing great concern that a young single woman was traveling with a group of unrelated men. In response, Acuff dropped Rachel Veach's earlier billing and created a comic sketch in which Rachel traded brother-sister quips with Pete Kirby, the dobro player. To accent his protective role, Acuff added "Bashful Brother" to his stage name, "Oswald." Fans accepted Oswald as her big, protective and personally circumspect brother, and this contrivance silenced the comments about carrying a woman with the band (Acuff 1983: 101–5).

One of the clearest examples of Acuff's concern with the visual representation of the band's identity occurred in 1940 when he and the band were asked to be part of the cast of the Republic Studio's film *The Grand Ole Opry*. Consonant with the movie's western theme, the wardrobe mistress issued the Smoky Mountain Boys cowboy outfits. Acuff, who had been delayed getting to the dressing room, found them trying on the western garb. As Elizabeth Schlappi recounts the incident:

He stood there with feet wide apart, eyes flashing, and hands fisted.
"What's this all about?" he demanded of his troupe.
"The movie folks told us to get into this garb."
"Take it off! We'll wear our regular 'Grand Ole Opry' clothes, or go
back home." Then turning to the studio officials, he added, "We are
just a bunch of country boys from Tennessee who have come out here
to put on our little country show like we do back home, and we intend to do exactly that and wear our regular clothes." (Schlappi 1978:
175–76)

And they did. Reflecting on the incident in 1943, Acuff affirmed: "I
am very annoyed when someone calls me a cowboy. You can see there
is nothing cowboy about me. . . . I don't intend for the public ever to
see me as a cowboy" (quoted in Schlappi 1978: 176).

Focus on Being Entertaining

Even if they did hark back to the string band, in 1938 Roy Acuff and
the Smoky Mountain Boys clearly were different from the Fruit Jar Drinkers and the numerous other "Grand Ole Opry" string bands of a decade
earlier. While Acuff self-consciously shaped the sound and image to fit
the nascent country string-band tradition, he clearly focused on doing
whatever it took to entertain the audience while the band was playing
by holding the center of attention himself, making loud comments, or
playing with his yo-yo, or posing for fan photos, or balancing his fiddle
bow on his chin, as can be seen in figure 14.1, taken on the Opryland
stage in 1979. In his autobiography he justifies these practices: "I figured
I needed to keep everybody's attention, so I was always doing something,
even if it was just moving around and talking to other performers. . . .
I've always tried to keep things as lively and entertaining as possible on
stage" (Acuff 1983: 85–86). Thus Acuff's efforts to craft the image of
the band were more in line with the exuberance of Uncle Dave Macon
than with the dead-pan delivery of the early Opry string bands.

The focus on being ever entertaining led Acuff by 1939 to ask every
member of the band both to be an excellent soloist and to take on an
identifiable character that could be brought into the frequent comedy
skits. This versatility made the band, unlike most others of the time, a
completely self-contained entertainment unit that could tour on its own
and not only as a specialized part in a larger package.

In this context, Acuff essentially played the part of master of ceremonies and bandleader always trying to keep order among this boisterous
set of musician hill folk. Given this role, he would dress slightly better
than the rest, by 1941 wearing slacks and an open shirt. This contrast

can clearly be seen in the gallery 3 publicity photo of Acuff with Lonnie Wilson. He would act the personable host, and play the surprised and slightly shocked superego for the group when the band members got into one of their more risqué skits, as, for example, when at the climax of a double-entendre interchange a huge, ten-foot-long phallic corncob exploded out of the front of a band member's pants, to the hysterical delight of Acuff and the audience.[14]

At the same time as he was revivifying and updating the string-band form, Acuff was providing a new content to that image through his heart-felt singing style. In counterpoint to the excellent musicianship and mad-cap antics of his band, Acuff was at great pains to sing each song with great clarity and raw emotion. All of the early accounts of Acuff's appeal echo Alton Delmore's assessment, quoted earlier, that Acuff seemed sincere. Perhaps not since Jimmie Rodgers had died five years earlier had a country music performer so clearly projected his personal feelings in a song.

Innovation in the Name of Tradition

The immediate strong response of the audience to this sense of authenticity in Roy Acuff's vocals had the effect of shifting the focus of attention in the string band. While a performance by one of the older groups consisted of ensemble instrumental play and a string of exciting instrumental solos interspersed with a vocal line sung by one or several of the instrumentalists, the Smoky Mountain Boys' performance consisted of a strong vocal augmented and complemented by instrumental interludes. In the process, Acuff as fiddler played fewer and fewer solos, and Acuff as vocalist became the center of attention. The shift became so pronounced that in 1943 he hired another hot fiddler and for over a decade used his own instrument only as a prop.

The difference between Roy Acuff's aggregation and earlier string bands is signaled in the name given top billing. Recall that many of the earlier string bands were known by a collective name—the Gully Jumpers, the Fruit Jar Drinkers, the Blue Sky Boys, the Skillet Lickers—with no single individual given headliner billing. But here we have "Roy Acuff and the (or "His") Smoky Mountain Boys." While the image may be hard core, it is ironic that the innovations made by Acuff exactly paralleled changes in the popular-music dance bands. Bands lead by instrumentalists such as Benny Goodman and Harry James were being displaced by aggregations known by the name of the vocalist, Frank Sinatra, Nat King Cole, Perry Como, Mel Torme, Dinah Shore, and the like.

Thus, while Acuff began by trying to revivify the string band and bring sincerity back into singing, his efforts ended in his becoming the prototype of the performer singing autobiographical songs and fronting a band—the model of the country music aggregation that has persisted to this day. As Bill Malone (1985: 205) puts it, with the advent of Acuff on the Opry, the star system was born. The success of Roy Acuff facilitated the success in country music of a whole new generation of autobiographical singers from Ernest Tubb and Kitty Wells to Hank Williams, Loretta Lynn, George Jones, and down to the present.

HARD-CORE AND SOFT-SHELL EXPRESSIONS

While the comparison of Roy Acuff with the Vagabonds clearly exemplifies the difference between hard-core and soft-shell expressions in country music, it is useful to draw back from these specific cases to better see the general features of hard core and soft shell and to show that they both represent recurrent tendencies in country music.

Few would question the authenticity of hard country, but it is not as widely acknowledged that the tradition of soft country has a distinctive aesthetic, has recurrent features, and extends as far back in time. The heritage of soft-core country is formidable. For example, Wendell Hall performed and recorded polished versions of country music in the early 1920s, years before the first hard country record by Fiddlin' John Carson was released in 1923. Carrying the argument back to the 1850s, the numerous nostalgic songs of Stephen Foster, such as "Swanee River," "Old Kentucky Home," and "Oh Susanna," represent a soft shell to the widely performed but largely undocumented hard-core Anglo-American ballads and African American songs of the time.

The basic justification for of hard country is that it represents the authentic tradition of the music called country and that it is by and for those steeped in the tradition. The corresponding justification for of soft country is that it melds countrywith pop music to make it enjoyable to the much larger numbers of those not born into or knowledgeable about country music.[15] The leading hard-core artists have received the most attention from contemporary commentators and later scholars as well. At the same time, the leading soft-shell artists of an era have tended to be more popular with audiences and to make more money than their hard-core counterparts.[16]

Characteristics of Hard Core and Soft Shell

In the following discussion the word "expression" is used as a generic term that may refer to a person, a musical rendition, a musical style, or some other collectivity. When stripped of all contextual clues, an expression may be impossible to classify unequivocally as one or the other. The following list suggests the range of factors that are important in differentiating between hard core and soft shell.[17] Rather than cite artists only from the first half of the twentieth century to illustrate the points, I shall also offer as examples artists active in recent years, because their sound, dress, deportment, and image may be better known to most readers.

SPEECH

Hard core: Southern or Southwestern accent, Southernisms in speech, white Southern grammar; informal, self-deprecating ("next we will try to play for you"). E.g., Fiddlin' John Carson, Hank Williams, Ernest Tubb, Loretta Lynn, George Jones, Randy Travis.

Soft shell: Standard American grammar; relatively unaccented or having a melodious regional accent with all the hard edges extracted; authoritative voice. E.g., Vernon Dalhart, Tex Ritter, Red Foley, Patsy Cline, Eddy Arnold, Vince Gill, Shania Twain.

SINGING STYLE

Hard core: Untrained voice with nasal tone; personal involvement in the song; out of meter to tell the story; rough harmonies, raw emotion. Sung as if telling personal experiences and expressing personally felt emotions. E.g., Jimmie Rodgers, Loretta Lynn, Hank Williams, George Jones, Merle Haggard, Marty Brown.

Soft shell: Trained voice with full tone; smooth harmonies; meter in sync with the instrumentation; songs sung, not emoted; singers interpret experiences and feelings of the songwriter in a way that they may be shared by all listeners. E.g., Red Foley, Crystal Gayle, Ray Charles, the Oak Ridge Boys, Kenny Rogers.

LYRICS

Hard core: Concrete situations, simple vocabulary; references are concrete and evoke specific personal experiences; singers perform songs that express a wide range of emotions, and these change with their own life experiences. E.g., Hank Williams, George Jones, Loretta Lynn, Johnny Cash.

Soft shell: General situation or specific situation stated in general terms; sets a mood; third-person voice, or if first-person, evoking feelings shared with the listener. Performers sing songs that fit their media persona as this changes with the musical fashions. E.g., Red Foley, Kenny Rogers, Dottie West, Alabama.

SONGWRITING

Hard core: Because their personal lives are often in the public eye, the best writers are either performers who tell about their own imaged life experiences, e.g., Hank Williams, Loretta Lynn, and Merle Haggard; or others who write lyrics tailored to the current imaged life experiences of a specific performer who makes the song her/his own, e.g., Willie Nelson for Patsy Cline and others, and Billy Sherrill for Barbara Mandrell.

Soft shell: Soft-shell artists are more likely to select songs composed by professional country music songwriters; e.g., Carson Robison, Felice and Boudleaux Bryant, Ben Peters, and Harlan Howard.

INSTRUMENTS

The signature instruments and styles change from era to era.

Hard core: Stringed instruments: fiddle, banjo, dobro.

Soft shell: Massed strings, ooh-aah vocal backing, swooping pedal steel, brass and woodwinds, synthesizers.

INSTRUMENTAL STYLE

Hard core: Rough, ragged, energized; backbeat guitar, bass, and drums; may musically refer to an earlier country style. E.g., Clayton McMichen referencing hoedown fiddle; Hank Williams using blues forms; George Strait referencing western swing; since 1975 artists may reference rockabilly. E.g., Hank Williams, Jr.

Soft shell: Smooth, harmonious, even-four or waltz beat. Often adopting recent pop song styles. E.g., Hawaiian guitars in the 1920s; crooning in the 1930–40s; swing in the 1950s; lush orchestrations since the 1960s.

SINGER'S ORIGIN

Hard core: Origin is stressed insofar as it is South, Southwest, farm or ranch (country, not city), humble beginnings, little education (education downplayed), or from a family of musicians. E.g., Fiddlin' John Carson, Bill Monroe, Loretta Lynn. Rustification may be augmented in image-making. E.g., Patsy Montana, Grandpa Jones.

Soft shell: Origin not stressed or tells of a conversion experience to country way of life. E.g., Ronnie Milsap, Kenny Rogers, Mary Chapin Carpenter. Soft-shell performers raised in the country music tradition, like Eddy Arnold and Bill Anderson, tend to stress their current refinement and note how far they have come from their youth of rural poverty. Anderson's "Po' Folks," for example, stresses wistful nostalgia for poverty origins and stresses how far he has come from them.

STAGE PRESENTATION

Hard core: Informal, friendly, accommodating, modest, including personal anecdotes about self and family; direct connection made with individual audience members; links to hard-core icons. In their stage banter about hunting, fishing, or housework, by their accent, vocabulary, grammar, and symbolically appropriate country roots, hard-core country performers establish their identity with the audience and suggest that they are no different from their own fans. As Alan Jackson has said of George Jones, "If you didn't know he was a star, you'd think he pumped gas somewhere." This "take me as I am, warts and all" stance has led some like Hank Williams, Jr., toward a surly stage presentation. Hard-country artists suggest that if they weren't performers they would be farmers, truck drivers, housewives, or hairdressers.

Soft shell: Formally packaged, distant, professional, unrevealing. Soft-shell county artists more often work, like pop artists, to distance themselves from the audience and then allow the audience to share an intimate moment with them. E.g., Vernon Dalhart, Eddy Arnold, Conway Twitty. Soft-shell country artists suggest that if they weren't in country music, they would be in some other aspect of the entertainment business.

PERSONAL LIFE

Hard core: Details widely known (even if partly fabricated) and often played out on stage; these artists "live the life they sing about." E.g., Hank Williams. George Jones and Tammy Wynette together and separately have sung about their troubled romantic life together. Jones has also capitalized on his own foibles in such songs as "No Show Jones," acknowledging his frequently being too drunk to perform much of the time for years following his divorce from Wynette.

Soft shell: Kept private as far as possible. Not played up in the music and career. Indiscretions and bad habits often covered in layers of hypocritical self-righteousness. E.g., Red Foley.

CLOTHES/HAIR STYLE

Dress codes vary widely from time to time, so it is difficult to characterize hard and soft clothing styles in general.

Hard core: Men tend to wear the currently appropriate version of hillbilly or western-style leather or denim outfits, while women may be dowdy, e.g., Kitty Wells; gaudy, e.g., Dolly Parton; or in-your-face sexy, e.g., Tanya Tucker.

Soft shell: Tailored reflections of the mature popular singer style of the time perhaps with an echo of the hard-core look of the time. For men these range from slacks and turtleneck sweaters, e.g., Eddy Arnold and Vince Gill, to formal evening wear, e.g., Jim Reeves. In the early 1950s, Reeves had dressed in cowboy outfits, but his big success began in the late 1950s when he switched to crooning and wearing formal wear. Other soft-shell artists, including Patsy Cline, also performed early in western outfits but switched to more urbane clothes as their soft-shell reputation became established. The clothes and hairstyling of women are much like those of the pop middle-of-the-road singer of the day. If present at all, western or hillbilly elements are muted and the look may be folksy, as with Emmylou Harris, Kathy Mattea, and Iris DeMent, but never folk. Dresses may be short or long as fashion dictates, pants suits tend to be tight. Hairstylings are often generous, bigger bouffants (Tammy Wynette), longer (Crystal Gayle), or teased out to form a mane (Barbara Mandrell, Reba McEntire), but they can also be very short (Lorrie Morgan). Overall, the focus, for women and men alike, is on what at the time is defined as sexy.

CAREER LONGEVITY

Hard core: Most, if not all, of career spent in country music because artists are committed to the field and, with the exception of gospel music, find it difficult to move into another form of music. More often than soft-shell artists, they die young, as the life lived catches up with the life sung about.

Soft shell: Soft-country performers may more easily come from or exit to popular or easy listening music. They are also more able to move into positions such as music producer or publisher.

Let me hasten to add that most expressions do not fit perfectly on one side or the other of the dividing line between hard core and soft shell. Think of Willie Nelson, the aging, long-haired redneck singing the sentimental pop ballad "Stardust," for example. The scheme just outlined is probably most helpful in highlighting differences in emphases and trends. It may also be used to show that a given expression is hard core in several of the preceding ways, but soft shell in others. Often it is helpful to compare an expression with others of the same time period. Comparisons over time must be made with care because the conventions of singing and image change. It is meaningless to ask: "Who is more hard core, Jimmie Rodgers, Hank Williams, or George Jones?"[18]

Why the Cycle of Hard Core and Soft Shell?

While hard core and soft shell are always present, one is usually predominant at any given time, and while their succession is not mechanistically determined, it is possible to suggest the forces—both aesthetic and commercial—that drive the dialectic.[19] The influences can be seen by briefly tracing the dialectic from the early 1920s to the late 1930s.

As was shown in chapter 2, it was the hard-core fiddlers and singers of racy and commentary songs who first attracted commercial attention in the early 1920s. The hard-core leaders included Fiddlin' John Carson, the Skillet Lickers, Uncle Dave Macon, and their ilk. Jimmie Rodgers was best able to fuse these hard elements in a more pop music package, creating a brief period of hyper-popularity for himself and the music.[20] At this point there were several forces that began the softening trend. First, aspiring artists, seeing the success of Jimmie Rodgers, began to copy him, but insofar as they were good copies, they appeared *less* authentic.[21] Second, the use of microphones facilitated the emergence of crooners and close-harmony groups. Third, the demands of 1930s-era radio advertisers, with their emphasis on clean family entertainment, purged the double-entendre lyrics and commentary songs while accenting sentimental and religious numbers.

If there had been journalistic commentators in the mid-1930s, they, like their equivalents in the more recent soft-shell turns of the dialectal cycle, would have bemoaned the "death of country music."

This atmosphere of soft shell was the environment in which Roy Acuff found immediate widespread popularity by accenting his neotraditionalism. As we have seen above, he offered a big, earnest voice singing old-fashioned songs while fronting a traditional string-band lineup, but he presented these in a form that worked perfectly both on a radio barn dance and on live show dates. Roy Acuff's hugely popular hard-core turn was answered by soft-shell artists such as Red Foley and Eddy Arnold, but it also opened the way for further development of what came to be called honky-tonk music, as we will see in the next chapter.

CONCLUSION

Part 3 of the book has focused on the 1930s era of the Great Depression, when country music was sustained and profoundly shaped by the opportunities and constraints afforded by radio broadcasting. We have seen the influence of the microphone in facilitating the careers of crooners and harmonizers, the role of radio sponsors in censoring the lyrics and shaping performers' deportment, and the influence of the migratory life in melding regional variations and rapidly professionalizing a generation of young performers. Finally we have outlined the dialectical interplay between hard-core and soft-shell tendencies which has served to continually revitalize country music.

The Evolving Hard-Core and Soft-Shell Look

G3.1 In 1937 the sharp-dressing, close-harmonizing crooners the Vagabonds (Harold Goodman, Dean Upson, and guitarist Curt Poulton), with their soft-shell sentimental songs, were the most popular artists on WSM's "Grand Ole Opry" barn-dance show.

G3.2 Roy Acuff and his band brought showmanship with their staged rusticity to the Opry in 1938, and when they dropped their more "pop" songs and concentrated on a hard-core sound and sentiment, they displaced the Vagabonds as the most popular act. Here the band is seen on the Opry stage with the program announcer barely visible above the stand on the right and the "Solemn Old Judge," George Hay, founder of the Opry, sounding his steamboat whistle. Acuff is on fiddle in white shirt and slacks while Lonnie "Pop" Wilson in checked shirt and false beard at the left. Pete Kirby (Bashful Brother Oswald), in a matching shirt playing dobro, has a tooth blackened, as does Rachel Veach, his stage sister. The bass player, Oral "Odie" Rhodes, the rube comedian, sports a beanie and painted freckles. Lewis Crook, with banjo in the left background, waits to perform with the Crook Brothers string band.

G3.3 Roy Acuff (with fiddle) and his Smoky Mountain Boys (and Girls) in a rustic setting.

G3.4 In this photo, taken on the same occasion as the prior one, it is clear that while Lonnie "Pop" Wilson is wearing hillbilly duds, old-timer makeup, and a false beard, the bandleader, Roy Acuff, has shed any semblance of a hillbilly outfit and is dressed in fashionable sportswear and a cravat.

G3.5 A young, open-faced Eddie Arnold in the casual outfit of the sort that would become an indicator of soft-shell performers down through the years.

Part Four

Making "Country" Reproducible

CHAPTER TEN

Honky-Tonk Firmament

Lives, Music, Lyrics

In part 4 I describe the changes in the music and in the ways in which it was made and merchandised that precipitated the final emergence of a field called "country music"—thirty years after the first commercial experiments in Atlanta, Georgia. Significantly, the five pillars of the emergent system were the same as those developed by Polk Brockman: record making, radio, touring, songwriting, and song publishing.

In this chapter we trace the emergence of western swing and honky-tonk music in the dance halls, roadhouses, and juke joints of the newly affluent working-class Texas and Oklahoma oil boomtowns of the mid-1930s, and we follow honky-tonk music through the post–World War II era, when, featuring new candid lyrics, it became the dominant form of country music. In chapter 11 we see how the honky-tonk image, creative songwriting, and sterling showmanship, punctuated by a tragically early death, fixed Hank Williams as the iconic representation of country music. Then in chapter 12 we complete the picture by seeing how a fully institutionalized system, increasingly called "country music" and self-consciously devoted to finding authenticity, finally emerged in 1953, the year of Hank Williams's death.

SOUTHWESTERN MUSIC NURTURED IN DANCE CLUBS

While the eastern musicians were evolving their hard-core and soft-shell musical styles shaped primarily by radio airplay, mid-1930s string bands in the Southwest found their music shaped more by the demands of playing in dance halls. These developments also took more hard-core and soft-shell forms which, in due time, came to be called "honky-tonk" and "western swing" respectively.

Dance Clubs

At a time when people in the rest of the fertile crescent of country music were suffering through the depths of the Great Depression and were able to afford few entertainments beyond that provided free over the radio airwaves, working-class people in the oil-rich boomtowns of Texas and Oklahoma, strong enough and willing to risk the danger, the dirt, and the smell, could get good jobs and, relative to their peers elsewhere, earn great amounts of money. As in all raw U.S. boomtowns, an array of entertainments sprang up, and many of these featured couple-dancing. With the repeal of Prohibition in December 1933, alcohol could be legally served and the number of clubs proliferated rapidly.

Three kinds of clubs can be distinguished: large dance halls featuring live bands and usually located on the outskirts of town which might, or might not, serve alcohol; roadhouses and honky-tonks serving alcohol and offering live dance music to attract drinking customers; and smaller drinking establishments featuring music played on a jukebox. In practice the difference between the latter two types was not great because roadhouses that featured bands might rely on a jukebox in off-hours, and joints that relied primarily on a jukebox for music might occasionally feature live entertainment.

Dance Halls Nurture Soft-Shell Western Swing

Like their Eastern cousins, the Southwestern performers played on the radio, but their live performances were not for communities that turned out occasionally to listen to their radio heroes or to take part in a periodic community square dance attended by people of all ages. The Southwestern boom-town string bands played at dance halls where singles and young married people paid to drink and couple-dance every weekend. A band that satisfied the dancers by including among its numbers the latest pop music could play at the same dance hall several nights every week and never have to travel great distances to a number of small towns, like performers back East. At the same time, these dance hall working conditions put a premium on keeping a perfectly regular dance beat and generating enough sound to be heard throughout the dance pavilion (Townsend 1976; Ginell 1994).

In the early 1930s public address systems were put in the large halls and ballparks where musicians performed[1] to help masters of ceremonies control the crowds and promote products, but these PA systems were quickly exploited by the musicians as well. With the amplification provided by microphones, singers could more easily be heard, and bands began to employ crooners who could sing in the relaxed pop style being made popular by Bing Crosby. Young dancers were particularly drawn to these handsome young band singers and to their songs of love.

Bob Wills, the grandson of an accomplished hoedown fiddler and son of a master string-band fiddler, was an architect of the "western swing" style that evolved in this special work context.[2] Working for Lee O'Daniel at Burrus Mills, Wills and Milton Brown experimented with using stringed instruments to duplicate the sound and feel of Dixieland jazz. As Wills's musical fortunes became more secure and he played ever larger dance halls, his band grew accordingly to create enough sound to fill the halls. When Wills left O'Daniel in 1933, his band numbered five, and later that year the number became seven, as electrified steel guitar and piano were added to the aggregation. Since a rock solid beat was fundamental to a dance band, Wills insisted that the piano, tenor banjo, guitar, and string bass all play on the beat. Finally in early 1935, Wills took the revolutionary step for a country music string band of hiring a Dixieland jazz-style drummer (Townsend 1976: 88–103). In the decade that followed, Wills and the other emerging western swing bands of the West and Southwest evolved a form that mirrored developments in popular dance band music while keeping a nasal tone with fiddle, steel guitar, and vocals that maintained the country music identity (Ginell 1994).

While western swing is most closely identified with Bob Wills, a number of people were involved in the evolution of the rustic hillbilly string band into the slick, polished, western-dressing, large western swing band featuring drums, brass, and reed instruments. The evolution of this sound can be traced from Jimmie Rodgers's white-blues recordings with jazz players, through Milton Brown's experiments in Dallas with crooning and what he called "country jazz." As we see in figure 10.1, a publicity photo of Milton Brown and his Brownies, they represented themselves in formal attire like any pop or jazz band of the day. The extensive work of Bob Wills in Tulsa, Oklahoma, which included dressing the band in western outfits (see gallery figure G4.1), evolved a decade later to the large soft-shell country sound exemplified by Spade Cooley's Los Angeles-based western swing band, which, with the addition of an accor-

Figure 10.1 Milton Brown (center), one of the architects of western swing, and his Brownies in their usual dance-band outfits, c. 1936

dion, sounded much like the middle-of-the-road pop song stylings of Lawrence Welk (Miller 1975; Malone 1985: 201; Ginell 1994).

Roadhouses Fostered Hard-Core Honky-Tonk Music

The patchwork of "wet" and "dry" jurisdictions created in the wake of the repeal of Prohibition fostered the development of a different kind of music. The clubs were called roadhouses because they were usually located on highways near city or county lines, where they tended to enjoy less police surveillance than clubs in the towns proper. Generally smaller than the dance halls, these roadhouses were primarily drinking establishments that provided live music to attract customers. Because patrons were loud and boisterous, and fights were frequent, the clubs were often called honky-tonks.[3]

Working in cramped conditions, the string-band musicians could not afford to increase the number of players, so they adapted by experimenting with every new development in the electronic amplification of instruments. It proved easier to amplify guitars than violins, and the electric guitar replaced the fiddle as the leading solo instrument. Acoustic guitar players, including Aaron (T Bone) Walker and Charlie Christian, began to tinker with electronic amplification by attaching "pick-ups" directly to their instruments (Malone 1985: 127), and by the fall of 1934, Bob Dunn, an accomplished guitarist and jazz trombonist, began playing a

Figure 10.2 A young Ernest Tubb shown here in Jimmie Rodgers's tuxedo, which, along with a signature guitar, had been presented to him by Rodgers's widow, Carrie. In the accompanying publicity, she said that she had chosen Tubb to carry on the Rodgers legacy.

guitar whose sound was heard directly through a portable PA system (Malone 1985: 157; Ginell 1994: 108–9). Within months many Texas guitarists, African American and white, were experimenting with playing "electric" guitars (Malone 1985: 157–58), and before long, electricians were tinkering with hard-bodied fully electric models (White 1991).

Roadhouse patrons were less interested in dancing than were dance hall audiences, so the evolving honky-tonk bands did not have to maintain a rock-steady beat. They could, therefore, rely on a bass and rhythm guitar and did not, like their western swing compatriots, add piano and drums. The photo of Ernest Tubb and his Texas Troubadours (gallery figure G4.2) shows this line-up, except that when this photo was taken in the 1950s, a snare drum had been added. The westernwear that typified the honky-tonk band is a far cry from the tuxedo shown in figure 10.2, which, emulating his hero Jimmie Rodgers, Tubb wore for his early publicity photos.

To entertain roadhouse patrons, honky-tonk bands offered a mix of fast instrumental numbers, slower dance numbers, and songs describing the life experiences of roadhouse patrons. In these increasingly personal and candid songs, instrumentalists moved to a supporting role, providing the context for the lyrics offered by the guitar-playing band-leader vocalist.

Thus the hard-core honky-tonk innovators, including Ernest Tubb, Floyd Tillman, and Al Dexter, were doing in the Southwest what Roy Acuff was doing at the same time in Tennessee, transforming the string-band sound to make it the complement of a featured vocalist. The sharp difference between Acuff on the "Grand Ole Opry" and the honky-tonkers is that while Acuff was changing the name of his band from the Crazy Tennesseans to the Smoky Mountain Boys and eliminating double-entendre songs from his repertoire to conform to the dictates of the conservative Opry radio program management, the Southwestern performers were crafting songs for honky-tonk audiences, songs that spoke ever more frankly of lusty love and its consequences.

THE RENAISSANCE OF RECORD MAKING

As we have just seen, the noise of the honky-tonk required that the band feature amplified instruments and sustain a high level of sound throughout each number. The records that bands made with this high-intensity electric sound soon outsold records made with the more relaxed string-band sound. Ernest Tubb's early recording experience provides a convenient case in point. His first few records, featuring acoustical instruments and Tubb singing in the style of Jimmie Rodgers, had only limited success, but this changed dramatically when, at the insistence of jukebox operators, he began to feature an electric guitar and recorded one of his own honky-tonk love songs, "I'm Walking the Floor over You" (Miller 1975: 226–27; Pugh 1996).

The Jukebox

"Juke joint"[4] is a name used in the Southeast for a small establishment like a honky-tonk, and "jukebox" is the name given to the automatic music-vending machines that small club proprietors placed in their establishments to supply music for their patrons. With the repeal of Prohibition in December 1933 there was a rapid expansion of clubs selling alcohol, and jukeboxes were installed in many clubs to provide inexpensive entertainment (Read and Welch 1959: 305–20). Most small club owners couldn't afford to buy a jukebox, but the machines were provided by syndicates of entrepreneurs who, in return, took part or all of the take from the boxes (Rasmussen 1994).

Jukeboxes used the standard 78 rpm records of the era, and the ever increasing number of jukeboxes created a great new demand for country music records. By the late 1930s as many as half of all country music record sales were for the more than 400,000 jukeboxes by then in use (Hurd 1940). Since many of these boxes were located in roadhouses and bars, upbeat songs of bravado and songs with explicit lyrics about love's laments proved far more popular than did either pop music offerings or the earlier styles of country music (Malone 1985: 153–54; Rasmussen 1994).

Independent Regional Record Companies

By 1940, there was a greatly increased potential market for honky-tonk country music records of a sort not then being played on the radio. But the dislocations caused by World War II, with musicians being drafted, a shortage of lacquer for making recordings, and in 1942–43 a protracted ban on any record making, disrupted incremental developments in the music and further increased the pent-up demand (Sanjek 1988: 217; Ennis 1992).

Taking advantage of a number of technical advances made during the war, and the availability of large numbers of young people with electronics experience gained in the military, entrepreneurs in cities across the country started record companies after the war's end (Gillett 1983). The best of these established direct ties with jukebox distributors and tried to make records that would garner heavy jukebox play.

The recording engineers found that the most popular records in the jukeboxes were "hot records," that is, they were recorded in such a way that the sound level was sustained at the same high volume throughout the song. Such songs commanded attention in the noisy honky-tonks. The made-for-jukebox hot recordings also sounded better than more balanced recordings when heard on the rapidly proliferating cheap personal radios. Thus as independent stations increasingly played phonograph records on the air and disk jockeys often became great promoters of (if not partners in) the local phonograph record companies (Escott 1991).

To produce hot records, the recording engineers had to continually change the volume controls during the recording process, and while this may now seem an obvious thing to do, it was anathema among the professional union recording engineers employed at the major record companies. The convention in recording then was to capture, as best one could, a "lifelike" sound that dictated setting all the microphone levels before recording began and then not touching the dials during the recording process.[5]

Another advantage that the small regional independent companies could have over the major firms was the more congenial atmosphere of their recording studios. From the earliest days, country music performers recording in New York, Chicago, and Los Angeles often complained about the cold, efficient recording environment in which they were treated at best as novelties.[6] The successful regional recording studios, such as those established by King Records in Cincinnati and later Sun Records in Memphis, provided a stimulating environment in which everyone was familiar with the music and worked together to produce a hit record (Rumble 1980; Escott 1991).[7]

The great competitive disadvantage experienced by the independent record companies was that they could not compete with the major firms in promoting their records or in distributing them quickly to the entire country music market. Many great songs of the decade following World War II first recorded on small labels were then "covered" by the major companies, and many artists who got their first break on an independent label moved to a major label after a successful record or two. For this reason the products of the independent record companies in the decade following World War II were numerically less important in the flowering of honky-tonk country music than were those of independent record companies in the success of rock music by 1955 (Gillett 1983; Peterson 1990; Ennis 1992). Nonetheless, their efforts to make records for the jukebox market, their exposing new talent, their forging links with the new breed of radio disk jockeys, and their experiments with more candid lyrics were essential to the eventual triumph of the honky-tonk style.

HONKY-TONK LYRICS: PERSONAL AND CANDID

Honky-tonk music evolved out of the hillbilly string-band music of the 1930s in the hothouse atmosphere of Southwestern roadhouses. Song lyrics were shaped by this atmosphere and by the changing larger world of which it was a part.

In the process, the honky-tonk lifestyle or worldview became dissociated from the roadhouse joint per se, and the image could be evoked without filling in all the details. Thus by 1938 Roy Acuff could sing about "Honky Tonk Mamas" in an updated version of the standard "Deep Elem Blues" about the hazards of the Dallas red-light district (Tosches 1985: 27); and Bob Wills could describe the remorse of lost love with a swanky western-swing beat through "Bubbles in My Beer."

Hillbilly Worldview in the Lyrics

Hillbilly song lyrics of the 1920s and early 1930s had been about finding and losing love, about the old folks at home, about tragedy, the travails of work, poverty, religion, violence, liquor, and a range of comedic themes.[8] The differences between men and women were seen to be essential, that is, rooted in biology. This view fit with the dualist view that divided all elements into good and evil, country and city, spouse and lover, poor and rich, then and now, sober and drunk, legal and illegal, South and North, West and East, home and road, day and night, God and human.

There had been many risqué songs in this mix of early commercial country music, but sexuality had usually been expressed euphemistically or was couched in cautionary ballad stories which, as in "Knoxville Girl," followed illicit love with pregnancy and the murder of the woman by the man. The most successful of the euphemistic sexual song performers in the 1930s was Jimmie Davis (the future governor of Louisiana) who recorded for RCA Victor such songs as "Tom Cat and Pussy Blues" which chronicles the heated interactions of "cock and pussy" (Tosches 1985: 123). Many such double-entendre recordings were made in the 1920s and 1930s (Tosches 1985; Wolfe 1993), but, as we have seen, risqué songs were excluded from performance on the radio.

Gender Relations in Changing Times

World War II gave most young working-class Americans, whether in the military, in defense plants, or in office jobs, an experience very much like that of the 1930s Southwest oil-boomtown residents, in that they were uprooted from their extended families and enjoyed the freedom to chart their own destinies. They found exciting though sometimes dangerous jobs, and earned far more money than they could have thought possible in the Depression-era conditions from which they came.

Women, as much as men, experienced exhilarating personal changes during the war, but their postwar experiences were quite divergent.[9] Men were expected to come home, marry, and better themselves with the skills learned in wartime or in the government-provided schooling offered to veterans. Women were legally required to give back to a man the factory or office job they had been encouraged to take during the war, and they were expected to go to a house that hubby would provide and to become full-time homemakers and mothers armed with all the labor-saving household devices flooding onto the postwar market.

Perhaps the single most telling statistic showing the social disruptions caused by the war and its aftermath is that there were more divorces in 1946 than in any other year. Men were distrustful of the women who had tasted freedom from the home and highly defensive of their male "prerogatives" in matters of employment, money management, and sex. Women, in turn, wanted to keep their new-found autonomy. For example, a poll made in 1945 found that 75 percent of working women wanted to keep their paying jobs, and a survey made the next year found that one-quarter of the women polled would prefer to have been born male. Few women were able to keep their jobs, but a third were married by age nineteen and had their first children by age twenty.

The popular psychology books of the time, from *Modern Women: The Lost Sex* to *A Generation of Vipers,* characterized women as being unmotherly. Instead they were found to be self-absorbed, predatory, money-hungry manipulators who emasculated their husbands and their sons (Bufwack and Oermann 1993: 166). In the decade following the war, popular male-oriented magazines from *Fortune* to *Playboy* blamed "modern" women for the country's ills, from family discord to juvenile delinquency, while at the same time merchandising products intended to help women emulate a female ideal based on the images of Marilyn Monroe, Lana Turner, Elizabeth Taylor, and Jayne Mansfield (Coontz 1992).

First-Person Honky-Tonk Lyrics

Gender roles and sexual relationships were continually being negotiated by the patrons of the roadhouses and honky-tonk clubs, and these posturing negotiations and laments began to enter into the lyrics of honky-tonk songs of the 1940s. Like popular music since the advent of the crooners in the 1930s, honky-tonk songs were expected to express personal feelings and singers were all the more attractive if they convinced their listeners that they personally felt the sentiment of the song. The honky-tonk was male turf and the singers were mostly men, so the lyrics represented the male side of the gender dualism.

"Honky Tonk Blues" of 1937, the first country recording to mention honky-tonks, describes the travails and temptations of the honky-tonking way of life. A number of songs such as Ted Daffan's "I've Got Five Dollars and It's Saturday Night," Tex Williams's "Smoke, Smoke, Smoke (That Cigarette)," Ernest Tubb's "Drivin' Nails in My Coffin (Every Time I Drink a Bottle of Booze)" express male bravado, and many, like Lefty Frizzell's "If You've Got the Money (I've Got the Time)," invite a woman to join in the revelry.

Borrowing from an advertisement for a brand of cigarettes, one hit song by Merle Travis viewed desirable women as "So Round! So Firm! So Fully Packed!" Many more songs chronicle in upbeat or sad tones the fickle, money-grubbing, or even treacherous characteristics of women. A sampling of hits popular during or just after World War II include the following: Al Dexter's "Pistol Packin' Mama" about a woman who enters a bar with murderous intent looking for her husband's girlfriend; Ernest Tubb's "Walking the Floor over You" about a woman who has broken her promise to return; "Whoa Sailor," Hank Thompson's song about a sailor who is rebuffed by a bar girl until he flashes a bankroll representing six months pay; Thompson's "The Wild Side of Life," about a married man who has tried in vain to keep his wife from going back to her earlier wicked ways; and Merle Travis's simple conclusion: "Divorce Me C.O.D."

Most men with the honky-tonk sensibility are not as upbeat over their woman problems as Travis. For example, in 1941 Ted Daffan got a "Worried Mind" from a woman who promised undying love, accepted his ring and home and took all the gifts he offered, but when he was down, just deserted him. Some years later, Daffan told Dorothy Horstman: "This song was an attempt to catch the mood of the people who haunted the little taverns where jukeboxes were the only source of entertainment. The title was suggested by a cheating girlfriend" (Horstman 1985: 194).

Two other hit songs of the war period written by Ted Daffan, "Born To Lose" and "Headed Down the Wrong Highway," express the honky-tonk sensibility of chronic defeatism and self-pity that begins with love problems and ends in total despair. This same geist can be traced in a number of other honky-tonk songs, including Ernest Tubb's "Wasting My Life Away" of 1941, Floyd Tillman's "It Makes No Difference Now" of 1938, and Rex Griffin's suicidal "The Last Letter" of 1937.

Explicit Songs of Infidelity

Even if women were seen by these men to be pivotal in life's travails, no commercially successful phonograph records were made through the whole war period which talked openly of the singer's infidelity, and the fate of "One Has My Name, The Other Has My Heart," one of the early postwar efforts in this direction, is instructive. Hal Blair, who wrote its lyrics out of his own experience, says that at the end of World War II: "I was engaged to a girl when I came home from overseas, and due to a misunderstanding, we were not married. I very brilliantly, on the rebound, married someone else. The story line is very simple and self-explanatory" (Horstman 1985: 204–5).

All of the major record companies rejected the song, but Eddie Dean, who wrote the song's music, was able to record it in 1946 on the fledgling West Coast label Crystal, over the strenuous objections of the company's owner. Although Dean promoted the song heavily, disk jockeys still wouldn't play it (Green 1976: 177). Then in 1948 the fledgling Capitol Records[10] released a version of the song by their singing cowboy movie star, Jimmy Wakely. It was an immediate smash hit and held the number-one spot on the country charts for eleven weeks, remaining on the charts for a total of thirty-two weeks.[11]

Based on the acceptance of "One Has My Name, The Other Has My

Heart," and while it was still on the charts, Floyd Tillman brought out a recording of his own "Slipping Around," which unblinkingly describes the experience of two married people carrying on an affair. His version charted on July 2, 1949, and four weeks later a version by Ernest Tubb charted and soon reached the top of the country chart. Seeing the early success of these records, Jimmy Wakely teamed with the popular band singer Margaret Whiting in a version that made clear that the partners in the affair shared both love and a sense of inconvenience about their legal predicament. The Whiting-Wakely version reached the country chart September 10 and was number one for seventeen of its twenty-eight weeks on that chart. The record also crossed over into the popular market, holding down the number-one spot there for three weeks.

With this million-selling record the informal taboo on candid lyrics about life problems dealing with sexual urges had been broken (Cherry 1985). But the flood of songs that followed tended to knit infidelity back into the web of dualistic sentiments mentioned above. Floyd Tillman began the process with his moderately successful 1949 follow-up song "I'll Never Slip Around Again" in which the singer's lover is now two-timing him, and he has resolved to go back to his wife, never to slip around again.

Women's Side of the Story

Excepting the Margaret Whiting duet on "Slipping Around" and her un-credited singing on "One Has My Name, The Other Has My Heart," no honky-tonk lyrics by women enjoyed national popularity until 1952.[12] When such a song did emerge, it fit exactly into the gendered dualistic worldview described above. The singer was not some hot ingenue on the periphery of the industry kicking to get in; it was Kitty Wells, an established artist who had long worked with her husband in a family band. She appeared on the Opry dressed in modest gingham dresses (see photo G4.3), and her producer was the rising talent Owen Bradley, who then also produced Ernest Tubb and Red Foley. Kitty Wells was at the center of the emerging country music industry establishment in Nashville, and there was no one better positioned to lyrically attack the honky-tonk male chauvinist predation of women.

The song had the strong title, "It Wasn't God Who Made Honky-Tonk Angels," but from all accounts it was not meant to be a feminist statement or open the female side of the dialectical opposition between the sexes. The writer, Jay Miller, explained that when "The Wild Side of Life" was a big hit in early 1952, topping the chart for fifteen weeks, he hoped to capitalize on it by writing a sequel or answer song, and "It Wasn't God" was the product (Horstman 1985: 224). Kitty Wells later said that since none of the songs from her first recording session with Owen Bradley had hit, she went in to record whatever he wanted just to get the money for making the session, and then forgot about it. Not till Hank Williams's wife Audrey told her several months later, did she realize that "It Wasn't God" was a hit (Bufwack and Oermann 1993: 178). And a hit it was, charting for eighteen weeks and topping the chart for six weeks.

The hard-core power of the first-person honky-tonk lyrics can be illustrated by detailing this pair of songs. "The Wild Side of Life" was written by William Warren and sung directly to his ex-wife (Horstman 1985: 227–28). As he explains in the song, she had asked him not to write or call, but he had seen her out having a wild time with men wearing suits and drinking expensive whiskey that he could not afford, so he decided to sing his thoughts to her. He rues the glamour of the gay life that has drawn her away from the only one who ever loved her, but he concludes that she'd never make a good wife, since he now realizes that God makes honky-tonk angels. In his hit rendition, Hank Thompson sings in a plaintive flat tone with sparse accompaniment that preserves the hatred, remorse, and sense of fatalism in the song's words.

In her response Kitty Wells maintains the same flat declarative tone. She explains that she is listening to the song on the jukebox and remembers when she was a trusting wife. Without detailing her own situation or directly blaming her ex-husband, she says that many married men act as if they are still single and that they are to blame for women going wrong. Refuting the ex-husband, she concludes with the title words of the song, "It Wasn't God Who Made Honky-Tonk Angels."

Minnie Pearl said that Kitty Wells always got a big response when she sang the song, but even when it was at the peak of its popularity she was not allowed to sing it on the "Grand Ole Opry" (Bufwack and Oermann 1993: 179). A number of songs followed elaborating women's points of view, but, as Bill Malone has noted, it was another decade before women would be allowed to stand alone as performers (Malone 1985: 224).

CONCLUSION

This chapter has traced the remarkable development of western swing and honky-tonk styles of music, which were born in the crucible of the working-class oil boom prosperity of the Southwest and spread to the rest of the nation along with the general economic prosperity engendered by the wartime production for World War II. The contribution of electronically amplified instruments was noted, and we traced the development of honky-tonk lyrics based in the dualities of good and evil. Increasingly honky-tonk lyrics became intimate, first-person confessionals, and they became rapidly more candid about sexual transgressions in the years following the war. As we will see in the next chapter, Hank Williams, who emerged out of obscurity in the late 1940s, became the leading exponent of these expressive personal songs.

CHAPTER ELEVEN

Hank Williams as the Personification of Country Music

Nothing in his life became him so much as the leaving of it.—William Shakespeare

When the twenty-nine-year-old Hank Williams died in the back seat of a Cadillac as he was being driven over icy roads toward a show date in Canton, Ohio, on January 1, 1953, his career and his personal life were in a shambles. Yet in the months that followed, the fans and the industry flacks transfigured Hank Williams. With the totally unprecedented fan response there was finally a definitive answer to the question posed back in 1923 by the music merchandisers—what do these people want? Now there was a single clear answer: In his work and his ways Hank Williams personified country music authenticity and was a model for those who followed.

It is not that Hank Williams invented anything new. Like all successful entrepreneurs, his achievements came from his unique recombination of existing elements. He did not develop a new style of music; his way of singing was not unique; his stage presentation, while arresting, was not original; he did not dress very differently from other country performers of the time; and his songs, while outstanding, did not depart stylistically from those of other writers of his time. The genius of Hank Williams was combining all the elements that we have discussed in the first ten chapters constituting country music in a way that bespoke authenticity.

We begin this chapter by looking at Hank Williams the performer, the songwriter, and describe the disastrous final year of his life, 1952. Finally we examine how in the early months of 1953, the timeliness of his untimely death was used to transform the fading earthly star into the icon of country music.

WHY HANK WILLIAMS? THE SENSE OF AUTHENTICITY

In many ways Hank Williams's origin and early career were like that of many other aspiring artists of the time.[1] And yet the stories about his coming-up and career served as a template for hundreds of later aspirants. In complaining decades later about the hard life of a hillbilly band, Waylon Jennings, for example, asked in song whether Hank Williams had really had to go through all the same experiences.

His Youth

Williams was born September 17, 1923, a few months after Fiddlin' John Carson cut that first commercial country music record in Atlanta. He saw the first light of day in a log house in Mount Olive West outside Georgiana, some sixty miles southwest of Montgomery, Alabama. His father was a World War I veteran who had been debilitated in France during a bar fight. Raised by his powerful mother, Lillie, Hank's earliest memories were of singing lustily beside her as she played the church organ.

A herniated spinal chord weakened Hank in his youth. It meant that he was unable to play boys' games and was unfit for most work. His mother packed peanuts in small bags and sent Hank to sell them on street corners. There he learned the huckstering ways of a street vendor, incorporating both fiddle and guitar-playing by the age of seven. Since there was neither a radio nor a record player in his home at the time, his musical influences were his mother's church organ and what he heard on the street around him. He learned to play from several old hoedown fiddlers, and from Rufe Payne, generally known as Tee Tot, an African American handyman and blues guitarist, whom Williams credits with being his greatest early influence.

The family moved several times from one town to another, with Hank continuing to sell peanuts, shine shoes, and play his guitar. Before he reached his teens Hank had made his regular spot the street in Montgomery right outside the studio of the NBC network affiliate, WSFA. After numerous entreaties, he was put on the air as "The Singing Kid" and played on the station off and on until at the age of nineteen he was kicked off the station for habitual drunkenness.

Performance Style

In his youth Williams honed all those skills and flaws that marked his "Grand Ole Opry" years of creative synthesis in Nashville. From the outset he had high expectations, telling everyone who would listen what a success he would be. With an ever-shifting aggregation of other young players he worked at developing a style grounded in the emerging honky-tonk band sound but accenting a heartfelt singing style like that of Roy Acuff.

Unlike Jimmie Rodgers, the Carter Family, Bob Wills, and Ernest Tubb, Hank Williams did not give life to a distinctive style of music. Rather, like Roy Acuff, he was distinctive in the intensity of feeling he put into each performance, and like Acuff, he sang with a high, piercing hillbilly voice unlike the sonorous western singers and leading artists of the barn dances of the early 1940s. As Williams told Ralph Gleason in 1952, "For drawing power in the South, it was Roy Acuff then God!! . . . He'd stand up there singing, tears running down his cheeks." Williams also mentioned the delivery of Johnny Ray, who had one huge hit in 1951, "Cry." "I like Johnny Ray. He's sincere and shows he's sincere. That's the reason he's popular" (Gleason 1969: 32).

Like Acuff, Williams learned to be a showman on stage, but their presentation was totally different. While Acuff would cry, clown, and orchestrate the actions of his band members, Williams, feeling the constant back pain, would lean forward into the microphone, knees bent, expressing sadness with his half-yodel breaking voice. Many report his ability to nod slightly, making direct eye contact with individuals in the audience so that each one of them was sure he was singing directly to them. On the up-tempo honky-tonk songs he would bend his knees, tap a foot, bounce, rock, and wiggle slightly. Something of this effect is captured in gallery photo G4.4, of Hank Williams on stage with Chet Atkins. Having seen nothing like this before in country music (although it was only a few years before Elvis Presley opened the flood gates), audiences went wild.[2] His performance gestures quickly became de rigueur for the spate of aspiring honky-tonk artists who followed him.

Westernwear

His older sister, Irene's, early memories are of Hank Williams dressing western and playing the cowboy. This was not unusual for any kid growing up in the mid-1930s. Like his peers he spent every moment of Saturday he could afford in the dark reaches of the neighborhood movie theater watching westerns. What is remarkable for an artist whose performance model was Roy Acuff, the "king of the hillbillies," is that he never looked the part of a hillbilly on stage. Hank Williams never ever appeared in bib overalls or anything remotely resembling a hillbilly outfit. Even in the early teen photo of him with his guitar during his street musician stage he is pictured in slacks and a wide-lapeled shirt. Like his model, Roy Acuff, Williams was a sharp dresser, but unlike Acuff, his stage out-fits were always western versions of the fashionable double-breasted suits of the day, cowboy hat, and fancy boots.

At least as early as 1938, he and his early co-bandleader, Hezzy (Smith) Adair, called their aggregation the Drifting Cowboys, and, even before he could afford to, Williams saw to it that the band always wore matching western outfits that complemented his own. The musical sound augmented the western look. Especially on his faster songs, as he readily admitted, Williams emulated the electric and steel guitar sounds of Er-nest Tubb's honky-tonk style (Escott 1994: 114).

Thus this rural Alabama boy whose outdoor recreations were hunting and fishing, rather than a westerner's riding and roping, and who could barely sit on a horse because of his back pain, early and completely em-braced the stage western cowboy look. In this, Williams was following the general trend of country music artists in wearing western outfits. He did not, however, wear a big hat and side arms and exaggerated outfits on stage like some of his contemporaries. His hats were more like the fedoras of the movie stars of the time, and like them, his clothes were cut to make him look "cool" rather than outlandish.[3]

Managed Career

While he occasionally showed good business judgment, Hank Williams had unbounded ego and generally focused on the felt need of the moment with scant concern for the consequences. Reading the biographical ac-counts and listening to the stories that circulate around Nashville, one finds the picture of a talented, streetwise, headstrong narcissist who at bottom was pretty lazy. The constant pressure to achieve came from those around him.

The accounts show that it was his mother, Lillie, who pushed Hank when he was young, often getting him engagements and collecting the receipts at the door. Repeatedly when he was down she cleaned him up and got him going again. His first wife, Audrey, who longed for a profes-sional career herself, fought with Lillie over Hank for eight years but played much the same role of pusher-minder-nurse. While these two women may have inspired most of Williams's songs of stark desperation, it seems very likely that the songs would never have been created if Lillie and Audrey had not repeatedly pushed Hank along.

If the prodding of Lillie and Audrey was necessary to making the Hank

Williams we all know, their efforts probably were not sufficient. Had Williams found a song publisher like Polk Brockman in Atlanta—and there were plenty of business people around in the late 1940s who focused on short-term profit—Williams's raw early efforts would have been bought from him, and, like most protean talents, he would have been left to fend for himself as best he could.

Luckily, Hank Williams met up with Fred Rose, himself a skilled pop and country songwriter working in Nashville as a song publisher in partnership with Roy Acuff.[4] Rose's prime talent was as a "song doctor," a person who could take the germ of another's idea or half-actualized lyric and turn it into a polished commercial song. From many years' experience working in Chicago, Hollywood, and Nashville, Rose had also learned that the best way to make money from music was not to go for a quick profit but rather to develop long-term mutually beneficial relationships with writers, performers, record companies, and even competing publishers. Like Ralph Peer, who two decades earlier had nourished Jimmie Rodgers, Rose helped Hank Williams with his songs and did all he could to protect Williams from himself.[5]

Expressing Dualistic Hillbilly Sentiments

While his stage outfit was western, Hank Williams never performed songs about the American West. Rather, his songs were set in the mode of candid, first-person lyrics, fatalistically accenting guilt and remorse in the honky-tonk style. In a way unique for the late 1940s and early 1950s, however, his repertoire expressed the full range of hillbilly sentiments from sacred to lusty.

Back in the 1930s the lusty songs and sentimental songs were generally performed by different artists or, if they were performed by the same artist, only in entirely different contexts.[6] The separation was maintained in recordings as well: artists who recorded both lusty and sentimental songs usually did so using two or more different names. Increasingly in the 1940s, however, artists performed both kinds of songs. One device was to end a boisterous show with a sacred song or two. But for most this was simply a show business formula, a way of signaling the end of a show and to make it more likely that patrons would leave peaceably and not fight in the parking lot.

Hank Williams was uniquely able to convincingly evoke in a single performance the dialectic in the epic struggle between good and evil. In the same set he could perform upbeat honky-tonkin' songs such as "Hey, Good Lookin' (What Ya Got Cookin')" and "If You've Got the Money (I've Got the Time)," guilt-drenched love laments including "Cold, Cold Heart" and "I'm So Lonesome I Could Cry," and sacred songs such as

"I Saw the Light" with equally convincing sincerity. "His heroes are undone by their own desires, tempted by illicit sex, plied with alcohol, rejected by a cooled lover, and left alone bathed in guilt and remorse, groping for eventual reunion with wife, home, and God" (Peterson 1979: 23). This mix of sentiments became the formula defining "country music" for the next generation and more (Ellison 1995).

Lived Authenticity: Writing Dualistic Lyrics

Hank Williams not only looked the part of a heroic western artist on stage, moved appealingly, and expressed the full range of hillbilly sentiments; he also wrote most of the songs he sang. Numerous songwriters had written a powerful song or two based on their own experience. Jimmie Rodgers, for example, had written to an unbelieving wife about how tuberculosis was killing him. However, more than any other songwriter, Hank Williams candidly detailed the highs and lows of his own personal life in a spate of good songs.

Consider the following songs he penned as a sequence in a single life: "Hey, Good Lookin' (What Ya Got Cookin')," "Settin' the World on Fire," "Baby, We're Really in Love," "Wedding Bells," "Crazy Heart," "Honky Tonkin'," "(You Don't Love Me) Half as Much (As I Love You)," "Your Cheatin' Heart (Will Tell on You)," "Honky Tonk Blues," "I Just Don't Like This Kind of Lovin'," "Why Should We Try Any More?," "You Win Again," "My Son Calls Another Man Daddy," "Take These Chains from My Heart," "Cold, Cold Heart," "I Can't Help It If I'm Still in Love with You," "I'm So Lonesome I Could Cry," and the song that was on the charts January 1, 1953, the day he died, "I'll Never Get Out of This World Alive" (McLaurin and Peterson 1992: ix).

Even Williams's novelty songs tended to be based in love's travails. For example "Howlin' at the Moon" details the experience of being besotted with new love, "Move on Over" is a man's request to share his dog's house, and "Kaw-Liga" is the lament of unrequited love between two cigar-store wooden Indians.

Counterbalanced with these earthy songs of love's course are somber recitations of life's travails (most recorded under Williams's nom de plume "Luke the Drifter"). These include jail-house laments such as "Lonesome Whistle," and religious songs such as "Pictures from Life's Other Side," "When God Comes and Gathers His Jewels," and the endearingly popular "I Saw The Light." More than any artist before him, Hank Williams exemplified in his song lyrics (as in his own brief life) the stark contrasts of hard work and dissipation, family loyalty and alienation, home and the open road, profound love and bitter hatred, good and evil, which characterized the dualistic worldview of country music fans. As Mo Bandy said in a song he made popular twenty years after Williams died, "Hank Williams, You Wrote My Life."

He Died Good

The final element in the answer to the question posed above, "Why Hank Williams?," is the imponderable influence of the timing and circumstance of his death that New Year's Day, 1953. As Don Helms, one of his Drifting Cowboy band members, has said: "Of course he died good. . . . Not old and ugly . . . Hank died right at the height of his career, so everybody remembers him when he was tops."[7] His biographer, Colin Escott (1994: 258), echoes and goes beyond this assessment. "It was a unique combination of circumstances that brought Hank Williams to the fore and allowed him to accomplish what he did when he did. . . . If he had lived a few years longer (even sober and productive), he would have become an embarrassment to the changing face of country music—too hillbilly by half. But in arriving when he did and dying when and how he did he became a prophet with honor."

THE DEATH AND TRANSFIGURATION OF HANK WILLIAMS

1952: Life Slipping Away

The year 1952 did not start well for Hank Williams. On January 3, Audrey threw him out of the house. She said he had shot at her, which he hotly denied, and he said she was being unfaithful, which she hotly denied. He went to Lillie's house in Montgomery and within days was taken to a local hospital after overdosing on pain pills. His pain had probably become more intense because on December 13 he had had an operation to fuse two vertebrae. Although he was supposed to be hospitalized for two months, he had checked himself out of the hospital after a week in order to be home for Christmas. Audrey chided him for checking out early, not staying in bed, and not wearing his prescribed back brace. In the ensuing fight Williams tried to throw a chair at Audrey, seriously aggravating his fused spine.

He was also soon back to performing, and although a companion was always sent with him to see that Williams got to shows sober, he regularly found ways to outwit his minder. Before a show in Richmond, Virginia, for example, he ordered tomato juice and asked for rubbing alcohol for leg pains. He vomited violently after drinking the mixture but later was given a beer to settle his stomach so he could perform. Existing in this macabre way he performed shows in New York, Boston, Texas, California, and Las Vegas, where his engagement was canceled after just a week.

He was so inept in his visit to the MGM studio in Hollywood that plans for moviemaking were scrapped.

Back in Nashville, Williams's personal life was in shambles. In January, Audrey's lawyers had served divorce papers and pressed to get an early judgment. Williams tried to convince her to come back—they had had an earlier divorce annulled—but this time Audrey was adamant. In the midst of this maelstrom Williams met Billy Jean Jones Eschliman at an Opry performance. Billie Jean had come to Nashville with Faron Young, then an aspiring young singer. Williams, the star and known to be a wild man with guns, simply said to the newcomer, "I'm taking that girl home," and in exchange gave Young a woman who had flown down from Pennsylvania intending to have a date with him. Within weeks Hank and Billie Jean were engaged to be married. Meanwhile, at what turned out to be his last recording session, another young woman, Bobbie Jett, entered the recording studio claiming that Williams had fathered her expected child. It seemed as likely that RCA executive Paul Cohen had fathered the child, but after some weeks' delay, Hank signed a formal agreement that said "Hank Williams may be the father of said child" and stipulated his contribution to the support of mother and child (Escott 1994: 219). Drinking heavily all the while, Williams was briefly committed to a hospital in Madison, Tennessee, to dry out.

After warning Williams repeatedly that he could not continue to miss performances, the "Grand Ole Opry" terminated his contract on August 11. Williams went beck to his mother, Lillie, and back to the "Louisiana Hayride" program that just three years earlier had been his stepping-stone to the Opry. He also went back to bingeing, songwriting, and engagements in small Southern roadhouses from Florida to Texas, and it is estimated that he made it to only half of the engagements. The one big show that he had after leaving the Opry was his October 19 pay-to-attend marriage to Billie Jean, depicted in figure 11.1, which, to swell the take, was staged twice at the New Orleans Municipal Auditorium. To anyone who cared to look it must have been clear that Williams's life was out of control.

1952: Career Sliding

Arguably Hank Williams had been the top country music act for three years, enjoying eight songs charted on the *Billboard* country music charts in 1949, 1950, and 1951.[8] His income was greater in 1952 than it had been in 1951 and in a class with that of Red Foley and Pee Wee King; it was exceeded only by Roy Acuff and Eddy Arnold.[9] Most of the increase, however, came from the royalties he was receiving from pop-artist recordings of songs he had written. Patti Page, Tony Bennett, Jo Stafford,

Figure 11.1 An estimated 14,000 people paid to attended the October 19, 1952, wedding of Hank Williams and Billie Jean Jones Eshliman. In seventy-four days he would be dead.

and Frankie Laine all scored pop music hits with Hank Williams songs in 1952.

It is difficult to tell how much Williams's personal popularity was falling in 1952, but there are a number of indications. He had six songs that charted in 1952, more than anyone except Eddy Arnold and Hank Snow. Yet he was no longer the hot young comer, and a number of young men were following his lead as a sensual performer and song stylist. Williams was most concerned about Lefty Frizzell.[10] Frizzell had seven charted songs in 1951, three of which became number-one hits, and in 1952 numerous handsome young men, including Carl Smith, Webb Pierce, Slim Whitman, Ray Price, Marty Robbins, and Faron Young, all tried to crowd into the niche Hank Williams had defined.

The *Billboard* columns devoted to country music regularly published the comments of disk jockeys on polls they had made of listeners' favorite artists. There was considerable regional variation in the rankings, but Williams was rarely mentioned first. An example is the national poll of fan favorites made by *Country Song Roundup*. In 1951, the first year of the poll, Williams was third behind Hank Snow and Eddy Arnold. In 1952 he was fourth behind Carl Smith, Hank Snow, and Lefty Frizzell (*Country Song Roundup* 1951, 1952).

The press seldom commented on his deterioration, and fan-oriented articles seemed to go out of their way to explain that the heartache he sang of did not come from his personal experience. An article in a 1950 issue of *National Hillbilly News,* for example, began "Got 'Lovesick Blues'?" No sir, not Hank Williams. . . . The real Hank Williams . . . is happily married to a beautiful girl and has two fine children" (Roe 1950: 51). Nonetheless, while his popularity with the fans held up better than he did personally, Hank Williams clearly wasn't the sensation he had been in the months after he first appeared on the "Grand Ole Opry" on June 11, 1949.

1953: The Biggest Year in Hank Williams's Life

One of his Drifting Cowboy bandsmen thought at the time of Hank Williams's death, "Well, this is the end of it. Before long it will all be gone and forgotten" (Rivers 1967: 2). But the reaction just kept building for months, reminding some of the popular reaction following the death of movie star Al Jolson (Gehman 1953b).

Williams's funeral was in Montgomery on January 4. Crowds estimated at between fifteen and twenty-five thousand tried to file past the open coffin. Many people around the country also wanted a remembrance of Hank Williams. In a *Billboard* story dated January 10, 1953, Frank Walker, president of the MGM record company for whom Williams recorded, reported that while an average of five requests per week were received for Williams's picture in the preceding months, MGM "was swamped with over 300 requests during the first three days following news of his death, local dealers were selling out of records, . . . [and] a flock of orders direct from customers had been received asking for a copy of every one of the records in the catalogue. One request which was accompanied by a signed blank check wanted three copies of everything issued by Williams" (Gehman 1953b: 25).

A follow-up article in the January 31 *Billboard* reported that practically all of the MGM distributors were back-ordered on Williams records, and in an attempt to keep up with the demand, MGM halved the number of scheduled new releases and operated its pressing plants around the clock. MGM also reported that the January requests for photos had passed the three-thousand mark. At the same time, the Acuff-Rose publishers reported that sales of Williams's song folios jumped from 700 to 5,000 a week, that many radio disk jockeys were block-programming Williams's songs in up to two-hour segments or playing one in each fifteen-minute segment, and that tribute records were beginning to be marketed (*Billboard* 1953a).

1953: Polishing the Image

Numerous people tried to take advantage of the interest in the earthy performer and turned him into a heavenly saint. Within weeks of the funeral, Williams's mother had commissioned an illustrated account of Hank's life entitled *Our Hank Williams*. Ignoring all his other problems entirely, Lillie attributed his death to his bad back and "the obsession to capture for himself and the world all the thousands of words and melodies that flew through his mind" (quoted in Williams 1970: 251). Lillie also converted her Montgomery boardinghouse into a memorial museum showcasing Williams's clothes, guitars, and guns. Within a week of the burial Audrey began the rewriting of history that would occupy her for the rest of her life. With Hank safely dead, she said, "I knew he would never hurt me or anyone else . . . . Everything I ever wanted or could desire I found in Hank Williams" (Escott 1994: 250). Within months Audrey and Billie Jean were each on the road performing as "*The* Widow of Hank Williams." Audrey clearly won the battle of the widows, inscribing her tribute on the back of Hank Williams's tomb, and portraying herself as the ever-devoted helpmate, while Billie Jean took the settlement money Audrey's lawyers offered not to act the part of the widow, and went off to marry Johnny Horton, a proto-rockabilly.

It wasn't just family members who worked to reconstruct the Williams image. Both the leading national country music fan magazines, *Cowboy Songs* and *Country Song Roundup,* devoted issues that appeared in February 1953 to Hank Williams, his life, his career, his song lyrics. They included written tributes from country music associates, lyrics of tribute songs, and the memories of those who had known him.[11] March 31 was established as "Hank Williams Day" for radio stations around the country (*Country Song Roundup,* 1953). By the end of 1953 at least sixteen tribute songs had been written, recorded, and commercially distributed (Metress 1995), several enjoying considerable commercial success. The rapidity and size of this outpouring was completely unprecedented and had its only parallel in the tribute songs released in the years following the death of Jimmie Rodgers.

The stark contrast between the myth of the fallen saint that was being created and insider memories of the man who had recently died is captured in the pronouncements of the manager of the WSM Artists Service, Jim Denny. Publicly he was grief-stricken and extremely laudatory of Hank Williams and his contributions (*Country Song Roundup* 1953: 9), but returning to Nashville from the funeral he is reported to have told his companions, "If Hank could raise up in his coffin, he'd look up toward the stage and say, 'I told you dumb sons of bitches I could draw more dead than you could alive'" (Escott 1994: 249). That sort of remembrance of Hank Williams didn't get aired in public. With Hank Williams dead, in 1953 it seems to have been in everyone's interest to accentuate the positive, eliminate the negative, and not to mess with anything in between.

CONCLUSION

In the months following Hank Williams's death, many in the industry wanted to distance themselves from the fallen stumble-bum, but the fan response was so overwhelming that once the first overblown round of eulogizing had subsided, they began to focus on his contributions, seeking out performers who could emulate him and songs like those he had written. By the end of 1953, as we will see in the next chapter, Hank Williams had become the implicit model of the authentic country music entertainer, and he was on the way to being the single most evocative representation of country music (Ellison 1995; Metress 1995).

Iconic Country

G4.1 Bob Wills (with fiddle, right center) and his band display the instrumentation and the westernwear of the western swing band of the early 1940s.

G4.2 There seem to be no surviving good photos of 1930s honky-tonk aggregations in action. Here we see an older Ernest Tubb and a latter-day spangled version of his Texas Troubadours, showing the instrumentation of the standard honky-tonk band.

G4.3 Kitty Wells in one of her gingham outfits, signaling that she was a good down-home gal even though she led the way for women singing candid songs about love relationships gone awry.

G4.4 Hank Williams, eyes riveted on the audience, knees bent, foot tapping, and leaning into the microphone, performs his crowd-pleasing magic with a young, admiring Chet Atkins looking on.

G4.5 Hank Williams "feeling his oats" in a backstage pose taken during a Thanksgiving 1949 tour of West Germany with tap dancer Thelma Acuff, daughter of Williams's early idol, Roy Acuff.

CHAPTER TWELVE

Creating a Field Called "Country"

While the huge, spontaneous outpouring of fan support for Hank Williams may have shown industry officials what most fans were interested in, having a model for country music look and practice did not mean that there was an organized system for reproducing his like. It had to be institutionalized. In this chapter we focus on the crisis in the mainstream pop music industry following World War II and the attempts to alleviate it. These efforts had the unintended consequence of more closely linking the country music business with the larger commercial music industry. We shall see how "authenticity and originality" became institutionalized as its core aesthetic, and why the field finally came to be widely called "country music" in 1953 just when the largest number of the genre's fans no longer lived in rural areas (Peterson and DiMaggio 1975). Urban migrant core fans needed assurance that they were still "country," and new, more cosmopolitan fans who were put off by the hillbilly stereotype embraced the positive image evoked by the word "country" (Peterson and Kern 1995).

THE FIELD IS INSTITUTIONALIZED

Discrimination against Country Music

In the 1920s and 1930s country music was thought to operate by its own rules for a distinct and esoteric market. While seen as an amusing curiosity by the pop music industry, it was considered largely irrelevant to their field (*Variety* 1929; Leamy 1929; Steele 1936). In practice, it was kept irrelevant, since country music and the artists who performed it were actively excluded from the pop music market.

This was accomplished in a number of ways, but one of the most blatant was to exclude country music songwriters from ASCAP membership. Thus country music songwriters could not receive compensation for the use of their work in public performances. In practice this also meant that their songs could not be played on network radio programs or used in Hollywood films (Ryan 1985). Even Gene Autry, the biggest singer/songwriter of western film songs, who applied for membership in 1930, was only grudgingly admitted to ASCAP eight years later. Even then he was a "nonparticipating" member, so that while ASCAP would collect fees for the use of his songs, he did not receive compensation for their use (Ryan 1985: 64). Pop songwriters who were ASCAP members were recruited to write the songs for most singing cowboy western films. The condescending attitude toward this work was clearly caught in the 1943 comment that "the composition of hillbilly music has always been regarded by Tin Pan Alley as a variety of unskilled labor" (*Time* 1943: 32).

In the 1920s and 1930s many American Federation of Musicians (AFM) union locals had not allowed country musicians to join because only "sight readers" were considered musicians, and the sounds that country bands produced did not fit their definition of "music" (Townsend 1976: 103). Then in the late 1940s many AFM locals moved to actively bar country acts from performing on the radio or at the major halls. For example, the local Cincinnati AFM local intervened when country music promoter J. L. Frank brought a package of "Grand Ole Opry" performers including Roy Acuff, Red Foley, and Ernest Tubb to Cincinnati in 1949. After the first night of the planned week's engagement the AFM local demanded that $1,000 be paid to the local in compensation for local musician's "lost income," since nonlocal union musicians were playing. They also specified that a number of local members equivalent to the number of the touring troupe be hired as "stand-ins." Since, as was customary, ticket prices were set low, the Opry group could not absorb these costs and canceled the rest of the week's engagement. The AFM local then claimed that the cancelation was due to poor attendance (Fantetti and Fantetti 1950). Concern over such practices came to a head that same year when a politically well-connected musician and major Washington, D.C., promoter, Connie B. Gay, quit the AFM, raised the specter of a federal government investigation of unfair labor practices, and moved to organize a rival labor union for country musicians

(*Billboard* 1949d). Following this, most AFM union locals moved more actively to enroll country music players.

Crisis in the Pop Music Industry

In the late 1940s the popular music industry trade press regularly reported that the business was in a state of crisis and that the highly profitable system for managing the introduction of new music, which had been developed in the early decades of the century, no longer worked as it should.[1] The center of the popular music industry was then, as it had been two decades earlier, a set of publishing houses whose associated writers produced songs for Broadway shows, the leading dance bands, and the major movie studios. Network radio was important because it provided the opportunity for the big-name bands to expose the latest songs to the public via their regular live radio broadcasts. Data compiled by Paul Lopes (1994) shows clearly why there was such great concern about the health of this system. From the mid-1930s through 1942 the big swing bands accounted for 75 percent of the hit records. But the figures show a dramatic decline thereafter, and by 1948 the big swing bands accounted for less than 25 percent of the hits.

A few hits that Lopes (1994) codes as country had appeared on the pop charts in earlier years, but in 1948 and in the five years that followed, country songs represented 4 to 7 percent of the market and, more significantly, included several of the biggest hits of the era. These conspicuous hits include "Pistol Packin' Mama," "Smoke, Smoke, Smoke (That Cigarette)," "(Ghost) Riders in the Sky (A Cowboy Legend)," "The Tennessee Waltz," "Mule Train," "Chattanoogie Shoe Shine Boy," "Goodnight Irene," and "Cold, Cold Heart." Several of these songs would not now be classed as country, but at the time they were seen as the most conspicuous members of a barrage of songs created outside Tin Pan Alley and a threat to the standard way of making hit songs (Churchill 1951; Ennis 1992).[2]

From the outside, the commercial music field looked like a welter of different sorts of firms and individuals acting on their own. Nonetheless their often contentious interaction was rationalized through the activities of a set of trade associations, including the American Society of Composers, Authors, and Publishers (ASCAP) representing the interests of song publishers and writers; the National Association of Broadcasters (NAB), representing the interests of radio networks; the American Federation of Musicians (AFM), speaking for the thousands of professional musicians; several associations representing moviemakers and distributors; and several trade magazines that facilitated coordination by rapidly exchanging information, most notably *Variety* and *Billboard*. The diverse and sometimes contending elements of the industry oligopoly had coordinated their efforts so well from the mid-1930s through the mid-1940s that industrial terms such as "hit tune factory" and "assembly line of songs" seemed appropriate and were widely used. As Neil Leonard correctly notes:

> This process of centralization gave a progressively smaller number of executives more and more control over the choice of material to be distributed. Owning or controlling affiliates in almost every phase of the entertainment business, the men in charge sought above all a standardized product which they could sell through every medium to as many people in as many places as possible. To be fully exploitable, music now had to be suitable not only for dance halls, the stage, and phonograph records but also radio and film. (Leonard 1962: 103)

This system depended primarily on the wages and performance rights fees paid for the music being performed around the country at dances and being broadcast live over the radio, but by 1947 "canned music," that is recorded music played on jukeboxes, at "sock hop" dances, by disk jockeys over the radio, and at social occasions in the home, was seriously eroding the employment of musicians and the sale of sheet music. The growth of recorded music was dramatic. In 1941 total record sales of all types of music amounted to $41 million dollars, but by 1947 sales had reached almost a quarter of a billion dollars.[3] Then even record sales turned down—17 percent in 1948 and another 8 percent in 1949. Industry pundits tried to identify the causes of the slide and to find fresh sources of musical inspiration that would bring the industry out of its slump.

Country Music's Role in the Crisis

Country music was cited on both counts. For example in a full-page, unsigned *Billboard* feature article of 1949 titled "Rustic Rhythm Reaps $$ Reward," the author begins by saying that the rise of country relative to pop music was due to the fact that the record companies were releasing more country records and spending more money to promote them. In addition, according to the author, movie studios were curtailing their releases of costly, big production films using pop music because of the growth of television, while ever more cheap-to-produce singing-cowboy films were being made. Also, country music was being featured on a large number of television variety shows at the expense of popular music. The author's conclusion that the success of country music would continue in the face of the pop music industry slump was based on a logic that seems to come out of the mid-1990s: he located the root of country music's success in excess federal government spending! (Following the press usage of the day, the author used the words "folk," and "rustic" interchangeably in referring to country music.) He found:

> A paramount factor in maintaining the steady climb of folk music, when all other branches of the music business are declining over the postwar years, has been the consistency of the farmers' incomes. As the federal program for subsidy payments to farmers has and will continue, rustic music has had a strong basis on which to base its expansion in all fields. (*Billboard* 1949c: 97)

Other articles of the time spoke of the spread of country music as if it were a disease that was infecting popular music. The following headlines from *DownBeat, Billboard,* and *Variety* exemplify their tone: "Hillbilly Boom Can Spread Like the Plague" (Emge 1949), "B'way Pubs Turn Song Revenooers But Hillbillies Get All the Gold" (Wexler 1950), and "Cornseed Crooners Reap B.O. Bonanza as City Slickers Lap Cider-Jug Tunes" (*Variety* 1951). In the industry B.O. means "box office," but a double entendre is suggested with a popular deodorant hand soap commercial of the day that referred to body odor as B.O.

Over the years there had been occasional national press stories about the money being made in country music. Representative examples include the 1938 *Colliers* magazine article titled "There's Gold in Them Hillbillies" (Crichton 1938) and *Time*'s 1943 piece "Bull Market in Corn" (*Time* 1943). Beginning in 1949, however, there was an explosion of articles in the music industry press showing how country music could be a source of profit for (or a part of) the popular music industry (*Billboard* 1949b, 1949c, 1950, 1953b, 1953c, 1953d; *Variety* 1949, 1951, 1953d; Wexler 1950; Sippel 1951). While some articles in the popular press continued to decry country music (Emge 1949; Churchill 1951) articles increasingly echoed the view that the country field was becoming integrated into the larger world of popular music (*Newsweek* 1949, 1952; McWethy 1951; Teeter 1952; Eddy 1952; Jarman 1953).

The contempt which most of those in the popular music industry held for country music was also being tempered. Trade magazine articles suggested with increasing frequency in the years following 1949 that it would be more profitable to incorporate country music into the larger commercial music business than to ridicule and try to suppress it. To this end the articles described how the country field operated and the opportunities that it held for wider exploitation.[4] While those in the world at large may still have held the music in low regard, by the early 1950s this strategy of co-optation had become the predominant point of view in the trade press. The 1949 *Billboard* feature article cited above on the profits to be reaped from country music was echoed in a 1951 *Wall Street Journal* article headlined "Hillbilly Tunes Boom Brings Big Business to the Melody Makers," and in a 1952 *Newsweek* feature "Country Music Is Big Business and Nashville Is Its Detroit."

The Five Elements of the "New" Country Field

As we saw in chapter 2, a five-element commercial country music system was developed in Atlanta by Polk Brockman in the mid-1920s.[5] This interdependent system consisted of performance on the radio, personal appearances in the area reached by the station's signal, songwriting, song publishing, and phonograph record making. But as we saw in chapters 3 through 11, different elements of this mix received more or less emphasis in different social settings over the next two decades. With Jimmie Rodgers in the late 1920s Ralph Peer relied primarily on record making, songwriting, and publishing. In the 1930s the focus in the Southeast was on radio performance and personal appearances, while establishments using jukeboxes in the Southwest meant that record making again became important in the late 1930s.

   In the late 1940s Hank Williams came to the fore as part of the reconstitution of the five-element self-reinforcing system developed in Atlanta. What is more, now there was an organized music industry that recognized the elements as a system, as is suggested in the title of a *Billboard* article of 1953 reviewing the country music business, "New Three R's Provide Success Formula—Radio, Routes, Records" (*Billboard* 1953e). The article went on to explain that songwriting and publishing were fundamental to the commercial music business as well (See also *Billboard* 1953b, 1953d; Denny 1954).

   If this system was a revival, it was also new in an important way because one element—radio—had been fundamentally altered by 1953. Artists no longer had to play live over the radio to gain the name recognition that would enable them to make money in live performances. Now prospective artists gained recognition by having their recordings played by radio disk jockeys (Sippel 1951). Thus by the 1950s aspiring artists needed to have their records become successful in order to raise their performance fees.[6]

   Through the 1930s country music records enhanced reputations more than they directly augmented incomes.[7] In 1953, and for another quarter of a century, money from live performances remained the prime source of income for country music performers, but money from record sales was growing in importance and, following the success of Hank Williams, records began to make considerable amounts of money for songwriters as well.

Linking Country with the Popular Music Industry

The commercial country music field that began to develop in the 1920s was distinct from the pop music market, and, as we have seen, owing in large part to the prejudices of those in the popular field, it was thought of as operating in a totally different way. Though the aesthetic and sound of country and pop *were* different, a number of forces conspired to make the industries that produced them operate in much the same ways. Increasingly shared technologies, organizational structures, legal constraints, and marketing strategies insured what Paul DiMaggio and Walter Powell (1991) call an "institutional isomorphism" between the pop and country fields.

With the 1940s crisis in popular music, deliberate efforts were made to ensure that the country and pop fields could be directly coordinated, and as Philip Ennis (1992) has clearly shown, the development of reliable information on the relative success of newly released phonograph records in the form of the weekly "record charts" published by *Billboard* magazine and others gave everyone concerned a way of "understanding" country music. Now, for the first time, a person did not need to like country music or even to have heard particular songs or artists to evaluate their market potential. They could simply turn to the weekly charts to infer trends. And the trade papers were important not simply for the charts they developed at this time. Their editorials and news stories (some of which are cited in the chapter on Hank Williams and here), together with the charts, as Anand and Peterson (1996) argue, created a web of information that not only facilitated isomorphism but *constituted* the commercial music field, as those in the system increasingly based their actions on the news reports and chart data they provided.

The most important specific point of articulation between country and pop—clearly illuminated by the charts—was the use of songs written for the country music market that, when sung by pop artists, helped revitalize the popular music business. "Pistol Packin' Mama," sung by Bing Crosby and the Andrews Sisters, led the way in 1943, followed by "Chattanoogie Shoe Shine Boy" sung by Crosby, Phil Harris, and Frank Sinatra in 1950;[8] and the biggest-selling song of 1951 in the pop music field was, according to Russell Sanjek, "the most successful song in 20 years," "The Tennessee Waltz" sung by Patti Page.[9] That same year, the Hank Williams song "Cold, Cold Heart" sung by Tony Bennett topped the pop charts for six weeks, the first of a set of songs by Williams to be major hits for popular music artists.

One of the pop writers recruited in 1938 to write songs for Gene Autry western films was Fred Rose, who, as we have seen, later settled in Nashville, established a country music publishing firm, and was instrumental in developing the songwriting abilities of Hank Williams. In switching his membership from ASCAP to its newly founded rival songwriters' collection agency, Broadcast Music Incorporated (BMI), Rose also helped to break the stranglehold on songs that the few largest ASCAP publishers enjoyed in the 1930s and early 1940s.[10]

The success of Hank Williams's songs on the popular music market at just this time was not an isolated phenomenon. As Ennis (1992) has carefully shown, by the early 1950s the pop, black-oriented rhythm and blues (R&B), and country music fields were coming to operate in much the same ways, so that it was relatively easy for songs (and less frequently artists) to "cross over" from one sector of the industry to the others. For example, in 1950 "Goodnight Irene" was a huge hit in the pop market as recorded by Gordon Jenkins and the Weavers, and within weeks cover pop versions were out by Frank Sinatra, Jo Stafford, and Dennis Day. Within two months the song had become a number-one country hit as performed by Red Foley and Ernest Tubb, and a month later it was a hit on the R&B charts in a version sung by Paul Gayten (Ennis 1992: 204). "Goodnight Irene" was one of the huge hit songs of the period—the *New York Times* estimated that in October 1950 it could be heard 1,400 times a minute across the United States (Wolfe and Lornell 1992: 257)—and was significant in another way because, like "Tennessee Waltz" and "Chattanoogie Shoe Shine Boy," the other monster hits of the time, it was not written or published by Tin Pan Alley people. "Irene" had been written by a man who had died the year before—African American "folk" singer Huddie Ledbetter, who performed as Leadbelly.

INSTITUTIONALIZING AUTHENTICITY

The Search for "Authenticity and Originality"

Back in the 1920s, Ralph Peer had searched for performers who were both "authentic" and "original," and in the 1930s Fred Rose was impressed with Roy Acuff because he would mist over in tears while delivering a sad song, but in the 1950s "authentic" and "original" became the key words used first by writers and then by business people generally in defining the country music field and in evaluating both artists and songs.

The best indication that this credo of country music authenticity was not simply huckstering hyperbole but explicitly shaping day-to-day decisions in the country music field comes from an article in the December 5, 1953, issue of *Billboard* reporting interviews with nine executives representing all of the major record companies then producing records for the country market. Among other things, they were each asked how they went about choosing new artists. In the one- or two-sentence answers that are reported, three actually used the word "authenticity" and two more used the phrase "the spirit of country music" or "sectional popularity," implying authenticity. Two others said "sincerity," and the last two used a term seemingly at variance with authenticity, that is "distinctive" (*Billboard* 1953h).

When the producers were asked how they chose new songs, the criteria seemed to shift somewhat. One used the word "authenticity"; one let the artist choose the material (presumably because an authentic artist will choose appropriate songs); three used the word "story"; and the others used a combination of the words "original," "fresh," or "different" (*Billboard* 1953h), and as we will see in the next chapter, these words are often used to indicate a performance that is authentic rather than a copy or fake.

Putting these statements about the desired qualities in a new artist together with those about the qualities of a desired song, we see that Ralph Peer's strategy, enunciated back in the 1920s, to seek authentic talent with original material had become the institutionalized practice of the people choosing who would make country music records.

Authenticity as Cliché

General-interest magazine writers in the early 1950s also characterized country music and its producers as unaffected and genuine. A 1952 *American Magazine* article on the "Grand Ole Opry" titled "Hillbilly Heaven," for example, notes that "the show retains an authentic backwoods flavor because it has neither phonies nor fakers" and goes on to say that while all of the big acts are too busy touring to work a farm, "every one of them owns a dirt farm and personally oversees it" (Eddy 1952).

Writing for the *New York Times Magazine,* Allen Churchill was more sensitive to authenticity being a contrivance. Noting that the biggest hit out of Nashville was sung without a discernible accent over a background that was as much pop as it was country, he continues:

> One thing calculated to enrage a country music addict is the suggestion that Nashville music is not as authentic as any dug up by the Weavers (the folk group that had a huge hit with "Good Night Irene")

simply because it is not as old. Says one Nashvillite: "people who write our songs were born right in folk-music territory. . . . The music they write is as authentic as any written hundreds of years ago. They capture the taste and depth of such music, and an honest and authentic hillbilly song, invented today, is still an authentic folk song." (Churchill 1951: 36)

THE NEW FIELD FINDS A NEW NAME: "COUNTRY MUSIC"

Interestingly, the final piece to fall into place in the institutionalization of the genre was the name of the field itself. While we have used the word all along, it was not until 1953 that "country" became the term generally used to define the field. And the inadvertent help of Senator Joseph McCarthy turned out to be crucial in determining which word would be chosen, as we will see.

Multiple Terms for Overlapping Fields

Back in the 1920s, people across the country played fiddles and an assortment of other instruments for dances and to accompany their singing, but there was no one distinct country music genre of song.[11] Insofar as labels were applied, they were functional, referring to the use made of the music (dance music, church music, fiddle contest, play songs, lullabies) or they were structural, referring to the form of the song (ballad, broadside, waltz, and the like).

Promoters went along with these practices in advertising events, and radio broadcasters like George Hay established the generic term "barn dance" to refer to the mix of genres that was heard on their rural-oriented variety radio shows, including the "National Barn Dance" and the "Grand Ole Opry." Record company executives, however, had the special problem of deciding how to classify the records in catalogues of releases and in setting up racks in their retail outlets. The stream of records we have been examining here—records featuring unschooled performers—began to be released in 1923, and in hindsight it would have been easy to coin a single name for them. At the time, however, there was a complex jumble of releases that might fit in one section or another depending on how the categories were drawn.

The historic first release by Fiddlin' John Carson, "The Little Old Log Cabin in the Lane," in 1923 was simply placed in Okeh Record Company's "Popular Music Series," which included records that were identified as "dance band," "sacred," "Hawaiian," "Broadway tunes," "novelties," "instrumentals," and "standards." With the rapid increase in the number of Okeh releases of all sorts, and Ralph Peer's desire to target the expanding new line of records, by late 1924 they were being listed separately as "'Old Time Tune' Records." The other record companies also categorized the music they were releasing to compete with Okeh. That year the Victor Talking Machine Company released a brochure announcing its new line of records featuring "Olde Time Fiddlin' Tunes," and Columbia Records released a booklet listing its "Familiar Tunes on Fiddle, Guitar, Banjo, Harmonica, and Accordion." The booklet did not define the genre or suggest its boundaries except indirectly, for it was said to include the songs and artists "whose names are best known where the square dance has not been supplanted by the fox-trot" (Quoted in Green 1976: 215). The fox-trot was the hot youth dance style of the time, but beyond implying generation, was this reference to a place also intended to suggest heartland not urban, white not African American, South not North, or ordinary working people not sophisticates? As we have seen in chapter 4, the record company promotion departments did not have a clear idea about the sources of the newly discovered interest in this music and so found it easiest to characterize the audience for the music negatively as not being intended for the "fox-trot" kind of person.

Differentiation from "Race Music"

Each phonograph record had several pieces of information printed on its label. In addition to the title of the song and the name of the performer, phonograph records were given a unique alphanumeric designation, and record companies used these designations to categorize records into distinct sets. These categories, in turn, were used to group records in media advertisements and on retail store displays. In time everyone in the trade came to identify song styles and artists by the series in which their records appeared.

All the recordings in the amorphous Columbia Records category described above, for example, were placed in its 15000-D series. If this category was musically heterogeneous, many of its number sounded much like recordings in the concurrent and equally heterogeneous 14000-D series. Virtually all the artists whose recordings were in the 15000 series were white, while those in the 14000 series were African American. Thus what determined the inclusion on one list rather than the other was the race of the performer, more than the sound of the music. Victor and the other record companies also grouped recordings by the race of the performer.

All of the prominent A&R men recording country music also recorded black artists, and it is not clear who dictated the differentiation at Columbia Records, but once instituted, people became sensitive to its connotation. The blues-singing white Allen brothers from Chattanooga, Tennessee, for example, threatened to sue Columbia for $25,000 because one of their records was placed in both the 14000 series and the 15000 series (Wolfe 1993).

By differentiating the music according to the race of the performer, the early record companies facilitated the bifurcation of the large, amorphous musical stock that was widely shared, to use the phrase of the Columbia Records booklet quoted above, "where the square dance has not been supplanted by the fox-trot." This is not to say that the creation of the racially separate categories of records *caused* the splitting in two of the common reservoir of music. Rather it facilitated a process of segregation that was already taking place. The music industry officials were following the practice of the spreading Jim Crow laws of the time that were pressing segregation down the social-class scale and outward from the cities into ever smaller towns where contacts between the races had been more informal and their cultural sharing less self-conscious (Russell 1970; see also Otto and Burns 1974; Malone 1979; Cantwell 1984).

To see the affinities between the music performed by whites and blacks one need go no further than the recorded work of Jimmie Rodgers—the father of "country" music. Many of the most popular pieces he performed were "blues" and some were "jazz" (Porterfield 1992). The similarities of musical styles is further suggested by the fact that African American string bands such as the Mississippi Sheiks were sometimes listed in the "Old Time" catalogues, and whites appeared in categories listing primarily African Americans (Otto and Burns 1974).

The record companies called the secular music that blacks recorded "blues," and later in the 1920s "race" music, a term which was singularly convenient from the racially segregated merchandiser's point of view. First, the term was widely used by the African American press in the mid-1920s as a positive term. To say a black man was a "race man," for example, was to say he took pride in his African American heritage (Green 1972: 36). Second, it was a convenient way of bracketing all popular music recordings by black performers irrespective of their musical style.

The Name "Hillbilly"

The record companies searched for a single convenient designation for the cognate records made by white performers. Ralph Peer had a hand in making the designation "hillbilly." In 1925 he was recording a group, and after the session asked them for their group name. They had none and the leader answered, "We're nothing but a bunch of hillbillies from

North Carolina and Virginia. Call us anything." Peer called them the "Hill Billies" (Green 1965: 213). Their music was well received, and in short order magazine articles began referring to "hillbilly music" as a generic term. Performers began to use the term to refer to themselves and their music, but this was often done with some reticence because, in popular parlance, the word had been a term of derision. Seeing that record buyers and concertgoers embraced the term without embarrassment, by 1930 the record companies and others in the business used the term "hillbilly" as the generic designation for the field.

Like the term "race," "hillbilly" was a very useful term. Its use did not rule out any form of music, but could be used to refer to any music performed by a "hillbilly" performer. Ideologically it served as a twin-edged distinction in that it was not actively resisted by consumers or performers (in the 1930s), and at the same time it carried a clearly negative connotation for many in the popular music industry as well as for the national press and its readership.

Seeing the pejorative connotation given the term, some connected with country music chafed at the use of the term "hillbilly." In the years that followed, Bradley Kincaid, the college-educated "National Barn Dance" and "Grand Ole Opry" performer, often spoke out against the use of the term (Green 1965), as did George Hay, who, ironically, as the impresario of the "Grand Ole Opry" had done so much to shape the hillbilly image (Hay 1945). In the 1930s and early 1940s a number of the rising artists, including Bob Wills (Townsend 1976), Johnny Bond (Bond 1976), and Ernest Tubb (Pugh 1996), tried to dissociate themselves from the word and its negative hayseed connotations.

That "hillbilly" did not wear well as the country music industry began to consolidate can be seen from the following statement in an August 3, 1946, open letter published in *Billboard*. Addressing "Mister Advertiser, Radio Agency and Program Director," country music publisher Fred Rose wrote a five-paragraph request that those in the entertainment business keep an open mind to what was being derisively called "hillbilly" music. He said it was genuine "folklore" created by and for "good American folks" who represented 75 percent of the U.S. population, "people who are your potential customers."

In the late 1940s with the greatly increasing interest in country music, the term "hillbilly" was used or avoided in the press *because of* its negative connotations. The jazz-oriented magazine *DownBeat*, for example, gleefully used the term in its 1949 report of alarm concerning the music's rising popularity titled "Hillbilly Boom Can Spread Like the Plague" (Emge 1949). Those writers who avoided the term searched for another to take its place. But if "hillbilly" was no longer politic or appropriate, no other single word immediately found acceptance. In the years from 1949 through 1953 a number of words were tried and often several of them were used in the same brief article. Pieces appearing in *Billboard* show this shift clearly. The 1949 articles all use the term "hillbilly" and sometimes other flip designations such as "oaters" and "oatunes" (*Billboard* 1949a, 1949b, 1949c, 1949d).

A 1950 *Billboard* article uses the term "hillbilly" in a snide way (Wexler 1950), but in another *Billboard* article of the same year the term "folk" was used to refer to the field (*Billboard* 1950). As if to cover all bets, this brief article, like most others of that year and the next two, used a large number of terms interchangeably in referring to the music, its practitioners, and its audience. In addition to "folk," the article used "rustic," "country," "hillbilly," "hillbilly and cowboy," "hillbilly and western," and "western and hillbilly." This profusion of terms was also evident in the pages of the fan magazines. In a single *Country Song Roundup* column, for example, "Grand Ole Opry" stalwart Pee Wee King uses "folk," "country," "country and western," "western and country," and "hillbilly" (King 1952). By 1951 "hillbilly" was sometimes abbreviated as "h.b." in *Billboard* (Sippel 1951). This usage, like the term that was coming into common usage in referring to the music market of African Americans, R&B (for Rhythm and Blues) had the great advantage of being brief. It had the disadvantage of retaining the "h" word.

"Folk Music," Red Scare, and Calling It "Country"

In 1950 the "folk group" called the Weavers sold over two million copies of their smash hit record, "Goodnight Irene," and between 1950 and 1952 they had nine more songs on the *Billboard* pop music charts. In the aura of this huge success the term "folk" was being used by many of those involved in the country field (including Hank Williams), by the trade press, and in advertisements for the music. It had also gained favor in the fan-oriented press, including the magazine called *Country Song Roundup*. "Folk" was desirable for several reasons. This one short word could be used elastically to include diverse varieties of music from bluegrass to movie western songs, and from honky-tonk to country gospel. It also had the clear advantage of implying a connection between current product and innumerable works that had come before, and, above all, it suggested authenticity (Churchill 1951: 36). Why then didn't this convenient, respectable, and symbolically convenient four-letter word stick as the name of the field?

Credit Senator Joseph R. McCarthy and the wave of anti-Communist hysteria that he rode to political prominence. McCarthy tainted the word "folk" by associating it with "Communist." He did this by attacking the

Weavers "folk" group as Communist sympathizers and summoning its most prominent member, Pete Seeger, to testify before his Committee on Un-American Activities (Wexler 1993: 66). Overnight the word "folk" was dropped from contention. In 1953 it was no longer used in the trade press, the fan magazines, or in advertisements for country music.

"Folk" was out and the word "country" was simply dropped in its place.[12] Along with many other terms, it had been used in the trade press for some years, but by December 5, 1953, the date of a forty-eight-page, advertisement-adorned special *Billboard* section devoted to the music, the term "country" is used virtually to the exclusion of all others (*Billboard* 1953d, 1953e, 1953f, 1953g, 1953h; Sippel 1953). The unsigned lead editorial of the section uses the term "folk" only in recalling the pioneering work of Ralph Peer and Jimmie Rodgers as the progenitors of a "growing folk tradition." Otherwise the article refers exclusively to "country" music, calling it "our native art [whose] inspiration springs from the heart of a nation" and invites readers to pay more attention to "this multi-faceted show business category which now constitutes one of the bright ornaments" of the entertainment business (*Billboard* 1953d). Thus the leading trade magazine of the industry dubbed the music and its makers "country"[13] and acknowledged their enterprise as an important element of the commercial entertainment industry.[14]

Forging a Collective Memory

One of the best ways to show that a field exists is to construct its past, and such efforts went forward on several fronts. Symbolically relating root to branch, *Billboard* published in the December 5 section devoted to country music an "Honor Roll of Artists" who had been selected by polling the "country music disk jockeys of America." The eight include "the father" Jimmie Rodgers, the recently martyred "son," Hank Williams, and six living performers: Roy Acuff, Eddy Arnold, Red Foley, Carl Smith, Hank Snow, and Ernest Tubb (*Billboard* 1953i). A number of alternative lineages were proposed in succeeding years, leading to the construction of a Hall of Fame that helped to consolidate a single orthodox pantheon of significant contributors to the development of country music.[15]

Talking daily to a mass audience, the leading disk jockeys of the mid-1950s did a great deal to facilitate the creation of a collective memory of a music with deep roots. Shedding the "Uncle Hayseed" image that many of the deejays affected in the 1940s, the rising generation of professional country music deejays talked to their listeners in a relaxed, knowledgeable tone of voice about the music.[16] Showing great enthusiasms for the work and familiarity with the performers, they introduced new records by linking the artist, the song, or the rendition to earlier country music works, and they helped to situate the current releases in the evolving country tradition by playing a good number of older recordings which complemented the current releases. Finally, the deejays tracked the local performances of groups so that fans could know what was happening locally in the world of country music. Thus this first generation of professional country music deejays, by focusing on the new releases and their links to the growing tradition, worked out the ways of presenting country music records on the air that got across the emergent credo of country music—"authenticity and originality" (Peterson 1978).

The field-defining strategy of exposing radio audiences to the diversity of musics that could be grouped under the emerging "country" umbrella is suggested by Philip Ennis's 1952 interview with one of these new professional country music deejays in Memphis:

> I use top hillbilly records and some western. As a whole about 20 per cent of the true mountain type, Bill Monroe. That Kentucky kind is the "countriest" with hymn, semi-religious, and more of folk music. Then about 10 per cent of the Western kind, which is like pop in such people like Pee Wee King and Spade Cooley. The rest, about 70 per cent is Nashville, the cross between Kentucky and Western. (Ennis 1992: 169)

The Field Forms a Trade Organization

1953 saw the transfiguration of Hank Williams into an icon and the consolidation of the newly defined field of country as a regular part of the commercial music business, but it was also the founding year of two further field-defining events that were to be annually renewed, the country music disk jockey convention and the memorial celebration of Jimmie Rodgers as the father of country music.

First, on May 26, 1953, the twentieth anniversary of Jimmie Rodgers's death, there was a memorial celebration attended by 30,000 people in his hometown, Meridian, Mississippi. At this event most of Rodgers's famous songs were performed by leading artists of the day, including Roy Acuff, Ernest Tubb, Bill Monroe, Webb Pierce, and Hank Snow, who all acknowledged the "father of country music." Widely noted in the press (*Newsweek* 1953), Jimmie Rodgers and his contributions in the early days of country music were celebrated in a special section of *Billboard* of May 16, 1953. This memorial signaled the beginning of the formal construction of roots for the newly designated county music field.

Second, in 1953 the first Country Music Disk Jockey Convention was convened by the WSM and Opry management at the time of the annual

October celebration of the founding of the "Grand Ole Opry" (*Variety* 1953c; *DownBeat* 1953).[17] Meeting in Nashville, this gathering became an annual event for all elements of the consolidating country music industry. They came together from all over the country to talk over common music programming problems, compare promotional techniques, swap job news, listen to young talent, preview forthcoming record releases, and briefly enjoy the largess of record company promoters. In a few years this grouping became a full-fledged industry trade association under the rubric of the Country Music Association.

CONCLUSION

In this chapter we have shown that in 1953, the year of Hank Williams's death, a number of efforts and trends came to fruition institutionalizing the field that was coming to be called "country," and fixing its ethos in "authenticity and originality." Few, if any, in 1953 had the sense that the problems besetting the popular music industry so soon would lead to the explosive emergence of Elvis Presley and rock music, and the serious consequences this would have for the fledgling country music industry.

Part Five

Authenticity and the Future
of Country Music

CHAPTER THIRTEEN

Authenticity

A Renewable Resource

Now we can return to a question posed at the outset. What is *authenticity*? The dead Hank Williams was the authentic iconic representation of country music in 1953, but if this rail-thin, flatland-accented Alabama boy wearing a stylized cowboy outfit had auditioned to record for Polk Brockman in 1923 singing his hillbilly cheating songs set in the honky-tonk mode, would Brockman have invited him to record? And if, forty years after he died in 1953, Hank Williams had auditioned at a Nashville writers' night in 1993, would he have been hailed as authentic country? I think not.[1]

To better understand authenticity and its dynamics in a music genre, this chapter addresses two questions. First, what does the word mean? And second, because the word is not often invoked unless the attribute is contested, we ask what are the politics inherent in the attribution of authenticity? In the light of these discussions, we consider in the final chapter the chances that country music can thrive in the twenty-first century.

DEFINING AUTHENTICITY

Six uses of the term "authenticity" can be drawn from the numerous examples given in the *Oxford English Dictionary*.[2]

1. Authenticated, not Pretense. A common sense of the idea of "authenticity," especially among critics and moralists, centrally involves the act of certifying what can be judged *authentic,* rather than *inauthentic,* a *fake,* a *forgery,* or a *pretense.* Unlike the other definitions given in the *OED,* this usage focuses attention on the authenticator, the judge, the institutional authority.

More than any other would-be arbiter of authenticity, the French Royal Academy of Music was able in the eighteenth century to develop the institutional apparatus necessary to define the authentic and to police against inauthentic art music. The cultural entrepreneurs of late-nineteenth-century Boston, as Paul DiMaggio (1982) has shown, were also remarkably successful in institutionalizing their particular ideas of what should constitute fine art music. These Boston promoters of the fine art/popular culture distinction found much of their intellectual justification in the speeches and writings of an English moralist and literary critic, Matthew Arnold, who contrasted what he called "culture"—(literary and artistic productions that he found to be authentic in leading people to the "sweetness and light"—the perfection of society)—with what he found to be "manufactured" (that is, created for some ulterior purpose). Arnold was quite generous in applying the label "manufactured" to the literary writing of his day, and he believed that the surfeit of inauthentic work was leading English society into anarchy. Arnold's principal work, *Culture and Anarchy* (1865), has been a touchstone of aesthetic and moralistic criticism ever since, even for those who utterly reject Arnold's assignment of particular works and ideas as authentic or inauthentic.

Many rock music scholars have differentiated between what they find to be authentic and inauthentic. (See in particular Simon Frith 1981, 1987, 1996; and Lawrence Grossberg 1992). The usual construction of rock is to see an early stage of innocent creativity and aesthetic renewal followed by co-optation, commercialism, and commodification. While many writers are explicit in saying that the music has been commercial from the outset and that its creators—at least those who attain any considerable reputation—are professionals, nonetheless they go on to make the question of authenticity an aesthetic and moral judgment.[3] While I agree with most of their analyses of aesthetic renewal and exhaustion, a process that Max Weber (1909: 246–50) called the "routinization of charisma," and which English music critic George Melly (1970) calls the decay of *revolt* into *style,* this work is not about my arguing for the authenticity of some styles of country music and not others. Rather, I report as best I can, how authenticity is fabricated in the field of country music.[4]

In fine-art fields, institutionalized standards are established by which authenticity can be judged at any particular time. Since country music has been institutionalized on a commercial basis, however, it has not been possible for any one group, whether critics, the state, creators, the industry, or audiences, to force its own aesthetic standards on the field.[5] Rather, authenticity emerges in the interplay within and between all these in concrete historical circumstances.[6]

2. Original, not Fake. The earliest cited meanings of the word "authentic" have to do with documents. The *authentic* is identified as the *original* and is set off against the *copy*, or when the intention is to mislead, the *fake* or *fraudulent*. As has been shown in the preceding chapters, no single artist originated all that by 1953 was understood to be country music. Rather the fully authentic was an assemblage from diverse sources. This idea of the authentic as *original* can most easily be applied to objects and ideas that have continuity over time. But it is not accurately applied to repeated performances of any kind because they are transient and any completely faithful later rendering is, per force, a copy.

3. Relic, not Changed. A closely related meaning of "authentic" is that of the *relic,* of the original. This was the authenticity claim that was made by Henry Ford and by many of the other promoters of old-time music discussed in chapter 4, who sought living fossils of authentic musical forms. Fanciful as this idea might seem today, it was widely held by the early anthropologists that "primitive" peoples represented earlier stages in cultural evolution, and this idea of "stone-age contemporaries" was applied to the peoples and the music of the Appalachian region, which was seen as cut-off from and uncorrupted by civilization. Thus, for example, in 1899 William Frost, the president of Berea College in Kentucky, wrote an article for the *Atlantic Monthly* titled "Our Contemporary Ancestors in the Southern Highlands," and two years later Ellen Sempel wrote an article for the *Geographical Journal* on "The Anglo-Saxons of the Kentucky Mountains."[7] As Whisnant (1983) has made clear in his careful analysis of the efforts of early social reformers in the Kentucky hills, many of the ideas of these writers were at best half-truths formulated out of their own ideas about the ills of contemporary urban society. But the fantasy views of mountain life did not go unchallenged even in the 1890s. For example, in 1896 Francis Land published an article in *Lippincott's Magazine* on "The Moonshiner of Fact," about a writer-friend of the author who fabricated from his own imagination stories about the lives of Appalachian mountain folk. None but the most hyperbolic of promoters since the 1930s has made the claim that country music is an authentic relic of an older primordial form.

4. Authentic Reproduction, not Kitsch. Many historical sites that have grown up across the country in recent decades are billed as *authentic reproductions.* These are counterpoised by reproductions that are *kitsch* (Eco 1986: 3–58). Colonial Williamsburg, Virginia, is probably the best known example of the former, and the latter is most spectacularly exemplified by the theme-park "America" once planned by the Disney Corporation to be sited near the Civil War battleground of Bull Run (Abramson 1995). The ironic pairing of the words "authentic" and "reproduction" is intended to suggest that the site is recently built or restored to be exactly what it was like at some specific point in the past. In practice, however, carbon-copy authenticity is repeatedly compromised, as Edward Bruner (1994) has shown in his detailed analysis of New Salem, Illinois, the carefully reconstituted town where Abraham Lincoln spent his early formative years. Compromise is inevitable, even when experts don't differ about what should be represented, because of modern building codes and the need to accommodate numerous staff and thousands of tourists.

Since, like every gourmet meal (Fine 1996), each musical performance is, in a sense, a reproduction, *authentic reproduction* can be claimed and contested in any self-conscious musical field. For the past several decades there have been bitter arguments in art music circles over how to perform Baroque and classical-era music.[8] Likewise there are enduring arguments over the differences between country and noncountry performance traditions. Within country music circles there have regularly been fights over whether particular genres of music are part of country music or not.[9] There have also been numerous heated debates about the appropriate instrumentation for a country music band[10] and about innovations in instrumental styles.[11]

5. Credible in Current Context. A distinct sense of "authentic" developed in the *Oxford English Dictionary* centers on being *believable* or *credible* to the contemporary general observer. The authentic in this sense may, but usually does not, accurately represent some object, person, or performance in the past. Thus, for example, the contemporary "authentic" representation of a witch available in any Halloween outfitter's shop would consist of an ankle-length black dress, a broad-brimmed hat with a tall, thin canonical peak, and a rough broom. This representation, though instantly identified today as a witch, does not fit the descriptions of any of the hundreds of women who were killed as witches in northern Europe and New England during the sixteenth and seventeenth centuries.[12] The "authentic" in this sense of "believable" also changes with time, as Bruner (1994) shows in his study of New Salem, Illinois. The reconstruction of the 1830s village that was credible in the 1930s was no longer credible in the 1990s. Authenticity for the latter, Bruner suggests, is informed in part by such television series as *Little House on the Prairie.*

6. Real, not Imitative. The final usage of "authentic," one that the *Oxford English Dictionary* calls "archaic," refers to that which is *true, consistent, sincere,* or *real* as opposed to the *imitative, artifactual, contrived,* or *phony.*[13] In this sense the measure of authenticity is the person or performance being judged. Hardly archaic, this usage is an important element in what is meant by authenticity in contemporary country music. In this usage, if any artist or performance is judged authentic, any reproduction of it is necessarily *in*authentic, because to be authentic, a person or a performance must be different from what has came before.

In recent years Ernest Tubb (Pugh 1996), Kitty Wells (Trott 1992), George Jones (Carlisle 1984), Loretta Lynn (Lynn 1976), and other venerable country music artists have been termed "authentic" in that they created their own personal style out of the expressions of others and their own experience, and they stayed true to the style they helped to develop rather than trying to keep up with each new change in country music style. At the same time, styles such as country boogie, tragedy songs, heart songs, and a capella ballads, which were thought of as authentic country when they flourished, are not now part of authentic country music. To be sure, these and other styles may be revived in the future and adapted by neotraditionalist devotees, thus making them central again.

Authenticity in Country Music: 1953

Echoes of all six uses of the term "authentic" just discussed can be found in the 1950s discourse of authenticity in country music, but it was the final two that clearly predominated. In the opening paragraphs of the first chapter we saw how country music recording company producers responded to the *Billboard* reporter. They sought new artists who were "authentic" and new songs that were "original." While their pairing of authentic and original seemed strange initially, it now makes perfect sense. Prospective performers had to have the marks of tradition to make them *credible,* and the songs that would make them successful had to be original enough to show that their singers were not *in*authentic copies of what had gone before, that is, that they were *real.*

The December 5, 1953, issue of *Billboard* that had the article about the desired country music artist and song was in the trade paper's first-ever section on country music, and it is interesting to see how authenticity was understood in the other ten articles in that section.[14] Entitled

"Country & Western Business Is BIG Business," the opening editorial says that the country music performers and songwriters have been so successful because, "they hitched their art to the proved philosophies of life and let their inspiration spring from the heart of a nation. . . . This certainty, that one's art is genuine, that it is pegged to more than surface considerations, and that it derives from the heart of a country—this is our assurance that country music will continue to attract even greater numbers" (*Billboard* 1953d: 41).

The first substantive article in the country music section of *Billboard* describes five subgenera of country music, saying that the history of the music "is the history of the people. It's the music that grew out of their lives—their sorrows and joys" (*Billboard* 1953f: 42). The next article asserts that it is the "genuine" quality that sets the country field apart from Tin Pan Alley music. "There is nothing synthetic about country music. Unlike Tin Pan Alley writers who create music solely as a means of earning a living, country music is not manufactured but rather bred by years of living and feeling a situation and then projected by the writer into song" (*Billboard* 1953g: 42). In the same article Bill McCall, president of Four Star Music, is quoted as saying: "In order to understand country music you have to know which end the milk comes out of, perhaps slop a few hogs, and maybe follow a mule down the row behind a plow." Silvester Cross cautions that "authenticity of material is all important in the country business. Country and Western people are the first to spot a 'phony' song." Joel Friedman (*Billboard* 1953g) says that proof of the need for authenticity is that while country music songs regularly become hits in the pop music field, pop songs do not become hits in the country music field.[15] Fred Rose, Hank Williams's Chicago-born publisher and sometime cowriter, underlines the importance of maintaining contact with the regional sources of the music: "If I'm away from the South for six months, I lose the feel and have to work my way back into it" (*Billboard* 1953g: 42, 62). The other articles in the set echo these evaluations. For example Sippel (1953) writing on country music's fans suggests that they respond to the artists as if they were real people, treating performers as family.

This view of the distinctive characteristics of country music was not unique to those reporting in *Billboard*. Writers for the national news, business, and opinion magazines of the time echoed these evaluations.[16] Thus, in 1953, informed outsiders understood the genre as expressing *authenticity,* and that authenticity was not contrived or copied but was based in the history of a people and was drawn from the experiences of those who lived in the everyday world. As we will show in the next section of the chapter, on the politics of authenticity, this unaffectedness was itself an affectation.

THE POLITICS OF AUTHENTICITY

Lionel Trilling (1972: 94) has cautioned: "Authenticity is implicitly a polemical concept." Here we intend to outline the politics of authenticity claims. Because the claim of authenticity imputes value relative to inauthenticity, one of the most effective ways to assert authenticity is to claim that an action, object, or person is "natural" and without "artifice."

Acting Naturally

In 1963 the song "Act Naturally" was a number-one country music hit for Buck Owens, host of the long-running country comedy TV show *Hee Haw*. Two years later the Beatles, with Ringo Starr singing, had a minor pop hit on the song, and in 1989 a version of the song cobbled together from the Owens and Starr versions was back on the country music charts. As Barbara Ching (1993) has noted, the song makes clear that authenticity through *naturalness* doesn't come naturally but rather, is a self-conscious *act* on the part of the person represented as singing the song. Buck Owens, of course, was not the first entertainer to be self-conscious about the art of seeming artless. Oscar Wilde, the camp English romantic playwright, had observed a hundred years earlier, "To be natural is such a hard pose to keep up" (Ching 1993: 122).

In an oft-cited 1936 essay "The Work of Art in the Age of Mechanical Reproduction," Walter Benjamin argues that in the industrial era originals are robbed of their "aura" of authenticity, and that only with the mass reproduction of symbols does authenticity emerge as a quality to be prized.[17] Indeed Miles Orvell (1989) has shown in his careful study of the changing attitudes about furniture and the decorative arts in the United States from 1880 to 1940 that before the mass production of furnishings, veneers and pine painted to look like fine wood or marble were the height of fashion, but that with industrialization and the prospect that anything could be made to look like anything else, the value shifted to "naturalness," so that objects came to be valued for showing what they were made of. Thus not only are authenticity and naturalness socially defined, their importance changes over time.

Naturalization: Elite French Wine

The "naturalization" of arbitrary distinctions is, as Antonio Gramsci (1971) and Pierre Bourdieu (1984) have shown, one of the most powerful tools of domination in society, and numerous careful studies have shown the corrosive consequences of essentializing differences of gender, class, race, and region. Consolidating authenticity claims requires building an institutional system, and one of the best ways to obscure this act of arbitrary power is to propagate the idea that the institutional system is part of the natural order of things.

Perhaps the best way to see the politics of fabricating authenticity is to examine a carefully researched case—one at some remove from country music. It is generally agreed that the chateau-made *grands crus* wines of the Bordeaux region of France are among the best in the world. But it was not always thus, as Robert Ulin (1995) has shown. As late as the fourteenth century, the wines of the interior east of Bordeaux along the Dordogne River were more highly prized in Paris. The Bordeaux winemakers and merchants persuaded the English, who controlled the port of Bordeaux and thus the riverain means of transporting heavy goods from the interior, to place differentially heavy taxes on wine from upstream. They also successfully lobbied for other restrictions that made the wine from the interior less palatable. As a consequence the land devoted to commercial winegrowing rapidly expanded in Bordeaux, and its international reputation for high quality was established. Spanish, Portuguese, and Italian commercial winegrowing expanded in the next several centuries, and the Bordeaux merchants found that because of the high shipping costs, they could not lower their prices sufficiently to compete in those markets. They collectively agreed to set standards for the preparation and aging of wines from select pieces of land, in order to identify this wine as having higher quality and thus command a higher price. This set of distinctions was officially codified in 1855, at the time of the Universal Exposition at Paris, which had as a goal the codification of the criteria for excellence in all fields of French national commerce and culture (Ulin 1995).

There were continual disputes over the proper designations of specific plots of land, and this helped to codify theories about what combinations of plant stock, soil, sun, heat, and rain naturally produced the best wine, and served to strengthen Bordeaux's reputation. As the standards were codified, the prices of the "best" wines increased, making it possible and profitable to cheat in the process of winemaking. Thus questions of what constituted authentic wine became consequential. Because of their concentrated taste and sweetness, for example, raisins were commonly used to make wine, and if raisins, why not other kinds of dried fruit? All such disputes helped in codifying what would be seen as the "natural" process of wine-grape growing and winemaking.

One further way of bringing order to the evaluation of wine, Ulin

(1995) explains, was for the merchants to organize the innumerable small *grand crus* plots of land into a few larger holdings, and to give the wine from them a unifying identity by associating them with the name of a neighboring country house or chateau. There continue to be bitter disputes over the chateau designations, but once established, they gave further gravity and sense of antiquity to the wine so designated, as the association between wine and chateau came to reinforce each other as part of the natural order of fine things.

Naturalization: Bluegrass Style

Having reviewed the politics of authenticity in the naturalization of the superiority of Bordeaux wine, it may be easier to see parallel processes in the formation of bluegrass as a distinct musical form, a form that some of its proponents see as the only true, natural, authentic form of country music (Cantwell 1984: 205). As Neil Rosenberg (1985) has shown in his carefully researched account of the development of bluegrass, the form coalesced in the mid-1940s as the "sound" created by Bill Monroe and his Blue Grass Boys, when Lester Flatt and Earl Scruggs were both in the band. The sound consisted of the extremely fast ensemble playing of acoustic stringed instruments with the individual instruments—including the human voice used much as an instrument[18]—exchanging solo choruses.[19] This new hot variant of the older string-band music was very popular among country music fans in the late 1940s and on into the early 1960s. Increasingly fans and promoters defined it as a form of music distinct from the amplified guitar sounds of honky-tonk country music and rockabilly. And when the lush, orchestrated strings of the Nashville sound began to reach wide popularity, bluegrass was no longer seen by radio programmers as being part of the mix of sounds to be played on commercial country radio stations. Bluegrass was shut out because it connoted old-time hayseeds to potential radio advertisers who were seeking younger, more affluent, if not urban, radio listeners (Peterson and Berger 1975; Peterson 1978). Bill Monroe felt that his style had been eclipsed by this amplified guitar music and he felt betrayed by his former band members, including Flatt and Scruggs, who had stolen his sound and profited from it themselves.

Like country boogie, country gospel, and big-band western swing, bluegrass might have disappeared as a living form of music except for the folk music revival of the 1950–60s. As Rosenberg (1985) and Cantwell (1996) show, a number of young, musically educated, folk-oriented performers and musicologists saw bluegrass as the living link back to the older acoustic forms of country and folk music. The most influential of these was Ralph Rinzler, who was the director of the Smithsonian

Institution's Festival of American Folklife and for a time served as Bill Monroe's manager. Just how clear Ralph Rinzler was about the strategy of making artists "authentic" in the eyes of this new audience can be seen in his comments about Clarence Ashley, a string-band performer and recording artist from the 1920s, and Doc Watson, who would become a leading light of the folk music revival but who, when Rinzler first met him at an early bluegrass event, was making a living in a rockabilly band. Rinzler said his strategy for attracting an urban audience for Ashley and Watson had two parts. "The first was to legitimize them by demonstrating the historic links between the two of them and musicians already acknowledged to be our nation's prime recording artists in their [folk] field. The second was to validate the folkness of their roots through detailed biographic notes and articles" (Rinzler 1993: 3).

Ralph Rinzler convinced Bill Monroe that he was not being robbed of his unique band sound by defecting band members, but rather that he was the founder of a perfectly unique form of music that had grown up naturally out of his own life experience. Rinzler said that the other performers weren't thieves but disciples of his music. And he convinced Monroe that there was a whole new educated, young Northern audience thirsting to hear his music and to pay him homage as its creator.[20] As a festival coordinator at the Smithsonian Institution, Rinzler was able to help deliver this new audience to Bill Monroe. The multiband bluegrass festivals that grew out of these early concerts came to feature a sort of ritual orchestrated by Rinzler and Monroe in which, with all the bands massed on stage the final evening, Monroe would introduce each of the other bandleaders who had earlier been Blue Grass Boys, at the same time showing the unity of bluegrass music and identifying its source.

The popular retelling of the bluegrass story down to this day echoes and simplifies this created tradition. All of the mechanisms of the creation of the genre are suppressed, and bluegrass is simply exalted as the product of a single man, Bill Monroe, an American original. He is depicted as a natural, authentic genius who simply drew his inspiration from life in the Kentucky hills.[21]

The combined efforts of Bill Monroe, Ralph Rinzler, and other folk-musicologists might be seen as inventing tradition for bluegrass, but the form has continued to evolve well beyond the orthodoxy they tried to establish in the 1970s (Rosenberg 1985). In recent decades other self-selected authenticating groups have worked to set standards for judging "old-time" fiddling, dancing, and singing styles (Blaustein 1975). Judge George Hay and the other managers of the "Grand Ole Opry" tried, as we have seen, to set the bounds of country music and the appropriate behavior of performers—going so far as dismissing the leading star of the form, Hank Williams, from the Opry—but these and similar efforts by other promoters such as John Lair (Yarber 1996) had no appreciable effect in shaping country music then or since.[22]

Regions of the Mind: Appalachia

As we saw in part 2, the images of hillbilly and singing cowboy were contrivances. The regions of the country they were meant to represent were in large part contrived products of memory work as well (Irwin-Zarecka 1994). There have been numerous treatments of the politics of imaging the South and the West and rural/small-town ways generally.[23] While these have to do with mass-mediated regions of the imagination, a class-biased view, alternately nostalgic and disparaging of the works of common people, has a long heritage in Britain, as shown in Harker (1985) and in Shiach's (1989) research on the evaluations of "folk" music and "popular" culture by intellectuals often unwittingly in the service of the ruling elite.

The concept of Appalachia as pristine remnant of a bygone natural environment peopled by British American stock, unspoiled by the modernist thrust of urbanization and industrialization, was a self-serving contrivance of the latter third of the nineteenth century. Descriptions of the region were used either to highlight the improvements of civilization or to show its depravity in despoiling pristine nature; to identify its residents as noble relics of Elizabethan England or debauched by contact with the wrong outside influences; and also to conceptually clear the region of all its other residents, including Native Americans, African-American slaves, central European immigrants, and well-to-do urban vacationers.[24]

In his analysis of the efforts of northern Christian missionaries in Appalachia to revive the old music and "native crafts" of the "Anglo-Saxons" they found living there, David Whisnant (1983) brings together all the themes involved in what he calls the politics of regional culture. The missionaries' views on music are encapsulated in the comments of Olive Dame Campbell, one of the social workers, writing to a colleague in 1916: the "folk movement in the mountains [of which her work was a part] . . . seeks the recognition and preservation of what is native and fine. We would like to have the people recognize the worth and beauty of their songs; we would like to have the singing of these songs encouraged in all the mountain schools and centers" (103). Some sense of what songs she thought were "fine" is suggested by the next sentence in her letter, "We would like to have them displace the inferior music that is now being sung there." The music of Fiddlin' John Carson and Jimmie Rodgers, as well as much of the Carter Family's work, were anathema to these reformers. In the name of ethnic song cleansing, one can imagine one of these Anglophile social workers seriously reprimanding a young Maybelle Carter for playing the Spanish guitar in a way that cruder folks of the time called "nigger picking" (Kahn 1970).

One of the most telling examples of regional invention has to do with the creation, mentioned briefly above, of that ancestor of both the hillbilly and the cowboy, the "leatherstocking" frontiersman of the West, when "West" meant virtually anything in or west of the Appalachian Mountains. This Daniel Boone-like character was personified in the popular imagination primarily through the novels of James Fenimore Cooper: *The Pioneers* of 1823, *The Last of the Mohicans* of 1826, and *The Deerslayer* of 1841.

As Alan Taylor (1994) has shown, Cooper's first novel was based on his own family experience and neatly illustrates the politics of authenticity. In 1807, James's father, William Cooper, wrote *A Guide to the Wilderness,* extolling the rich, unclaimed bounty of the untouched and empty land that would become the settlement he founded as Cooper's Town, New York. Cooper says he was in a deserted land and wished by settling it to complete "a divine task left undone at the creation" (Taylor 1994: 6).

In point of fact there were large Native American towns close to Cooper's settlements with battlements, orchards, woven weirs for catching fish, and lines of brush extending for hundreds of yards to guide deer to traps. White trappers and traders had moved through the area for a century and there were other permanent settlements of whites on contiguous land that were forty years old when William Cooper arrived to play God. Even the thousands of acres he claimed as "his land" had earlier been surveyed in 1785 as part of another, larger land claim. His patently false assertion that the land was "empty" can be understood as a way of buttressing William Cooper's own property rights to the land.

In his novel *The Pioneers,* James Fenimore Cooper began the revision of his father's construction of the founding of Cooper's Town. James writes about a character much like his enterprising father, but he also reintroduces the rival land claimants, the Native Americans, the leatherstocking squatter-settlers, and the land speculators. At the end of the novel the elderly Native American dies on what, for him, is still "his" land, while the mythic leatherstocking strikes out West and South seeking regions of the mind free of land speculators and white settlers.

Invented Tradition and Emergent Custom

The articles in the anthology edited by Eric Hobsbawm and Terence Ranger (1983), *The Invention of Tradition,* detail a number of examples

of how groups in power self-consciously naturalize the antiquity of artifacts, practices, and beliefs that they have "invented" to buttress their
own claims to power and respect. While in his introduction Hobsbawm
draws a hard line between such invented traditions and traditions based
in venerable custom, in practice it is often impossible to draw such a
line.

While there may be instances of fabrication, such as the Scots Highland clan kilt, which are invented out of whole cloth (Trevor-Roper
1983), in most instances it is not so easy to draw a clear line because
most inventions are in part based on customs—and vice versa (Zerubavel
1991). Sewell (1994) has shown this in the invention of the idea that
there was a battle to take the Parisian fortress of the Bastille and that
this battle was the start of the French Revolution. Anderson (1983) has
also shown the mix of fact and invention in the worldwide spread of the
idea of nationalism, and Biernacki (1995) has shown how their differing
cultures shaped the ideas about the emerging industrial working class
in England and Germany.

Invention can become customary practice over time. For example,
Native American Pueblo women were well known among anthropologists for the distinctive decorations they put on the pots they made.
When the railroads brought increasing numbers of tourists to the area
early in the twentieth century, Pueblo women found that the best-selling
items were flowerpots, animals, and ashtrays painted with "non-Indian"
designs. A mixed group of white archaeologists, writers, and social reformers banded together in 1923 to form the Indian Art Fund (AIF),
which was joined by others, including agents of the U.S. Bureau of Indian
Affairs. The AIF set out to preserve what they believed to be the genuine
Indian artifacts by telling the tourists what was authentic and what was
kitsch and by showing the Pueblo women what they should present for
sale and how it should be made. Both tourists and potters were quite
resistant to this "expert" advice in the early part of the century, but with
the increasing Native American self-consciousness in recent decades, the
patterns that the Indian Arts Fund claimed were distinctive of individual
pueblos and the pot-making techniques that they described have become
accepted by the pot makers and "serious" collectors as the standard of
the tradition.[25] Thus a more or less invented tradition can be naturalized
into custom.

The Authentic Voice

As Hank Williams was fond of saying, not just anyone could sing country
music. "You have to plow a lot of ground and look at the back side of
a mule for a lot of years to sing a country song."[26] In *Meaning and Authen-*

ticity, César Graña (1989) is also concerned with identifying the characteristics that give persons the right to speak with authenticity. Like Hank
Williams, he finds that this right is inscribed in the signifiers of group
membership, and represents a naturalized display of force and domination. Graña's primary concern is with the role of the European aristocracy
in substantiating the fine arts, but attempts to naturalize the right to
speak can be seen in all situations where the right to speak for a group
is contested, as it is in country music.

Stephen Cornell (1995) argues that claims of ethnic group membership in this country now are often made in order to establish the right
to speak authentically as a group member and, at least implicitly, for the
group. In his parallel analysis of four major historical sites, Joseph Rhea
(1995) carefully shows how in the 1980s ethnic groups were able to gain
much greater control over the ways in which they are represented for
the national collective memory at the historical monuments run by the
National Park Service. He focuses on two cases of revised telling: the
role of Native Americans in the reinterpretation of the Little Bighorn
(formerly called the Custer Battlefield) in Montana, and the role of
Latinos in the reinterpretation of the Alamo in San Antonio, Texas. His
other two cases involve recently established sites whose meaning has
been shaped by the interested ethnic group from the outset. These are
Martin Luther King, Jr.'s birth home and burial site in Atlanta, Georgia,
and the World War II camp in Manzaner, California, where Japanese
Americans were interned. These instances show the importance in the
present era of establishing authenticity through ethnic group identity
rather than through an assumed general American identity—the dominant bases of legitimation from the time of the American Civil War
through the Second World War (Kammen 1991).[27]

Identification with country music today is like identification with an
ethnic group in this way. Indeed, being a fan of country music and its
associated way of life may serve as a way that millions of people of mixed
ethnic identity can express their imagined place in society against urbane
corporate ways and in distinction from other nation- race- and religion-
based ethnic identities.

All would-be country music performers have to authenticate their
claim to speak for the country identity. Following a mule doesn't signify
any more. For musicians, establishing the right to speak involves know-
ing all the conventions of making the music (Becker 1982; Berliner 1994)
and the nuances of voice and gesture that make their work sound "country" (Ellison 1995). Music and performance are vital to the audience,
but signifiers are also vital. The boots, the hat, the outfit, a soft rural
Southern accent, as well as the sound and subjects of the songs, all help.[28]

Figure 13.1 Randall Hank Williams (Hank Williams, Jr.), seen here with his father, lent authenticity to the hard-core neotraditional revival of country music in the late 1980s.

Finally, being able to show a family heritage in country music is perhaps the strongest asset among authenticity claims. Many artists recall learning first from their mothers or playing in a family band. Perhaps no one has made more out of his heritage than Hank Williams, Jr. Shown in figure 13.1 with his famous father, Hank Jr. has continually reminded his fans of his "family tradition" of hard-core country performance and hell-raising.

But fealty to country music identity has not always been important. Jimmie Rodgers, for example, didn't dress "country" or always play with a "country" band. Following the custom for professional entertainers of the day, he tried to deliver each song in the mood that was appropriate for the song. To suggest how far this role-taking went at the time, Rodgers sometimes sang songs voiced in a woman's experience, and Sara Carter likewise sang some of her songs from the perspective of a man. As a harbinger of changing expectations about authenticity, it is interesting to note, however, that Jimmie Rodgers did write and sing about the tragedy of tuberculosis, the disease from which he was dying.

The insistence on fealty to a particular country identity and speaking from personal experience came to the fore, as we have seen, in the era of Hank Williams. By the late 1930s the elements of the hard-core and soft-shell styles had become clear, the hillbilly and singing cowboy images had coalesced, and the honky-tonk sound had developed. By the 1950s these served well in establishing Williams's singing of his own life in song as the model for the would-be authentic country music entertainer.[29]

Once fabricated, has the model of authenticity represented by Hank Williams remained unchanged down to the present? As suggested at the outset, I think not. After all, as early as the 1970s, Waylon Jennings was asking in song, "Are you sure Hank done it this way?" And if the icon of authenticity is in question, can the circle of authenticity remain unbroken? These are the concerns with which we bring the book full circle in the final chapter.

CONCLUSION

Authenticity in a living art form can have a number of meanings, but as we have seen, in popular culture, where experts and authorities do not control the particulars of the word's meaning, the definition centers on being *believable* relative to a more or less explicit model, and at the same time being *original,* that is not being an imitation of the model. Thus what is taken to be authentic does not remain static but is continually renewed over the years. The changing meaning of authenticity is not random, but is renegotiated in a continual political struggle in which the goal of each contending interest is to naturalize a particular construction of authenticity.

In the final chapter we will see just how far the particular meaning of "authenticity" which has been constructed out of the contending meanings of "believable" and "original" has changed in country music over the years since 1953, and we spell out the conditions that could make possible the further development of the music well into the twenty-first century.

CHAPTER FOURTEEN

Can the Circle Be Unbroken?

I n 1935 the Carter Family recorded a traditional hymn that uses the occasion of the death of a family member to reflect on the continuity of the family after death. For some unexplained reason in their version of the song the specific empirical question "*Will* the circle be unbroken?" is changed to the more general structural question "*Can* the circle be unbroken?"[1] In a parallel fashion we ask here not whether country music will continue in the twenty-first century, but what structural conditions are necessary for it to do so. Central in addressing this concern is the question of authenticity.

THE CIRCLE OF DEATH AND REBIRTH

It's All Over

Continuity cannot be taken for granted, and, in fact, statements about the death of authentic country music have a venerable history. As early as 1910 it was said that authentic "traditional" music—meaning English-type balladry—was being displaced by crassly commercial, string-band styles exemplified by the likes of Gid Tanner and the Skillet Lickers (Whisnant 1983). In 1929 the fledgling commercial genre was said by industry pundits to be "finished." In a special sense it was true, because the string of disaster-song hits sung by Fiddlin' John Carson, Vernon Dalhart, and others *had* played out (Wolfe 1995). Nonetheless the "classic country" sounds of Jimmie Rodgers and the Carter Family were just becoming widely popular in 1929.

In the 1940s "purists" bemoaned the encroachments of honky-tonkers with electrified instruments who were crowding out the now-established string bands who had been the interlopers a generation before (Rosenberg 1985), and by 1980 the fans of honky-tonkers Ernest Tubb and Webb Pierce were denouncing the plasticity of Barbara Mandrell and the Oak Ridge Boys (Corbin 1980). Finally, in 1994 critics were once more decrying the inauthenticity of much of the music coming out of Nashville, saying "It's just a matter of time" until the boom in country music goes bust (Ridley 1994).[2]

Looking back, one might view this series of statements and conclude that the music has gone, and will continue to go, through unbroken circles of death and renewal. This view is supported by what we have seen earlier with regard to career stages and the dialectic of hard-core versus soft-shell styles. It is not inevitable, however, that the cycle will continue, and Tony Scherman wrote in a 1994 essay that the circle of country music authenticity was already broken. He bases this conclusion on two assertions. The first is that "the generation of George Jones, Merle Haggard, Willie Nelson, and Waylon Jennings [made] the last great infusion of country-music creativity" (1994: 54), an argument that might be dismissed as personal prejudice. But his second assertion is quite different. He argues that the social conditions that spawned the waves of country music are no longer present. "Country music was born of the trauma of rural people's adjustment to industrial society, but that fight has been fought. . . . Severed from its working-class origins, country music is becoming a refuge for culturally homeless Americans everywhere" (1994: 55, 57). The difference between these new fans and the old, Scherman argues, is that the new fans can choose whether to like country music or not, while for the earlier fans country music was not a choice but was part of their *lived experience*. Scherman was not the first to make this point about a liking for country music becoming discretionary. In 1976, Hugh Cherry suggested to me that "anyone who is a hillbilly today, is a hillbilly by choice," so that what had been the structural fate of poor white rural people had become, for their descendants and others, one lifestyle choice among many. Scherman concludes that if liking country music is discretionary, "'Authenticity' is a meaningless criterion in country music. . . . So it looks like it's good-bye to country music" (1994: 57). Scherman may well prove correct, but the evidence of this study suggests otherwise, since authenticity seems open to change.

A vastly wider array of music is part and parcel of the lived experience of most people today, but earlier generations in the 1920s and 1950s didn't just mechanically accept the music around them either. To say that they did is to naturalize what was for people a set of choices about what to accept and what to reject. Who would have predicted, for example, that an important element of Hawaiian music played on steel guitars would become a signature sound of country music? Each stylistic turn, from the Carter Family and Jimmie Rodgers on down, has been a tentative offering, and in the interplay between audiences, industry, and performers, the efforts of many experimentalists were rejected, and older forms of music were regularly sloughed off as no longer authentic.

Authenticity Work

Maintaining the sense of authenticity takes work.[3] As we have seen, Jimmie Rodgers, the "Father of Country Music," was quite an actor, arguably the genre's most consummate actor. But for a young person today to act just like him or like Sara Carter, Hank Williams, or Loretta Lynn, wouldn't be accepted as authentic.[4] Authenticity in the 1990s takes work, just as it did in earlier eras, but the job has changed because the times have changed, and so too have the signifiers of authenticity.

The most obvious change from 1923 is that there was then no clear tradition of country music with its own past, its own iconic progenitors, its own institutional delivery system, and its own self-conscious fan community. There was then no shared understanding of what constituted country music as a distinct genre. Beginning in the 1950s and growing rapidly in the final decades of the twentieth century, a huge body of information on what constitutes country music has accumulated and become available for reference on records, in still pictures, in movies, in television programs, in biographies, and in scholarly reports. What is more, representations of the traditions are now often incorporated in video and live performances (Ellison 1995).

While country music lyrics have always referred back to earlier times, it was not until the 1950s that concerted efforts were made to preserve and display earlier representations of country music itself. The first dramatic evidence that there was commercial value in evoking past artists as icons was the 1953 celebration of the twentieth anniversary of Jimmie Rodgers's death, promoted by Ernest Tubb and Hank Snow. This event drew upwards of 75,000 people to Meridian, Mississippi (*Billboard* 1953j), and there were over 100,000 who attended the Hank Williams memorial in Montgomery, Alabama, a year and a half after his death (Terry 1954).

The explosion of rockabilly music in the years just following Hank Williams's death forced those in the industry, and fans as well, to become more self-reflective about what constituted country music and what fell outside the bounds of the genre. In the process, most of a generation of rising young artists, including Elvis Presley, Jerry Lee Lewis, Johnny Cash, Conway Twitty, and many more, absented themselves or were temporarily banished from country.

Country music industry leaders, fighting to recover the integrity of country music following the drastic decline in business caused by the first wave of rock music in the late 1950s, became committed to the idea of a country music heritage linking past performers and styles with contemporary country music.[5] One of the most conspicuous of the early efforts was the founding in 1961 of the Country Music Hall of Fame, which in 1967 was housed in a grand building containing both a country music museum and a research archive (Green and Ivey 1980). One of the early displays in the museum was a large chart showing all the diverse styles that had culminated in the commercial country music of the day. The following year Bill Malone published the first edition of his encyclopedic and profoundly influential *Country Music, U.S.A.* It clearly grounded the efforts of contemporary artists in the works of hundreds of named predecessors stretching back to the beginning of the twentieth century.

Ironically, it was young hippie freaks, including Gram Parsons, Jerry Garcia, and John McEuen, who engaged in a great deal of authenticity work for country music in the early 1970s. They were thoroughly familiar with the work of the country rockers, but they sought to celebrate older country styles from the 1920s and 1930s in their work and to acknowledge the contributions of gifted older performers.[6] In 1971 John McEuen and his Nitty Gritty Dirt Band created a set of recordings featuring Maybelle Carter, Roy Acuff, Earl Scruggs, Merle Travis, and a number of other older artists. Called "Will the Circle Be Unbroken," the front cover of the elegant United Artists three-album set features an etching of an unidentified full-bearded Civil War general flanked by Confederate and Union battle flags. The sixty-eight photos inside and on the back cover intermix scenes of nature with recording-studio shots of the older musicians playing with their Dirt Band disciples. Just as the oval-shaped front-cover etching suggests the meeting of forces following the Civil War, the photographs inside show young hippies and traditionalists coming together in their love of the music. To further accent the point that the circle is being re-formed, dust-cover sleeves reprinted hippie *Rolling Stone* and straight *Nashville Tennessean* accounts by Chet Flippo and Jack Hurst respectively of the meeting of youth and traditional worlds in their shared love for the music and respect for each other's dedication to keeping the tradition alive. This set of records outsold all expectations and spawned a series of albums down through the years, pairing rising country artists with their heroes, and featuring established artists singing the songs identified with an earlier great.

In the 1980s another form of authenticity work began to be important, as copiously illustrated and well-researched fan-oriented histories of country music began to appear, and in the 1990s these were augmented by television programs devoted to telling part or all of the country music story.[7] Roy Acuff, Bill Monroe, Merle Haggard, Johnny Cash, and among somewhat younger musicians Marty Stewart, Emmylou Harris, and Dwight Yoakam have been most conspicuous in playing the role of teacher-of-the-tradition, but it is not unusual for other artists to tell an audience of their own heroes and to indicate their own place in the tradition. This is often done in the process of introducing a song or a guest artist. The introducer typically indicates how a tradition is being carried from generation to generation, and the audience is typically asked to participate in this quasi-religious process of laying on of hands, as Curtis Ellison (1995) has clearly shown.

Signifiers of Artistic Authenticity

Many of the signifiers that show an audience that an artist has the right to perform country music have changed little since 1953. The verbal accent, vocabulary, grammar, and prior rough work experience affirm that a person is from the great geographic cradle of country music and hasn't let education get the better of a working-class identification. Performers without this full pedigree have to do special authenticity work to gain acceptance.

Artists seeking to establish the bona fides of authenticity now have available a set of signifiers that had not been codified in 1953. The codification of a country music heritage in the decades since 1953 means that the artists of the 1990s can affirm authenticity by showing that they know and respect the tradition and want to carry it forward. For example, at a 1992 Temple Theater concert in Meridian, Mississippi, Karon Blackwell, who grew up in Chicago and had worked mostly in California making singing commercials for 7UP and others, carefully pronounced her name KAY-ron and told an initially skeptical audience of her birth in Mississippi, saying just how proud she was to be able to perform in Meridian, where one of her all-time favorites, Jimmie Rodgers, had been born.[8]

By watching a band's action on stage, it is possible to tell a country music band from a band of any other genre of music because of performance conventions (Becker 1982). Typically the band comes out very nearly on time, the lead singer greets the crowd warmly, and the band

Figure 14.1 Shot from behind, Roy Acuff and His Smoky Mountain Boys performing in 1979 on the Grand Ole Opry stage in Opryland. Note that, balancing his fiddle bow on his nose, Acuff was ever the entertainer.

orients its performance to the audience in a way that looks spontaneous rather than choreographed. The hometowns of band members are mentioned as they are introduced, and jokes are made about how the Southerners are educating any "Yankees" in the group. The authenticity markers of guest performers are lavishly described, showing both the bandleader's knowledge of the tradition and her/his respect for it. As in no other genre, the latest record release and upcoming show dates are promoted from the stage, a legacy of the days when country radio performers regularly advertised products and promoted their upcoming appearances. In addition older artists reprise their earlier hits in live performances and render them in a fashion as close to the hit version as they can. Figure 14.1 shows Roy Acuff and his Smoky Mountain Boys performing on the Opryland stage during the broadcast of the "Grand Ole Opry" in 1979. The song being played is likely one of their old favorites and Acuff can be seen in center stage balancing his fiddle bow on his chin much as he did forty years earlier.

Again, very unlike the stage performance style of stars in most other genres, country music artists approach fans at the edge of the stage, touching hands, exchanging comments, receiving messages, and posing for photos. All these little gestures signal that the artist has not lost the common touch. Perhaps the most important signifier of this common touch is the time after the show, when the star artist sits at a table to sign autographs on hats, T-shirts, souvenir programs, and body parts while having his or her photo taken arm-around-the-fan. Artists are known among fans by how many hours they are willing and able to endure this postshow ritual. Garth Brooks, who at the time was not only the biggest-selling country music artist, but was outselling all artists in every other field as well, spent twenty-three straight hours signing autographs for fans attending the 1996 International Country Music Fan Fair in Nashville (*Close-Up* 1996).

Music industry publicists don't rely on performance conventions alone to do the authenticity work for their aspiring artists. Press packs are regularly made for each artist. Particularly in the case of new artists, these highlight signs of authenticity that are consistent with the stereotype, including hometown, family musical experience, musical apprenticeship, hobbies, prior rough work experience, and so forth. Also included are favorable comments by established artists and notices of riotous acceptance by patrons of venues in the South. These press packs are written so that writers for local newspaper entertainment sections don't have to compose stories but can lift whole passages for their own articles. Album liner notes and jacket art are also crafted to do authenticity work.

Country music stage outfits were already well-worked-out signifiers with completely understood traditions in the 1950s. Though the specific signs have changed somewhat year to year since then, the stage clothes and hairdos that clearly signify that a performer is making a claim to being hard-core or soft-shell country are well understood in the 1990s.

Authenticity Signifiers in the Music

There is at least one clear difference between the signifiers of authenticity in the lyrics of the 1950s and those of half a century later.[9] Hank Williams and his peers relied on all the characteristics mentioned above, from accent to outfits, in order to establish authenticity, so that their songs could express personal feelings. Song lyrics written in the decades since Williams's death increasingly load up on signifiers that unambiguously locate the song—and by inference the singer—squarely within the country music tradition. In order to set the appropriate scene, songs make mention of well-known past performers, including Jimmie Rodgers, Bob Wills, Ernest Tubb, Patsy Cline, and Hank Williams. In the 1970s, for example, the aspiring white performer Mo Bandy, had a hit with "Hank Williams, You Wrote My Life," which cleverly wove the titles of Williams's songs into the story line. In the same decade, the aspiring performer of black, Indian, and Irish extraction, Stony Edwards, sang "Hank and Lefty, You Raised My Country Soul." Over the years songs referring to another song, or to a particular style, performance situation, or performance site, have proliferated.[10] These songs facilitate the singer's claim to be a country performer and help to naturalize the tradition that is being fabricated.

There is one final way of linking new work to the growing mythic tradition. This is through the music itself. Instrumental sounds of the dobro, fiddle, banjo, and rockabilly piano can contextualize and help to authenticate current offerings. Instrumental riffs, yodels, and melodic fragments can serve the same purpose. Such musical quotes are purposefully coordinated with the appropriate lyrical references to more tightly weld the new song and its singer into the fabricated authenticity.

INSTITUTIONAL MECHANISMS OF STASIS AND RENEWAL

Institutional Stasis and the Dissipation of Authenticity

The institutional system of the industry tends to resist change. Since the 1950s, the record company executives who select which performers and songs will be recorded have said that—like it or not—country music is whatever is currently being played on country music radio. Country radio programmers in turn say that they will play whatever music draws the largest elements of the audience that is sought by their potential advertisers, but that they can choose only from the music that the record companies decide to produce and then to promote. Promoters of live music shows try to book the artists currently getting the most airplay and selling the most records. These same acts are most likely to be featured in magazine stories and on television. Finally, aspiring artists and songwriters, hoping to be successful, mold their work to fit with what is currently hot.

This institutionalized commercial music machine is inherently conservative, acting as a giant gyroscope that keeps country music on a fairly narrow track, since each new song and each new artist created in this way is a close copy of the one before. Thus every active person in the industry tends to copy from those who are enjoying current success. A Roger Miller song of 1971 neatly expresses the idea: "If You're Hot, You're Hot (And If You're Not, You're Not)." But this system of reproduction does not insure that country music can survive indefinitely, because as we have seen in the discussion of the meaning of authenticity, there is an accent on being "real," and yet in the mechanical system each copy is a paler replica of the authentic original. Thus, ironically, even the most faithful attempt to preserve authenticity works to dissipate it because to copy the authentic creates what is necessarily inauthentic.

Does this mean that Tony Scherman (1994) and the other doomsayers are correct, that country music's vital life is over? Not necessarily. There are at least three other processes that in interaction pose challenges to the static institutional system.[11] Together they make possible innovations in authenticity which allow the circle to remain unbroken. Each of the processes has been discussed in earlier chapters, so these concluding comments can be brief.

The Dialectic of Hard Core and Soft Shell

As shown in chapter 9, hard-core and soft-shell traditions in music antedate the commercial country music that has been the focus of this inquiry. At least since the 1930s, when radio-based country music was firmly established as "family entertainment," commercial interests have worked to smooth over the raw, hard edges of country music to increase its commercial success, particularly with fans who may say that they don't like "country music" but do like the predominant soft-shell artist of the time, be it Red Foley, Eddy Arnold, Olivia Newton-John, Kenny Rogers, or Vince Gill (Peterson and Kern 1995). If this process of compromise gone on unabated, country music would long since have become indistinguishable from sentimental middle-of-the-road popular music. But there is also a countervailing hard-core force at work.

As this "popularizing" thrust continues, country imagery merges with the middle-of-the-road music of the time, and for some months this hyperfad "country music" may be hailed as sweeping all other forms of music before it.[12] As soon as the fad wanes, country music again seems to be on the point of extinction. But meanwhile elements of the audience craving hard-core country have long since shunned what is superpopular and have turned to emerging acts who express the hard edge in ways that are understandable to audiences of that particular time. Discovered playing in bars, honky-tonks, and college-area clubs, these "neotraditionalists" of the moment gain critical acclaim, and the most commercial of their number go on to stardom. In a few years when their style is set, their more soft-shell imitators are even more commercially successful than in the last cycle, and the impetus for softening-for-sales has returned.

This dialectic of hard core and soft shell ensures the renewal of the sense of authenticity.[13] It does not suggest why experimentation with hard-core elements takes place, and for this we turn to the recurrent conflict between generations.

The Dialectic of Generations

Innovative young artists, that is, those who fabricate a contemporary way of expressing authenticity, commonly feel that they are doing so in opposition to the music they have grown up with, finding inspiration in sources outside country music as then defined.[14] This can clearly be traced in the conflicts experienced by Jimmie Rodgers, the Delmore Brothers, Rose Maddox, Bob Wills, Ernest Tubb, Patsy Cline, Elvis Presley, and many since their time and before. For country music innovators these sources often come from the African American music of their time.[15]

The oedipal conflict between generations thus provides a wellspring of innovation. It also ensures that most of the survivors among these rebellious innovators later in life become stout defenders of the "heritage of country music," defined as all those leading up to and including the music of their generation. Shunned as bothersome "has-beens" by most among their musical children's generation, some of those who stay true to their original thrust eventually are hailed as paragons of roots-authenticity for the rising generation of their musical grandchildren and are elected into the Country Music Hall of Fame.

The Changing Production System

While the institutional field of commercial music might be considered static at any single point in time, devoted to the production of a standard product, some interests in the field as well as some outside are always working to change the structure of the field to their own advantage, while those who identify their interests with the current system staunchly defend the status quo. Changes caused by this tug-of-war are aperiodic, but from time to time they are large enough to dramatically disadvantage some types of performers and advantage others and in so doing to influence the direction of country music. All the changes in law, technology, and organizational structure have been made for some commercial purpose, but these have not always come from within the country field, and they have usually had consequences not intended by the early champions of the change. The best way to suggest briefly the change-making potential inherent in changes in the production system is with a few loosely linked illustrations.[16]

As we saw in chapter 10, the 1940s witnessed an outwelling of personal country music songs expressing love's joys and laments. Their emergence has been interpreted as a consequence of the dislocations of World War II, and the war was undoubtedly a factor. But earlier dislocations, including those surrounding World War I and the Great Depression, did not evoke a comparable outwelling of candid love songs. Up through the 1930s the structure and aesthetic of new songs was tightly controlled by a few largely New York–based song publishing firms through the performance rights collection agency ASCAP, which effectively shut out creative efforts in the blues and country fields, as John Ryan (1985) has clearly shown. He also shows that their hold was broken by the radio industry, which established a rival collection agency, Broadcast Music Incorporated (BMI). Because most of the music not under license was in blues, jazz, and country music, BMI moved into these fields, and its prime client, the radio stations, were able to program candid love music in the 1940s as never before.[17] It was thus possible for the first time to establish competitive country music publishing firms and for a large number of people to aspire to careers as country music songwriters (Ivey 1994). One of the early beneficiaries of this shift was the Acuff-Rose publishing firm and its most acclaimed songwriter, Hank Williams (Rumble 1980).

In the late 1940s the number of independent radio stations exploded and many played country music records, thus creating a means of exposing the record output of the numerous new regional recording companies that used the cheap new tape-recording technologies to produce 45-rpm records at a very low cost. This competition accelerated the experimentation with candid country music lyrics and led directly to the development of the rockabilly styles that with the rapid rise to popularity of Elvis Presley and his cohort in the 1950s, severely threatened the very existence of commercial country music (Tosches 1980).

Reacting to the threat of rock, the Country Music Association was formed in 1959. It worked to get more country music played on the radio and was so effective that by the 1970s most of the new recruits to country music radio were disk jockeys with experience in rock and pop music. Bringing their hit-oriented rock sensibilities to country music, they effectively ended the idea of country radio as a mix of new songs, old standards, bluegrass, and gospel. In the process, staples of the medium, including the likes of Ernest Tubb, Kitty Wells, and Hank Snow, were not often played on country radio. Those who happened to be at the top of the charts at the time, including Johnny Cash and Loretta Lynn, were made into superstars, and the "outlaws," including Waylon Jennings, Jessie Colter, Willie Nelson, and their followers, moved from the periphery of what was considered country music to center stage (Peterson 1978).

Beginning in Hank Williams's final years, country music began to be exposed via television, and the new medium might have quickly become a major addition to the five-element system of country music. Television was vital in exposing Elvis Presley and the other early rockers, but it was of no great importance in country music for decades because country music television of the 1950s through 1980s was produced as if it were a radio barn dance with pictures, or a videotaped live performance. Not until the big success of made-for-television music videos of popular music in the mid-1980s were country videos made that began to exploit the unique potential of the medium for reinforcing the story line of the song. More important, the tight shots that focused on facial expressions and the movements of body parts also put a great premium on youthful good looks and dancelike movements in the 1990s. The demands of video destabilized the careers of many radio artists and at the same time made possible the careers of a number of newcomers. The video close-ups also made for an updating of the old stock cowboy and hillbilly images. Singing cowboys were represented by numerous so called "hat acts," and the hillbilly image was updated in "country hunks" the likes of Billy Ray Cyrus. By the 1990s, therefore, television had joined radio, personal appearances, songwriting, publishing, and record making as a major element of the country music field.

The destabilizing influences of changes in the production system will undoubtedly continue, but they should not be considered in isolation because they usually interact with the dialectic of hard core and soft shell, with generational cycles, and with the societal changes that foster alterations in audience tastes. Initially production-system changes tend to privilege hard-core over soft-shell tendencies, but soft-shell creators quickly take advantage of the changes. In the early 1950s, for example, hard-shell innovators were the first to exploit a whole set of changes then taking place in the electrification of instruments and developments in recording studio technology—and in the process gave birth to rockabilly. But by the end of the 1950s soft-shell producers used the new technologies to create the mellow Nashville sound as well. Finally, production-system changes always tend to facilitate the breakthrough of a young generation of "roots" performers who share their construction of authenticity with a rising generation of fans and communicate their recasting of the memory of the icons of country music, including the

Carter Family, Jimmie Rodgers, Hank Williams, and more recent additions to the pantheon.[18]

CONCLUSION

In this final brief chapter I do not claim to have adequately explained how, since 1953, country music has managed to keep its identity distinct from "popular music" on the one hand and from "art" or "folk" music on the other, or how it can keep its identity in the twenty-first century. Nonetheless, the processes explored in this book, including institutionalization, generational cycles, the dialectic of hard core and soft shell, and above all, the sense of authenticity that allows something new to be plausibly represented as something unchanging, will be vital in any such effort. All that can be said with certainty is that, so long as country music remains the shared property of performers, the industry, and fans, the sense of authenticity will be preserved as it is changed.

Notes

CHAPTER ONE

1. The "southernness" of country music has been hotly contested. It is undoubtedly true that most of the notable performers come from the South and Southwest, cultivate a regional air, and most often sing of places in that region (Peterson and Gowan 1971; Peterson and Davis 1975; McLaurin and Peterson 1992; Malone 1993). At the same time it is also true that the antecedents of country music were played all across North America in the nineteenth century and gave way to commercial popular music only in the rapidly expanding centers of urban development (Peterson and DiMaggio 1975). By 1923, when the commercialization of country music began, the largest region where the older music traditions still flourished was that largely rural fertile crescent of country music starting in West Virginia, expanding down through the South (but not including peninsular Florida or New Orleans), moving west through Texas and Oklahoma, and coming to an end in Bakersfield, California (Peterson and Davis 1975). Thus the "southernness" of country music was an historical accident, but once fixed in the ichnography and in the regional styles of music that survived, white rustic southernness became an essential element of the genre.

2. This commercial decision, made at the high tide of Jim Crow racism, had the effect of obscuring the common heritage shared by American-born working-class African Americans and whites and facilitated its separation into distinct streams (Cantwell 1984). This act of segregation also set up the dialectic between black and white music in which innovators in country music from Jimmie Rodgers, Bob Wills, Hank Williams, and Elvis Presley on down to present-day performers are said, with surprise, to have been inspired by African American performers. It would be more accurate to say that both races had contributed to and drawn from a common rural working-class heritage (Rooney 1971; Otto and Burns 1974).

3. Significantly, the term "country music" was coming into general usage just at the time when most of the music's fans no longer lived in the "country." But then, as Cantwell (1984), Malone (1993), and Tichi (1994), among others, have

shown, nostalgia for elements of an imagined simpler past time have been, since before the time of Stephen Foster, an important theme in the music now called "country."

4. There had been field records made by ethnomusicologists, but these were not offered for sale on the commercial market. There had been earlier commercial records, but these had been performed by trained musicians who sang in a rustic fashion, most notably Vernon Dalhart and Wendell Hall. And there had been one earlier commercial recording by a pair of rustics, but it was not released until well after the success of the Atlanta recording by Fiddlin' John Carson. Carson's was, therefore, the first record released by a rustic (Malone 1985: 35–38; Daniel 1990: 68).

5. The systematic reshaping of collective memory has been seen as a deliberate manipulation of the past by authorities interested in justifying their own claims to power and prestige (Hobsbawm and Ranger 1983; Altheide and Johnson 1980; Gusfield 1981). It has been seen as the effort of a dominant class to subvert the interests of the working class (Ewen 1976; Coontz 1992). It has been seen as a form of marginal group resistance to domination (Lipsitz 1990; Willis 1990). It has been seen as a way ethnic groups reposition their place in society (Rhea 1995). And the misremembering of the past has been seen as a product of the unpremeditated and gradual restructuring of group identity (Zelinsky 1988; Orvell 1989; Kammen 1991; Portelli 1991).

6. It's not simply that performers, the industry, and the audience interact to create the authentic image. Each of the first three helps to shape each of the others, and the image-of-the-moment also shapes the other three. For example, as I have shown earlier (Peterson 1978), in the early 1970s, radio advertisers wanted to attract younger, more affluent listeners to country radio stations. Radio programmers decided that some popular artists, including Porter Wagoner, were "too country" for the young demographics they were seeking. The disk jockeys played numerous performers who had been defined as marginal to country music, including the "outlaws" Waylon Jennings and Willie Nelson along with crooners like Kenny Rogers and Barbara Mandrell. Many small-town fans withdrew from contemporary country music in disgust and many new, more cosmopolitan fans were attracted. The major record companies dropped most of their "too country" acts and sought out artists more in tune with the new sense of authenticity. Now, of course, all the innovative artists, disk jockeys, and record producers of the 1970s are passé, and authenticity wears a new face.

7. Jazz shared much of the same stigma as a Southern music originated by poor African Americans, but it was explicitly avant-gardist, focusing on musical innovation and the latest urbane fashions in dress, dance, and language. Thus, by the late 1920s, jazz was embraced by many in the commercial music industry as the benchmark of what was cool (Peterson 1972; Vincent 1995).

8. On the origins and use of the term "hillbilly," see Green (1965: 204–28).

9. For excellent reviews of the general characteristics of the process of institutionalization, see DiMaggio and Powell (1991), Powell and DiMaggio (1991), and Dobbin (1992).

10. It is conventional to write that these four musics "borrow" from each other, but until the mid-1920s when the workings of the music industry began

to clearly institutionalize the differences (Ennis 1992), it is probably more accurate to think of there being one caldron out of which creative efforts are drawn. Thus, for example, when Jimmie Rodgers, Maybelle Carter, Bob Wills, Bill Monroe, Hank Williams, Chet Atkins, and many others said that they learned particular elements of their style from black performers, it meant something quite different from Paul McCartney's learning his falsetto yell from Little Richard. The country performers were being honest about the specific sources, but, unlike the Liverpudlian Paul McCartney, who was learning a vocal expression foreign to his background, by acknowledging a specific African American source, they are distancing themselves from the Southern working-class cultural heritage shared with African Americans.

11. For the details of my view of the evolution of jazz from folk to popular to fine art music up through the early 1970s, see Peterson (1972). The institutionalization of symphonic music "fine art" in the latter part of the nineteenth century necessitated the financial support of wealthy patrons of magnificent concert halls, symphonic orchestras, and conservatories for the training of performers (DiMaggio 1982).

12. Some intellectuals do not use the term "folk" in describing the blues because they do not separate any African American–based music from the rest. Rather they tend to see the blues, ragtime, jazz, rhythm and blues, soul, funk, and rap as elements of the continuing black experience in America (George 1988; Henry Lewis Gates interview with the author, December 3, 1989, at the National Humanities Center).

Diverse sorts of music are now called "blues," but blues is called folk music here because of the way it is now created, enjoyed, and preserved. By "folk" music I mean the various kinds of music that are studied, collected, composed, or performed by those interested in the oral music of any group of people. These include traditional performers, scholars and students in academic departments of folklife, ethnomusicologists, the staffs of various government agencies, including the Folklife Division of the National Endowment for the Arts, the Folk Division of the Smithsonian Institution, the Library of Congress, the National Folklife Endowment, and the many people who make a living by presenting one or another form of folk music for the edification and enjoyment of diverse audiences. The question of authenticity is hotly contested in these circles. For widely contrasting views, see Harker (1985), and Cantwell (1996).

Over the years there has been a lively debate among folklorists over what should be considered folk music. Frances James Child, working in the latter part of the nineteenth century, tried to differentiate traditional English and Scottish ballads from more recent compositions produced for sale as broadsides and in songbooks. The fruits of his painstaking detective work can be seen in the monumental five-volume *English and Scottish Popular Ballads* published between 1882 and 1897. More recent scholars recognize that many songs produced for sale by the commercial music industry, both while Child was working and since, now pass from musician to musician by word of mouth and thus have entered the oral tradition. What is more, some oral-tradition songs have been adapted for commercial recording and have subsequently reentered the oral tradition as performers learned the songs from commercial phonograph records and subsequently taught them to others. See Green (1972), and Dugaw (1987) for examples of this complex exchange between commercial and oral streams.

Further complicating the question of what folk music is, professional "folk musicians," including Pete Seeger, Joan Baez, Jack Elliot, and many more, have since the 1940s been reviving old songs and composing new ones in one or another folk style (Schmidt and Rooney 1979; Rosenberg 1985: 109–12, 143–61; Eyerman and Baretta 1996). Thus "folk music" has become a recognized species of commercial entertainment (Brand 1962; Ennis 1992). The authenticity of such *commercial* folk music is found by probing the aesthetic choices of this music's creators, critics, and connoisseurs rather than by assessing the response of a social group or category of people whose music it is said to represent.

13. As they have dropped from wide popularity, some country music styles have been preserved and perpetuated in ways similar to those of folk and art music. Bluegrass is the best documented case in point.

14. For discussions of the lyrical themes in country music see Gaillard (1978), Horstman (1986), Rogers (1989), McLaurin and Peterson (1992), and Tichi (1994). Patricia Averill (1975) provides a wide range of fascinating speculations about the meanings of lyrics in her dissertation on the evolving worldview of rural-born Southern whites since World War I as seen in the lyrics of country music. A number of worthwhile studies could be spawned from the questions she raises.

15. Country music's continuation in the twenty-first century is not inevitable. To say that country music has not been coopted or absorbed into commercial popular music is not to say that it will not be in the future. There are precedents for major forms of communally based commercial music being absorbed. For example, in his book *The Death of Rhythm and Blues* (1988), Nelson George shows how this vigorous cognate musical form lost its autonomy and was absorbed. With the exception of gospel music, popular black musical forms have been avant-gardist in orientation, thus systematically turning the face of the rising generations away from their rich musical heritage. Ironically, insisting on being traditional may facilitate country music's survival into the future.

16. The elements of the production perspective basic to this paragraph, and indeed to the entire book, can be found in Peterson (1976, 1990, 1994), Crane (1992), and Fine (1996).

17. One example of each will suggest their importance. *Law:* The enforcement of copyright law helped to focus the attention of early producers on finding new and therefore copyrightable songs, and from the late 1940s on, made it possible for many people to make a living as country music songwriters. *Technology:* The era of commercial country music was launched by the development of radio and of field-recording equipment that made it possible to record prospective country music artists in Atlanta, Bristol, and wherever else they could be congregated. *Careers:* The early artists were recruited haphazardly, and mostly from the ranks of amateurs, but based on the success of Jimmie Rodgers and others, a younger generation of aspirants, including Roy Acuff and Ernest Tubb, had clear models of how to make a career in country music. *Market:* Market refers to the industry's always incomplete conception of audience preferences. The idea of many early impresarios, for example, that audiences wanted to see old men play-

ing traditional tunes, led them to seek out cranky old geezers, most of whom enjoyed very little success. *Industry Structure:* Before World War I very few country music artists could get full-time employment as performers, and then usually as novelty acts on the vaudeville stage circuit (Bufwack and Oermann 1982; Childers 1988). An industry based on radio appearances, touring, record making, song publishing, and the movies was developed from the ground up by a large number of entrepreneurs, and each chapter in this book can be read as a stage in the institutionalization of the country music industry.

18. I have argued elsewhere that the limit on the rate of innovation is never determined by the supply of entrepreneurial talent. It is limited by the structural arrangements that facilitate or frustrate that talent (Peterson 1981).

CHAPTER TWO

I particularly want to thank Wayne Daniel, Ed Kahn and Nolan Porterfield for their helpful comments on an earlier version of this and the next chapter.

1. As David Whisnant has shown, from 1890 on, numerous folklorists and social workers had been coming to the Southern mountain regions to collect, preserve, and, when necessary, teach what he calls in the words of one of their number, Olive Dame Campbell, "all that is native and fine" (1983: 103). On the extent of these efforts to instruct highlanders in "their own culture" see also Shapiro (1978: 130–31, 218–43).

2. Some serious scholars argue that because what they think of as "country music" is by definition music played in an appropriate setting before a live audience, no electronically transmitted performance can be authentic. Others argue that many of the recordings made in the 1920s are authentic transcriptions of such music but that most of the recorded music since is so changed by the constraints of commercialism that it has lost its authenticity.

3. Phonograph record sales were in decline and many in the industry concluded that the phonograph was a novelty whose time was passing (Sanjek 1988: 63–64). In 1923 radio was an exciting prospect, but it was not then seen primarily as a vehicle for exploiting music or making careers in music. In a 1922 letter sent from Kashmir, India, by a young woman to her farming relatives in southern Ohio, one can begin to sense what a wonder radio was considered to be and how powerful its projected consequences. "What leaps and bounds radio telephony etc. are taking all of a sudden. The *Literary Digest* is full of it. If I was a boy, I'd be awfully excited and anxious to have my fingers on it all. As it is I'm excited enough! In a few years we'll talk to you from [India] and sakes only knows what you will be able to do in the States—having market reports, concerts, lectures, sermons, etc. right at home while you sit with your feet by the fire" (Edna Peterson, personal letter written home to her parents and siblings June 2, 1922).

4. In order to become professionals, aspiring young musicians had to forsake country music and go into the popular music field, and it is impossible to say how many creative performers were lost to the genre by these constraints.

5. One of the few who worked full-time as a musician was "Uncle" Dave Macon of Woodbury, Tennessee, who traveled on the Southern vaudeville circuit in the years just before the coming of radio. In a sense, Macon was not really an exception to the rule of semiprofessionalism. He began touring in 1921 at

the age of fifty-one soon after he sold his (mule-driven) contract freight-hauling business and had grown sons who worked the family farm (Wolfe 1975a).

6. In the 1930s McMichen fronted another hot band, the Georgia Wildcats, and in the 1945–55 period he converted the string band to a Dixieland band (Cohen 1975: 27–34; Daniel 1990: 105–8). Why was his string-Dixieland band of the 1920s not more popular? If it had been, McMichen could now be considered the father of a music much like what two decades later emerged as bluegrass.

7. This story may be true as Wiggins recounts it, but as Charles Wolfe has cautioned in personal correspondence, Uncle Dave Macon, Prince Albert Hunt, Grandpa Jones, and others all tell a similar story about their early performing experience.

8. Charles Townsend's (1976) book on Bob Wills gives an excellent description of the hard-scrabble life of string-band groups playing for ranch parties and dances.

9. These contests, however, were important for the development of country music because they brought together artists playing in a number of different styles and fostered rapid innovation in showy fiddle-playing techniques. In particular, the contests disadvantaged those who, like John Carson, played with short bow strokes the highly rhythmic square-dance music, and who played with the fiddle on the shoulder so they could sing at the same time. This gave the advantage to those who played with the more melodic "long bow" technique, holding the fiddle under the chin (Spielman 1975).

10. Gordon Tanner's recollection of his father's being asked to play in front of stores to draw a crowd to the location includes passing the hat for tips. While this may well have happened, store owners would not have appreciated the disturbance of street musicians unless the entertainment was defined as a service that would draw customers into the store. The financial arrangements between the store owner and his father might well have escaped the attention of Gordon, who was only "five or six" at the time (Burrison 1977). The practice of having country-style entertainment for special commercial events was practiced widely on an organized basis at the turn of the century. In Nashville, for example, Lower Broad Street was closed to traffic during the annual spring festival held by the local furniture stores then congregated in the area, and musicians played for the crowds (interview with Herman Crook by Paul DiMaggio and me, 1973, supplemented by an interview with Fred Beesley, owner of one of those stores, both in Nashville).

11. This reasoning persisted through the 1930s. Many phonograph records made in that era, for example, included on their labels, "Not licensed for radio air play."

12. Unless otherwise indicated, all the information for this section comes from the transcripts of interviews held in Atlanta with Polk Brockman by Archie Green, Ed Kahn, and sometimes Helen Sewell between August 11, 1961, and August 27, 1963, supplemented by my interview and exchange of letters with Brockman in September and October 1973.

13. This "Atlanta story" is conventionally told with John Carson at the center of the piece (Burrison 1977; Daniel 1984, 1985; Wiggins 1987) and with Brock-

man seen as a minor player, but Brockman's insights and his failings more uniquely capture the essence of commercial developments and failures there.

14. With encouragement from Brockman, some country music scholars have considered this the first case of a commercial firm making field recordings. Actually, this was a widespread practice. As Gronow (1981) notes, in the first decade of this century the major record companies made tens of thousands of commercial records under field conditions for markets in Asia. For example, between 1900 and 1910, the Gramophone Company made 4,410 records in India. Gronow reprints a picture of the Beka Company portable recording equipment in Rangoon mounted on a bullock cart.

15. Four notable disputes are as follows: (1) Was Carson a last-minute substitute, or did Brockman leave him off the agreed performer list so that Peer could not object to spending the company money to record an unknown type of performer?

(2) Did Peer pronounce the result "plu perfect awful?" And if he did, was he making an aesthetic judgment about Carson's performance, or was he referring to the poor technical quality of the recording? Most later commentators have assumed it was an aesthetic judgment, but in an interview with Hugh Cherry years later, referring to the Fiddlin' John session, Peer said, "This was a very difficult recording proposition because it was before the invention of the so-called electrical recording system. We had to use large horns and it was really troublesome getting both the fiddle played by Carson and his voice all into the mouth of the one [recording] horn. When the wax recording got back to New York and had been processed, I listened to those two items, and believe me they were terrible" (Cherry 1970: hour 1, section 2).

(3) Was the original pressing for 500 copies, as Brockman said; or for 1000, as Peer, near the end of his life, said? Robert Pinson (personal communication June 21, 1996) says the latter number would have been highly unusual in 1923 for an unknown artist. Sometimes as few as 100 records were pressed.

(4) Did Peer originally refuse to release the song with an Okeh master number and give it an Okeh label only when its popularity had been demonstrated? This is the standard story, but Pinson says that as far as he knows no copies of the original 500/1000 custom pressings have been unearthed in the past forty years of intensive record hunting. Reading through these questions, one can see that the common theme is a dispute over whether Brockman or Peer deserves the prime credit for "finding" Carson and "starting" country music.

16. Many early artists were payed a flat fee of ten or twenty-five dollars for each song cut, while others like John Carson were paid a royalty of two cents on each record sold. Vernon Dalhart and Jimmie Rodgers were the only artists singing country songs who made any considerable amount of money from their record sales in the 1920s (Haden 1975; Porterfield 1992).

17. Unless otherwise indicated, the details of how Brockman commissioned, transcribed, and published songs is taken from the remarkable series of letters written between July 30, 1957, and September 13, 1960, to Archie Green and John Edwards by Irene Spain, the step-daughter of Reverend Andrew Jenkins, who was employed to render the songs composed by Jenkins into standard musi-

cal notation for later sale as sheet music. Irene Spain also transcribed from phono-graph records onto sheet music for Brockman many of the songs by other coun-try, blues, and gospel artists whom he was recording. These letters are in the John Edwards Memorial Foundation Archive.

18. Interview with Polk Brockman conducted by Archie Green and Ed Kahn, August 11, 1961, on file in the John Edwards Memorial Foundation.

19. Ibid.; also my interviews with Cotton Carrier and Jack Stapp in 1972. See also the letters by Irene Spain referenced in note 17 above.

20. Green and Kahn interviews with Polk Brockman. See note 12.

21. Unlike the later "National Barn Dance" broadcast from WLS in Chicago, which was a sort of rural variety show, the early WBAP broadcasts were simulated barn dances with a string band and square-dance calling fiddler.

22. Lambdin Kay came from a musical family whose tastes did not include country music. Kay was born in Brooklyn, New York. His mother was billed as a "noted pianist/composer" in her frequent WSB appearances in the 1920s, and his brother was the conductor of an Atlanta theater orchestra (Personal corre-spondence from Wayne W. Daniel, June 23, 1987). According to Cotton Carrier, long-time employee of WSB whom I interviewed in 1972, "WSB never did have an owner or general manager who liked country music. They wanted just enough to satisfy local advertisers and weren't interested in building the reputation of the station on country music." For more on Cotton Carrier see Daniel (1981). The WSB "Barn Dance" folded early in 1950 (Malone 1985).

23. Ernest Rogers, a doctor's son and Emery University graduate, did assist Lambdin Kay in selecting musical groups. Rogers played and sang country music from time to time, but apparently in a tongue-in-cheek manner (Daniel 1990: 49). Daniel's evaluation of his attitude has been contested, but the fact remains that in his work at the station through 1940 Rogers did not play an important role in developing country music on the radio, as did a number of others.

24. WSB's interest in country music revived in the 1940s after Austin Cox, former governor of Ohio, became the publisher of the *Atlanta Journal,* the news-paper that owned WSB. He believed that supporting country music in the South would bolster his run for the presidency of the United States. Cox called in John Lair, who had years of experience in programming country music radio at WLS in Chicago and WLW in Cincinnati (Daniel 1990).

25. When he talked with me in 1973, Brockman denied that he had ever published any songs, though he was quick to claim priority in developing other aspects of the commercialization of country music. Perhaps by 1973 he had be-come sensitive to the exploitation implicit in publishing the songs of others with-out adequately compensating them. In 1961, he told Archie Green and Ed Kahn that although he had paid for many of Andrew Jenkins's songs, he had only "got his money out of a few."

26. I have no direct evidence that the writers of songs that Brockman bought felt exploited, but this sense of pride in creativity and fear of having work stolen was often voiced to John Ryan and me in our study of country music songwriters (Ryan and Peterson 1982; Peterson and Ryan 1983). Perhaps it is significant that the only songwriter with whom Polk Brockman developed a lasting relationship was the preacher Andrew Jenkins. Jenkins apparently felt that the songs were a

gift of God and not his property. For more details on this remarkably prolific man, see the letters available in the Southern Folklife Collection at the University of North Carolina, Chapel Hill, which his step-daughter and collaborator, Irene Spain, wrote to John Edwards and to Archie Green.

CHAPTER THREE

1. The appellation "A&R man" is said as one word, and the "man" part was accurate because no women served in this capacity in country music for about fifty years.

2. This model of the role didn't enter the popular music field until the advent of rock music in the 1950s, when the A&R man came to be referred to as the "producer" (Peterson and Berger 1971).

3. The sales figures come from Charles Wolfe in a private communication, July 1996.

4. Two of the categories created by Wolfe, Comedy and Gospel, do not distinguish between traditional (Wolfe categories A and B), popular music (Wolfe categories C and D), and original country songs (Wolfe categories E, H, and I) and so they have been eliminated from this analysis. The eight Cajun songs recorded in 1928 have also been eliminated.

5. David Evans has analyzed the record production of blues artist Blind Lemon Jefferson on a year-by-year basis, so it is easy to see any changes taking place. Jefferson's career was tragically short. He suffered a heart attack and froze to death in a Chicago blizzard in 1930 at the age of thirty-five. His first releases in 1926 were billed by Paramount Records as "a real old-fashioned blues by a real old-fashioned blues singer" (Evans 1982: 76). In 1926 the billing was accurate. As Evans shows, that year thirteen sides were traditional, three were adaptations of traditional material, and none were original. By 1929, his last year to record, none were traditional, only one was an adaptation of traditional material, and twenty-one were original compositions (Evans 1982: 77).

6. Since of all the A&R men, Ralph Peer was the most eager to record new material, it would be interesting to examine a year-by-year comparison of the sources of the songs that he supervised. Unfortunately, no one has yet made such a comparison. And since the available evidence suggests that the change to new songs came faster for the blues (Evans 1982) than for country music (Wolfe 1972), it would be good to compare the recorded results of Peer's works in these two fields.

7. The corporate frugality was a facade. Peer later learned that the treasurer earned an additional annual "bonus" of $25,000. Personal communication of September 11, 1995, from Nolan Porterfield.

8. The information on how Ralph Peer came to see the importance of using copyrights is drawn from Porterfield (1992) supplemented by the remarkable set of rambling interviews conducted with Peer in 1959 by Lillian Borgeson.

9. Peer later said that he "worked for nothing," but Ed Kahn says he agreed to work for one dollar a year. This latter seems likely because the token salary was a standard way that persons whose services were volunteered could avoid violating labor laws. During both world wars many people were loaned to the government by corporations and they were called "dollar-a-year" employees.

10. Peer did encourage artists to buy songs. That way, the artist would get writer royalties and the animus of the original songwriter would be directed at the performer, not at Peer.

11. This element of Peer's "generosity" was both at Victor's expense and at its prompting. Ironically, the executives at Victor were shocked when Peer suggested paying hillbillies just twenty-five dollars per side. Victor was the premier record company then, and felt it had a reputation to maintain. Peer quotes executive Nat Shilkret as saying, "You can't make any recordings for Victor at $25 apiece. That's entirely too cheap. It might get out and we can't stand that kind of publicity" (Porterfield 1992: 104).

12. In the depths of the Depression when record sales fell dramatically Peer did resort to buying songs outright even from such notable artists as the Carter Family (Wolfe, forthcoming).

13. When an artist would come with a song in the public domain, Peer would have it changed enough so that he could copyright it as an original or at least as a unique arrangement.

14. An unsigned article in the February 18, 1926, *Musical Courier* (1926) is also instructive because it describes a song-hunting trip taken by Nathaniel Shilkret, who would be a close Victor associate of Ralph Peer.

15. By "overarranged" jazz offerings the author would not have had in mind the freewheeling recordings of Louis Armstrong and the other early jazz greats whose records, at the time, sold primarily to blacks. He would have been referring to the insipid and formulaic offerings of the white dance bands such as the various units directed by Paul Whiteman, who, riding the jazz craze, had dubbed himself the "king of Jazz" (Leonard 1962).

16. The prime sources for this section are Charles Wolfe's extensive liner notes for the Rounder Records reissue "The Carter Family: Their Complete Victor Recordings." As of this writing, the first five of nine of the projected CDs are commercially available, and Charles Wolfe has shown me his text for the sixth. Supplementary sources include Kahn (1970), Wolfe (1972, 1987), Koon (1974), and Atkins (1975).

17. It was customary for country folk of that time to wear their very best clothes whenever they went to town. A. P. is pictured in a conservative suit, white shirt, and tie in all the group publicity photos, even when the group is pictured in a rural scene (see gallery figure G1.3).

18. It was not until 1938 that the Carter Family began an association with a powerful radio station. And this one was located in Mexico just across the border from Del Reo, Texas, beamed at rural audiences in the United States. The increased exposure the family received probably stimulated record sales, but did not lead to lucrative touring opportunities because they broadcast from such a remote location.

19. In the 1930s the Carters did not have professional managers and they did not work on the established Southern vaudeville and theater circuits. Promotion consisted entirely of small handbills that A. P. Carter had printed himself. Their performances typically began with a brief introductory number. Then A. P. would introduce the group and the next number. The women sat and A. P. stood, often pacing or wandering offstage while the women were performing. A sense of his

halting and humorless style can be heard in the announcements he made for station XERA. Selected transcriptions are available on "The Carter Family on Border Radio," JEMF LP 101.

20. The word "original" is used here to differentiate this working threesome from later combinations of the family that performed together. The Carter Family name is now known among fans primarily through the later work of Maybelle Carter and her three performing daughters on the "Grand Ole Opry" (and touring with Elvis Presley). One of these daughters, June, continued to tour in the 1990s with her husband, Johnny Cash, and June's daughter, Carlene, has carried the family name forward into a third generation of country music performers.

21. The prime source for the material in this section is Nolan Porterfield's (1992) excellent biography of Jimmie Rodgers and his (1995) essay accompanying the complete Rodgers recordings released by the Bear Family. Unless otherwise noted, all direct quotations in this section are from Lillian Borgeson's 1959 interviews with Ralph Peer.

22. In the course of the interviews with Lillian Borgeson, Peer also said that he "invented" Louis Armstrong.

23. Rodgers's first wife, Stella Kelly, reemerged years later with an eleven-year-old daughter. Rodgers was willing to accept paternity and pay support, but when Stella pressed for much more, the case went to court and her claims were denied.

24. Accounts vary as to the cause of the rupture. Did Rodgers dump the group, did they dump him, or did Ralph Peer split them up? My sense is that the musicians fought over who would get top billing and the leader's cut of the session money for recording. Rodgers wanted the money very much to take his wife and daughter to Washington, D.C. In any case, at the first sessions Peer cut three songs on the reconstituted Tennava Ramblers and two on Jimmie Rodgers.

25. Twenty-six years later in Meridian, Mississippi, for the unveiling of the Jimmie Rodgers memorial, Ralph Peer remembered his reaction to Rodgers's recording a bit differently. He told a *Meridian Star* reporter, "I was elated when I heard [Rodgers] perform without the unsuitable accompaniment. . . . I thought his yodeling alone might spell success. . . . I considered Rodgers to be one of my best bets" (May 26, 1953: 24). Thanks to Nolan Porterfield for this excerpt.

26. A plantation owner would provide housing tools and seed for a crop and allow the sharecropper to charge expenses at the general store (which he may have owned). The sharecroppers had a great incentive to work as hard as possible because they got a proportion of the profits from the crop. When the crop was harvested the money due to the sharecropper was computed by the plantation owner and it would generally pay off the accumulated charges but little more, so the sharecropper would have to contract for another year.

27. This conclusion about what aspects of the recording process the A&R men controlled and the freedom they gave to their artists is derived from a wide range of sources, including interviews with Art Satherley, Polk Brockman, Frank Walker, and Ralph Peer, as well as the published accounts in Cohen (1965), Wolfe (1972), Seeger (1973), Wiggins (1987), and Porterfield (1992).

28. Sara Carter's half-hearted Jimmie Rodgers–style yodeling can be heard in several songs cut in 1928. Listen to "The Foggy Mountain Top" and "Sweet

Fern" available on Rounder Records' CD *The Carter Family: Their Complete Victor Recordings,* vol. 2.

29. Recording producers of the 1920s did not make aesthetic judgments about which of the recorded country or blues songs to release. Rather these decisions were made by company functionaries on the basis of the technical quality of the reproduction process and on the prior sales success of the particular performer (Oliver 1984). It would be interesting to know who decided not to release Jimmie Rodgers's one recorded social protest song, "Prohibition Has Done Me Wrong." Of all the songs he ever. cut, it is the only one never released, and, in fact, the master was lost. The song says that many people vote dry and drink wet and that preachers too are hypocrites. It cautions that when people can't get alcohol they turn to "dope, cocaine, and morphine" so that "Prohibition has killed more folks than Sherman ever seen." The song concludes that Prohibition is just a scheme, a money-making machine. Ironically, the song is known today only because it was earlier recorded by Clayton McMichen, its author (as Bob Nichols) (Wolfe 1993). In that rendition McMichen sings and yodels in a way very reminiscent of Jimmie Rodgers.

30. Peer's attitude toward the music he was recording on field trips was not unusual. F. W. Gaisberg, recording with field equipment in Shanghai, China, in 1903, most candidly expressed the aesthetic blindness of the early field-recording A&R men when he said, "On the first day, after making ten records we had to stop. The din had so paralyzed my wits that I could not think. . . . Up to the 27th of March we made 325 records for which we paid $4 each. To me the differences between the tunes of any two records were too slight for me to detect" (Gaisberg 1942: 62–63).

31. This quotation is from the interview between Hugh Cherry and Ernest Tubb for the radio show called the "Jimmie Rodgers Story."

32. There is no substitute for listening to Rodgers's music to show that most of it sounds like blues. Rodgers's oeuvre is now readily available because in 1995 the Bear Family Corporation of Hamburg, Germany, released a complete set of all of the songs recorded for Victor by Jimmie Rodgers. These include hitherto unreleased alternate takes of numbers, the sound-track of a movie short, and a blackface comedy routine, "The Pullman Reporters," which Rodgers made in 1930.

33. It is known from the record that Jimmie Rodgers selected the songs he chose to record and the backing aggregations, but it is not as clear who crafted the other elements that made up the "Jimmie Rodgers image," the image that proved attractive to so many millions of people and influenced singers, popular as well as country, for decades. Although Porterfield (1992) does not say so in so many words, the conclusion that emerges from his detailed study of Rodgers's career is that Jimmie Rodgers, working virtually on his own, produced the Rodgers image. While Ralph Peer was nominally his manager, he seems to have taken no lead in crafting an image. Rodgers worked with a number of bookers and promoters, but like other country artists of the time, he did not have a manager who had a financial stake in building Rodgers's long-run career. No one, as far as I know, has researched the sources of inspiration for Rodgers's publicity photo shoots (sampled in gallery 1) in which he is pictured in a wide range of attire.

It may well be that no one gave a great deal of thought to the overall image the photos helped to create. The particular garb may have been dictated by the publicity needs of the moment.

34. When this mix of music reemerged again it did so, of course, under the rubric of "rock 'n' roll."

35. To the amazement of music industry analysts, the sales of country music records did not fall proportionately. *Variety* headlined a 1933 article "Billy Tunes Still Bullish," but a rapidly increasing number of these represented mail-order sales of records that had been recorded years earlier (Porterfield 1992: 338).

CHAPTER FOUR

1. These include *The Deerslayer, The Last of the Mohicans, The Pathfinder, The Prairie,* and *The Pioneers.* The latter casts a character very much like Cooper's father as a leading modernist destroyer of the leatherstocking's way of life.

2. The word "western" is properly capitalized when it refers to a geographical region such as the Western United States. In this discussion, however, it refers to a way of dress, a kind of music, or a way of life. As such, it no more deserves to be capitalized than does hillbilly, rockabilly, or crooner.

3. Given Carson's usual performance style, "shall we say," was probably a coy way of conveying to the knowledgeable Atlanta reader of the time, "until Carson was too drunk to continue" (Wiggins: 1987).

4. The association between the Benét poem and the newspaper account of Lowe Stokes's victory was suggested by Bill Harrison (1969). A readily available version of the fiddling contest between the Devil and the brash youth can be heard in the Charlie Daniels Band's "Devil Went Down to Georgia."

5. Throughout the nation's history the West has been the prime locus of the imagined unspoiled land, but for the fifty years following 1880 the Appalachian region rivaled the West for this honor (Shapiro 1978; McNeil 1995).

6. The fiddling convention rapidly lost popularity by 1935 as string bands fronted by vocalists came to predominate in popularity. Old-time fiddling has enjoyed a renaissance of popularity since 1960 as a form of preservationist music where legitimate styles and the bounds of orthodoxy are carefully monitored by contest judges and devoted listeners alike (Blaustein 1975).

7. Henry Ford was hardly alone in his view of the city. In the eyes of the leading architect of the time, Frank Lloyd Wright, the city was "a place fit for banking and prostitution and not much else. . . . Is this not Anti-Christ? The Moloch that knows no God but more?" (Kimmel 1994: 19).

8. Ford was serious in his support of anti-Semitism. He kept on the payroll Fritz Kuhn, the pro-Nazi leader of the German-American Bund, and accepted the Grand Cross of the German Eagle from Hitler in 1938 (Dahlinger 1977: 108).

9. Personal communication from Donald V. Baut, Curator of Research for the Dearborn Historical Museum, September 10, 1973.

10. In reviewing a number of interviews, I have noted the high level of anger felt by fiddlers interviewed thirty or forty years after the events of 1925–26. See for example Bob Pinson's 1963 interview of Charlie Stripling of Kennedy, Alabama. While some fiddling contests of the preceding decades had been fixed, the sense of unfairness probably more often came from the fact that aesthetic stan-

dards varied widely from area to area. Thus when a local favorite ventured into the territory of another, the second would have the advantage on aesthetic grounds irrespective of any conscious bias. Only in the 1950s were organizations established that fixed what was allowable as "old-time" fiddling (Blaustein 1975; Spielman 1975).

11. The information on the activities of Jean Thomas and J. W. Day, a.k.a. Jilson Setters, comes from Jean Thomas (1930), *Literary Digest* (1932), *American Magazine* (1933), *Time* (1934), *Newsweek* (1935a, 1935b), Archie Green (1972: 174–82), and Stephen F. Davis (1978).

12. See the liner notes to Rounder Records LP 1010, "Parkersberg Landing," for the details of her offer to Ed Haley. One can imagine how this Faustian offer might have seemed to the old fiddler.

13. Day's best-known event song is "Coal Creek Troubles," chronicling aspects of the war that raged intermittently in the 1890s on the Cumberland plateau of eastern Tennessee between free coal miners and those supporting the mine owners' use of convict labor. See Archie Green (1972: 175–84) for a description of the war and the various versions of the song.

14. He did record twice again for the Library of Congress. Under the direction of Jean Thomas in 1934 he recorded several traditional ballads and one about his stage character, "Fiddler of Lost Hope Hollow." Then in 1937 he recorded fifteen songs for John A. Lomax. These were primarily event and commentary songs, which ranged from "The Nigger's Wedding" to "Assassination of Governor Gobel," "Coal Creek Troubles," and "Franklin Roosevelt" (Davis 1978).

15. Stringfield, thirty-three at the time of the publication of the bulletin, was the son of a Raleigh, North Carolina, Baptist minister. He attended Wake Forest College and studied flute and composition at the Institute of Musical Art in New York City. Stringfield had been guest conductor for a number of orchestras and had held conducting appointments with the Newark and Nashville symphony orchestras as well as with the Washington National Opera Association. Among his many compositions on American themes was "From the Southern Mountains," which won the 1928 Pulitzer Prize for composition.

16. I don't mean to suggest that the University of North Carolina Press was more prejudiced than any other of the time. In fact in the mid-1920s, it published two excellent anthologies of Southern black songs collected and edited by sociologists Howard Odum and Guy B. Johnson (1925, 1926).

17. All quotations in this and the next two paragraphs are drawn from the *University of North Carolina Extension Bulletin* (Stringfield 1931). Page numbers for quotations are given in the text.

18. Though he recorded operatic arias, blackface minstrel songs, and traditional country music, Dalhart was never depicted in the garb of the characters he sang. He always appeared in a well-tailored business suit, pudgy and looking very much a solid banker (Walsh 1955, 1960; Haden 1975).

19. Rodgers never appeared in the conservative wedding-church-and-burial suit of the old-timer or the bib overalls of a hillbilly. He did, of course, appear in the work clothes of his pre–music career job, that of an up-to-date industrial railroad worker. There are snapshots of him in a cowboy hat and boots, but

these appear only after he built his dream house in Kerrville, Texas, and as his biographer, Nolan Porterfield (1992: 211), notes, there is no evidence Rodgers ever performed in western garb.

CHAPTER FIVE

1. Moore (1957) shows that the Kentucky frontiersman was portrayed as a Noble Savage both in the fictional literature of the nineteenth century and in the newspapers of the day. One of the most quickly mythologized frontiersmen of the trans-Appalachian West was Davy Crockett, who in 1831, when he was forty-five and a U.S. Congressman, was made larger than life in the hit play "Lion of the West."

2. Thompson was not the first country music performer to appear on WSM. Humphrey Bate and several others had appeared in the months before as part of the brand-new station's mix of programming (Peterson 1975; Wolfe 1975b).

3. Old-time fiddler John Carson had been the featured country music performer on WSB in Atlanta, but his radio performances were not like those of Uncle Jimmy Thompson. Carson's fiddling style did represent the older style of playing (Spielman 1975), but he performed a wide range of types of songs. He played with a number of other artists, and, holding the base of the fiddle against his shoulder, he often sang while playing. Carson's versatility was due to the fact that during most of his preradio performances he had been a featured entertainer rather than an accompanist for square dancing (Wiggins 1987).

4. This is the impression given in Hay's book and in the numerous popular articles written about the program. For a representative sampling of these, see Gentry (1969). A similar view is also presented in Malone (1985).

5. For that year, and that year alone, the complete WSM program "Diary" has been preserved. The "Diary" is held in a special collection of Vanderbilt's Central Library. This record of the Opry in 1928 is augmented by material found in the Country Music Foundation Archives in Nashville, Tennessee. Finally, much valuable insight has been gained through talking with people familiar with the Opry and WSM in the late 1920s. Interviewees included DeFord Bailey, Alcyone Bate Beasley, Norm Cohen, Herman and Helen Crook, John DeWitt, Sid Harkreader, Bert Hutcherson, Claude Lamply, Bert Layne, Kirk McGee, Ed Poplin, Jr., Bob Pinson, Blythe Poteete, Aaron Shelton, and Charles Wolfe. Information gleaned from the "Diary" proved particularly valuable in helping our informants recall the details of the early era.

6. As Wolfe (1973) notes, two other Nashville radio stations, WDAD and WLAC, had regular evening country music shows in 1928.

7. A good description of how roads, records, and radio served to professionalize country music groups is presented by Rorrer (1972).

8. Apparently Hay and McConnell never recorded any of their courtroom skits, and no transcripts have been found. According to our informants they were not unlike the judge-and-defendant skits revived on TV by Sammy Davis, Jr. and Flip Wilson in the 1970s. In 1926, however, George Hay did publish a most remarkable book, *Howdy Judge* (Hay 1926). It is a series of brief, fictionalized courtroom encounters between a white judge and a series of black defendants

which Hay wrote for the Memphis *Commercial Appeal* while he was a court reporter in that city before becoming a radio announcer. A remarkable portrayal
of race relations, a number of these stories could easily be adapted as radio skits.
One such example follows:

> "I sells sea food, jedge," testified a witness James Wright, negro, charged
> with larceny. "Sounds like a fish story to me," commented the judge. "Who
> did you say took that watch?" "I says a boy by de name o' Hamp Funny
> Face stole it f'm de gen'man." "What do they call the defendant?" "Calls
> him Geetch." "All right, we'll hold Geetch to the State. He's got a mighty
> shifty eye on him. Think the grand jury ought to look into them." (p. 45)

and another:

> "When were you twenty-one?" the court asked Albert Menfield, negro,
> charged with a misdemeanor. "Yistiddy." "Yes, but you drove a car before
> yesterday, didn't you?" "I reckon so." "Why didn't you get a license?" "Jes'
> kep' on puttin' it off." "You put it on," advised the court, as he fined him
> $10. (pp. 27–28)

Not only was "live" Negro dialect humor part of the Opry in 1928, but in the
early 1930s, a fifteen-minute segment of the "Amos 'n' Andy" show was presented
weekly in the midst of the Opry. According to Aaron Shelton, WSM engineer of
that time, the "Amos 'n' Andy" show from NBC was simply too popular not to
air, and it had to be broadcast live when transmitted because stations then did
not have the ability to transcribe programs for airing at a later time.

9. It is interesting to note that while the "Grand Ole Opry" is often called
the oldest continuous program on radio, there was no Opry on September 22,
1928. That night U. S. Senator William Borah, Republican, gave a political speech
that was rebutted by Governor Alfred E. Smith, Democrat. Again in 1969, following the assassination of Martin Luther King, Jr., troops of the Tennessee National
Guard occupied Nashville, the city was under curfew, and there was no live Opry
performance. WSM listeners heard the rebroadcast of a show that had been taped
earlier. That afternoon, Roy Acuff and several other Opry regulars put on a benefit concert in the Ryman auditorium as their contribution to the diffusing of racial
tensions.

10. Others who played twenty or more Saturday nights in 1928 include Ar-
thur and Homer Smith (29), Paul Warmack and His Gully Jumpers (28), Dr.
Humphrey Bate and His Possum Hunters (25), the Crook Brothers (22), the Clod
Hoppers (22), Bert Hutcherson (22), and Obed Pickard (20).

11. Kirk McGee told Paul DiMaggio and me that he and his brother Sam had
spent much of 1928 on an extended tour of vaudeville theaters and schoolhouses
throughout the South, Midwest, and Northeast with Uncle Dave Macon.

12. The only forms of popular music that are conspicuous in their absence
are the fox-trot dance orchestras and jazz groups, which used brass, reed instruments, piano, and drums. What was apparently acceptable on the Opry, then as
now, seems to be determined more by instrumentation than by lyrical, rhythmic,
or melodic content. Thus in format, the 1928 "Grand Ole Opry" struck a sort
of balance. It was not as much a variety show as the Chicago WLS "National

Barn Dance" and not as exclusively an old-time music show as the Atlanta WSB and the Fort Worth WBAP barn-dance shows (Malone 1985). In summary, the Opry in its early years was neither as rustic nor as pure as some have suggested. Rather it offered variety entertainment with a rural accent.

13. While Hay was associated with the Opry for another twenty years, intermittent illness later prevented him from personally selecting the groups that would appear. In 1928, or soon thereafter according to our informants, Harry Stone took over the task of auditioning and booking artists. Hay increasingly devoted himself to the role of Opry master of ceremonies.

14. In association with Uncle Dave Macon, who had worked in vaudeville shows for several years before the Opry began, the McGee Brothers, Arthur Smith, Sid Harkreader, and several others became full-time touring professionals. Obed Pickard brought his family into his one-man band and then left the Opry to become one of the major country music radio acts of the era between the two world wars. In contrast, Herman Crook kept his day job as a cigar maker while remaining an Opry regular until his death. In like fashion, Dr. Humphrey Bate eschewed the rigors of extensive professional touring for the sake of his family and his profession. He continued to appear on the Opry for many years, and one member of his Possum Hunters, daughter Alcyone Bate Beasley, still appeared on the Opry fifty years later.

15. Characterizations of the stratification in the South in the era between the world wars are given by John Dollard (1937). See also James West (1945). The cultural isolation of a small town just thirty miles from Nashville in the days when radio and the automobile were just becoming important is well described by Walter King Hoover (1968).

16. On the nature of ethnic stock characters in American popular theater, see Goldberg (1930: 31–138), Ewen (1961: 20–107), and Toll (1974). The degree to which the music industry was already carefully attuned to changing consumer tastes is documented by the December 15, 1925, article in *Talking Machine World* "What the Popularity of Hill-Billy Songs Means in Retail Profit Possibility."

17. In 1972 our informants seemed unaware of the commercial reasons why the comedic names were created. When asked why a group was named the Gully Jumpers, for example, Herman Crook said, "Well, they had to be called something."

18. Personal communication, May 1996, from Charles Wolfe. Presumably in that era when gangsters were ever in the headlines, the name Crook had a notorious ring.

19. The "National Barn Dance" of WLS in Chicago, the most widely heard barn dance of the time, created more broadly stereotyped characters in the mold of vaudeville stock characters. Among others, these included Arkie the Arkansas Woodchopper, Amos 'n' Andy (blackface comedy), the Kentucky Wonder Bean, the Little Cowboy (George Goebel), Olaf the Swede, Pie Plate Pete, the Maple City Four (barbershop), and a character calling himself Ralph Waldo Emerson (Evans 1969: 216–21; Steele 1936).

20. For many of these later performers, including Eddy Arnold, George Jones, Loretta Lynn, and Johnny Cash, country music represented the most likely

means of escaping from a life of chopping cotton, truck driving, and assembly-line work. The function of a music career as an escape route is less important in the 1920s.

21. Unless otherwise noted, the following account of the creation and early days of the Beverly Hill Billies is given by Griffis (1972, 1980), supplemented by personal correspondence in January 1990 with Griffis. Glen Rice's Beverly Hill Billies should not be confused with the CBS network situation comedy featuring the backwoods Clampett family of Bug Tussle who struck it rich on oil and moved to Beverly Hills, California. The success of the television program shows the national audience's continuing fascination with comedic hillfolk. As late as 1993, *The Beverly Hillbillies* was still the highest-rated half-hour show in television history, and the show was responsible for fully nineteen of the one hundred top-rated episodes (Cox 1993).

22. The lasting power of the hillbilly image can be seen in the continuity of symbolism even as the specific descriptors change. For example "hillbilly" has become "redneck." The humor of Rod Brasfield and Minnie Pearl has evolved through "Hee Haw" to Jeff Foxworthy. And the singer of love laments has evolved from the Carter Family through the likes of Loretta Lynn to Lorrie Morgan and Reba McEntire. Hillbilly aggression has generally been censored out of songs or channeled into a perennial battle between the sexes (Peterson 1992). It finds its fullest expression in movies such as *Deliverance* and the recurrent image of the corrupt good-ole-boy sheriff (Kirby 1986).

23. Of course P. T. Barnum did find a way of institutionalizing sensationalism in the form of the three-ring circus. Rather than having to promote the unique skills of separate acts as he had done for years, Barnum used the three-ring circus as a kind of empty shell, advertised as "the greatest show on earth," into which he could introduce a continual succession of "spectacular" acts. The parallel with Barnum would have been complete if Glen Rice had gotten the job taken by Ed Sullivan and become the impresario and host of a television variety show.

CHAPTER SIX

1. The extended 1996 PBS video presentation "The West," a film by Stephen Ives produced by Ken Burns, shows the complex interplay between all these groups and more. It shows how the clash of interests and worldviews created a West that is more myth than reality.

2. In the passage quoted, Lomax is stating what he purports to be the reality of the cowboy's existence rather than a romantic image of it. In showing Lomax's mythologizing, Mark Fenster (1989) notes that in the years following the publication of the book, Lomax toured widely, giving lectures on cowboy songs all around the country. He had a number of means of increasing the dramatic impact of his presentations. For example, before a series of lectures he coached college students to appear at the end of his presentation garbed as cowboys and singing selections from his anthology (Fenster 1989: 269).

3. We will not focus on the touring singing cowboy shows, but they did spring up in the 1920s. The most widely known was run by Otto Gray out of Stillwater, Oklahoma. Gray took over the seven-person Billy McGinty Cowboy Band in 1924 and created a nine-person, self-contained, vaudeville tent-show

performance group (McRill 1960). Gray was quite an aggressive image promoter. By 1930 his unit was traveling in two touring cars with large trailers and a larger bus that featured a brilliant spotlight. There were regular short stories about the aggregation in *Billboard,* and in 1934 the magazine featured a full-page picture of Gray on its cover.

4. This account of John Wayne's experience of being cast as a singing cowboy is drawn from Young (1980: 145–46).

5. Autry's nonacting way of acting was, in effect, the B-film version of the American male actor's naively sincere style as exemplified with differing nuances by the youthful Jimmy Stewart, Gary Cooper, Henry Fonda, Marlon Brando, and James Dean.

6. Unless otherwise noted, the details of Gene Autry's career come from Green (1975a, 1976, 1994). Douglas Green earned a Ph.D. in folklore and published a number of articles on western music and western music-makers (cf. Green 1975a, 1985c, 1976, 1994; and with Robert Pinson 1980). He is also "Ranger Doug," founder and lead singer of the highly successful western music group Riders in the Sky.

7. In these years the link between WLS and Sears was close, even though Sears had divested itself of WLS (standing for "World's Largest Store") in 1928 because many competing retail merchandise advertisers didn't want to place ads on what was felt to be "the Sears station" (Evans 1969).

8. This is not to say that songs with western themes could not be popular if properly diluted. Bing Crosby, the premier popular music crooner of the era, charted eighteen songs with western themes, from "The Last Round-up" in 1933 to "All Along the Navajo Trail" in 1945 (Whitburn 1986: 104–13).

9. As Holden (1990) notes, the trend featuring the western image without western songs continued into the 1980s. The movie *Urban Cowboy* spawned a revival of fashion interest in westernwear, but none of the songs on the soundtrack evoked western imagery.

10. Autry's mix of songs is not unusual. In addition to singing songs evoking the West, the leading cowboy show-band aggregations of the mid-1930s, such as Otto Gray and His Oklahoma Cowboys, performed a mixture of sentimental weepers, comedy-novelty pieces, romantic ballads, and older popular songs (Gray 1930). Thus the mix of songs performed by cowboy and hillbilly bands of the 1930s did not differ greatly.

11. Personal communication to my Vanderbilt University freshman seminar, "Country Music in Social Context," October 1994.

12. On the place of the cowboy in the American psyche see also Elkin (1950), Emery (1959), Cawelti (1970, 1976), Tompkins (1992), and Tichi (1994).

13. This is not to say that no one has been successful playing the geezer. The most prominent example is Louis Marshall Jones. One early morning when Jones was very sleepy from working a show and then driving the long way home the night before, Bradley Kincaid chided the twenty-two-year-old Jones on the air: "You're just like an old grandpa." People wrote in asking just how old Grandpa Jones was, and they decided to build the character into the act (Jones 1984: 52). Over the decades since, the man has come to be the character for millions of "Hee Haw" and "Grand Ole Opry" listeners.

CHAPTER SEVEN

1. U.S. record sales for the entire phonograph record industry reached $106 million in 1921, the year before the introduction of radio, and then trended sharply down through 1925 to $59 million. By 1929 sales had recovered to $75 million, but then, with the Depression, plummeted to just $6 million in 1933. The dollar value of record sales did not reach the 1921 level again until 1945 (*Billboard* 1967: 12).

2. For example, all four of Nashville's commercial radio stations founded in the 1920s programmed country music performers, and for a while in 1928 there was a barn-dance program on Thursdays (WBAW), and Fridays (WLAC), as well as on Saturdays (WSM) (Wolfe 1973: 7).

3. In the 1920s the term "barn dance" referred to the type of dancing that was distinguished from "ballroom dancing." Barn dancing included any of the forms of round, square, and line dancing in groups, or solo as in the case of dancing to jigs and hornpipes. What was ruled out were any of the "urban" forms of couple dancing such as the fox-trot, waltz, or Charleston, and for this reason the various styles of barn dancing were often referred to as "country dancing" (Nevell 1977). The fiddle was the premier instrumental accompaniment, but a wide range of bowed, plucked, struck, blown, or hammered instruments might be used with or instead of the fiddle to provide melody and to keep a steady rhythm. At the same time brass instruments, such as the trumpet and tuba, as well as reed instruments, such as the saxophone and clarinet, were virtually absent from barn-dance accompaniment up through the 1920s. The only reed instruments that were at all common were the metal reeds of the harmonica and the accordion (Nevell 1977).

4. No transcriptions or recordings of the barn dances of the early 1930s were made, so the sound is inferred from the reports of witnesses and from phonograph records made by participants.

5. This quotation is drawn from a personal communication from George C. Biggar, June 1973. The other quotations from Biggar in this section, which are not given more detailed citation, are also from this personal communication. Biggar, though he does not take credit for having conceived of the barn-dance idea, became one of its biggest promoters over the course of four decades, and it is thanks to him that much information on programming the barn dance has been preserved. See especially Biggar (1940, 1949, 1950, 1964) and WLS ([n.d.], 1937).

6. This section is based on an analysis of the "Grand Ole Opry" listings in the *Nashville Tennessean* newspaper, supplemented by Hay (1945), Wolfe (1975b), Green (1975b, 1975c), personal interviews with knowledgeable persons, and the standard reference works. The various sources are often in conflict with each other on details. For example Zeke Clements and his Bronco Busters are reported to have become a part of the Opry as early as 1930 and as late as 1939 (Hay 1945). It is clear from the *Tennessean* that Zeke came to WSM with Texas Ruby in 1934 after working at WLS and WHO.

7. Even the trained opera vocal style is a refined form of shouting.

8. In popular music the first great crooner was Bing Crosby, who emerged in 1931. His most accomplished disciples included Red Foley, Eddy Arnold, Frank Sinatra, and Tony Bennett.

9. One of the best-known radio comics working this style of comedy in the pop field was Gracie Allen, who played off her straight man, George Burns. Ventriloquists like Edgar Bergen also played straight to the comedy of their dummies, such as Charlie McCarthy.

10. In the early 1930s, the American Federation of Musicians forbade the playing of recorded music on the networks and on network station local broadcasts (Sanjek 1988).

11. In addition to the "National Barn Dance" and the "Grand Ole Opry," Wolfe (1994: 57) lists ten major radio barn dances in the 1930s. In all, there were probably no more than two dozen.

12. As Roy Acuff recalls, Bailey was very popular on live appearances and was notable for playing the guitar left-handed, that is upside down and backward. According to Bailey, he was asked to leave the Opry in 1941 because he knew only eleven tunes and wouldn't learn any more. Bailey was bitterly resentful because he had a wide-ranging repertoire and played guitar and piano as well as the harmonica. He never seems to have understood that he was not being singled out for special treatment (Horton 1991). The harmonica tunes he played on the Opry were all licensed by ASCAP and when the radio industry formed a rival song-licensing agency, BMI, and refused for some months in 1941 to play any ASCAP songs on the air, all American radio artists had to scramble to find songs not licensed by ASCAP (Ryan 1985).

13. This structure of self-protective relationships is much like the "simplex" described by Peterson and White (1979) by which a few musicians are able to control access to the numerous lucrative jobs backing up artists and jingle makers.

14. Even so great an actor as Charlie Chaplin, for example, received a cool reception from moviegoers when he stepped out of his "spunky little hobo" role.

15. Serendipity in field research is illustrated by the discovery of a fascinating four-page document on the 1933 WLS Artists Bureau. I found it in 1973 in Bert Layne's fiddle case while interviewing him about the Skillet Lickers of Atlanta in the 1920s.

16. Quoted from a 1978 letter signed "Grandma Bootsie." It is from Betty Waggoner to her grand daughter, archived at the Country Music Foundation in the file with the material of Curt Poulton, who was the baritone in the Vagabonds. I am grateful to John Rumble for the clue that lead me to correctly link the names.

17. This is expressed most forcefully in print in Alton Delmore's (1977: 52–62) autobiography.

18. Ruth Loring Tanksley, Hay's secretary at the Artist Bureau, wrote in 1979 personal correspondence, "The Judge was a real character, and a marvelous individual. I loved him and had the highest respect for him as a human being who loved his fellow man." Alton Delmore (1977) is the most critical of George Hay in print.

19. Based on several interviews with John DeWitt, who as a young engineer

helped to build the WSM transmitter and eventually became its director; and with Bud Wendell, who was manager of the "Grand Ole Opry" in the early 1970s when we talked about this. See also Peterson (1975).

CHAPTER EIGHT

1. There is no complete listing of all the stations that included one or more live country music programs in the thirties, but there must have been three to five hundred. As late as 1949, *Billboard* magazine estimated that there were 650 radio stations that were using "live hillbilly talent" across the country, and Peterson and Gowan (1971) found 396 radio stations listed by *Country Song Roundup* as playing live country music in 1950.

2. Unless otherwise noted, the material for this section of the chapter comes from Erik Barnouw's (1966) detailed history of the development of radio in the United States. The specific figures come from Leblebici et al. (1991).

3. Most of these large independents served the political and/or mercantile interests of their principal owners, and all were snuffed out by the mid-1930s through the combined weight of political, professional association, and religious group pressure (Carson 1960; Kahn 1973; Pusateri 1976).

4. Such national spot advertising began to be economically important in the late 1930s (Leblebici 1991).

5. One unit with the name "Ray-O-Vac Twins" (named after a kind of flashlight battery) appeared on the "Grand Ole Opry" in 1928 (Peterson and DiMaggio 1973).

6. Country music performers were generally not eligible for AFM membership because, for reasons discussed below, they were not considered to be musicians.

7. All of the details for this story are drawn from Charles Townsend's biography of Bob Wills (1976: 68–82).

8. As Bill Malone commented in 1971, a study of the nationwide activities of the Crazy Water Crystals company would be illuminating. Now, as then, none has been made. These comments are drawn from Ahrens (1970a, b), Malone (1971), Wolfe (1994) and Grundy (1995).

9. Elizabeth Schlappi (1975: 186) has explained why in 1935 the group, then playing over WROL, Knoxville, was first referred to by this name. One day, the program went on the air before it's allotted time as the band was tuning up. Allen Stout, the announcer, feeling he had to explain the cacophony to the audience, said, "Listeners, these are just a bunch of crazy Tennesseans." Thus, while Acuff did not originate the name, he did embrace it as a commercially useful band name when it was casually offered.

10. This information comes from Alcyone Bate Beasley, Roy Acuff, and Blythe Poteete. See also Hay (1945) and Wolfe (1975a).

11. I appreciate Charles Wolfe's pointing out this practice to me.

12. Though it may seem hard to believe, there was an absolute ban against using any recorded programming (other than sound effects) on network programming through the 1940s (Barnouw 1968: 163).

13. The LP "The Carter Family on Border Radio" (JEMF 101) issued by the John Edwards Memorial Foundation in 1974 provides a good sampling of the

early transcriptions. It also shows the lengths to which the makers of the transcription went to make the transcriptions sound as if they were live broadcasts.

CHAPTER NINE

1. An earlier version of this chapter that puts more weight on recent developments in hard-core and soft-shell music and musicianship appeared as "The Dialectic of Hard-Core and Soft-Shell Country Music," in *South Atlantic Quarterly* 94 (Winter 1995) (Peterson 1995). An analysis of the differences between hard-core and soft-shell country fans can be found in Peterson and Kern (1995).

2. The information on the Pickard Family comes from Kahn (1968) and Wolfe (1975b), supplemented by information in the files of the John Edwards Memorial Foundation Archive.

3. Spelling and capitalization as in the original song folio are reproduced as page 99 in Wolfe (1975b).

4. This observation is evidenced by the numerous WLS surveys made during the 1930s and by Alton Delmore, who says that during his time on the Opry he was strongly advised against even talking to representatives of WLS who were visiting WSM and the Opry. See Delmore (1977: 59–60).

5. The information on the Vagabonds, unless otherwise noted, comes from Wolfe (1975b), and Rumble (1980), supplemented by information in the Country Music Foundation archives as well as my interviews with Roy Acuff, Alcyone Bate Beasley, Herman Crook, and John DeWitt.

6. Actually, by this point in their careers, Curt Poulton's guitar was not homemade. Rather it was a monogrammed promotional model specially handcrafted by the Martin company to Poulton's specifications. This according to a letter in the Poulton folder in the Country Music Foundation archive.

7. Curt Poulton's wife, Betty Waggoner, reports that Atkins said this in a 1957 radio interview with Poulton. This information found at the County Music Foundation archive.

8. According to the rate book, the single-show performance rate for solo popular music artists was no more than twenty dollars, except for one theater organist who was a local celebrity and received twenty-five dollars. The rate for duos was twenty-five dollars and a female trio, thirty-five. Among country string bands, the Dixieliners' rate was thirty-five dollars and that of Paul Warmack and the Gully Jumpers, forty. Uncle Dave Macon is pictured but no rate is given. Perhaps he wanted to negotiate a rate on his own, and it is true that this onetime vaudeville celebrity preferred to work for a percentage of the gate rather than for a set fee. The 1933 WSM Artist Service Bureau Rate Book is archived in the Country Music Foundation Library, Nashville, Tennessee.

9. June (Elviry) Weaver was perhaps the most outstanding strong female vaudeville comic. Married first to one Weaver brother then the other in real life, she played "Elviry" in an act called "The Weaver Brothers and Elviry." Formed in 1913, the troupe eventually numbered twenty persons. Between 1937 and 1943 they starred in a number of B films, including the *The "Grand Ole Opry,"* in which most of the cast of the Opry also appeared. See the winter 1988 issue of *Old Time Country,* which is devoted to the Weaver Brothers and Elviry. See also Bufwack and Oermann (1993: 36–38).

10. More important for the future development of the Opry—and the development of the music industry in Nashville—than the western swing music of the Golden West Cowboys was the fact that King's father-in-law, J. L. (Joe) Frank, accompanied him to Nashville. Frank was a concert promoter who, working out of Chicago, had launched the careers of Gene Autry and others. Unlike many promoters, who from the beginning took all the money they could get from an artist, Frank saw to it that artists were fairly compensated. Like music publisher Ralph Peer, Frank worked to develop artists in the belief that in the long run he could make much more money from artists who were successful. Transferring his base operations to Nashville, Frank is credited with taking "Opry performers' small-time schoolhouse shows to big-city auditoriums" (Ivey 1994: 284) and in the process, building the careers not only of Pee Wee King, but, among others, Ernest Tubb, Eddy Arnold, and Roy Acuff. Acknowledgment of Frank's role in promoting artists' careers came with his election into the Country Music Hall of Fame in 1967.

11. Dizzy Dean dubbed Acuff "King of the Hillbillies" (Schlappi 1978: 216). The other appellations were made in the *American Magazine* of May 1944 and *Colliers* of March 5, 1949.

12. Unless otherwise noted, this account of Roy Acuff's early years is drawn from Acuff's (1983) autobiography and Schlappi's (1978) biography, supplemented by my interviews with Schlappi and Acuff.

13. Alton Delmore (1977: 115–22) asserts that since Arthur Smith had been scheduled to tour as part of a WSM package with the Delmore Brothers, Alton was given the privilege of choosing which of several Opry guests he would like as a replacement. Acuff never confirmed Delmore's story, but as Charles Wolfe has suggested in personal correspondence, Acuff probably never knew the true story. Alton Delmore's account is consistent with the events that are known from other sources and with what Acuff could recall.

14. A picture of this phallic sight gag can be found on page 17 of the July 1953 issue of *Cowboy Songs*. Thanks to John Rumble for alerting me to the existence of this picture.

15. Most, if not all, forms of music have soft and hard components. Thus, soft country is to hard country as semiclassical music is to classical music, as pop-rock is to hard rock, and as cocktail and funk jazz are to serious jazz.

16. Soft-shell artists Eddy Arnold, Jim Reeves, and Vince Gill sold more records over a comparable span of years than their hard-core counterparts Hank Williams, George Jones, and Randy Travis, but hard-living hard-core artists tend to attract more press attention. Always a "good boy," since he emerged in the late 1930s, Eddy Arnold appreciates the money, but has been extremely unhappy that he has received little scholarly attention while some of those who were "falling-down drunk" have been lionized. This latter is from Don Cusic, who is writing a biography on Eddy Arnold (personal communication, August 31, 1996).

17. The concepts "hard core" and "soft shell" were developed in discussions with five delightful groups of freshman seminar students between 1992 and 1996. An earlier version of the classification that follows was presented at the Eleventh

Annual Meeting of the International Conference on Country Music held in Meridian, Mississippi, in June 1994.

18. Some readers have commented that the differences between hard core and soft shell became obscure in the 1990s because, by then, all performers were so clearly acting a part, even if, in the words of the Buck Owens song, they were "acting naturally." But what we have seen so far suggests that Uncle Dave Macon, Jimmie Rodgers, George Hay, Patsy Montana, the Vagabonds, Roy Acuff, and many others were quite self-conscious in their image-making. The indicators of hard and soft may be in flux, but the conditions that make for the distinctions have not gone out of existence.

19. A more detailed analysis of the dialectical cycle in country music from the early 1970s to the early 1990s is made in Peterson (1995: 291–97). See also Malone (1985: 369–415), Peterson (1978: 292–314), and Peterson and Kern (1995).

20. In this, Rodgers's role in fostering great popular interest in country music is not unlike that of the *Urban Cowboy* movie in 1980 and Garth Brooks's showmanship in the early 1990s.

21. Ernest Tubb is a good example of an early strict imitator of Jimmie Rodgers, and one who became popular only when he found his own authentic voice.

CHAPTER TEN

1. Portable, efficient, and relatively inexpensive public address systems and instrument amplifiers became practical only after the invention in 1928 of alternating current-driven vacuum power tubes (White 1991).

2. The relative contributions of Bob Wills and other early innovators such as Milton Brown have been hotly contested (Townsend 1976; Ginell 1994). Certainly Wills was able to sense what the audience wanted and draw creative players to his band. He also had the advantage of working for well over a quarter of a century, while Milton Brown was killed in an auto accident in 1936 at a time when his Musical Brownies were the most popular Southwestern musical organization (Malone 1985).

3. Nick Tosches (1994a: 153) provides a brief but detailed etymology of the word "honky-tonk," tracing it from its first known use in print in 1894 to its first use in a country music song of 1937, Al Dexter's "Honky Tonk Blues."

4. The term "juke joint" was first applied to working-class African American places of entertainment devoted to "jooking," that is to say, fast couple-dancing (Hazzard-Gordon 1990).

5. This was first explained to me by Randy Wood, founder of Dot Records. Further insights were obtained in interviews with Jim Bulleit, Harold Bradley, Hugh Cherry, James Fogelsong, and Ronnie Light. By the 1960s this "hot sound" was achieved by a number of electronic devices, such as equalizers. By then it was understood that record music was uniquely created in the recording studio and was essentially different from live music.

6. Harold Bradley reported to me in 1973 that, as exemplified by the experiences of Jimmy Dean in New York and Washington, D.C., this disdain of East Coast studio personnel for country music artists lasted well into the 1970s.

7. The major record companies were not insensitive to the advantages of recording country music artists in an atmosphere comfortable to them. They continued to record in Southern and Southwestern cities long after the system of "field recording," with equipment temporarily installed in vacant rooms rented for the purpose, had been abandoned (Interview with Arthur Satherley). This also led the major companies in the 1950s to begin to locate recording studios in a single regional location, Nashville, Tennessee (Malone 1985: 209–11).

8. For my thoughts on the dualistic nature of the country music worldview, see Peterson and McLaurin (1992) and Peterson (1992). For a broader treatment of the complexities of the dualistic worldview in country music, see Gaillard (1978), Guralnick (1979), Rogers (1989), Tichi (1994), and Ellison (1995).

9. This characterization of female-male relationships in the war and postwar periods comes from Amott and Matthaei (1991: 128–33), Coontz (1992), and Bufwack and Oermann (1993: 164–68).

10. Capital Records of Los Angeles had been formed in 1942 by three men with eclectic tastes interested in capitalizing on innovative trends in all fields of music (Gillett 1983: 70). Though new, it had the market power of a major firm because it distributed its own records.

11. Unless otherwise noted, references to a record on the "chart" or "charting" have to do with the records appearing on the weekly *Billboard* magazine country music performance listings as these are summarized in Whitburn (1994).

12. Several women did make honky-tonk songs in the 1940s. Texas Ruby, a self-described "hard drinking good-timing mama," recorded for Columbia and King. Her honky-tonk issue-songs written from a woman's perspective included "You've Been Cheating on Me," "Have You Got Someone Else on the String?" and "Don't Let That Man Get You Down." Rose Maddox sang a number of honky-tonk numbers, including "Hangover Blues," "I Wish I Was a Single Girl Again," and "(Pay Me) Alimony." None of these charted in the 1940s.

CHAPTER ELEVEN

1. The account of Hank Williams's life recounted in this chapter is taken from Escott (1994) unless otherwise indicated. Escott's biography is the best researched and most dispassionate account available. I also gained much insight from those who knew Hank Williams or saw him perform. Most revealing have been the numerous conversations held between 1975 and 1996 with Hugh Cherry, who knew Williams well during his years in Nashville. I also consulted the works by Rivers (1967), R. M. Williams (1970, 1975), H. Williams (1979), Williams and Vinicur (1989), Rumble (1980), Koon (1983), Sutton (1987), and Flippo (1981). On occasion Flippo creates conversations between Williams and others, especially his first wife, Audrey. While fabricated, they convey much of the character of both Hank Williams and those around him, according to Cherry.

2. Eye witnesses attest to Hank Williams's riveting performance style. Recorded live performances include audience responses that do not fit climaxes in the lyric line and must come from his stage movements. (Thanks to Charles

Wolfe for sharing these tapes.) Remarkable as it seems in this multimedia age, there is only one known surviving video of Williams performing. Made less than three months after major surgery on his spine, it is his restrained rendition of "Hey, Good Lookin'" from the March 26, 1952, *Kate Smith Show* in which he is shown to lean and rock but not roll his hips. It's amazing to remember that Elvis Presley's gyrations were to be televised just three years later.

3. Offstage Hank Williams dressed well in the latest New York fashions of the day. Vain about his thinning hair, he wore a hat even around the house (Escott 1994).

4. John Rumble (1980) provides an exhaustively researched and well-documented account of Fred Rose the songwriter, song publisher, and helpful confidant whom Hank Williams called Pappy.

5. Rose, like Ralph Peer before him, realized that he could make more money in the long run as the publisher of songs written by Hank Williams and his other writers than he could by buying songs from them. Rose applied this philosophy of long-term collective gain not only to his dealings with writers but in the numerous actions he took in helping other local firms in their efforts to develop the country music industry in Nashville (Rumble 1980). I think he is more responsible for the development of Nashville as the center of the country music industry that any other individual. Perhaps the only rival for this distinction is Edwin Craig, who encouraged the National Life and Accident Insurance Company to found WSM and who strongly supported the "Grand Ole Opry" because it helped to bring business to the insurance company (Peterson 1975).

6. Many 1930s performers of sexually tinged songs turned to sentimental and sacred songs later in their careers. The most notable of these was Jimmie Davis (Tosches 1985). This career-prolonging move has been repeated by numerous artists in the decades since.

7. This quotation is taken from the 1993 production "Long Gone Lonesome Blues: The Music of Hank Williams," written and produced by Margaret House and aired over National Public Radio.

8. The figures in this paragraph are compiled from Whitburn (1994).

9. These figures are according to *Newsweek* (1952), whose estimates came from Nashville publishers and booking agents, as do the comparable figures of Eddy (1952). They obviously do not include the leading singing cowboys who made Hollywood movies, including Eddy Arnold, Roy Rogers, and Tex Ritter. Hank Williams's rapid rise in popularity is suggested by figures published October 26, 1949, in the entertainment industry magazine *Variety*. Only five months after joining the Opry, Williams had sold more total records than all but six Opry artists, all of whom had been selling records for many years (*Variety* 1949), and the phenomenal rise in his fortunes were noted in a *Wall Street Journal* article (McWethy 1951).

10. This according to Hugh Cherry, who says that Williams greatly admired Frizzell because this younger prodigy was the only other artist who charted his own course and wasn't just a pawn of the music managers. As if still following his mentor, Lefty Frizzell's personal life self-destructed after 1952.

11. These magazines were both dated June 1953 in the common practice of pulp magazine publishers to increase their shelf life on newsstands.

CHAPTER TWELVE

1. The prime source of information for this section is Sanjek (1988). Other sources have been useful on details, most notably Barnouw (1968), Ryan (1984), Ennis (1992), and Lopes (1994). For my earlier assessment of how this turmoil in the popular music industry created the conditions for the emergence of rock music, see Peterson and Berger (1975) and Peterson (1990).

2. The lead front-page article of the January 3, 1953, *Billboard* shows the depth of the concern about the state of the music business and also how poorly the "problem" was understood. Noting that only eighty-one records made it into the twenty-position weekly "best-selling" chart of the 2,868 records released, the author wrote approvingly of cutting the number of records released (Gehman 1953). The article also mentions without comment the increased representation among the hits of records by independent companies, but it does not note that, with few exceptions, the hits coming from the independent companies did not fit the Tin Pan Alley mold but were rhythm and blues, country, and proto-rock. They were, as it proved, harbingers of things to come.

3. The source of the figures quoted in this paragraph is the Recording Industry Association of America's listings printed in the *Billboard 1967–1968 International Buyer's Guide*. The 1941 figures were somewhat depressed by a dispute between the AFM and the record companies, but the five-fold increase in revenues nonetheless had a huge impact on the record industry.

4. See, for example, *Billboard* 1949b, 1949c, 1950, 1953b, 1953d, 1953e, and 1953h.

5. Bill Ivey (1994) gives a concise account of the development of country music as an industry.

6. This change was reflected at the barn-dance radio shows as well. While in the 1930s, appearing on the "National Barn Dance" or "Grand Ole Opry" helped an aspiring performer get live engagements, in the 1950s, having a hit record was prerequisite to being asked to appear on the "Grand Ole Opry" (Malone 1985).

7. Of course, some artists in the 1930s had made considerable money playing in western films, but Jimmie Rodgers was the only performer who had made any considerable amount of money from writing songs and selling records.

8. The top country artist of the time, crooner Red Foley, had far and away the biggest pop hit on the song. His version was in the top position on *Billboard*'s popular music chart for eight weeks.

9. Sanjek 1988: 288. The phenomenal success of "The Tennessee Waltz" is indicated by the fact that 4,225,000 copies of it were sold between December 1950 and September 1951, while the next two best-selling songs, "Mule Train" (which has a western theme) and "Some Enchanted Evening" (from the Broadway musical *South Pacific*), sold 2,663,000 and 2,565,000 records respectively (ibid., 305).

10. Ryan (1985: 71) reports that in the late 1930s fifteen publishing companies controlled the rights to 90 percent of all popular music.

11. Unless otherwise noted, the information contained in the following paragraphs about the early attempts to find a name for the music are drawn

from Archie Green's (1965) excellent article, "Hillbilly Music: Source and Symbol."

12. The *Annual Accumulation* of the *Music Index* is a bibliographic compilation of all periodical articles dealing with music of all sorts. In 1952 articles dealing with country music are listed as "Folk" but in 1953 none are. That same year the category "Country Music" appears for the first time.

13. While the word "country" became *Billboard*'s most frequently used term for the genre in 1953, the term "country and western" and even its abbreviation "C&W" were also used in the trade press and elsewhere for some years as well. A detailed analysis might be able to show that the latter terms were used most often in stories whose sources emanated from California and Texas while "country" was used as the all-inclusive term in reports from Nashville, which was in 1953 the emerging center of the music's business. In 1952 a *Newsweek* reporter found that people around the Opry said they preferred the word "country" but in practice often used "hillbilly" (*Newsweek* 1952).

14. This editorial is unsigned but probably was written by *Billboard* general editor Paul Ackerman. Russell Sanjek and Murry Nash have both noted in interviews with me that Ackerman was very interested in creating a positive view of the genre, thus facilitating the incorporation of country music into the commercial music fold.

15. There has been continual debate over how Hall of Fame members are chosen and who is left out. While many individuals have their advocates, the most systematic and continuing critique has been that persons associated with the "Grand Ole Opry" or based out of Nashville have been advantaged at the expense of those based elsewhere. The concern that persons based on the West Coast were systematically excluded became so intense in the early 1960s that a group calling itself the Academy of Country and *Western* Music was formed in 1964 to redress the balance and make its own awards. While this association still exists and makes annual awards, the fact that it no longer stood in opposition to the Nashville interests was signaled when in the 1980s it took the word "Western" out of its own name. Thus the accepted name within the industry became "country" from coast to coast.

16. Leaders among this first generation of professional deejays included Randy Blake, Hugh Cherry, Biff Collie, Eddie Hill, Nelson King, and Lee Moore.

17. The Disk Jockey Convention, which in a few years evolved into the Country Music Association, a trade association for all the elements of the field, later traced its beginning from a hastily prepared hotel party hosted by WSM management for deejays at the 1952 celebration. We focus on the 1953 meeting because that year the event became a weekend full of didactic and social events (Moore 1960).

CHAPTER THIRTEEN

I particularly appreciate the help of Hugh Cherry, Wendy Griswold, Larry Grossberg, Michèle Lamont, Lynnette Spielman, and Janet Wolff in preparing this chapter. Please do not hold them responsible, however, because I fear that none will agree with all that I have said here. I hope that at least my view of authenticity is more clearly stated as a result of their comments.

1. Hank Williams's slow, deliberate way of speaking, his grammar, pronunciation, and accent would have been quite acceptable, but the opinion would have changed when the music began. In 1923 any serious artist wore a white shirt, tie, and suit, so his outfit would have been seen as that of a comic, but, as his audience would have noted with surprise, he did not act at all like a comic. His own secular song lyrics were like none of the conventional styles of the 1920s (Cusic 1992). And as shocking for 1923 would have been the sound of the band. The audience expecting a straight string band would have been startled, to say the least, by the swooping steel sound and the heavily accented honky-tonk back-beat rhythms. As of 1993 no one with all the characteristics of Hank Williams has been signed to a major country music label in the 1990s. The one who came closest is the singer-songwriter son of a Kentucky tobacco farmer, Marty Brown, who recorded three albums for MCA before losing his major label deal.

2. The *Oxford English Dictionary* defines "authenticity" by suggesting synonyms and giving brief quotations from the earliest examples of the particular usage. The quotations are so short that it is often difficult to see that the meanings are as distinct as is suggested; thus I do not claim that this is an authentic representation of the meanings found in the *OED.* Bruner (1994) gives an excellent rendering of the usages in the *OED,* and while it has been very helpful, I do not follow it exactly here because he is concerned with the uses of the authenticity claim about New Salem, Illinois, a village reconstructed to look as it did when Abraham Lincoln lived there. As Crutchfield (1986) has suggested, the locus of authenticity for a performance (such as country music) is quite different from that for a physical object (such as a village) or historical person (such as Abraham Lincoln).

3. In addition to the works by Frith and Grossberg see for example Laing (1985), Chambers (1986), Curtis (1987), and Friedlander (1996).

4. I do understand that by highlighting some elements and performers and not others, this work, like any other discussion of country music, can have some small part in molding what is seen as authentic country (Baudrillard 1981).

5. In the 1940s and 1950s an affiliation with the "Grand Ole Opry" was so important to artists' careers nationally that the management of the Opry then was more successful than at any other time in authenticating what constituted country music (Peterson 1975, 1978). But its hegemony was never complete. Of all forms of commercial music, bluegrass has perhaps been most successful in developing an institutional system that serves to police the boundaries of authenticity, and as Neil Rosenberg (1985) has shown, it was able to convert what at first was an acoustic "sound" within country music into a distinct "style" beyond the bounds of commercial country music.

6. The sociological way of understanding the differences between fine and popular culture are much more subtle than is suggested here. For four quite different approaches to the sociological view, see Becker (1982), DiMaggio (1987), Crane (1992), and Fine (1996).

7. The three turn-of-the-century articles mentioned in this paragraph are all reprinted in the sterling editorial harvest edited by William McNeil (1995) which

samples from over a hundred years of urban intellectuals' views of Southern mountain people.

8. Greatly oversimplified, the debate has been over whether to use scores that exactly represent the composer's intentions and play the music on period instruments or to play the music on more versatile and full-sounding modern instruments, interpreting the compositions in the manner that has grown up around the music in the past several centuries of performance (Crutchfield 1986; Frith 1996).

9. For example, in the 1930s western swing was not considered part of country music, nor did its proponents consider it as such. Bob Wills explicitly aspired to be a jazz performer and sought to distance his work from country music (Townsend 1976). In the early 1970s the song stylings (and personal behavior) of Waylon Jennings and Willie Nelson were considered by many in the country music field to be closer to rock than to country music (Peterson 1978).

10. In the 1930s and 1940s, for example, drums and brass were virtually excluded from the stage of the "Grand Ole Opry."

11. Chet Atkins, as a case in point, was fired from the "Grand Ole Opry" in 1946 because his hot style of guitar playing was considered to be jazz, not country, and he got back on the Opry in 1950 only as the accompanist to the traditionalist Carter Family (personal interview with Chet Atkins, February 1973).

12. This according to Gary Jensen (interview, July 14, 1996), who has carefully researched the evolving standardization of the representation of witches in the half century following the end of religiously sanctioned witch-killing by the state.

13. This meaning is still in use today. Jonathan Adler (1992: 31) talks about the American electorate's "search for authenticity" in comparing contemporary politicians who have a consistent presentation of self with those who are continually changing their statements in an effort to please their constituents.

14. Why use a commercial music trade magazine to find the meaning of authenticity in country music? Those in the country music field "knew it when they saw it" and didn't need to verbalize its characteristics. But the music industry reporters had to objectify the characteristics of authentic country music in a way that would be understandable to their music industry readers. In a parallel fashion, Americans have turned to sophisticated Europeans writing for a European audience, from Alexis de Toqueville (1835) to Umberto Eco (1986) and Jean Baudrillard (1988), for a judgment on what is distinctive about the United States. In using such reports the reader should keep in mind the intended audiences in both instances. The Europeans have seen U.S. society as an extension of European civilization, and the music industry reporters saw country music in relation to the rest of the commercial music industry of the time.

15. Friedman in *Billboard* (1953g) notes one exception, Slim Whitman's "Indian Love Call," but, in fact, a goodly number of the songs performed by country music artists of the time had been created by popular music songwriters.

16. See for example Allen Churchill (1951) writing in the *New York Times Magazine,* John McWethy (1951) writing in the *Wall Street Journal,* an unsigned article in *Newsweek* (1952), and Don Eddy (1952) in *American Magazine.*

17. Wendy Griswold made this comment to me about reinterpreting Benjamin. She explores the complexities of authenticity in her research on the distinctly different ways in which African novelists have been evaluated in Africa, Great Britain, and the United States (Griswold 1987).

18. In stark contrast to country music where elements of rhythmic, chordal, and orchestral complexity are sacrificed to accent the story being sung by the lead singer (Peterson and McLaurin 1992), there is no lead singer in bluegrass. Each band member is an instrumentalist, and vocal lines are rendered in the manner of another instrument in the band, rather than to accent the sincere feeling of the singer.

19. The form of a bluegrass number is very similar to that of New Orleans jazz in the 1920s.

20. I am grateful to Scott Baretta for pointing out this statement.

21. The visually stunning video "High and Lonesome" (created by Rachel Liebling in 1991) on the history of bluegrass music mentions numerous musical and economic influences. Although the video is more accurate than any other available, Liebling sets the story visually in the mountains, not in the bluegrass country of Kentucky, and builds the story around Bill Monroe—as a kindly old visionary. In his introduction to the anthology *Transforming Tradition*, Neil Rosenberg (1993) points to the role that folklorists have played in changing the music they have set out to study. Many of the authors describe the mix of idealism for the "folk" and pessimism about "industrial society" that shaped the work of folkmusicologists in the "folk music" revival following World War II. See also Cantwell (1996). For a more exuberant view of the mixing of cultures in the "folk revival" era, see Schmidt and Rooney (1979).

22. The continuity of the "Grand Ole Opry," as well as the locating of the Country Music Association and its associated Country Music Foundation Archive in Nashville, have, however, meant that the importance of the "Grand Ole Opry" and events taking place in Nashville *before* 1950 have received more prominence than they deserve. I thank Hugh Cherry for convincing me of this point.

23. Recent analyses of the media-made South can be found in Kirby (1986) and Campbell (1981). Recent books on the media image of the West include Tompkins (1992), Slotkin (1992), and Tichi (1994). On the politics of small-town virtues see Goldman and Dickens (1983) and Larson and Oravec (1987).

24. Bill McNeil (1995) has anthologized a comprehensive collection of early popular magazine essays on the region and its people. His work is notable in telling something about each author so it is easier to gauge their slant on the topic. Henry Shapiro (1978) provides an excellent analysis of the creation of the idea of Appalachia and the diverse interests that the idea has been used to serve since 1870. His final chapter is on the "folksong revival" of the years 1880–1920.

25. Elements of this remarkable chapter in the invention of tradition can be found in Frost (1980), Wade (1985), and Bodkin (1987).

26. Thanks to Hugh Cherry, who knew Hank Williams well, for this quotation.

27. Once established, the "group voice" can serve as a trap, as judgments of merit become hostage to a particular construction of the authentic voice. Henry Lewis Gates (1991) cites a series of examples. Some involve acclaimed African

American and Native-American writings that are found to be trash when their nonethnic authorship is exposed. He also cites numerous examples showing that the works of particular African American, Jewish American, and Euro-American artists are highly acclaimed only when the author writes about the ethnic group's own experience, whereas when the same authors write about another group's experience, their works are discredited as derivative or they are ignored by critics.

Parallel to the discussions of slave narratives described by Gates, the articles in the anthology edited by Georg Gugelberger (1997), on the *testimonio* of Latin America's disenfranchised and oppressed, nicely illustrate the political struggle to establish the authenticity of the *testimonio* and the ironies involved in its becoming identified as an established literary form.

28. At the same time, the country label can become a hindrance. Some performers identified as country have had difficulty trying to establish a claim to be taken seriously in other genres of music. Examples include Bob Wills's difficulty being accepted as a jazz player in the 1940s, Roger Miller's belated recognition as a Broadway musical writer in the 1970s, and Mark O'Connor's cool reception as a classical music composer in the 1990s; and some artists have claimed that being labeled "country" early in their careers has seriously hurt their commercial success. I have been told this by several artists. Three who have said it publicly are Marshall Chapman, Rosanne Cash, and Steve Earl.

29. The idea of authenticity to one's own personal experience as written in song came to the fore in popular music some years later. This is part of what the rock revolution of the 1950s was about, but the emergence of the singer-songwriter did not reach iconic form until Bob Dylan, a decade after Hank Williams's death.

CHAPTER FOURTEEN

1. Patricia Averill (1975) gives the most complete analysis of the various versions of the song and uses "Can" in her title. Fine and Stoker (1985) also use "can" in asking how social movement groups maintain their unity.

2. As Everett Corbin's "case against modern country music" (1980) says clearly in the chapter titled "Fighting for My 'Country,'" many commentators find it easiest to see authenticity in the styles they learned to love in their youth, and to see what has come after as derivative or sham. As they say on the other side of this generational divide, "If it's too loud, you're too old" (Epstein 1994).

3. The word "work" is used here to signal that authenticity is a contrivance that takes conscious effort to achieve and to maintain. A major part of authenticity work is to make the "act" seem "natural." The term "work" is used in a roughly cognate way by Michèle Lamont (1992) and Kelly Moore (1996) in speaking of "boundary work."

4. It might be argued that Loretta Lynn, or any of the others, was unselfconsciously natural and unaffected. Even if one accepts this as true, these performers came to the fore because those around them recognized, shaped, and promoted their natural appeal.

5. These industry efforts were led by the newly founded Country Music Association (CMA). It has been argued that the CMA has had a greater influence than any of the trade associations for other genres of music (Peterson 1978), but so

far there has been no extended study of the CMA and its influence in the institutionalization of country music.

6. To date there is no thorough analysis of the 1970s fusing of West Coast rock and Nashville-based country music that takes into account the fusion's influence on Bakersfield country music, the Austin music scene, redneck rock, and via these developments, country music down through the 1990s.

7. To date the most comprehensive video history of country music is the six-hour 1996 TBS program titled "Roots of Country." The mid-1990s also saw well-produced television programs that showed the place of women in the development of country music and the musical links between country and African American music. See especially "Rhythm, Country, and Blues," both a video presentation and a CD produced by Don Was and Tony Brown, MCA MCAV-10876; and "The Women of Country," ABC Video 42098 and 42099, a two-volume video written by Robert Oermann and produced for High Five Entertainment by Bud Schaetzle in 1993.

8. This was observed by me. Curtis Ellison (1995) provides a number of detailed descriptions of how country music artists continually reaffirm their connection with the musical heritage and with their fans.

9. For a fuller discussion of the nature of country music songs and the differences between country songs and those of other genres, see the articles in Peterson and McLaurin (1992).

10. One of the first self-referential songs was perhaps the most successful: "The Tennessee Waltz," first recorded in 1948 by its cowriter Pee Wee King. Recorded in November 1950 by Patti Page, her rendition had sold over four million copies in the United States by May 1951. The song is strictly self-referential because in the song titled "The Tennessee Waltz," the singer makes reference to a song called "The Tennessee Waltz," which he/she danced to with his/her sweetheart.

The perceptive reader may have noticed that I have not quoted directly from any song lyrics in this book. Sadly, according to the current interpretation of copyright laws made by most scholarly book publishers, even the briefest quotation from a lyric is not considered a "fair use," meaning that the author citing the work must pay the copyright holder the requisite fees, which often are considerable.

11. The social and economic state of society influences the themes of country music lyrics (Rogers 1989). It has also influenced its geographic confinement and spread (Peterson and DiMaggio 1975). These factors have been mentioned when appropriate throughout the book. The direct influence of the audience in the years up to 1953, though vital, has received less systematic attention than it deserves because there remain only scattered bits of direct evidence of the desires and interests of fans. No systematic regional or national surveys were made, and fan magazines didn't emerge until the 1940s. A number of fan scrapbooks have been collected and would give an insight into the psychodynamics of superfans, but these generally cover the period after 1950. Concert promoters, radio barn-dance managers, and other business people of the period did form their own commercial views of fans, but none committed their observations to paper until decades later and then in the form of a few clichés.

12. The two most recent hyperfad peaks of country music were reached in 1979–80 and 1993–94. As in the 1949–53 period, the super popularity of country music in recent times has occurred at times of aesthetic crisis in the popular music field. As far as I know, no one has carefully examined the available evidence to see whether the ebb and flow of these genres is always linked and opposite.

13. While we argue that the dialectical relationship between hard core and soft shell has helped to renew country music and to keep it from being submerged in popular, art, or folk music, Frith (1987: 136) argues that rock music is seen by critics as keeping its authentic credibility by appealing to both folk and art sensibilities. It is *folk,* he suggests, by representing the music of the youth community, and it is *art* in focusing on individual creative sensibility.

14. This section is based on an unpublished analysis of a cycle of six career stages that ensure that young performers schooled in the tradition will at first revolt against it, then introduce elements from other music traditions, and finally be proud to be defined as carriers of the tradition. I first became aware of this dialectic of generations in conversations over the years since 1975 with Country Music Disk Jockey Hall of Fame member Hugh Cherry. Cantwell (1996) and Eyerman and Baretta (1996) treat the ideological clash of generations in folk music.

15. Direct African American sources are most clearly seen for creative artists of the 1923–53 period that has been focal in this book. In the time since the rockabilly rupture of country music in the mid-1950s, the outside innovative influences have as often come indirectly via rock music.

16. For more extended discussions showing the power of the production-of-culture perspective see Ryan (1985), Peterson (1990, 1992) and Crane (1992).

17. This brief statement greatly oversimplifies the factors involved in the development of candidly personal love songs. Another important factor was the jukebox. Box operators had accepted more risqué songs than those that were played over the air, and by the 1940s there were nearly half a million boxes located in bars, pool halls, and soda fountains across the country (Sanjek 1988). They provided a ready market for the candid recorded honky-tonk love laments, and their success in jukeboxes encouraged disk jockeys to play them on the radio as well.

18. The continual recasting of the memory of Hank Williams suggests how authenticity claims can change. While Hank Williams has remained an icon down the decades, what is highlighted as his marks of authenticity has changed profoundly. Christopher Metress (1995) has chronicled four decades of changes, in his analysis of the continuing outwelling of songs paying homage to Williams.

References

Abramson, Rudy. 1995. "Rare Alliance Defeats Disney at Manassas." *Reckon* 1 (1): 26.

Acuff, Roy. 1983. *Roy Acuff's Nashville: The Life and Good Times of Country Music.* New York: Perigee.

Adler, Jonathan. 1992. "Searching for Authenticity." *Newsweek,* March 2: 31.

Ahrens, Pat J. 1970a. "The Role of the Crazy Water Crystals Company in Promoting Hillbilly Music." *JEMF Quarterly* 6: 107-9.

———. 1970b. *The History of the Musical Careers of DeWitt "Snuffy" Jenkins, Banjoist, and Homer "Pappy" Sherrill, Fiddler.* West Columbia, SC: Wentworth.

Altheide, David L., and John M. Johnson. 1980. *Bureaucratic Propaganda.* Boston: Allyn and Bacon.

American Magazine. 1933. "Minstrel: Jilson Setters." May: 115–41.

Amott, Teresa, and Julie Matthaei. 1991. *Race, Gender, and Work: A Multicultural Economic History of Women in the United States.* Boston: South End Press.

Anand, Narasimhan, and Richard A. Peterson. 1996. "Market Information Constitutes Fields: The Music Industry Case." Manuscript. Vanderbilt University, Owen Graduate School of Management.

Anderson, Benedict. 1983. *Imagined Communities: Reflections on the Origin and Spread of Nationalism.* London: Verso.

Arnold, Matthew. 1865 [1994]. *Culture and Anarchy.* New Haven, CT: Yale University Press.

Asbel, Bernard L. 1954. "The National Barn Dance." *Chicago,* October: 20–25.

Atkins, John. 1975. "The Carter Family." Pp. 95–120 in *Stars of Country Music,* edited by Bill C. Malone and Judith McCulloh. Urbana: University of Illinois Press.

Averill, Patricia A. 1975. "Can the Circle Be Unbroken: A Study of the Modernization of Rural-Born Southern Whites since World War I Using Country Music." Ph.D. diss. University of Pennsylvania, Department of Folklore.

Barnouw, Erik. 1966. *A Tower in Babel*. New York: Oxford.

———. 1968. *The Golden Web*. New York: Oxford.

Baudrillard, Jean. 1981. *For a Critique of the Political Economy of the Sign*. St. Louis: Telos.

———. 1988. *America*. London: Verso.

Becker, Howard S. 1982. *Art Worlds*. Berkeley: University of California Press.

Benét, Stephen Vincent. 1925. "The Mountain Whippoorwill." *Century*, March: 635–39.

Benjamin, Walter. 1936 [1968]. "The Work of Art in the Age of Mechanical Reproduction." Pp. 109–32 in *Illuminations*, edited by Hannah Arendt. New York: Harcourt, Brace.

Berliner, Paul. 1994. *Thinking in Jazz: The Infinite Art of Improvisation*. Chicago: University of Chicago Press.

Biernacki, Richard. 1995. *The Fabrication of Labor: Germany and Britain, 1640–1940*. Berkeley: University of California Press.

Biggar, George C. 1940. "The Case for Hillbillies: Biggar of WLW Says They Help Theaters, Vaudeville, Stations, Instrument Firms, You 'n Me." *Billboard*, April 30.

———. 1949. "Material for 'Everybody's Music' Feature." Memo to Joe Koehler, *Sponsor* magazine. New York.

———. 1950. "Grand Ol' Opry at WSM." Internal memo to Glenn Snyder of WLS, March 27.

———. 1964. "Forty Years in the Right Business." Typescript of a speech given to the South Dakota Broadcasters Association Convention, May 22.

Billboard. 1949a. "Gay Hypes Live Oaters in D.C. Via "Korncert." April 23: 22.

———. 1949b. "Hillbilly Personals Harvesting Big Moola a la Disking Names." April 23: 46.

———. 1949c. "Rustic Rhythm Reaps $$ Reward." October 22: 97.

———. 1949d. "Gay Secedes from AFM over Radio Interview Fuss; Wants Union for Hillbillies." November 26: 18, 39.

———. 1950. "Signs Say Folk Music's Comin'." April 8: 28.

———. 1952. "Folk Music Well Received but Poor B.O." October 11: 19–20.

———. 1953a. "In-Pouring of Tributes to Williams Continues." January 31: 15.

———. 1953b. "New Trends Evolve in Hillbilly Field." February 14: l6, 44.

———. 1953c. "Disk Men Pan Country Gold." October 3: 1, 18.

———. 1953d. "Country & Western Business Is BIG Business: Editorial." December 5: 41.

———. 1953e. "New Three R's Provide Success Formula—Radio, Routes, Records." December 5: 42.

———. 1953f. "Country Songs Reflect the Life of a People." December 5: 42.

———. 1953g. "'Genuine' Quality Sets Country Field Apart from Tin Pan Alley Music." December 5: 42, 64.

———. 1953h. "Questions and Answers Reveal Approach, Policies of A&R Men." December 5: 54.

———. 1953i. "Honor Roll of C&W Artists." December 5: 48.

———. 1953j. "Jimmie Rodgers: Hillbilly World to Honor His Memory." May 16: 1, 6.

————. 1967. *Billboard 1967–68 International Buyer's Guide.* New York: Billboard Publications.

Blaustein, Richard J. 1975. "Traditional Music and Social Change: The Old Time Fiddlers Association Movement in the United States." Ph.D. diss., Indiana University, Department of Folklore.

————. 1996. "Before the Myth Was Born: Claud Grant of the Tennava Ramblers Remembers Jimmie Rodgers." Presented at the Tenth Anniversary Conference of the Center for Popular Music, Middle Tennessee State University, Murfreesboro.

Bodkin, Jonathan. 1987. *Pottery of the Pueblos of New Mexico, 1700–1940.* Colorado Springs, CO: Taylor Museum.

Bond, Johnny. 1976. *Reflections: The Autobiography of Johnny Bond.* Los Angeles: John Edwards Memorial Foundation, University of California.

Boorstein, Daniel J. 1973. *The Americans: The Democratic Experience.* New York: Random House.

Bourdieu, Pierre. 1984. *Distinction: A Social Critique of the Judgment of Taste.* Cambridge, MA: Harvard University Press.

Brand, Oscar. 1962. *The Ballad Mongers: Rise of the Modern Folk Song.* New York: Funk and Wagnalls.

Branyan, Helen B. 1991. "Medical Charlatanism: The Goat Gland Wizard of Milford, Kansas." *Journal of Popular Culture* 25: 31–37.

Bruner, Edward M. 1994. "Abraham Lincoln as Authentic Reproduction: A Critique of Postmodernism." *American Anthropologist* 96: 397–415.

Bufwack, Mary A., and Robert K. Oermann. 1982. "Adelyne Hood: The Amalgamation of Vaudeville and Folk Traditions in Early Country Music." *JEMF Quarterly* 18: 116–30.

————. 1993. *Finding Her Voice: The Saga of Women in Country Music.* New York: Crown.

Burrison, John A. 1977. "Fiddlers in the Alley: Atlanta as an Early Country Music Center." *Atlanta Historical Bulletin* 21: 59–87.

Business Week. 1935. "Medicine Men Take to the Air." February 9: 10.

Campbell, Edward D. C. Jr. 1981. *The Celluloid South: Hollywood and the Southern Myth.* Knoxville: University of Tennessee Press.

Cantwell, Robert. 1984. *Bluegrass Breakdown: The Making of the Old Southern Sound.* Urbana: University of Illinois Press.

————. 1996. *When We Were Good: The Folk Revival.* Cambridge: Harvard University Press.

Carlisle, Dolly. 1984. *Ragged but Right: The Life and Times of George Jones.* Chicago: Contemporary Books.

Carr, Patrick. 1994. "Will the Circle Be Unbroken: The Changing Image of Country Music." Pp. 328–59 in *Country: The Music and the Musicians,* edited by Paul Kingsbury, Alan Axelrod, and Susan Costello. New York: Abbeville.

Carson, Gerald. 1960. *The Roguish World of Dr. Brinkley.* New York: Rinehart.

Cawelti, John G. 1970. *The Six-Gun Mystique.* Bowling Green, OH: Bowling Green State University Press.

————. 1976. *Adventure, Mystery, and Romance.* Chicago: University of Chicago Press.

Chambers, Iain. 1986. *Urban Rhythms*. London: Macmillan.

Cherry, Hugh. 1970. "The History of Country Music: The Forty-Eight Hour Radio Documentary." Los Angeles: John Thayer & Don Bruce, Together Production. Audio tape.

———. 1985. "Rex Griffin, Hank Williams, and the 'Lovesick Blues.'" *Country Songs* 1 (September): 70.

Childers, James S. 1988. "Professional Rubes Tell Adventures: Old Fashioned Show Still Liked by Public." *Old Time Country* 5 (4): 4–6.

Ching, Barbara. 1993. "Acting Naturally: Cultural Distinction and Critiques of Pure Country." *Arizona Quarterly:* 107–25.B.

Churchill, Allen. 1951. "Tin Pan Alley's Git-tar Blues." *New York Times Magazine* July 15: 8, 36–37.

Close-Up. 1996. "International Country Music Fan Fair Celebrates 25th Year." *Country Music Association: Close-Up* 27 (8): 10–15.

Cohen, John. 1964. "Introduction to Styles in Old-Time Music." In the *New Lost City Ramblers Song Book,* edited by John Cohen and Mike Seeger. New York: Oak Publications.

Cohen, Lizbeth. 1989. "Encountering Mass Culture at the Grassroots: The Experience of Chicago Workers in the 1920s." *American Quarterly* 41: 6–33.

Cohen, Norm. 1965. "The Skillet Lickers: A Study of a Hillbilly String Band and Its Repertoire." *Journal of American Folklore* 78: 229–44.

———. 1967. "Polk 9000 Numerical." *JEMF Quarterly* 6 (2–3): 61–67.

———. 1974. "Fiddlin' John Carson: An Appreciation and a Discography." *JEMF Quarterly* 10: 138–56.

———. 1975. "Early Pioneers." Pp. 1–39 in *Stars of Country Music,* edited by Bill C. Malone and Judith McCulloh. Urbana: University of Illinois Press.

Coltman, Robert. 1976a. "Roots of the Country Yodel: Notes toward a Life History." *JEMF Quarterly* 12: 91–94.

———. 1976b. "Across the Chasm: How the Depression Changed Country Music." *Old Time Music* 23 (Winter): 6–12.

Coontz, Stephanie. 1992. *The Way We Never Were*. New York: Basic Books.

Corbin, Everett J. 1980. *Storm over Nashville: A Case against Modern Country Music*. Nashville: Ashler.

Cornell, Stephen. 1995. "Ethnicity as Narrative: Identity Construction, Pan-Ethnicity, and American Indian Supertribalism." Manuscript.

Country Song Roundup. 1951. "Hillbilly Popularity Winners." August: 8.

———. 1952. "Hillbilly Popularity Winners." August: 14.

———. 1953. "Special Announcement." June: 11.

Cox, Steve. 1993. "Hillbilly Brainbusters." *TV Guide,* May 22: 21.

Crane, Diana. 1992. *The Production of Culture Perspective*. Newbury Park, CA: Sage.

Crichton, Kyle. 1938. "There's Gold in Them Hillbillies." *Colliers,* April 30: 24–25.

Crutchfield, Will. 1986. "The Meaning of 'Authenticity.'" *Oberlin Alumni Magazine,* Fall: 4–8.

Curtis, Jim. 1987. *Rock Eras: Interpretations of Music and Society, 1954–1984.* Bowling Green, OH: Popular Press.

Cusic, Don. 1992. *Hank Williams: The Complete Lyrics.* New York: St. Martins.

Dahlinger, John C. 1977. *The Secret Life of Henry Ford.* New York: Bobbs Merrill.

Daniel, Wayne W. 1981. "Old Time Fiddlers' Contests on Early Radio." *JEMF Quarterly* 17: 159–65.

———. 1985. "Fiddlin' John Carson: The World's First Commercial Country Artist." *Bluegrass Unlimited* 20 (1): 40–43.

———. 1986. "Mechanics and Musicians: Henry Ford and Old-Time Music." *Devil's Box* 20 (3): 17–25.

———. 1990. *Pickin' on Peachtree.* Urbana: University of Illinois Press.

———. 1993. "The WLS National Barn Dance: Uptown Downhome Music in the Old Hayloft." Paper presented to the Tenth International Country Music Conference, Meridian, MS, May.

Daugherty, Margaret Hay. 1982. "George D. Hay: The Solemn Ole Judge—A Pioneer P-R Man." *Bluegrass Unlimited* 17 (July): 28–33.

Davis, Skeeter. 1993. *Bus Fare to Kentucky: The Autobiography of Skeeter Davis.* New York: Birch Lane.

Davis, Stephen F. 1978. "Jilson Setters: The Man of Many Names." *Devil's Box* 12 (1): 42–45.

Delmore, Alton. 1977. *Truth Is Stranger Than Publicity: Alton Delmore's Autobiography.* Edited with an introduction, commentary, and discography by Charles K. Wolfe. Nashville: Country Music Foundation Press.

Denny, James R. 1954. "Why the Upsurge in Country Music?" *DownBeat* June 30: 66.

DeWitt, John H. Jr. 1972. "Early Radio Broadcasting in Middle Tennessee." *Tennessee Historical Quarterly* 31: 80–94.

DiMaggio, Paul J. 1982. "Cultural Entrepreneurship in Nineteenth Century Boston, Part 1: The Creation of an Organizational Base for High Culture in America." *Media, Culture, and Society* 4: 33–50.

———. 1987. "Classification in Art." *American Sociological Review* 52: 440–55.

DiMaggio, Paul J., and Walter W. Powell. 1991. "The Iron Cage Revisited: Institutional Isomorphism and Collective Rationality." Pp. 63–82 in *The New Institutionalism in Organizational Analysis,* edited by Walter W. Powell and Paul J. DiMaggio. Chicago: University of Chicago Press.

Dixon, Robert, and John Godrich. 1970. *Recording the Blues.* New York: Stein and Day.

Dobbin, Frank R. 1992. "Cultural Models of Organizations: The Social Construction of Rational Organizing Principles." Pp. 117–42 in *The Sociology of Culture,* edited by Diana Crane. Oxford: Blackwell.

Dollard, John. 1937. *Caste and Class in a Southern Town.* New Haven: Yale University Press.

DownBeat. 1953. "C&W Deejays Organize." December 30: 17.

Dugaw, Dianne. 1987. "The Popular Marketing of 'Old Ballads': The Ballad Revival and Eighteenth-Century Antiquarianism Reconsidered." *Eighteenth-Century Studies* 21: 71–90.

Eco, Umberto. 1986. *Travels in Hyperreality: Essays.* San Diego: Harcourt Brace Jovanovich.

Eddy, Don. 1952. "Hillbilly Heaven." *American Magazine,* March.

Elkin, Friedreich. 1950. "The Psychological Appeal of the Hollywood Westerns." *Journal of Educational Sociology* 24: 72–86.

Ellison, Curtis W. 1995. *Country Music Culture.* Jackson: University Press of Mississippi.

Emery, P. E. 1959. "The Psychological Effects of the Western Film: A Study in TV Viewing." *Human Relations* 12: 195–231.

Emge, Charles. 1949. "Hillbilly Boom Can Spread Like the Plague." *DownBeat* May 6: 1.

Ennis, Philip H. 1992. *The Seventh Stream: The Emergence of Rocknroll in American Popular Music.* Hanover, NH: Wesleyan University Press.

Epstein, Jonathon S., ed. 1994. *Adolescents and Their Music: If It's Too Loud, You're Too Old.* New York: Garland.

Escott, Colin. 1991. *Good Rockin' Tonight: Sun Records and the Birth of Rock'n'Roll.* New York: St. Martins.

———. 1994. *Hank Williams: The Biography.* New York: Little Brown.

Evans, David. 1982. *Big Road Blues: Tradition and Creativity in the Folk Blues.* Berkeley: University of California Press.

Evans, James F. 1969. *Prairie Farmer and WLS.* Urbana: University of Illinois Press.

Ewen, David. 1961. *The History of Popular Music.* New York: Barnes and Noble.

Ewen, Stewart. 1976. *Captains of Consciousness: Advertising and the Social Roots of Consumer Culture.* New York: McGraw Hill.

Eyerman, Ron, and Scott Baretta. 1996. "From the 30s to the 60s: The Folk Music Revival in the United States." Manuscript. University of Lund, Sweden, Department of Sociology.

Fantetti, Nicola, and Rose Fantetti. 1950. "Behind the Scenes." *National Hillbilly News,* March-April: 32–33.

Fenster, Mark. 1989. "Preparing the Audience, Informing the Performers: John A. Lomax and *Cowboy Songs and Other Frontier Ballads.*" *American Music* 28: 260–77.

Fessier, Mike Jr. 1967. "It's Just Ol' Gene Autry." *Los Angeles Times West Magazine,* February 19: 25–28.

Fine, Gary Alan. 1996. *Kitchens: The Culture of Restaurant Work.* Berkeley: University of California Press.

Fine, Gary Alan, and Randy Stoker. 1985. "Can the Circle Be Unbroken? Small Groups and Social Movements." *Advances in Group Processes* 2: 1–28.

Flippo, Chet. 1981. *Your Cheatin' Heart: A Biography of Hank Williams.* New York: Simon and Schuster.

———. 1994. "From the Bump-Bump Room to the Barricades: Waylon, Tompaull, and the Outlaw Revolution." Pp. 312–27 in *Country: The Music and the Musicians,* edited by Paul Kingsbury, Alan Axelrod, and Susan Costello. New York: A bbeville.

Fowler, Gene, and Bill Crawford. 1987. *Border Radio: Quacks, Yodelers, Pitchmen, Psychics, and Other Amazing Broadcasters of the American Airwaves.* Austin: Texas Monthly Press.

French, Warren. 1951. "The Cowboy in the Dime Novel." *Texas Studies in English* 30: 219–34.

Friedlander, Paul. 1996. *Rock and Roll: A Social History.* Boulder, CO: Westview.

Frith, Simon. 1981. *Sound Effects: Youth, Leisure, and the Politics of Rock'n'Roll.* New York: Pantheon.

———. 1987. "Toward an Aesthetics of Popular Music." Pp. 133–49 in *Music and Society,* edited by Richard Leppert and Susan McClary. Cambridge: University of Cambridge Press.

———. 1996. *Performing Rights: On the Value of Popular Music.* Cambridge: Harvard University Press.

Frost, Richard H. 1980. "The Romantic Inflation of Indian Culture." *American West* 17: 5–9, 56–60.

Gaillard, Frye. 1978. *Watermelon Wine: The Spirit of Country Music.* New York: St. Martin's.

Gaisberg, F. W. 1942. *The Music Goes Around.* New York: Macmillan.

Gans, Herbert J. 1979. "Symbolic Ethnicity: The Future of Ethnic Groups and Cultures in America." Pp. 193–220 in *On the Making of Americans,* edited by Herbert J. Gans, Nathan Glazer, Joseph R. Gusfield, and Christopher Jenks. P hiladelphia: University of Pennsylvania Press.

Gates, Henry Lewis, Jr. 1991. "'Authenticity,' or the Lesson of Little Tree." *New York Times Magazine,* November 24: 1, 26–29.

Gehman, Nev. 1953a. "Poll Clocks 35 Also-Rans for Every Solid-Selling Disk Hit." *Billboard,* January 3: 1, 12.

———. 1953b. "Fans Clamor for Disks of Late Singer." *Billboard,* January 17: 1, 25.

Gentry, Linnell. 1969. *A History and Encyclopedia of Country, Western, and Gospel Music.* 2d ed. Nashville: Clairmont.

George, Nelson. 1988. *The Death of Rhythm and Blues.* New York: Pantheon.

Gillett, Charlie. 1983. *The Sound of the City: The Rise of Rock and Roll.* Rev. ed. London: Souvenir Press.

Ginell, Cary. 1994. *Milton Brown and the Founding of Western Swing.* Urbana: University of Illinois Press.

Gleason, Ralph J. 1969. "Hank Williams, Roy Acuff, and Then God." *Rolling Stone,* June 28: 32.

Goldberg, Isaac. 1930. *Tin Pan Alley.* New York: Frederick Ungar.

Goldman, Robert, and David R. Dickens. 1983. "The Selling of Rural America." *Rural Sociology* 48: 585–606.

Gramsci, Antonio. 1971. *Selections from the Prison Notebooks.* London: Lawrence and Wishart.

Graña, César. 1989. *Meaning and Authenticity.* New Brunswick, CT: Transaction.

Gray, Otto. 1930. "Songs: Otto Gray and His Oklahoma Cowboys." Stillwater, OK: privately published by Gray.

Green, Archie. 1965. "Hillbilly Music: Source and Symbol." *Journal of American Folklore* 78: 204–28.

———. 1972. *Only a Miner: Studies in Recorded Coal-Mining Songs.* Urbana: University of Illinois Press.

Green, Douglas B. 1975a. "Gene Autry." Pp. 143–56 in *Stars of Country Music,* edited by Bill C. Malone and Judith McCulloh. Urbana: University of Illinois Press.

————. 1975b. "Pop Acts Graced Opry." *Music City News,* October: A-24.

————. 1975c. "Western Swing Hit Opry in 40s." *Music City News,* October: A–31.

————. 1976. *Country Roots: The Origins of Country Music.* New York: Hawthorne Books.

————. 1994. "Tumbling Tumbleweeds: Gene Autry, Bob Wills, and the Dream of the West." Pp. 78–104 in *Country: The Music and the Musicians,* edited by Paul Kingsbury, Alan Axelrod, and Susan Costello. New York: Abbeville.

Green, Douglas B., and William Ivey. 1980. "The Death of Rock, the Rise of Country." Pp. 257–76 in *The Illustrated History of Country Music,* edited by Patrick Carr. Garden City, NY: Doubleday.

Green, Douglas B., and Robert Pinson. 1980. "Music from the Lone Star State." Pp. 102–37 in *The Illustrated History of Country Music,* edited by Patrick Carr. Garden City, NY: Doubleday.

Griffis, Ken. 1970. "The Johnny Bond Story." *JEMF Quarterly* 6: 96–100.

————. 1972. "The Charlie Quirk Story and the Beginnings of the Beverly Hill Billies." *JEMF Quarterly* 8: 173–78.

————. 1980. "The Beverly Hill Billies." *JEMF Quarterly* 16: 3–17.

Griswold, Wendy. 1987. "The Fabrication of Meaning: Literary Interpretation in the United States, Great Britain, and the West Indies." *American Journal of Sociology* 92: 1077–1117.

Gronow, Pekka. 1981. "The Record Industry Comes to the Orient." *Ethnomusicology* 25: 251–84.

————. 1983. "The Record Industry: The Growth of a Mass Medium." *Popular Music* 3: 53–75.

Grossberg, Lawrence. 1992. *We Gotta Get Out of This Place: Popular Consumerism and Post Modern Culture.* London: Routledge.

Grundy, Pamela. 1995. "'We Always Tried to Be Good People': Respectability, Crazy Water Crystals, and Hillbilly Music on the Air, 1933–1935." *Journal of American History* 81: 1591–1620.

Gugelberger, Georg M. 1997. *The 'Real' Thing: Testimonial Discourse in Latin America.* Durham, NC: Duke University Press.

Guralnick, Peter. 1979. *Lost Highway: Journeys and Arrivals of American Musicians.* Boston: Godine.

Gusfield, Joseph. 1981. *The Culture of Public Problems: Drinking-Driving and the Symbolic Order.* Chicago: University of Chicago Press.

————. 1986. *Symbolic Crusade: Status Politics and the American Temperance Movement.* Urbana: University of Illinois Press.

Haden, Walter D. 1975. "Vernon Dalhart." Pp. 64–85 in *Stars of Country Music,* edited by Bill C. Malone and Judith McCulloh. Urbana: University of Illinois Press.

Halbwachs, Maurice. 1992. *On Collective Memory.* Chicago: University of Chicago Press.

Handler, Richard. 1986. "Authenticity." *Anthropology Today* 2: 79–81.

Harker, Dave. 1985. *Fakesong: The Manufacture of British "Folksong" 1700 to the Present.* Milton Keynes: Open University Press.

Harkreader, Sidney J. 1976. "Fiddlin' Sid's Memories: The Autobiography of Sidney J. Harkreader." JEMF special ser. no. 9. Los Angeles: University of California.

Harrison, Bill. 1969. "Hell's Broke Loose in Georgia." *Devil's Box* 10: 6.

Hay, George. 1926. *Howdy Judge.* Nashville: McQuiddy.

———. 1945. *A History of the Grand Ole Opry.* Nashville: N.p.

Hazzard-Gordon, Katrina. 1990. *Jookin': The Rise of Social Dance Formations in African-American Culture.* Philadelphia: Temple University Press.

Hegeman, Susan. 1989. "Native American 'Texts' and the Problem of Authenticity." *American Quarterly* 41: 265–83.

Hobsbawm, Eric, and Terence Ranger, eds. 1983. *The Invention of Tradition.* Cambridge: Cambridge University Press.

Hoeptner, Fred, and Bob Pinson. 1971. "Clayton McMichen Talking: Part 2." *Old Time Music* 2: 13–15.

Holden, Stephen. 1990. "As the Sun Sets Slowly in the West . . ." *New York Times,* January 21.

Holston, Noel. 1973. "The Man from the South with a Cigar in His Mouth." *Sentinel Star, Florida Magazine,* Orlando, February 25.

Hoover, Walter K. 1968. *The History of Smyrna, Tennessee.* Nashville: McQuiddy.

Horstman, Dorothy. 1986. *Sing Your Heart Out, Country Boy.* Nashville: Country Music Foundation.

Horton, David C. 1991. *DeFord Bailey: A Black Star in Early Country Music.* Knoxville: University of Tennessee Press.

Hughbanks, Leroy. 1945. *Talking Wax; or, The Story of the Phonograph.* New York: Hobson Book Press.

Hurd, Walter. 1940. "Talent and Tunes on Music Machines." *Billboard* suppl., September 28: 3.

Hurst, Jack. 1975. *Grand Ole Opry.* New York: Abrams.

Irwin-Zarecka, Iwona. 1994. *Frames of Remembrance: The Dynamics of Collective Memory.* New Brunswick, NJ: Transaction Books.

Ivey, Bill. 1994. "The Bottom Line: Business Practices That Shaped Country Music." Pp. 280–311 in *Country: The Music and the Musicians,* edited by Paul Kingsbury, Alan Axelrod, and Susan Costello. New York: Abbeville.

Jardim, Anne. 1970. *The First Henry Ford: A Study in Personality and Business Leadership.* Cambridge: MIT Press.

Jarman, Rufus. 1953. "Country Music Goes to Town." *Nation's Business* 41 (2) (February).

Johnson, Thomas F. 1981. "That Ain't Country: The Distinctiveness of Commercial Western Music." *JEMF Quarterly* 17: 75–84.

Johnston, Alva. 1939. "Tenor on Horseback." *Saturday Evening Post,* September 2: 18, 74–76.

Jones, Louis M. 1984. *Everybody's Grandpa: Fifty Years Behind the Mike.* Knoxville: University of Tennessee Press.

Jones, Loyal. 1980. *Radio's Kentucky Mountain Boy.* Berea, KY: Appalachian Center, Berea College.

Kahn, Ed. 1968. "Interview with Charlie, Bubb, Lucille Pickard." *JEMF Quarterly* 4: 136–41.

———. 1970. "The Carter Family: A Reflection of Changes in Society." Ph.D. diss., University of Southern California.

———. 1973. "International Relations, Dr. Brinkley, and Hillbilly Music." *JEMF Quarterly* 9 (2): 47–55.

Kammen, Michael. 1991. *Mystic Chords of Memory*. New York: Knopf.

Kimmel, Michael S. 1994. "Consuming Manhood: The Feminization of American Culture and the Recreation of the Male Body." *Michigan Quarterly Review* 32: 7–36.

King, Pee Wee. 1952. "Pee Wee King's Corn Fab." *Country Song Roundup*, June: 18.

Kirby, Jack T. 1986. *Media-Made Dixie: The South in the American Imagination*. Athens: University of Georgia Press.

Koon, George W. 1983. *Hank Williams: A Bio-Discography*. Westport, CT: Greenwood.

Koon, William H. 1974. "The Carter Family: A Brief History." Booklet accompanying "The Carter Family on Border Radio." LP 101 of the John Edwards Memorial Foundation.

Laing, Dave. 1985. *One Chord Wonders: Power and Meaning in Punk Rock*. Milton Keynes, England: Open University Press.

Lamont, Michèle. 1992. *Money, Morals, and Manners*. Chicago: University of Chicago Press.

Larson, Charles U., and Christine Oravec. 1987. "'A Prairie Home Companion' and the Fabrication of Community." *Critical Studies in Mass Communication* 4: 221–44.

Leamy, Hugh. 1929. "Now Come All You Good People." *Colliers,* November 2: 20, 58–59.

Leblebici, Huseyin, Gerald R. Salancik, Anne Copay, and Tom King. 1991. "Institutional Change and the Transformation of Interorganizational Fields: An Organizational Analysis of the U.S. Radio Broadcasting Industry." *Administrative Scienc e Quarterly* 36: 333–63.

Lenihan, John H. 1980. *Showdown: Confronting Modern America in the Western Film*. Urbana: University of Illinois Press.

Leonard, Neil. 1962. *Jazz and the White Americans*. Chicago: University of Chicago Press.

Lewis, David L. 1972. "The Square Dance Master." *Devil's Box* l7: 4–6.

———. 1976. *The Public Image of Henry Ford: An American Folk Hero and His Company*. Detroit: Wayne State University Press.

Lipsitz, George. 1990. *Time Passages: Collective Memory and American Popular Culture*. Minneapolis: University of Minnesota Press.

Literary Digest. 1924. "The Fiddlin' Champion Receives His Crown." December 6: 70–71.

———. 1926. "Fiddling to Henry Ford." January 2: 33–38.

———. 1932. "Kentucky's Ancient Minstrel Wanders Afar from His Folks." December 24: 26–27.

Lomax, John. 1910. *Cowboy Songs and Other Frontier Ballads*. New York: Sturgis & Walton.

Lopes, Paul D. 1994. "The Creation of a Jazz Art World and the Modern Jazz

Renaissance." PhD. diss., Department of Sociology, University of California, Berkeley.

Lynn, Loretta. 1976. *Loretta Lynn: Coal Miner's Daughter.* Chicago: Regnery.

Malone, Bill C. 1971. "Radio and Personal Appearances: Sources and Resources." *Western Folklore* 30: 215–25.

———. 1979. *Southern Music: American Music.* Lexington: University of Kentucky Press.

———. 1985. *Country Music U.S.A.* Austin: University of Texas Press.

———. 1993. *Singing Cowboys and Musical Mountaineers.* Athens: University of Georgia Press.

Marre, Jeremy, and Hannah Charlton. 1985. *Beats of the Heart.* London: Pluto.

McCulloh, Judith. 1967. "Hillbilly Records and Tune Transcriptions." *Western Folklore* 26: 225–44.

McLaurin, Melton A., and Richard A. Peterson, eds. 1992. *You Wrote My Life: Lyrical Themes in Country Music.* Philadelphia: Gordon and Breach.

McNeil, W. C. 1995. *Appalachian Images in Folk and Popular Culture.* Knoxville: University of Tennessee Press.

McNeil, William K. 1987. "The New London, Texas, School Tragedy: The History of the Disaster and Its Songs." Paper presented at the Fourth Annual Country Music Conference, Meridian, MS, May.

McRill, Leslie A. 1960. "Music in Oklahoma by the Billy McGinty Cowboy Band." *Chronicles of Oklahoma* 38: 66–74.

McWethy, John A. 1951. "Hillbilly Tunes Boom Brings Big Business to the Melody Makers." *Wall Street Journal,* October 2: 1, 3.

Melly, George. 1970. *Revolt into Style: The Pop Arts.* London: Penguin.

Metress, Christopher. 1995. "Sing Me a Song about a Ramblin' Man: Visions and Revisions of Hank Williams in Country Music." *South Atlantic Quarterly* 94: 7–28.

Miller, Townsend. 1975. "Ernest Tubb." Pp. 222–36 in *Stars of Country Music,* edited by Bill C. Malone and Judith McCulloh. Urbana: University of Illinois Press.

Moore, Arthur K. 1957. *The Frontier Mind: A Cultural Analysis of the Kentucky Frontiersman.* Lexington: University of Kentucky Press.

Moore, Kelly. 1996. "Organizing Integrity: American Science and the Creation of Public Interest Organizations, 1955–1975." *American Journal of Sociology* 101: 1592–1627.

Moore, Thurston. 1960. "Disc Jockey Festival." *Country Music Who's Who* 1: 33.

Morris, Edward. 1994. "New, Improved, Homogenized: Country Radio since 1950." Pp. 64–77 in *Country: The Music and the Musicians,* edited by Paul Kingsbury, Alan Axelrod, and Susan Costello. New York: Abbeville.

Morton, David C. 1982. "Every Day's Been Sunday." *Nashville!* February: 50–55.

———. 1991. *DeFord Bailey: A Black Star in Early Country Music.* Knoxville: University of Tennessee Press.

Musical Courier. 1926. "Song Hunting in the Southern Highlands." February 18: 45.

Nash, Alanna. 1994. "Home Is Where the Gig Is: Life on and off the Road."

Pp. 176–91 in *Country: The Music and the Musicians,* edited by Paul Kingsbury, Alan Axelrod, and Susan Costello. New York: Abbeville.

Nash, Roderick. 1970. *The Nervous Generation: American Thought, 1917–1930.* Chicago: Rand McNally.

Nevell, Richard. 1977. *A Time to Dance.* New York: St. Martin's.

Newsweek. 1935a. "Bow with Antic Ways Put Hillbilly Fiddler at Top of Bill." May 18: 20.

———. 1935b. "Mountaineer Sets Folklore to Opera Score." August 24: 30–31.

———. 1949. "Corn of Plenty." June 13.

———. 1952. "Country Music Is Big Business and Nashville Is Its Detroit." August 11: 82–85.

———. 1953. "Rodgers Remembered." June 8: 32.

Odum, Howard W., and Guy B. Johnson. 1925. *The Negro and His Songs: A Study of Typical Negro Songs in the South.* Chapel Hill: University of North Carolina Press.

———. 1926. *Negro Workday Songs.* Chapel Hill: University of North Carolina Press.

Oermann, Robert K. 1994. "Honky-Tonk Angels: Kitty Wells and Patsy Cline." Pp. 212–33 in *Country: The Music and the Musicians,* edited by Paul Kingsbury, Alan Axelrod, and Susan Costello. New York: Abbeville.

Oermann, Robert K., and Mary A. Bufwack. 1981. "Patsy Montana and the Development of the Cowgirl Image." *Journal of Country Music* 8: 18–32.

Oliver, Paul. 1984. *Songsters and Saints: Vocal Traditions on Race Records.* Cambridge: Cambridge University Press.

Orvell, Miles. 1989. *The Real Thing: Imitation and Authenticity in American Culture: 1880–1940.* Chapel Hill: University of North Carolina Press.

Otto, John S., and Augustus M. Burns. 1974. "Black and White Cultural Interaction in the Early Twentieth Century South: Race and Hillbilly Music." *Phylon* 35: 407–17.

Page, Don. 1965. "Autry: Cowhand with a $ Brand." *Los Angeles Times,* October 22.

Palmer, Robert. 1994. "Get Rhythm: Elvis Presley, Johnny Cash, and the Rockabillies." Pp. 192–211 in *Country: The Music and the Musicians,* edited by Paul Kingsbury, Alan Axelrod, and Susan Costello. New York: Abbeville.

Parton, Dolly. 1994. *Dolly: My Life and Other Unfinished Business.* New York: HarperCollins.

Patterson, Timothy A. 1975. "Hillbilly Music among the Flatlanders: Early Midwestern Radio Barn Dances." *Journal of Country Music* 6: 12–18.

Peer, Ralph. 1953. "Discovery of the 1st Hillbilly Great." *Billboard,* May 16: 20–21, 35.

Peterson, Richard A. 1972. "A Process Model of the Folk, Pop, and Fine Art Phases of Jazz." Pp. 135–51 in *American Music: From Storyville to Woodstock,* edited by Charles Nanry. New Brunswick, NJ: Trans-Action Books.

———. 1975. "Single-industry Firm to Conglomerate Synergistics: Alternative Strategies for Selling Insurance and Country Music." Pp. 341–57 in *Growing Metropolis: Aspects of Development in Nashville,* edited by James Blumstein and Benjamin Walter. Nashville: Vanderbilt University Press.

———. 1978. "The Production of Cultural Change: The Case of Contemporary Country Music." *Social Research* 45: 292–314.

———. 1979. "Has Country Lost Its Homespun Charm?" *Chronicle of Higher Education,* May 29: 26–27.

———. 1981. "Entrepreneurship and Organization." Pp. 65–83 in *Handbook of Organizational Design,* vol. 1, edited by Paul C. Nystrom and William H. Starbuck. New York: Oxford University Press.

———. 1990. "Why 1955? Explaining the Advent of Rock Music." *Popular Music* 9: 97–116.

———. 1992. "Class Unconsciousness in Country Music." Pp. 35–62 in *You Wrote My Life: Lyrical Themes in Country Music,* edited by Melton McLaurin and Richard Peterson. Philadelphia: Gordon and Breach.

———. 1994. "Culture Studies through the Production Perspective." Pp. 163–90 in *The Sociology of Culture,* edited by Diana Crane. Oxford: Blackwell.

———. 1995. "The Dialectic of Hard-Core and Soft-Shell Country Music." *South Atlantic Quarterly* 94 (Winter): 273–300.

———., ed. 1976. *The Production of Culture.* Beverly Hills, CA: Sage.

Peterson, Richard A., and David G. Berger. 1971. "Entrepreneurship in Organizations: Evidence from the Popular Music Industry." *Administrative Science Quarterly* 16: 97–107.

———. 1975. "Cycles in Symbol Production: The Case of Popular Music." *American Sociological Review* 40: 158–73.

Peterson, Richard A., and Russell Davis, Jr. 1975. "The Fertile Crescent of Country Music." *Journal of Country Music* 6: 19–27.

Peterson, Richard A., and Paul J. DiMaggio. 1973. "The Early Opry: Its Hillbilly Image in Fact and Fancy." *Journal of Country Music* 4: 39–51.

———. 1975. "From Region to Class, the Changing Locus of Country Music: A Test of the Massification Hypothesis." *Social Forces* 53: 497–506.

Peterson, Richard A., and Marcus V. Gowan. 1971. "What's in a Country Music Band Name?" *Journal of Country Music* 2: 1–9.

Peterson, Richard A., and Roger M. Kern. 1995. "Hard-Core and Soft-Shell Country Fans." *Journal of Country Music* 17 (3): 3–6.

Peterson, Richard A., and Melton McLaurin. 1992. "Introduction: Country Music Tells Stories." Pp. 1–14 in *You Wrote My Life: Lyrical Themes in Country Music,* edited by Melton McLaurin and Richard Peterson. Philadelphia: Gordon and Breach.

Peterson, Richard A., and John Ryan. 1983. "Success, Failure, and Anomie in Art and Crafts Work: Breaking in to Commercial Country Music Songwriting." *Research in the Sociology of Work* 2: 301–23.

Peterson, Richard A., and Howard G. White. 1979. "The Simplex Located in Art Worlds." *Urban Life* 7: 411–39.

Portelli, Alessandro. 1991. *The Death of Luigi Trastulli: Form and Meaning in Oral History.* Albany: State University of New York.

Porterfield, Nolan. 1992. *Jimmie Rodgers: The Life and Times of America's Blue Yodeler.* Urbana: University of Illinois Press.

———. 1994. "Hey, Hey, Tell 'em about Us: Jimmie Rodgers Visits the Carter

Family." Pp. 12–39 in *Country: The Music and the Musicians,* edited by Paul Kingsbury, Alan Axelrod, and Susan Costello. New York: Abbeville.

———. 1995. "Stranger through Your Town." Essay accompanying *Jimmie Rodgers: Singing Brakeman.* Hamburg, Germany: Bear Family Records.

Powell, Walter W., and Paul J. DiMaggio, eds. 1991. *The New Institutionalism in Organizational Analysis.* Chicago: University of Chicago Press.

Pugh, Ronnie. 1987. "Gene Autry: The Jimmie Rodgers Influence." Paper presented to the Fourth Annual Country Music Conference, Meridian, MS, May 29–30.

———. 1996. *Ernest Tubb: The Texas Troubadour.* Durham, NC: Duke University Press.

Pusataeri, C. Joseph. 1976. "FDR, Huey Long, and the Politics of Radio Regulation." Paper presented at the Popular Culture Association–South meetings. Knoxville, TN, October.

Radio Digest. 1928. "Who's Who in Broadcasting." October.

Randall, Richard S. 1968. *Censorship of the Movies.* Madison: University of Wisconsin Press.

Rasmussen, Chris. 1994. "The People's Orchestra: Juke Boxes and the Reorientation of American Popular Music." Paper presented to the Annual Meetings of the American Studies Association, Nashville, TN, October.

Read, Oliver, and Walter L. Welch. 1959. *From Tin Foil to Stereo: Evolution of the Phonograph.* Indianapolis: Bobbs-Merrill.

Rhea, Joseph T. 1995. "Memory of a Nation: The Race Pride Movement and American Collective Memory." Ph.D. diss., Harvard University, Department of Sociology.

Ridley, Jim. 1994. "It's Just a Matter of Time." *Nashville Scene,* July 14: 17–18, 20–21.

Rinzler, Ralph. 1993. Liner Notes to "Bill Monroe and Doc Watson: Live Duet Recordings 1963–1980." Smithsonian/Folkways CD: SF CD 40064.

Rivers, Jerry. 1967. *Hank Williams: From Life to Legend.* Denver: Heather Enterprises.

Roach, Joseph. 1996. *Cities of the Dead: Circum-Atlantic Performance.* New York: Columbia University Press.

Roe, Gene L. 1950. "Got 'Lovesick Blues?' No Sir, not Hank Williams." *National Hillbilly News,* January-February: 51–52.

Rogers, Jimmie N. 1989. *The Country Music Message.* Fayetteville: University of Arkansas Press.

Rooney, James. 1971. *Bossmen: Bill Monroe and Muddy Waters.* New York: Hayden.

Rorrer, Clifford K. 1972. "Charlie Poole and the North Carolina Ramblers." *Country Music Who's Who: 1972,* pp. H-3–H-5.

Rose, Fred. 1946. "Open Letter to Mr. Advertiser, Radio Agency, and Program Director." *Billboard,* August 3: 123.

Rosenberg, Neil V. 1985. *Bluegrass: A History.* Urbana: University of Illinois Press.

———. 1994. "Blue Moon of Kentucky: Bill Monroe, Flatt & Scruggs, and the Birth of Bluegrass." Pp. 126–51 in *Country: The Music and the Musicians,* edited by Paul Kingsbury, Alan Axelrod, and Susan Costello. New York: Abbeville.

————, ed. 1993. *Transforming Tradition: Folk Music Revivals Examined.* Urbana: University of Illinois Press.

Rumble, John W. 1980. "Fred Rose and the Development of the Nashville Music Industry, 1942–1954." Ph.D. diss., Vanderbilt University, Department of History.

Russell, Oland D. 1937. "Floyd Collins in the Sand Cave." *American Mercury,* November: 289–97.

Russell, Tony. 1970. *Blacks, Whites, and Blues.* New York: Stein and Day.

Ryan, John. 1985. *The Production of Culture in the Music Industry: The ASCAP-BMI Controversy.* Lanham, MD: University Press of America.

Ryan, John, and Richard A. Peterson. 1982. "The Product Image: The Fate of Creativity in Country Music Song Writing." *Sage Annual Reviews of Communication Research* 10: 11–32.

Samuelson, Dave. 1995. "Linda Parker: WLS's Sunbonnet Girl." *Journal of the American Academy for the Preservation of Old-Time Country Music* 30: 17.

Sanjek, Russell. 1988. *American Popular Music and Its Business: The First Four Hundred Years,* vol. 3, *From 1900 to 1988.*New York: Oxford.

Scherman, Tony. 1994. "Country: Its Story Is Over." *American Heritage,* November: 38–57.

Schlappi, Elizabeth. 1975. "Roy Acuff." Pp. 179–201 in *Stars of Country Music,* edited by Bill C. Malone and Judith McCulloh. Urbana: University of Illinois Press.

————. 1978. *Roy Acuff: The Smoky Mountain Boy.* Gretna, LA: Pelican.

Schmidt, Eric von, and Jim Rooney. 1979. *Baby Let Me Follow You Down: The Illustrated Story of the Cambridge Folk Years.* Garden City, NY: Doubleday.

Seeger, Mike. 1973. "Who Chose Those Records?" Pp. 8–17 in *Anthology of American Folk Music,* edited by Josh Duncan. New York: Oak.

Sewell, William H. 1994. "Political Events as Cultural Transformations: Insecurity, Collective Effervescence, and Collective Creativity in the Summer of 1789." Manuscript. University of Chicago, Department of History.

Shapiro, Henry D. 1978. *Appalachia on Our Mind: The Southern Mountains and Mountaineers in the American Consciousness, 1870–1920.* Chapel Hill: University of North Carolina Press.

Shaw, Arnold. 1987. *The Rockin' 50s: The Decade That Transformed the Pop Music Scene.* New York: De Capo.

Shiach, Morag. 1989. *Discourse on Popular Culture: Class, Gender, and History in Cultural Analysis, 1730 to the Present.* Stanford, CA: Stanford University Press.

Sippel, Johnny. 1951. "The Hillbilly Deejay Prime Asset to Country & Western Field." *Billboard,* September 15: 61.

————. 1953. "Strong Bonds Unite Artist and His Fans." *Billboard,* December 5: 48, 88.

Slotkin, Richard. 1992. *Gunfighter Nation: The Myth of the Frontier in Twentieth-Century America.* New York: HarperCollins.

Spielman, Earl V. 1975. "Traditional North American Fiddling." Ph.D. diss. University of Wisconsin, Department of Musicology.

Stanley, Robert. 1978. *The Celluloid Empire.* New York: Hastings House.

Steele, Harry. 1936. "The Inside Story of the Hillbilly Business." *Radio Guide,* January 25: 20–21, 42.

Strasser, Susan. 1989. *Satisfaction Guaranteed.* New York: Pantheon.

Stringfield, Lamar. 1931. "America and Her Music." *University of North Carolina Extension Bulletin* 10 (7) (March).

Sutton, Juanealya McCormick. 1987. *The Man Behind the Scenes: Neal (Pappy) McCormick and Hank Williams.* DeFuniak Springs, FL: Juanealya Sutton.

Talking Machine World. 1925. "What the Popularity of Hill-Billy Songs Means in Retail Profit Possibility." December 15.

———. 1929. "Mail Order Songs." January 14: 22.

Taylor, Alan. 1994. "The Creation of Cooper's Town: In Fact and in Fiction." *Ideas* 2 (2): 5–14.

Teeter, H. B. 1952. "Nashville, Broadway of Country Music." *Coronet,* August: 28–32.

Terry, B. 1954. "100,000 Jam Montgomery, Alabama, for Hank Williams' Memorial." *DownBeat,* October: 34.

Thomas, Jean. 1930. "Blind Jilson: The Singing Fiddler of Lost Hope Hollow." *American Magazine,* February: 62–65, 166–67.

Tichi, Cecelia. 1994. *High Lonesome: The American Culture of Country Music.* Chapel Hill: University of North Carolina Press.

Time. 1934. "Traipsin' Woman." June 18: 54.

———. 1943. "Bull Market in Corn." October 4: 32.

Toll, Robert C. 1974. *Blacking Up: The Minstrel Show in Nineteenth Century America.* New York: Oxford University Press.

Tompkins, Jane. 1992. *West of Everything: The Inner Life of Westerns.* New York: Oxford University Press.

Toqueville, Alexis de. 1835 [1945]. *Democracy in America.* New York: Vintage.

Tosches, Nick. 1980. "Rockabilly!" Pp. 217–37 in *The Illustrated History of Country Music,* edited by Patrick Carr. Garden City, NY: Doubleday.

———. 1985. *Country.* New York: Scribners.

———. 1994a. "Honky-Tonkin': Ernest Tubb, Hank Williams, and the Bartender's Muse." Pp. 152–76 in *Country: The Music and the Musicians,* edited by Paul Kingsbury, Alan Axelrod, and Susan Costello. New York: Abbeville.

———. 1994b. "The Strange and Hermetical Case of Emmett Miller." *Journal of Country Music* 17 (1): 39–47.

Townsend, Charles R. 1976. *San Antonio Rose: The Life and Music of Bob Wills.* Urbana: University of Illinois Press.

Trevor-Roper, Hugh. 1983. "The Invention of Tradition: The Highland Tradition of Scotland." Pp. 15–42 in *The Invention of Tradition,* edited by Eric Hobsbawm and Terence Ranger. Cambridge: Cambridge University Press.

Tribe, Ivan M. 1984. *Mountaineer Jamboree: Country Music in West Virginia.* Lexington: University Press of Kentucky.

Trilling, Lionel. 1972. *Sincerity and Authenticity.* Cambridge, MA: Harvard University Press.

Trott, Walt. 1992. *Honky-Tonk Angel.* Nashville: Nova.

Tuska, Jon. 1982. *The Vanishing Legion: A History of Mascot Pictures, 1927–1935.* Jefferson, NC: McFarland.

Ulin, Robert C. 1995. "Invention and Representation as Cultural Capital: Southwest French Winegrowing History." *American Anthropologist* 97: 519–27.

Variety. 1929. "Hill-Billy Music." December 29: 28–32.

———. 1949. "Fort Knox No Longer Has Exclusive on Pot of Gold: WSM, Nashville, Talent Corners a Good Chunk of It." October 26: 38.

———. 1951. "Cornseed Crooners Reap B.O. Bonanza as City Slickers Lap Cider-Jug Tunes." June 27: 1.

———. 1953a. "Impact of Williams' Death Cues O.O. for New Backwoods Berlin." February 11: 1, 61.

———. 1953b. "Hank Williams Immortal to Cornball Fans." April 19: 1, 52.

———. 1953c. "100 Country Disk Jockeys Launch Hillbilly Protection Association." November 25: 58.

———. 1953d. "Jazz Plays Second Fiddle to Corn as Hillbillies Make Hay Abroad." November 25: 1.

Vincent, Ted. 1995. *Keep Cool: The Black Activists Who Built the Jazz Age.* London: Pluto.

Wade, Edwin L. 1985. "The Ethnic Art Market in the American Southwest, 1890–1980." Pp. 167–91 in *Objects and Others: Essays on Museums and Material Culture,* edited by George L. Stocking. Madison: University of Wisconsin Press.

Wallis, Roger, and Krister Malm. 1984. *Big Sounds from Small Peoples: The Music Industry in Small Countries.* London: Constable.

Walsh, Jim. 1955. "Musicologist Jim Walsh on Hillbilly Champs: Dalhart vs. Rodgers, et al." *Variety,* September 21: 51, 54.

———. 1960. "Favorite Pioneer Recording Artists: Vernon Dalhart." *Hobbies,* May: 33–35, 45; June: 34–36, 60; July: 34–37, 55; August: 33–35, 60; September: 34–36, 45, 49; October: 34–36, 44; November: 32–35, 44–45; December: 32–33.

Weatherbee, Wilson J. 1924. "Good Evening, Everybody! This is Station KYW." *American Magazine,* March: 60–61, 208–11.

Weber, Max. 1909 [1978]. *Economy and Society: An Outline of Interpretive Sociology,* vol. 1. Berkeley: University of California Press.

West, James. 1945. *Plainville, U.S.A.* New York: Columbia University Press.

Wexler, Jerry. 1950. "B'way Pubs Turn Song Revenooers But Hillbillies Get All the Gold." *Billboard,* August 19: 1, 13.

———. 1993. *Rhythm and the Blues: A Life in American Music.* New York: Knopf.

Whisnant, David E. 1983. *All That Is Native and Fine: The Politics of Culture in an American Region.* Chapel Hill: University of North Carolina Press.

Whitehorse, David. 1988. *Pow-Wow: The Contemporary Pan-Indian Celebration.* Publications in American Indian Studies 5. San Diego: San Diego State University.

Whitburn, Joel. 1986. *Pop Memories: 1890–1954.* Menomonee Falls, WI: Record Research.

———. 1989. *Top Country Singles: 1944–1988.* Menomonee Falls, WI: Record Research.

————. 1994. *Top Country Singles: 1944–1993*. Menomonee Falls, WI: Record Research.

White, Forrest. 1991. *Fender: The Inside Story*. San Francisco: Miller Freeman.

Wiggins, Gene. 1975. "Benét's 'Mountain Whippoorwill': Folklore atop Folklore." *Tennessee Folklore Society Bulletin* 41: 99–114.

————. 1977. "The Socio-political Works of Fiddlin' John and Moonshine Kate." *Southern Folklore Quarterly* 41: 106–28.

————. 1987. *Fiddlin' Georgia Crazy: Fiddlin' John Carson, His Real World, and the World of His Songs*. Urbana: University of Illinois Press.

Wik, Reynold M. 1972. *Henry Ford and Grass-Roots America*. Ann Arbor: University of Michigan Press.

Williams, Hank Jr. 1979. *Living Proof: An Autobiography*. New York: Putnam.

Williams, Lycretia, and Dale Vinicur. 1989. *Still in Love with You: Hank and Audrey Williams*. Nashville: Rutledge Hill.

Williams, Roger M. 1970. *Sing a Sad Song: The Life of Hank Williams*. Garden City, NY: Doubleday.

————. 1975. "Hank Williams." Pp. 237–54 in *Stars of Country Music*, edited by Bill C. Malone and Judith McCulloh. Urbana: University of Illinois Press.

Willis, Paul. 1990. *Common Culture: Symbolic Work and Play in the Everyday Cultures of the Young*. Boulder, CO: Westview.

Witmark, Isidore, and Isaac Goldberg. 1975. *The Story of Witmark*. New York: DeCappo.

————. 1937. "Listeners' Ideal National Barn Dance Program." Chicago: WLS, The *Prairie Farmer* Station.

WLS. [n.d.]. "Important Dates: WLS National Barn Dance." [No attribution but extremely detailed through October 23, 1950]

Wolfe, Charles K. 1972. "Ralph Peer at Work: The Victor 1927 Bristol Sessions." *Old Time Music* 5: 10–15.

————. 1973. "Nashville and Country Music, 1925–1930: Notes on Early Nashville Media and Its Response to Old-Time Music." *Journal of Country Music* 4 (Spring): 2–16.

————. 1975a. "Uncle Dave Macon." Pp. 40–63 in *Stars of Country Music*, edited by Bill C. Malone and Judith McCulloh. Urbana: University of Illinois Press.

————. 1975b. *The Grand Ole Opry: The Early Years, 1925–1935*. London: Old Time Music.

————. 1977a. "McMichen in Kentucky: The Sunset Years." *Devil's Box* 11 (2): 10–18.

————. 1977b. "Fiddler's Dream: The Legend of Arthur Smith." *Devil's Box* 11 (4): 26–67.

————. 1979. "Columbia Records and Old-Time Music." *JEMF Quarterly* 14: 118–21.

————. 1980. "The Birth of an Industry." In *The Illustrated History of Country Music*, edited by Patrick Carr. Garden City, NY: Doubleday.

————. 1982. *Kentucky Country: Folk and Country Music of Kentucky*. Lexington: University Press of Kentucky.

————. 1987. "Pre-War Melodies and Mountain Songs." Essay accompanying *The Bristol Sessions*. Country Music Foundation: Nashville.

————. 1993. "The White Man's Blues, 1922–1940." *Journal of Country Music* 17 (3): 38–44.

————. 1994. "The Triumph of the Hills: Country Radio, 1920–50." Pp. 40–63 in *Country: The Music and the Musicians,* edited by Paul Kingsbury, Alan Axelrod, and Susan Costello. New York: Abbeville.

————. 1995. "Event Songs." *South Atlantic Quarterly* 94: 217–30.

————. Forthcoming. "Give Me the Roses While I Live." Essay accompanying *The Carter Family: Their Complete Victor Recordings,* vol. 6. Rounder Records 1069.

Wolfe, Charles K., and Kip Lornell. 1992. *The Life and Legend of Leadbelly.* New York: Harper.

Yarber, Lisa. 1996. "Just Plain Old Country Girls: John Lair and the Construction of the Coon Creek Girls." Presented at the International Country Music Conference, May 10–11.

Young, R. J. 1980. "The Singing Cowboy." Pp. 138–63 in *The Illustrated History of Country Music,* edited by Patrick Carr. Garden City, NY: Doubleday.

Zelinsky, Wilbur. 1988. *Nation into State: The Shifting Symbolic Foundations of American Nationalism.* Chapel Hill: University of North Carolina Press.

Zerubavel, Eviatar. 1991. *The Fine Line: Making Distinctions in Everyday Life.* New York: Free Press.

Credits

TEXT FIGURES

Fig. 1.1. Photo courtesy of the Country Music Foundation. Fig. 2.1. Photo courtesy of the Charles K. Wolfe Archive. Fig. 2.2. Photo courtesy University of North Carolina Southern Folklife Collection, Wilson Library Manuscripts Department. Fig. 3.1. Photo courtesy of Nolan Porterfield. Fig. 3.2. Photo courtesy of Nolan Porterfield. Fig. 4.1. Photo courtesy of the Country Music Foundation. Fig. 5.1. Photo courtesy of the Charles K. Wolfe Archive. Fig. 5.2. Photo courtesy of Bob Pinson. Fig. 6.1. Photo courtesy of the Country Music Foundation. Fig. 7.1. Photo courtesy of the Country Music Foundation. Fig. 7.2. Photo courtesy of the Charles K. Wolfe Archive. Fig. 8.1. Photo courtesy of the Country Music Foundation. Fig. 10.1. Photo courtesy University of North Carolina Southern Folklife Collection, Wilson Library Manuscripts Department. Fig. 10.2. Photo courtesy of Ronnie Pugh. Fig. 11.1. Photo courtesy of the Country Music Foundation. Fig. 13.1. Photo courtesy of the Country Music Foundation. Fig. 14.1. Photo courtesy of Roger Weiss.

GALLERY FIGURES

Fig. G1.1. Photo courtesy University of North Carolina Southern Folklife Collection, Wilson Library Manuscripts Department. Fig. G1.2. Photo courtesy of the Charles K. Wolfe Archive. Fig. G1.3. Photo courtesy University of North Carolina Southern Folklife Collection, Wilson Library Manuscripts Department. Fig. G1.4. Photo courtesy of Nolan Porterfield. Fig. G1.6. Photo courtesy of Nolan Porterfield. Fig. G1.5. Photo courtesy of Nolan Porterfield. Fig. G1.7. Photo courtesy University of North Carolina Southern Folklife Collection, Wilson Library Manuscripts Department. Fig. G2.1. Photo courtesy of the Country Music Foundation. Fig. G2.2. Photo courtesy University of North Carolina Southern Folklife Collection, Wilson Library Manuscripts Department. Fig. G2.3. Photo courtesy of the Charles K. Wolfe Archive. Fig. G2.4. Photo courtesy of the Charles K. Wolfe Archive. Fig. G2.5. Photo courtesy of the Country Music Foundation. Fig. G2.6. Photo courtesy of the Country Music Foundation. Fig. G2.7.

Photo courtesy of Robert K. Oermann. Fig. G3.1. Photo courtesy of the Country Music Foundation. Fig. G3.2. Photo courtesy of Les Leverett. Fig. G3.3. Photo courtesy University of North Carolina Southern Folklife Collection, Wilson Library Manuscripts Department. Fig. G3.4. Photo courtesy of the Country Music Foundation. Fig. G3.5. Photo courtesy of the Country Music Foundation. Fig. G4.1. Photo courtesy of Bob Pinson. Fig. G4.2. Photo courtesy of the Country Music Foundation. Fig. G4.3. Photo courtesy University of North Carolina Southern Folklife Collection, Wilson Library Manuscripts Department. Fig. G4.4. Photo courtesy of the Country Music Foundation. Fig. G4.5. Photo courtesy of Les Leverett.

General Index

A&R producer: 37, 41, 46; sources of information on, 245n. 27; aesthetic judgments of, 246n. 28
Academy of Country and Western Music:
263
Acuff, Roy: 50, 117, 139, 142–143, 144–
150, 155, 164, 224, 226–227, 231,
250n. 9; band name Crazy Tennesseans, 123, 256n. 9; and Roy Acuff Flour,
125; sings "Honky-tonk Woman," 166;
Hank Williams's early model, 175
image: 25; resists westernwear, 91; of
authenticity, 129, 149, 192; as hillbilly not cowboy, 147–148; as entertainer, 148; showmanship, 175; as
"King of the Hillbillies," 258n. 11
photos of: 226, G3.2, G3.3, G3.4
Acuff, Thelma: Roy's daughter, photo of,
G4.5
Acuff-Rose Publishing Company: 39; Hank
Williams's popularity, 183
advertisers: product name used in group
name, 120, 121
aesthetic mobility: 9
AFM (American Federation of Musicians):
excludes country music performers,
13
African-American music: derivative, 64;
235n. 2, 237n. 12
Alabama: band, 137, 151
Alamo (San Antonio, TX): 218
Allen Brothers: 196
Allen, Gracie: 255n. 9

"Amos 'n' Andy": radio series, 143, 250n. 8
Anderson, Bill: 152
Andrews Sisters: 191
Appalachian region: 207, 215–216; as un-
spoiled land, 247n. 5
Arkie the Arkansas Woodchopper: 101
Armstrong, Louis: 18; recorded with Jim-
mie Rodgers, 47
Arnold, Eddy: 151, 152, 153, 154, 155,
251n. 20, 258n. 16; photo of, G3.5
Arnold, Matthew: 206
ASCAP (American Society of Composers,
Authors, and Publishers): exclusion of
country music writers and publishers,
13, 186, 187, 192, 231
Ashley, Clarence: 214
Atkins, Chet: 46, 142; influence of Curt
Poulton on, 142; dropped from the
"Grand Ole Opry," 265n. 11; photo of,
G4.4
Atlanta: role played by John Carson in
country music development, 15; rural
migrants in, 17–18; first field recording
in, 19; early country music industry in,
25–27, 29–34
Atlanta Journal: role in promoting John Carson, 20
audience: bluegrass, 214; country music,
268n. 11; *See also* country music: audience
Austin music scene: 268
authentic voice: 217–220; of a group,
266–267

Song Index

Act Naturally: 211
(Pay Me) Alimony: 260n. 12
All Along the Navajo Trail: 253n. 8
Assassination of Governor Gobel: 248n. 14
At My Mother's Grave: 40

Baby, We're Really in Love: 178
Back in the Saddle Again: 92
Barbara Allen: 56
Be Honest with Me: 92
Born to Lose: 169
Bubbles in My Beer: 166

Can the Circle Be Unbroken?: 221
Chattanoogie Shoe Shine Boy: 187, 191, 192
Cimaroon: 92
Coal Creek Troubles: 248n. 13
Cold, Cold Heart: 177, 178, 187, 191
Cool Water: 92
Crazy Heart: 178

Death of Mother Jones, The: 87
Death of Little Kathie Fiscus, The: 31
Death of Floyd Collins, The: 24–25, 40, 69
Deep Elem Blues: 166
Devil Went Down to Georgia: 247n. 4
Divorce Me C.O.D.: 169
Don't Let That Man Get You Down: 260n. 12
Drivin' Nails in My Coffin (Every Time I Drink a Bottle of Booze): 168
Dust: 92

Give Me a Pinto Pal: 92
Good-night Irene: 187, 192, 198
Great Speckled Bird, The: 145, 146

(You Don't Love Me) Half as Much (As I Love You): 178
Hangover Blues: 260n. 12
Hank and Lefty, You Raised My Country Soul: 228
Hank Williams, You Wrote My Life: 179, 228
Have You Got Someone Else on the String?: 260n. 12
Headed Down the Wrong Highway: 169
Hell's Broke Loose in Georgia: 58
Hey Good Lookin' (What Ya Got Cookin'): 177, 178, 261n. 2
Honky Tonkin': 178
Honky Tonk Blues: 168, 178, 259n. 3
Honky Tonk Mamas: 166
Howlin' at the Moon: 178

I Saw the Light: 178
I Wish I Was a Single Girl Again: 260n. 12
I Just Don't Like This Kind of Lovin': 178
I'd Love to Live in Loveland with You: 100
I'll Never Get Out of This World Alive: 178
I'm a Stern Old Bachelor: 100
I'm So Lonesome I Could Cry: 177, 178
I'm Walking the Floor over You: 164, 168
I've Got Five Dollars and It's Saturday Night: 168